Sustainability in the Gig Economy

Ashish Gupta · Tavishi Tewary ·
Badri Narayanan Gopalakrishnan
Editors

Sustainability in the Gig Economy

Perspectives, Challenges and Opportunities in Industry 4.0

Springer

Editors
Ashish Gupta
Department of Marketing
Indian Institute of Foreign Trade
New Delhi, Delhi, India

Tavishi Tewary
Department of Economics
Jaipuria Institute of Management
Noida, Uttar Pradesh, India

Badri Narayanan Gopalakrishnan
School of Environment and Forest Sciences
University of Washington
Seattle, WA, USA

ISBN 978-981-16-8405-0 ISBN 978-981-16-8406-7 (eBook)
https://doi.org/10.1007/978-981-16-8406-7

This Springer imprint is published by the registered company Springer Nature Singapore Pte Ltd.
The registered company address is: 152 Beach Road, #21-01/04 Gateway East, Singapore 189721, Singapore

To my parents (Shri Ramesh Chandra Gupta and Smt. Kamla Devi Gupta), sister (Mrs. Kanchan Gupta), wife (Mrs. Pooja Gupta), and lovely son (Aradhay Gupta) for their never-ending love, unwavering and continued support, and belief in me.

I am truly thankful for all your support and trust in me and for the inspiration that constantly drew from you at different junctures.

- Ashish Gupta

To Shivji, my grandfather, and all my friends, with all my love. Blessed to have you all in my life.

- Tavishi Tewary

To my parents, loving wife, Sumathi, and two beautiful children, Anagha and Hari, for their support and inspiration.

- Badri Narayanan Gopalakrishnan

Preface

The gig economy has emerged as one of the most significant and much-discussed phenomena in work. The definitions of the gig economy vary from consisting of all non-traditional and less structured work arrangements to a more specific focus on work performed via online platforms and crowdsourcing marketplaces. These online/digital platforms create opportunities for new microwork, which encompasses a series of smaller distributed tasks performed by the workers in different locations. The gig economy has facilitated multiple jobs simultaneously with ease. For example, a gig can be used to supplement income from a traditional job, or a worker can register on multiple platforms simultaneously. The gig economy platform is redefining the labour market and our conceptualization of work by leveraging the transformative power of digitalization.

The gig economy can also be classified based on geography into the localized and delocalized gig economy. The delocalized gig economy refers to the services offered by gig workers irrespective of the location of the gig worker. It includes crowd work platforms, while localized gig economy refers to the on-demand peer-to-peer economy that requires the jobseekers to be physically situated within a shared geographical area. Freelancer, Uber, and Deliveroo are considered examples of the gig economy.

Advancement in technology has played the role of the catalyst in promoting the gig economy. The digitization and use of IoT have made it increasingly lucrative for companies to reorganize their processes and workflow. A huge chunk of the work can be delegated to the non-employees of the company. These technologies are more flexible and make it feasible to restructure the traditional work on a project-specific basis. It allows hiring temporary workers with a mix of skills appropriate for each project. It has also helped the companies reduce their cost and respond quickly to any shift in demand in the market. The segmentation of work has facilitated the spread of the gig economy in almost all the sectors of the economy.

On the other hand, this popularity of the gig economy has challenges as well. The new economy has increased the reliance on outsourcing, and it further implies that the companies are reducing their human and social capital in the long run. It is a novel form of working arrangement that exclusively focuses on fragmentation of work wherein independent workers partner with digital platforms to provide a range of on-demand services to the customers.

This book, Sustainability in the Gig Economy: Perspectives, Challenges and Opportunities in Industry 4.0, provides a concise overview of the gig economy concept and its key features. It covers three core themes: the brighter and darker side of the gig economy; it also discusses making this economy sustainable for future jobseekers by protecting their interests. As an interdisciplinary work, contributions stem from various perspectives, including sociology, law, technology, human resource, economics, and sustainability. The book critically reviews the literature on the gig economy. The book summarizes key elements and debates that encompass the gig economy. It provides an expert map to guide the readers with challenges in the gig economy and for navigating to a sustainable solution. It helps the readers to understand how the theory interacts with practice. It provides a library of intellectual insights into the future of the gig economy. It introduces the audience to novel research tools that aid in better understanding the concept of the gig economy and its applicability in different sectors.

The chapters synthesize the key themes and thinking emerging in the field of the gig economy and the complex relationship found in work. It also highlights the opportunities presented by the gig economy and how they can be utilized to improve the performance of the businesses. It provides a direction to the students, scholars, academicians, and policymakers by presenting an expansive body of literature on the gig economy.

The book comprises conceptual and empirical papers and has contributions from countries like Italy, South Korea, the USA, France, Pakistan, Turkey, etc. The 24 chapters are organized into 3 sections in this book. We believe that these 24 chapters outline a rich tapestry of the gig economy issues related to various parts of the world. They offer a multidisciplinary view as they provide a comprehensive collection of cases across different sectors by various authors working on different themes of the gig economy. We hope that this book will become a popular and trusted resource for the readers who wish to understand the concept of the gig economy and its dimensions in a detailed manner.

New Delhi, India — Ashish Gupta
Noida, India — Tavishi Tewary
Seattle, USA — Badri Narayanan Gopalakrishnan

Contents

Sustainability of Gig Era and Industry 4.0

Future Challenges of Sustaining a Gig Economy

Editors and Contributors

About the Editors

Dr. Ashish Gupta is presently working as a full-time faculty in marketing area at Indian Institute of Foreign Trade (IIFT), New Delhi, an autonomous institution of Ministry of Commerce and Industry, Govt. of India. His research interests are in marketing, customer relationship management, service quality, branding and consumer behaviour. He has almost a decade of teaching and research experience in the area of marketing and management. He has more than 40 research papers to his credit published in international and national journals like *Journal of Internet Commerce; International Journal of Quality and Service Sciences; Young Consumers; American Business Review; Journal of Retailing and Consumer Services; Asia Pacific Journal of Marketing and Logistics; Emerald Emerging Markets Cases; Journal of Direct, Data and Digital Marketing Practice; International Journal of Customer Relationship Marketing and Management; International Journal of Electronic Customer Relationship Management; International Journal of Indian Culture and Business Management* etc.

Dr. Gupta has also presented more than 25 research papers in international and national conferences. He conducted / completed several workshops, FDP and MDPs such as Six- Month Online Professional Training Programme on 'International Business Analytics and Market Intelligence' during January to June 2022; AICTE-ATAL Sponsored FDP on 'Leadership and Excellence in Professional Education' in July 2021; International Faculty Development Program from Aston Business School, Aston University, Birmingham, UK in August 2019. In 2018, Dr. Gupta conducted Six-month Management Development Program on 'International Business' for Armed Forces Personnel sponsored by Directorate General of Resettlement and Welfare, Ministry of Defence, Govt. of India during August 2018- January 2019. Dr. Gupta has also conducted one-week MHRD-GIAN Program on 'Digital and Social Media Marketing in Emerging Markets' Sponsored by Ministry of Human Resource Development (Govt. of India), New Delhi during 14-20 October 2016.

He is actively engaged in government funded projects and currently doing a project for Khadi and Village Industries Commission (KVIC), Ministry of Micro, Small and Medium Enterprises, Govt. of India.

Recently Indian Council of Social Science Research awarded a project on 'Internationalization of Indian Higher Education Institutions (HEIs): Identification of the Strategic, Structural and Policy Dimensions, Challenges, and Solutions for Management Institutions'

Dr. Tavishi Tewary is Assistant Professor and Area Chair-Department of Economics at Jaipuria Institute of Management, Noida, India. She obtained her PhD from the National Institute of Industrial Engineering, India. Her area of interest covers international trade analysis; sustainability; international economics; socio-economic development, energy, circular economy, Industry 4.0. She is Advisor at the Infinite Sum Modeling, USA. She is also visiting faculty at UDLAP, Mexico. She has taught students from over 50 countries in the Pan Africa e-network Project. She has also conducted FDPs on Data Analysis using SPSS, PLS-SEM, and EVIEWS students, research scholars and faculty members. Further, she has experience in providing scientific leadership to high-profile strategic sustainability and conservation initiatives with several years of research experience.

Dr. Badri Narayanan Gopalakrishnan is the Lead Adviser at NITI Aayog – Government of India, wherein he heads the vertical of Trade and Commerce. Prior to joining the GoI, he has been an economist working to analyse a wide range of economic (mainly international trade), disruptive technology (blockchain, AI, drones, robotics, IoT, etc.), environmental/energy and public health policies. He has informed the process of decision making in several major economic policies such as free trade agreements, technology regulations, etc., both through his academic research and consulting/advisory projects.

Badri has also been a Senior Economist and Affiliate Professor with University of Washington Seattle, Senior Fellow with European Center for International Political Economy, Brussels, National Council for Applied Economic Research (NCAER) and Center for Social and Economic Progress (formerly Brookings India), New Delhi. He is on the Board of Directors of British American Business Council. He has also been a consultant with the UN, World Bank, ILO, FAO, WHO, ICRIER, IMF and several other international organizations as well as government/private bodies across the world. He has also been engaged with the startup community across the world as an advisor and co-founder. He had founded a consulting firm named "Infinite Sum Modelling" in 2015, which has a global presence, with offices in Vancouver, Seattle, Los Angeles, Coimbatore, Bangalore, Hyderabad, Chennai, and New Delhi. He has been a consultant to several organizations such as McKinsey, KPMG, PWC, World Bank, UN, ADB, Harvard University, LSE, the Commonwealth Secretariat, etc. He has published over 100 papers and 5 books cited thousands of times in journals as well as popular media (FT, BBC, CNN, WP, The Economist, etc.), in reputed journals such as *Nature Communication, Energy Economics, Network and Spatial*

Economics, Economic Modelling, Applied Economics, Agricultural Economics, etc., and presented his work in over 30 countries across the world.

List of Contributors

Alpana Agarwal Amity University, Noida, U.P., India

Himanshu Ahuja Delhi Technological University, Delhi, India

Sumathi Chakravarthy Infinite-Sum Modeling Inc., Washington, USA

Walid Chaouali Carthage Business School, University of Tunis Carthage, Member of ARBRE, Higher Institute of Management of Tunis, Tunis, Tunisia

Ginni Chawla Indian Institute of Foreign Trade (IIFT), New Delhi, India

Miloslava Chovancova Faculty of Management and Economics, Tomas Bata University in Zlin, Zlin, Czech Republic

Arabella Mocciaro Li Destri Department of Economics, Business and Statistics, University of Palermo, Palermo, Italy

Sandeep Kumar Dey Faculty of Management and Economics, Tomas Bata University in Zlin, Zlin, Czech Republic

Ashish Mohan Dubey Department of Management, Birla Institute of Technology, Patna, Bihar, India

Jose I. Galan University of Salamanca, Salamanca, Spain

S. Girish Department of Commerce, School of Commerce, Finance and Accountancy, CHRIST (Deemed To Be University), Bangalore, India

Badri Narayanan Gopalakrishnan Infinite-Sum Modeling Inc., Washington, USA

Ritika Gugnani Department of Economics, Jaipuria Institute of Management, Noida, Uttar Pradesh, India

Om Prakash Gusai Department of Commerce, Motilal Nehru College, University of Delhi, New Delhi, India

Harinderpal Hanspal Thing Company LLC, Mercer Island, WA, USA

Mahrane Hofaidhllaoui ESSCA School of Management, 69007 Lyon, France

Isha Jaswal Delhi Metropolitan Education (GGSIPU), New Delhi, India

Sonali Jindal Indian Institute of Foreign Trade (IIFT), New Delhi, India

Noonu Mary Jose Department of Commerce, School of Commerce, Finance and Accountancy, CHRIST (Deemed To Be University), Bangalore, India

David Joseph Department of Commerce, School of Commerce, Finance and Accountancy, CHRIST (Deemed To Be University), Bangalore, India

Harrshit M. Kansal Indian Institute of Foreign Trade (IIFT), New Delhi, India

Komal Kapoor IMSUC, Ghaziabad, India

Anukaran Khanna Department of Management, United College of Engineering, and Management D-II, UPSIDC Industrial Area, Prayagraj, Uttar Pradesh, India

Prateek Khanna Department of Business Administration, Shambhunath Institute of Engineering and Technology, Prayagraj, Uttar Pradesh, India

A. V. Akshay Kumar Department of Commerce, Jain College, Bengaluru, India

Senthil Kumar Professor of Research & Business Analytics, School of Management, Presidency University, Bangalore, India

Neha Makkar Institute of Innovation in Technology and Management, Delhi, India

Mehreen Malik NUST Business School, National University of Sciences and Technology (NUST), Islamabad, Pakistan

Sindhu Bharathi Mandharachalam Infinite-Sum Modeling Inc., Washington, USA

Dávid Adrián Máté University of Miskolc, Miskolc, Hungary

Jelena Mazaj Department of Economics, Business and Statistics, University of Palermo, Palermo, Italy

Gábor Mélypataki University of Miskolc, Miskolc, Hungary

Istadeva Mishra Amity Business School, Noida, Uttar Pradesh, India

Samiha Mjahed King Saud University, Riyadh, Kingdom of Saudi Arabia

Mohamed Mousa Department of Management Sciences, Pontifical Catholic University of Peru, Lima, Peru

R. Kiruba Nagini Department of Management Studies, Pondicherry University, Pondicherry, India

Mohammad Faraz Naim Department of Management, Birla Institute of Technology & Science Pilani, Pilani, India

Sagar Venkateshwar Nemani Indian Institute of Foreign Trade (IIFT), New Delhi, India

Panggih Kusuma Ningrum HeyLaw Indonesia, Kota Tangerang Selatan, Indonesia

Joseph Odhiambo Onyango Strathmore University Business School, Nairobi, Kenya

K. Pallavi Maulana Azad National Institute of Technology, Bhopal, India

Sunil Kumar Pandey Birla Institute of Technology Mesra, Patna Campus, Patna, India

Pasquale Massimo Picone Department of Economics, Business and Statistics, University of Palermo, Palermo, Italy

Padma Priya Indian Institute of Foreign Trade (IIFT), New Delhi, India

Geetanjali Purswani Department of Commerce, School of Commerce, Finance and Accountancy, CHRIST (Deemed To Be University), Bangalore, India

L. C. Raghavan Infinite-Sum Modeling Inc., Washington, USA

M. Anand Shankar Raja Department of Commerce, CHRIST (Deemed To Be University), Bangalore, India

Ankur Rani Department of Commerce, Baba Mastnath University, Rohtak, Haryana, India

Mark Ratilla Faculty of Management and Economics, Tomas Bata University in Zlin, Zlin, Czech Republic

Muhammad Mustafa Raziq NUST Business School, National University of Sciences and Technology (NUST), Islamabad, Pakistan

S. Riasudeen Department of Management Studies, Pondicherry University, Pondicherry, India

Zsófia Riczu University of Miskolc, Miskolc, Hungary

Harsh Vardhan Samalia National Institute of Technical Teachers Training & Research, Chandigarh, India

Reetika Sehgal Department of Management, United College of Engineering ,and Management D-II, UPSIDC Industrial Area, Prayagraj, Uttar Pradesh, India

Nidhi Divyesh Shah Indian Institute of Foreign Trade (IIFT), New Delhi, India

Deep Shree Delhi Technological University, Delhi, India

Ashutosh Shukla School of Management Sciences, Varanasi, India

Olga Shvetsova Korea University of Technology and Education, Cheonan, South Korea

Hergovind Singh Maulana Azad National Institute of Technology, Bhopal, India

Upasana Singh Delhi Metropolitan Education (GGSIPU), New Delhi, India

S. Bhargav Varma Department of Economics, Meghanad Desai Academy of Economics, Mumbai, India;
Ottoman's Turkish Restaurant, Chennai, India

R. Venkatesakumar Department of Management Studies, Pondicherry University, Pondicherry, India

Anhsu Yadav Amity Business School, Noida, Uttar Pradesh, India

Preeti Yadav Department of Commerce, Kamal Institute of Higher Education and Advance Technology, GGSIPU, New Delhi, India

Jose Angel Zuñiga-Vicente Rey Juan Carlos University, Madrid, Spain

Background to the Gig Economy

The Gig Economy: A Preliminary Proposal of Some Distinctive Forms

Jose I. Galan and Jose Angel Zuñiga-Vicente

1 Introduction

Since the financial crisis at the end of the 2000s, the global market has undergone a great deal of change. This has led to a steady increase in new forms of work and an acceleration in technological innovation. Many jobs involving physical interaction are disappearing (Fayard, 2021; Friedman, 2014; Gandini, 2019; Healy et al., 2017; Ungemah, 2021; Vallas & Schor, 2020; Zwick, 2018). Recent technological developments (e.g., the gradual implementation of blockchain, 5G, artificial intelligence, and the Internet of Things) are leading to what is termed the Fourth Industrial Revolution (or Industry 4.0), which will see the implementation of a new economic model called the gig economy (hereafter, GE) based on digital platforms, and the existence of a new type of employee: the gig worker (hereafter, GW).

Over the last few years, many workplaces have become virtual or remote, partly in the belief that they would be more productive, efficient, and sustainable as a result (e.g., Graham et al., 2017; Lojeski & Reilly, 2020; Richardson, 2020; Schwellnus et al., 2019). Many people now have a priori a great deal of freedom to decide when to work and what projects to work on. The economic turbulence caused by the COVID-19 pandemic has led large swathes of the workforce either to place their trust in or to move away from gig work.

The term GE encompasses a range of different terminologies and conceptualizations. It goes by many names and has many variants: for example, the 'platform economy', 'on-demand (digital) economy', 'peer-to-peer economy', 'sharing

J. I. Galan (✉)
University of Salamanca, Campus Miguel de Unamuno, Edificio FES, 37007 Salamanca, Spain
e-mail: jigalan@usal.es

J. A. Zuñiga-Vicente
Rey Juan Carlos University, Paseo de los Artilleros, s/n, 28032 Madrid, Spain
e-mail: joseangel.zuniga@urjc.es

A. Gupta et al. (eds.), *Sustainability in the Gig Economy*,
https://doi.org/10.1007/978-981-16-8406-7_1

economy', or 'crowd-sourcing economy'. It has been the subject of much controversy in the mass media over the past few years. There is no academic consensus on the term; researchers attach different meanings to it depending on their analytical approach and field of study. Richardson (2015) suggests that the associated semantic confusion allows the GE to be the subject of both academic and popular discourse. Most scholars argue that the GE is becoming an established market-based economy (e.g., Friedman, 2014; Goods et al., 2019; Healy et al., 2017; Ukolov et al., 2016; Zwick, 2018). However, despite the enormous controversy surrounding it, one thing seems clear: the GE has great potential.

The main aim of the present study is to present a preliminary characterization of the GE to improve understanding of it and to explain the heterogeneity of previous perspectives and/or results. While some studies have tended to be optimistic about the concept and its potential effects on GWs, others have been more circumspect, pointing out the harmful effects of working conditions and even on people's dignity (e.g., Anwar & Graham, 2020; Barratt et al., 2020; Christie & Ward, 2019; Friedman, 2014; Graham et al., 2017; Prassl, 2018; Schwellnus et al., 2019; Wood et al., 2019). In the present study, we attempt to resolve this dichotomy by proposing the existence of two types of GE: the *strong form* and the *weak form*. However, we recognize that these represent the two extremes of a continuum on which intermediate forms also exist. We argue that each of these forms is contingent on specific conditions of labor supply and demand as well as on people's skillsets, which will partly determine their employability, bargaining power, and rights at work.

Each of these forms refers to a specific context and will therefore have a differential impact on working conditions and human dignity. A virtue of our taxonomy is that it allows us to classify the GE into different typologies and therefore to understand it more. The GE is not a uniform concept but a contextual one, with varying economic and social effects (especially on workers) depending on the form that pertains. Our model also enables us to synthesize the representations of the GE (either positive or negative) in the extant literature on this booming phenomenon.

2 Main Characteristics and Magnitude of the Gig Economy and Gig Workers

2.1 Identifying Distinctive Aspects of the Gig Economy

The concept of the GE emerged in the USA shortly after the 2007 subprime mortgage crisis. A drastic reduction in liquidity led to the search for alternative sources of income, both for those who did not have permanent or full-time jobs and for those who needed extra income. Some of the main companies (i.e., employers or platforms) who are representative of this category then emerged, for example, TaskRabbit, Thumbtack, Rocket Lawyer, and the so-called unicorns like Airbnb and Uber. Terms that refer to their approach include the 'sharing economy'—primarily in allusion to platforms such as Uber or Airbnb—and the 'crowd-sourcing economy', or even 'collaborative economy'. Most of these companies use app-based platforms via which they hand out work in small chunks—cleaning homes, hiring caregivers, ferrying passengers, delivering goods, and so on—leading some to prefer terms such as 'platform economy', 'on-demand digital economy', or 'peer-to-peer economy'. At this point, it should be noted that not all GE roles are based on tech platforms. For example, many GWs also work for more traditional firms that have radically transformed their staffing schemes.

The word 'gig' originally referred to a performance by musicians, but it is now applied more broadly to jobs that are carried out on an ad hoc basis. The person hired to do the job in question is responsible for fulfilling a specific role within a project/task/activity. The GE symbolizes a free market structure that rests on short-lived work agreements between independent workers and companies or platforms with the main purpose of offering certain services to customers. It is therefore typically made up of three major groups of economic agents (Barratt et al., 2020; Hauben et al., 2020; Jabagi et al., 2019): (a) independent workers, in other words, GWs, who are paid by the 'gig' (i.e., a project, a task, or an activity), unlike fixed-term or permanent workers who receive a fixed salary; (b) consumers who require a specific service, for example, the delivery of a particular item; and (c) companies that connect the GWs to the end customers in a direct manner, normally via app-based technology platforms. Figure 1 presents the main characteristics of the GE.

The GE may be viewed as an important driver of innovation because companies that are linked with it tend to be highly innovative. They have been able to identify a need in the market and, using modern technology, transform that need into a business opportunity. They often enjoy the benefit of incorporating new perspectives, especially when they hire skilled GWs. The evidence shows that the GE is changing the way many companies do business.

The GE has substantially increased labor flexibility. It has been suggested that individuals who provide their services through this type of platform can organize their agenda and time as they see fit. For the most part, they can choose only the projects they are interested in. This goes hand in hand with the freedom to select the days and slots to carry them out.

The GE means that work does not have to be tied to a specific geographical location. New platforms provide work that is scalable and global, though some sectors of the GE can be narrowed down to particular areas. Many jobs can be carried out remotely across borders; all the GW needs is an internet connection. Freelancers, for example, can use mobile devices to provide their services from home or elsewhere, while they are traveling, or when they are on holiday.

The GE now exists in high- and low-wage and developed and developing economies (Ford & Honan, 2019; Goods et al., 2019). It is embracing more and more sectors. It emerged in the accommodation, transport, and food delivery industries, and is presently most prevalent in services, but there are now platforms linking virtually every type of provider with end-users (i.e., customers). It is expected to develop further with the wider implementation of blockchain technology, which

Fig. 1 Main distinctive characteristics of the gig economy. *Source* The authors

allows the decentralization and monetization of all production and service activities, connecting professionals with end-users and eliminating the intermediation that was a core element of the traditional economy.

The GE can help to simplify the relationship between parties, that is, between employer (i.e., the platform) and worker. Projects/tasks/activities are simply communicated through messaging. The individual registers on a platform and the platform communicates the availability of projects/tasks/activities to them through the mobile device(s) of their choice.

The GE can generate a fixed or extra income. Some GWs start out with the aim of earning extra income in addition to their regular jobs but many then make it a way of life. Below, we explain how this feature of the GE depends largely on the particular form we have proposed.

The GE does not create labor ties between the different parties. The relationship is exclusively linked to a specific project/task/activity. Once the project/task/activity ends, the relationship ends. There are no obligations on either the progenitor of the project/task/activity or the person providing the service. Both parties have to agree upon the value of this.

The GE can facilitate direct contact between different economic agents through digital platforms because, ordinarily, it eliminates intermediation. Digital platforms make it possible to link the needs of potential customers with the services provided by several professionals, which generates a new economic relationship with a clear trend toward decentralization. Blockchain technology will accentuate this disintermediation and decentralization. Trust is generated by the use of classification systems for both potential service providers and potential users or customers. This represents an important cost saving that can benefit not only the users or customers but also those who provide the service.

The GE facilitates greater transparency in payment. Most payments are made online, which permits the adoption of new payment systems. In particular, the use of blockchain technology and cryptocurrencies are becoming a secure means of decentralized transactions, guaranteeing unparalleled transparency. While the use of cryptocurrency is based on anonymity, all the transactions are stored on an open ledger (namely, the blockchain). All the data associated with a particular transaction can therefore be seen by any party at any time, a fundamental advantage in the eyes of those who are committed to an increasingly transparent banking system.

The GE can create substantial 'value' for customers. It is commonly argued that, besides generating potential gains for job-seekers and firms (or platforms), digital business models can create value for customers too. Transaction costs for clients can be significantly reduced and most products can be supplied to any place and practically at any time, and so the concept of convenience reaches an entirely new level.

2.2 The Global Prevalence of the Gig Economy

The growth of the GE over the last few years has been exponential. However, governments and/or official data sources have difficulty in counting how many GWs there are. This indicates the difficulty in establishing the magnitude of the GE. In addition, the current global crisis caused by COVID-19 has created further uncertainty.

The following statistics provide evidence of and an insight into the state of the global GE pre-COVID-19. The United States (US) Bureau of Economic Analysis (BEA) estimated that the so-called digital economy grew by an average of 5.6% per year in the period 2006–2016 compared with a 1.5% increase in the economy as a whole. According to the US Bureau of Labor Statistics, in 2017 the US GE had about 55 million participants. It is estimated that about 36% of US workers were part of the GE and around 33% of firms used GWs extensively. In 2018, freelancers in the USA contributed almost $1.28 trillion to the economy (this year, the US GDP was around $20.5 trillion), which is approximately the same as the total GDP of a middle-size developed country like Spain. The number of workers participating in America's GE was expected to balloon to 43% by the end of 2020. According to the predictions of MBO Partners (2020), if the GE keeps growing at its current rate, it is likely that more than 50% of the US workforce will be participating in it by 2025; this means almost tripling the growth of employment projected for this year. On the other hand, the results of a survey conducted by Rowe Price (2018) showed that around 26% of millennials in the USA deemed that work related to the GE (i.e., independent full or part-time work) was economically more secure than full-time ones. However, this percentage was significantly lower among baby boomers (around 15%) and Generation Xers (around 18%). Interestingly, the baby boomers expressed the most positive feelings about the GE.

According to the Association of Independent Professionals and the Self Employed (IPSE), the number of independent workers in the EU countries increased by about 24% in the period 2008–2015, rising from approximately 7.7 million to 9.6 million. A more recent study that examined 16 European Union (EU) countries reported that around 1.4% of people between 16 and 74 years old claimed that their main job was working via a platform. However, the proportion of the population who had carried out platform work at any time ranged from under 6% in Czechia to around 18% in Spain and averaged around 11% for the countries as a whole (Brancati et al., 2019).

In the United Kingdom (UK), the Office for National Statistics (ONS) claimed that the GE workforce in 2017 was approximately 4.4% of the whole population. In fact, according to some statistics, the UK economy seemed to be following the same path as the USA. The UK's self-employment economy almost doubled in size for the period 2016–2019.

In 2018, approximately 15% of China's workforce, representing over 110 million people, was involved in the GE. For example, Zhaopin.com (China's largest online recruiting firm) estimated that demand for freelance or part-time jobs almost doubled between 2015 and 2016, which was greater than that for full-time jobs. Working in the GE was proving a feasible option for many millennials who preferred flexible work schedules and, at the other extreme, for an increasing number of elderly persons looking for additional income. Fueled by the tech boom, it is expected that the number of workers in China's GE will nearly quadruple by 2036 (Rothschild, 2018).

In 2019, Queensland University of Technology published a report stating that around 7% of the Australian workforce participated in the GE (Carey, 2019). In 2019, according to a Bank of Canada report, approximately 18% of Canadians worked in the GE for non-recreational motives (Kostyshyna & Luu, 2019).

Finally, according to a survey conducted by Deloitte (2014), millennials—that is, those born between about 1980 and 2000—are forecast to comprise around 75% of the global total workforce by 2025. Because these young people tend to be more confident about freelancing than other generations, a promising future for the GE is assured.

As was noted above, all prior estimates refer to the pre-COVID-19 situation, so it is essential to highlight how the world of work and the GE might change post-pandemic. Some recent quantitative and qualitative studies have shown that COVID-19 may have a positive effect on job openings in the GE and on GWs (see, e.g., Apouey et al., 2020; Polkowska, 2020; Umar et al., 2020). In a similar vein, Cao et al., (2020), using data from a large online education platform with more than 100,000

GWs, examined the effect of COVID-19 on the GE labor supply and quantified how much of this effect was attributable to lockdown policies. Their results reveal that the average labor supply in the GE increased by 25% during the pandemic. On the other hand, many companies in the GE have been forced (like more traditional companies) to carry out mass layoffs as a result of the economic crisis caused by COVID-19. Finally, according to recent statistics provided by MBO Partners (2020), with the advent of COVID-19 and associated economic crisis, in the USA the number of GWs fell 7%—from around 41.1 million in 2019 to around 38.2 million in 2020.

2.3 Gig Workers: A New Type of Employee

In general, it can be argued that for employers (i.e., platforms), the GE is viewed mostly as a win–win game. Most businesses can contact professionals quickly and contract them to carry out individual projects/tasks/activities without having to bear the associated cost burdens, such as training, office space, or any other privileges linked with the more traditional fixed-term employee (e.g., health and unemployment insurance, retirement plans, paid vacations, or sick days, as is the case in many countries). Gig work, however, can be a mixed bag of advantages and disadvantages (e.g., Anwar & Graham, 2020; Bajwa et al., 2018; Fabo et al., 2017; Lehdonvirta, 2018; Petriglieri et al., 2019).

Some of the major advantages that most GWs enjoy are the following. First, the work is more flexible. Compared with more traditional employees, GWs are in many cases free to choose what jobs they are really interested in doing and when and where they wish to do them. In many instances, the possibility of working from home allows them to achieve a proper work-life balance. As Barratt et al., (2020: 1651) argue, 'the new economic reality is reinforced by many workers' self-conceptualization shifting from a dependent employee to 'their own boss' or a micro-entrepreneur'. Certainly, flexible schedules are highly appreciated by most workers but, since the beginning of COVID-19, many full-time workers have likely been forced to join GE out of necessity.

Second, it offers greater independence. It is ideal for people who prefer to be alone when they are carrying out specific assignments because in many cases they feel free to do the assigned project/task/activity in the way they think it should be done.

Third, it permits people to carry out a greater variety of projects/tasks/activities for a wider range of customers. This can help to keep the work interesting and therefore many GWs exhibit a higher level of enthusiasm, motivation, and creativity in their work.

Fourth, GWs can specialize in what they prefer or know how to do best. A priori, this again should make them more committed/motivated and, hence, raise their productivity. A survey conducted by BCG Henderson Institute shows the three main reasons why people opt for the GE: (1) meaningful and interesting tasks; (2) self-employment; and (3) flexibility in organizing work (Wallenstein et al., 2019).

According to another survey conducted by MBO Partners, around 79% of full-time GWs said they were happier when they were working on their own than doing a more traditional job (MBO Partners, 2018).

Finally, the GE makes it easier for people to earn an income in times of severe economic crisis. For example, in a recent study, Polkowska (2020) found that during the pandemic and the 2020 lockdown of the Polish economy, working as a rider was considered to be at least a partial 'remedy' for the serious problems in the labor market. Their findings highlighted the fact that the riders themselves generally did not feel any negative effect of the coronavirus on their occupational situation. In a similar vein, Apouey et al. (2020), using a sample of precarious workers in France between March and April 2020, showed that stress and anxiety levels were no higher for GWs than other groups. Furthermore, riders also reported significantly lower stress levels during the lockdown.

Potential disadvantages include the following: first, gig work tends to be associated with modest pay. For example, two surveys conducted in 2019 and 2018 by the Economic Well-Being of US Households and Edison Research, respectively, showed that approximately 58% and 80% of the GE respondents for whom this sort of work has become the principal source of revenue found serious difficulty in meeting an unanticipated bill of $400 or $1,000.

Second, the GE tends to provide less social protection. Traditional employment typically offers numerous protections and privileges (such as health and unemployment insurance, retirement plans, paid vacation or sick days, the possibility of a company car, and having one's fuel/lunch paid for) that GWs do not enjoy. Gig work is widely regarded as precarious, and this is why the system has been roundly criticized and denounced in many countries' mass media.

Third, gig work can be very stressful. While it affords greater flexibility in most cases, it can also be unpredictable because of the short-term nature of many jobs, which leaves employees with real concerns about how long the work will last. Incomes are also much less stable. Moreover, having to look for the next task or gig and adjusting to the change can generate even more stress.

According to a survey by Edison Research (2018), approximately 45% of persons for whom gig work is the principal source of revenue tend to score more than 50 points on an Economic Anxiety Index (from zero to 100) compared with only 24% of persons in traditional jobs. In many services, pricing can change significantly on a daily (or even hourly) basis, so GWs are often required to adapt to irregular and at the same time rigid work methods and are thus subject to constant pressure. Also, since the beginning of COVID-19, rivalry among GWs may have risen significantly. This is because workers who originally were confident in the GE as their major source of revenue must now compete not only with each other but also with a growing number of previously permanent employees who have been forced into gig work, most likely because they have been made redundant. Finally, GWs have to be highly disciplined and resilient and to adapt—for example to new technologies—to survive in the new economy.

3 Forms of the Gig Economy: A Preliminary Proposal

As noted above, we have proposed two extreme forms of the GE—the strong and the weak—while recognizing that they exist on a continuum containing intermediate forms. All of them are contingent on the values that can be described using two key variables employed to understand the functioning of the relationships between employers (i.e., platforms) and workers. The one is related to labor demand and supply and is linked to the principle of labor scarcity and value. The other is the level of skills required to deliver the different services involved in the different transactions or exchanges in question. In the first case, depending on whether the demand exceeds or is less than the supply of jobs in the sector or in the specific geographic location, we distinguish between two different scenarios or contexts. Likewise, the level of skills (in terms of high and low) required to carry out the service/task/activity in question also conditions the specific form of the GE. We note the role exerted by employers or platforms in each situation and the labor conditions that workers are more likely to face. Online companies or labor platforms may generally be distinguished by the skills required by the GW to undertake the projects/tasks/activities. On-demand work can be low- or high-skilled. For example, a great number of projects/tasks/activities involve low skills—food delivery from fast-food restaurants or goods from retail stores—or services such as facilitating accommodation, house cleaning, moving, dog walking, and pet sitting among others. By contrast, jobs for designers, coders, software developers, robotics engineers, care workers, doctors, accountants, consultants, or lawyers, require high skills.

When the supply of jobs is lower than the demand (which, in general, in the case when a high level of skill is involved), we argue that the dominant form of GE is the strong form. When the supply of jobs is greater than the demand (which, in general, is the case when a lower level of skill is involved), the dominant form of GE is the weak form. Figure 2 summarizes these forms. The figure also indicates that intermediate forms can coexist between the extremes.

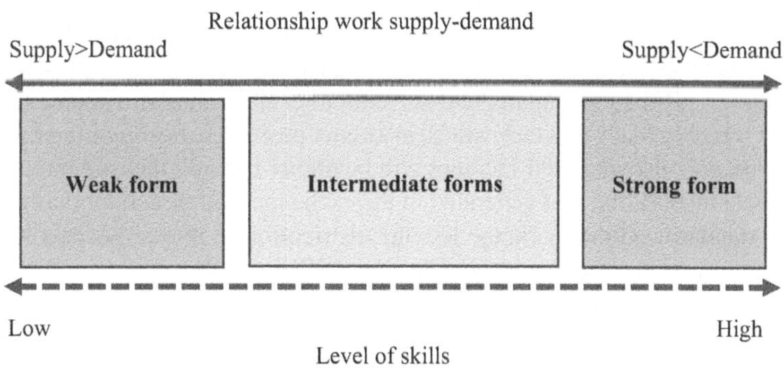

Fig. 2 Forms of the gig economy. *Source* The authors

Next, we explain the potential impact of the GE on working conditions and on GWs themselves, depending on the dominant form.

3.1 The Strong Form of the Gig Economy

As was stated above, the strong form corresponds to a situation in which the supply of labor is lower than the demand, that is, where there is a need for skills possessed by fewer people and where the jobs are more difficult to come by. Workers in these circumstances can become high-value service providers. For example, nowadays, most information workers (e.g., in data science, big data, or legal services) are in high demand among both traditional and non-traditional companies, and they tend to be scarce because their skills involve a high technical and sometimes multidisciplinary component. Firms are continually advertising in the business press for these types of GWs.

In general, highly skilled individuals perform projects/tasks/activities that are difficult to automate. This explains why these workers a priori are invariably in a position to be discriminant in their choice of projects/tasks/activities. They also generate high value for the companies that hire them. They therefore have certain bargaining power. As a result, their working conditions and wages are generally good, and they can enjoy freedom and professional development through the various projects/tasks/activities they carry out. Furthermore, digital platforms allow most of them to reach out to a critical mass of clients that might have been less within their reach before the GE boom.

Highly skilled GWs, especially those linked to information services, may join several platforms to supplement other sources of revenue. This leaves them less vulnerable to potential labor abuse arising from discretionary policy changes by either the platforms or the companies engaging them. Substitution is also less likely because they are less replaceable. Online platforms that act as intermediaries of high-skilled work cannot afford high turnover rates among their employee base, and so it might be expected that they are much more committed to worker-friendly labor policies (Van Doorn, 2017). Because a GW in this situation can be considered to be a scarce/rare, difficult to imitate, non-substitutable, and valuable resource (Barney, 1991), it is highly likely that they will be in a better position to negotiate their working conditions, and also that their incomes will be higher because they are more able to appropriate most of the rent generated in the exchange or transaction. Furthermore, the less standardized the work, the less the distribution of power moves toward the client and away from the employee (Choudary, 2018).

Some examples of companies that might play a role in this form of GE are the following: Pager, a mobile technology company that connects healthcare providers and patients with different types of urgent healthcare services; Heal, an online platform that arranges for physicians to make house calls; Tongal, which connects businesses looking for innovative ideas with directors, producers, or writers; Expert360, a company that matches independent business consultants (highly qualified workers with extensive experience in executive or senior management positions in large corporations or investment companies) with clients for short- or long-term projects; Gigster, which, as its website states, helps other "companies expand their ability to innovate by building dynamic teams made up of top global talent that create industry-changing custom software"; UpCounsel, an online marketplace for legal services that allows users (primarily entrepreneurs and businesses) to find and hire attorneys according to their specific requirements; and Andela, a firm that builds software engineering teams using the world's top talent and introduces them to a worldwide client base.

3.2 The Weak Form of the Gig Economy

This corresponds to an unbalanced situation where the supply of labor is greater than the demand; it is therefore detrimental to the worker, who has barely any bargaining power over conditions or wages. In some cases, this generates semi-slavery threatens people's dignity. The greater the imbalance, the greater the offense to the worker. In addition, the jobs involved usually require few skills and can be performed by large numbers of people (Choudary, 2018). Even in the medium term, many of these tasks could be easily automated.

Because the provision of certain services follows standard procedures, platforms (i.e., employers) tend to exercise a substantial amount of control over the conditions of exchange or transaction. For example, they can design and employ surveillance systems to track deliveries (Heiland, 2021). The more highly marketed the service is, the more control the platform can apply over its delivery. A plausible explanation for this is that such services are ordinarily associated with lower bargaining costs. Highly standardized jobs can be more easily and successfully monitored using certain technological devices, and employees are subsequently less empowered (Choudary, 2018). In such circumstances, agency problems are more likely to arise between employers or platforms and workers because the former are quite likely to behave more opportunistically. Weak form GE jobs carry more risk than opportunity compared with strong form GE jobs.

Employers such as Uber, Deliveroo, and Glovo fix the price for jobs, which means that the GW can neither bargain with the employer nor with the client (Rosenblat & Stark, 2016). The policies of these employers are usually designed to preclude the possibility of the employees working on their own terms. It is widely acknowledged that low-skilled GW power and influence within such companies are negligible (Van Buren & Greenwood, 2008). Furthermore, low-skilled workers, especially those in a more precarious situation (for instance, temporary workers), are very likely to become increasingly dependent on these types of employers (platforms) for their main source of revenue (Choudary, 2018).

In general, the position of low-skilled GWs is more precarious than that of their high-skilled peers in several respects. For example, they often do not have the same degree of income and social security protection (particularly in the event of illness or unemployment); their working conditions are inferior; they have few training opportunities; their career prospects are poor; and they lack collective bargaining rights and representation (Pesole et al., 2018).

Uber is currently one of the largest companies in the GE. It provides taxi, package and/or food delivery, courier, and freight transportation services (among others). Online food delivery companies include Deliveroo, Glovo, Just Eat, and Swiggy. In Spain, the food delivery sector is dominated by four large companies or platforms: Glovo, Deliveroo, Just Eat, and Uber Eats. They have often abused their position, according to the Spanish consumer organization FACUA. It is common to hear their GWs in Spain and elsewhere protesting poor working conditions. Furthermore, the Spanish restaurants and shopkeepers who have joined apps of these platforms have also denounced that this modality of delivering is not profitable due to the 'abusive' commissions that platforms charge them, which can reach, in some cases, up to 40%.

Numerous academic studies have pointed to the negative consequences of the GE for workers (e.g., Aloisi, 2016; Aroles et al., 2019; Graham et al., 2017; Scholz, 2017; Stanford, 2017; Van Doorn, 2017; Wood et al., 2019). Their situation is often worse than is found in traditional call centers (Woodcock, 2016). Most of the above studies refer to the weak form.

4 Conclusions

The present study has reviewed relevant aspects of the GE. Its principal characteristics, its importance in various countries, and various contingent features have been discussed. Previous literature has treated the GE as if it were a homogeneous phenomenon, adopting both optimistic and pessimistic positions concerning the labor relations that exist within it. Scholars have also failed to agree on a common definition of the term, either in terms of content or scope. We have proposed an original categorization that can help resolve the problem of a lack of consensus on a definition and the generalization of arguments concerning the GE.

We have presented two extreme forms of GE: the strong form and the weak form. These have been characterized according to the relationship between labor supply and demand and the principles of scarcity and value. The level of skills that are necessary for GWs to carry out their projects/tasks/activities has also been considered. We have argued that the strong form of the GE can benefit GWs by creating a wider range of opportunities. By contrast, the weak form of the GE negatively affects employment relationships to such a degree that less skilled GWs have none of the rights that have been acquired by employees over the last decades. This form currently presents more risks than opportunities for workers. The weak form of GE resembles a quasi-master–slave relationship in which the principle of basic survival brushes up against the principle of the dignity of the human being. Accordingly, the weak form could be viewed as less socially responsible than the strong form.

The massive surge of COVID-19-related layoffs has raised questions about how technology should be applied. While many companies related to the GE are having to lay workers off (as are traditional firms), others are trying to help get people back into employment. The current global economic and health crisis has highlighted the need to pay more attention to rights, protections, and benefits for all employees, and especially for those facing a more precarious situation. A growing number of people around the world do not want to be hired as employees in the traditional manner and are opting for more flexible ways of living. However, there is a continuing debate about which particular social protections and economic benefits businesses (especially those operating in the GE) should provide. Certainly, the shift in workforce attitudes and continuous calls for greater protection for GWs (which have grown as a result of COVID-19) have placed the issue on the political agenda in many countries.

In light of the present study and the typology proposed, it is clear that protection should be extended to both types of GWs in the different forms of the GE, but more especially for those who operate in the weak form because they have often been forced to work in conditions of semi-slavery. They may also have more difficulty (given their low level of skills in many cases) in finding new jobs immediately if they are fired. For example, the food delivery sector (whose companies are part of the so-called weak form of the GE) has been one of the worst hit during the pandemic. It has witnessed massive indiscriminate layoffs, and unions of workers on digital platforms are urging governments in countries where food delivery companies operate to introduce labor rights for GWs. Some experts have suggested that policymakers should work toward more GW empowerment and protection and guarantee that the appropriate measures are applied not only at the point of entry but also thereafter. This could be achieved through the monitoring of all available data.

While we recognize that policymakers play a fundamental role in improving workers' conditions (by introducing the relevant regulations), we—along with Healy et al. (2020) and others—suggest that ethical consumer behavior might also help. It is clear that in the weak form of the GE, GWs are the most vulnerable group and, therefore, consumers through their purchasing decisions could force some companies (or platforms) to adopt more worker-friendly policies.

Acknowledgements This paper has been supported by Project RTI2018-097447-B-I00 of the Ministry of Science, Innovation and Universities (Spain). Any errors are our own responsibility.

References

Aloisi, A. (2016). Commoditized workers: Case study research on labor law issues arising from a set of "on-demand/gig economy" platforms. *Comparative Labor Law and Policy Journal, 37*(3), 620–653.

Anwar, M. A., & Graham, M. (2020). Between a rock and a hard place: Freedom, flexibility, precarity and vulnerability in the gig economy in Africa. *Competition and Change*, 1024529420914473. Retrieved from https://doi.org/10.1177/1024529420914473

Apouey, B., Roulet, A., Solal, I., & Stabile, M. (2020). Gig workers during the COVID-19 crisis in France: Financial precarity and mental well-being. *Journal of Urban Health, 97*(6), 776–795.

Aroles, J., Mitev, N., & de Vaujany, F. X. (2019). Mapping themes in the study of new work practices. *New Technology, Work and Employment, 34*(3), 285–299.

Bajwa, U., Gastaldo, D., Di Ruggiero, E., & Knorr, L. (2018). The health of workers in the global gig economy. *Globalization and Health, 14*(1), 1–4.

Barney, J. (1991). Firm resources and sustained competitive advantage. *Journal of Management, 17*(1), 99–120.

Barratt, T., Goods, C., & Veen, A. (2020). 'I'm my own boss…': Active intermediation and 'entrepreneurial' worker agency in the Australian gig-economy. *Environment and Planning a: Economy and Space, 52*(8), 1643–1661.

Brancati, C. U., Pesole, A., & Fernández-Macías, E. (2019). Digital labour platforms in Europe: Numbers, profiles, and employment status of platform workers. *JCR Technical Reports*, Luxembourg: European Commission. Retrieved from https://ec.europa.eu/jrc/en/publication/digital-labour-platforms-europe-numbersprofiles-and-employment-status-platform-workers

Cao, X., Zhang, D., & Huang, L. (2020). The impact of COVID-19 pandemic on gig economy labor supply (August 4, 2020). NYU Stern School of Business, Retrieved from https://ssrn.com/abstract=3666725 or https://doi.org/10.2139/ssrn.3666725

Carey, R. (2019). The so-called 'gig economy' changing the Australian workforce. *Special Broadcasting Service*. Archived from the original on 2019–09–23. Retrieved 2019–09–23

Choudary, S. P. (2018). The architecture of digital labour platforms: Policy recommendations on platform design for worker well-being. *ILO Future of Work Research Paper Series, 3*. Geneva: International Labour Organization.

Christie, N., & Ward, H. (2019). The health and safety risks for people who drive for work in the gig economy. *Journal of Transport and Health, 13*, 115–127.

Deloitte (2014). *Big demands and high expectations. The Deloitte millennial survey*. Executive Summary, January. Retrieved from https://www2.deloitte.com/content/dam/Deloitte/global/Documents/About-Deloitte/gx-dttl-2014-millennial-survey-report.pdf

Edison Research (2018). *The gig economy*. Marketplace-Edison Research Poll, December. Retrieved from http://www.edisonresearch.com/wp-content/uploads/2019/01/Gig-Economy-2018-Marketplace-Edison-Research-Poll-FINAL.pdf

Fabo, B., Karanovic, J., & Dukova, K. (2017). In search of an adequate European policy response to the platform economy. *Transfer: European Review of Labour and Research, 23*(2), 163–175

Fayard, A. L. (2021). Notes on the meaning of work: Labor, work, and action in the 21st century. *Journal of Management Inquiry, 30*(2), 207–220.

Ford, M., & Honan, V. (2019). The limits of mutual aid: Emerging forms of collectivity among app-based transport workers in Indonesia. *Journal of Industrial Relations, 61*(4), 528–548.

Friedman, G. (2014). Workers without employers: Shadow corporations and the rise of the gig economy. *Review of Keynesian Economics, 2*(2), 171–188.

Gandini, A. (2019). Labour process theory and the gig economy. *Human Relations, 72*(6), 1039–1056.

Goods, C., Veen, A., & Barratt, T. (2019). "Is your gig any good?" Analysing job quality in the Australian platform-based food-delivery sector. *Journal of Industrial Relations, 61*(4), 502–527.

Graham, M., Hjorth, I., & Lehdonvirta, V. (2017). Digital labour and development: Impacts of global digital labour platforms and the gig economy on worker livelihoods. *Transfer: European Review of Labour and Research, 23*(2), 135–162.

Hauben, H., Lenaerts, K., & Waeyaert, W. (2020). *The platform economy and precarious work*. Publication for the committee on Employment and Social Affairs, Policy Department for Economic, Scientific and Quality of Life Policies. Luxembourg: European Parliament.

Healy, J., Nicholson, D., & Pekarek, A. (2017). Should we take the gig economy seriously? *Labour and Industry: A Journal of the Social and Economic Relations of Work, 27*(3), 232–248.

Healy, J., Pekarek, A., & Vromen, A. (2020). Sceptics or supporters? Consumers' views of work in the gig economy. *New Technology, Work and Employment, 35*(1), 1–19.

Heiland, H. (2021). Controlling space, controlling labour? Contested space in food delivery gig work. *New Technology, Work and Employment*. Retrieved from https://doi.org/10.1111/ntwe.12183

Jabagi, N., Croteau, A.-M., Audebrand, L. K., & Marsan, J. (2019). Gig-workers' motivation: Thinking beyond carrots and sticks. *Journal of Managerial Psychology, 34*(4), 192–213. Available at: https://doi.org/10.1108/JMP-06-2018-0255

Kostyshyna, O., & Luu, C. (2019). The size and characteristics of informal ("Gig") work in Canada. *Staff Analytical Note 2019–6. Bank of Canada*. Retrieved from https://www.bankofcanada.ca/wp-content/uploads/2019/02/san2019-6.pdf

Lehdonvirta, V. (2018). Flexibility in the gig economy: Managing time on three online piecework platforms. *New Technology, Work and Employment, 33*(1), 13–29.

Lojeski, K. S., & Reilly, R. R. (2020). *The power of virtual distance: A guide to productivity and happiness in the age of remote work*. Wiley.

MBO Partners (2018). *The new normal*. Retrieved from https://www.mbopartners.com/wp-content/uploads/2019/02/State_of_Independence_2018.pdf

MBO Partners (2020). *A decade of independence: Ten trends that matter*. Retrieved from https://info.mbopartners.com/rs/mbo/images/MBO_Partners_State_of_Independence_2020_Report.pdf

Pesole, A., Urzí Brancati, M. C., Fernández-Maciás, E., Biagi, F., & Gonzalez Vasquez, I. (2018). Platform workers in Europe: Evidence from the COLLEEM survey. *EUR- Scientific and Technical Research Reports*, Publications Office of the European Union. Retrieved from http://publications.jrc.ec.europa.eu/repository/handle/111111111/52393

Petriglieri, G., Ashford, S. J., & Wrzesniewski, A. (2019). Agony and ecstasy in the gig economy: Cultivating holding environments for precarious and personalized work identities. *Administrative Science Quarterly, 64*(1), 124–170.

Polkowska, D. (2020). Platform work during the COVID-19 pandemic: A case study of Glovo couriers in Poland. *European Societies*. Retrieved from https://doi.org/10.1080/14616696.2020.1826554

Prassl, J. (2018). *Humans as a service: The promise and perils of work in the gig economy*. Oxford University Press.

Richardson, L. (2015). Performing the sharing economy. *Geoforum, 67*, 121–129.

Richardson, L. (2020). Coordinating office space: Digital technologies and the platformization of work. *Environment and Planning D: Society and Space*, 0263775820959677. Retrieved from https://doi.org/10.1177/0263775820959677

Rosenblat, A., & Stark, L. (2016). Algorithmic labor and information asymmetries: A case study of Uber's drivers. *International Journal of Communication, 10*, 3758–3784.

Rothschild, V. (2018). China's gig economy is driving close to the edge. Foreign Policy, Retrieved 29 January, 2021, from https://foreignpolicy.com/2018/09/07/chinas-gig-economy-is-driving-close-to-the-edge/

Rowe Price, T. (2018). *2018 Financial attitudes and behaviors toward the gig economy*. April, Baltimore.

Scholz, T. (2017). *Uberworked and underpaid: How workers are disrupting the digital economy*. Polity Press.

Schwellnus, C., Geva, A., Pak, M., & Veiel, R. (2019). Gig economy platforms: Boon or bane? *Economics Department Working Papers*, No. 1550, OECD Publishing, Paris. Retrieved from https://doi.org/10.1787/fdb0570b-en

Stanford, J. (2017). The resurgence of gig work: Historical and theoretical perspectives. *The Economic and Labour Relations Review, 28*(3), 382–401.

Ukolov, V. F., Solomatin, A. V., Solomatin, Y. V., Chernikov, S. U., & Ukolov, A. V. (2016). Food-sharing economy pattern comparison in UK and Russian markets. *International Business Management, 10*, 4268–4282.

Umar, M., Xu, Y., & Mirza, S. S. (2020). The impact of Covid-19 on gig economy. *Economic Research-Ekonomska Istraživanja*. Retrieved from https://doi.org/10.1080/1331677X.2020.1862688

Ungemah, J. (2021). *Punching the clock: Adapting to the new future of work*. Oxford University Press.

Vallas, S., & Schor, J. B. (2020). What do platforms do? Understanding the gig economy. *Annual Review of Sociology, 46*, 273–294.

Van Doorn, N. (2017). Platform labor: On the gendered and racialized exploitation of low-income service work in the 'on-demand' economy. *Information, Communication and Society, 20*(6), 898–914.

Van Buren, H. J., & Greenwood, M. (2008). Enhancing employee voice: Are voluntary employer–employee partnerships enough? *Journal of Business Ethics, 81*(1), 209–221.

Wallenstein, J., de Chalendar, A., Reeves, M., & Bailey, A. (2019). *The new freelancers: Tapping talent in the gig economy*. BCG Henderson Institute. Retrieved from https://www.bcg.com/en-us/publications/2019/new-freelancers-tapping-talent-gig-economy

Wood, A. J., Graham, M., Lehdonvirta, V., & Hjorth, I. (2019). Good gig, bad gig: Autonomy and algorithmic control in the global gig economy. *Work, Employment and Society, 33*(1), 56–75.

Woodcock, J. (2016). *Working the phones: Control and resistance in call centres*. Pluto Press.

Zwick, A. (2018). Welcome to the gig economy: Neoliberal industrial relations and the case of Uber. *GeoJournal, 83*(4), 679–691.

Jose I. Galan is Full Professor in Management at the University of Salamanca (Spain) and Chair of the Iberoamerican Project of Management and Corporate Social Responsibility (University of Salamanca/Santander Bank). He has also been visiting professor in different universities: University of Warwick, Oxford, Bath, or Unicamp. He has served as consultant for the United Nations, European Commission, Santander Bank, SEGIB, and Regional Government of Castilla y Leon. He has published in *Journal of International Business Studies, Journal of World Business, Strategic Management Journal, Journal of Management Studies, Journal of Business Ethics, Business & Society, Organization Studies* or *British Journal of Management* among others.

Jose Angel Zuñiga-Vicente is Full Professor in Management at the Rey Juan Carlos University (Spain). He has also been visiting professor (fellow) in different universities: Warwick Business School, Copenhagen Business School, or Middlesex University London, among others. His research is currently focused on different aspects related to human resources, internationalization, and innovation. He has published in *Journal of International Business Studies, Journal of Management Studies, Long Range Planning, Journal of Business Research, British Journal of Management, International Business Review, Journal of International Management* or *The International Journal of Human Resource Management* among others.

Gig Economy: Trends and Perspectives. How to Define Advantages and Disadvantages of Gig Economy?

Olga Shvetsova

1 Introduction

1.1 Characteristics of Gig Economy

The term "gig economy" (GIGE) refers to a free market system in which traditional businesses employ independent contractors, freelancers, and short-term employees to complete individual tasks, assignments, or jobs. The term comes from the performing arts world in which musicians, comedians, etc., are paid for their individual performances, called "performances".

Gig economy implies short-term, temporary, and project employment of civilian workers. Regardless of the world of work, such performers work on small tasks for a certain amount of time (e.g., on shifts) or on a project basis. Once the task or shift is complete, the contractor switches to another task. It can be a new task from the same employer or a completely different job. At the same time, as noted by FlexJobs, both men and women are equally involved in gig economy. Men are more likely to be employed in manufacturing, while women are more likely to work in marketing and online sales.

Despite the fact that the term "gig economy" itself is relatively new, this form of working relationship has been around for a long time. According to a 2017 American Personnel Association study, 78% of Americans surveyed see gig economics as a new name for non-traditional forms of employment (ACPA, 2021).

The term "gig worker" can include freelancers, temporary workers, and contractors. According to a CIPD study, 1.3 million Britons were employed in the gig economy in 2017 (CIPD, 2021). The American Personnel Association reports that there were 10.6 million independent contractors in the USA as of May 2017 or 6.9%

O. Shvetsova (✉)
Korea University of Technology and Education, Cheonan 31254, South Korea
e-mail: shvetsova@koreatech.ac.kr

A. Gupta et al. (eds.), *Sustainability in the Gig Economy*,
https://doi.org/10.1007/978-981-16-8406-7_2

of all workers in the country. An organization survey found that less than half of these workers rely on part-time jobs as their main source of income (ACPA, 2021).

Main characteristics of GIGE are as follows:

- Gig economy drives businesses to hire independent contractors to perform individual jobs called "concerts".
- Hired and assigned via the Internet and smartphone apps, GIG employees work remotely.
- Although contract workers have great schedule flexibility and additional income, they suffer from relatively low wages, lack of benefits, and increased stress.
- In 2018, about 57 million Americans—nearly 36% of the total US workforce—worked full time or part time (Harris & Krueger, 2019).

While such temporary arrangements offer tremendous benefits, such as freedom and flexibility, workers in a booming gig economy find that they face an increased risk of financial hardship because they are solely responsible for their own income and benefits. Just like traditional jobs, gig economy jobs are great as long as they are not.

Humanity now lives at high speeds. And the larger they are, the more urgent becomes the issue of employees' efficiency and their focus on results.

The gig economy is a relatively new concept in business. Often referred to as the freelance economy, this term refers to the environment in which people are temporarily recruited to complete specific projects.

At the moment, this relationship model is the most popular among IT professionals. However, representatives of scientific and creative professions are beginning to adopt this format. For example, in the USA, more than 30% of employees are already working on this principle (Harris & Krueger, 2019).

The basics of the gig economy are moving away from the standard schedule from 9 to 18, work outside the state, the ability to work on several projects at the same time. Working in this format motivates people to complete the task faster. The company receives its profit—it does not spend money on the maintenance of the state.

Working according to new business principles, people become more responsible and conscious, because their activities are not limited to routine and encourage constant development. With advanced training, the number of orders and areas where you can apply and improve your skills also increases. As a result, business profits grow.

1.2 How Does Gig Economy Work?

"Gig economy" or "freelance economy" gives gig workers opportunity to receive all or part of their income from short-term contracts that are paid them for individual tasks, assignments, or jobs. These individual assignments only reflect only a proportion of total income. By summing multiple tasks from different companies, the total income is high for these gig workers. For example, taxi drivers register themselves with various platforms to supplement their income.

Gig economy provides a flexible work environment and helps in attaining work–life balance. Role of Internet is the most crucial factor that helped the economy evolve and thrive in the contemporary world. They are digital earning platforms and allow people to earn money by simply selling their used items on eBay and OLX or having online handyman services such as TaskRabbit.

A report published in 2018 by Gallup that 29% of the workforce in America have alternate works as their main job and around 57 million Americans have one or more jobs (Mas & Pallais, 2017). The United States Bureau of Economic Analysis estimates that there is an increase in digital economy at 5.6% annually from 2006 to 2016. This digital economy supports nearly six million in industries such as warehousing, finance, and wholesale (Horton, 2017).

A report by Pew Research Center (USA) forecasts a rapid growth due to greater usage of mobile devices for buying and selling products and providing personal services. A study done by Digital Trends predicted a sharp increase in smartphone users by 2020 (Horton, 2017).

Wired publishers noted the similarities between gig economy and zero-contract work in the absence of guaranteed wages and in the fact that both forms of employment are a consequence of companies' desire to reduce personnel costs. At the same time, in gig economics, payment occurs upon completion of the task (e.g., the delivery of an order or a taxi), and payment under a zero contract occurs according to the number of hours worked.

The gig economy is a truly progressive approach that should bring positive changes for:

- Employers and managers—they will be able to form a team depending on the actual needs of the enterprise;
- Consumers—companies will more quickly respond to their requests and fill the market with really popular goods and services;
- Narrow and qualified specialists—they will be able to work for several employers at once, and they will be able to regulate the cost of their services and the level of profit.

But there is an opinion that the popularization of such a business model may cause a devaluation of traditional stability and social guarantees. There is a risk that highly skilled workers will indeed be replaced by less skilled independent workers.

Traditional work is not only a source of income, but also a place for socialization and constant communication. According to the principles of gig economy, the composition of the team working on a project can constantly change. Because of this, employees will constantly be in the process of adaptation, and this is additional stress.

Now you can freely choose whether to join a project team or work in a traditional job. But what will happen when this opportunity is gone? Only part of the existing workers adapts to the new conditions.

With the transition to the gig economy, the role of HR will increase. He will need to notice the roughness in the team's work in time and correct them. If in traditional collectives these processes could self-regulate, in new conditions they will become more noticeable.

How do gig workers appear?

1. A positive option: People find that they need to change or take more than one job to allow themselves the lifestyle they want. Such professionals can work in the office from nine to six, and then move on to a second job from six to nine. Or they could be a nine to six gig worker all day.
2. Negative option: Distributed among workers who have been laid off, as well as among residents of countries with emerging economies.

Gig economy is called a kind of "virtual migration," when everyone can work from anywhere. Internet geography Professor Mark Graham in his article on digital work and development says it can bring good jobs to regions of the world where work is difficult. In reality, everything turned out to be a little more complicated (MBO Partners, Inc, 2018). Researchers at the Oxford Internet Institute interviewed 456 workers in Africa and Southeast Asia and found that digital platforms play an important role in the gig economy (MBO Partners, Inc, 2018).

Such online platforms like Freelancer, Fiverr, Uber, and Upwork act as a link between the business and the professional, but their operating principles isolate workers socially and deprive them of a number of safety benefits.

The gig economy is a logical consequence of the massive changes that have taken place in the world over the past 20 years. This is the economy of efficiency, the desire to achieve more, and the ability to think freely. This is a real evolution in business and cannot be stopped.

2 Pandemic and the Gig Economy

Because of the pandemic, the World Economic Forum has witnessed a fall in demand for its services. Security has become the major concern of the gig workers during this time. Majority of the employees (70%) are not content with the support extended by their employers and expected government support. The saving was negligent among the workers (23%), and 70% of them had no income as they had lost their jobs. Around 89% of the existing gig workers are searching for new avenues of income generation (Katz & Krueger, 2019).

The situation is stable for the freelancers as per the internal study by Payoneer payment system which surveyed more than 1000 freelancers. Nearly ¾ of the respondents experienced stable hourly rate. The freelancers (40%) believed that the demand for their service was either constant or in some situations it also increased while 32% found a drop in new orders placed by the employers. This fall in demand was more prominent in North America and Europe (53%) as compared to Asia and Australia (45%) (Katz & Krueger, 2019; Cook et al., 2019).

3 Advantages and Disadvantages of Gig Economy

3.1 GIGE Advantages

For employers, the gig economy is basically a win–win. Companies can quickly contract experts for customized projects without overhead costs such as office space, training, and perks. For freelancers, however, this can be a mixture of pros and cons.

Benefits of GIG working are as follows:

1. Flexibility: Unlike traditional employees, gig workers are free to choose what types of work they will do, when, and where they will do it. The ability to work from home helps balance work and family schedules and needs.
2. Independence: For people who like to be left alone while they complete a task, working at a concert is ideal. Without the hassle of traditional office interruptions such as staff meetings, progress reviews, and gossip about coolers, gig economy workers are usually given almost unlimited independence to do their jobs when and how they think they should.
3. Variety: The old office insect of monotony is rare in concert work. The variety of tasks and clients makes the job interesting every day, helping the concert workers to be more enthusiastic and creative in their work. There are never boring working days if you do not want to.

Various opportunities are created because of the gig economy. New sources of completion can be formed with the growth of technology-driven talent markets operationalizing through various online platforms. There are several examples in transportation sector including Uber and Lyft. There are companies like Handy dealing in repairing appliances, Tongal for catering ads and videos, and Hourlynerd for consultation. There is a need to strategize how to compete with firms hiring gig workers from the online platforms (Chen et al., 2019).

Another question arises as to how the companies can use this platform to improve their talent strategies. Alignment with the new model of the gig economy is very important, and the creative and traditional teams should work toward it. Tongal, the gig platform providing ad and videos has positioned itself as the first on demand studio in the world. Various freelancers from the field of music and advertisement can come together to search for better opportunities on this platform. They cater to some of the biggest companies like LEGO, Lenevo and Dannon (Chen et al., 2019; Cook et al., 2019). This requires integration and collaboration across departments to implement new models such as talent on demand and outdoor advertising and crowdsourcing.

One more example can be Thomson Reuters which has launched an in-house crowdfunding model offering works to company's engineers in its other division and overcoming deep internal stagnation and generation of ideas within the country's internal network (Thompson Reuters annual report Homepage, 2021).

3.2 GIGE Disadvantages

While the growth of the digital economy shows that consumers are enjoying and demanding convenience, choice and potential cost savings on gig services and sales, the gig economy also poses a threat to public safety.

Due to the remote hiring processes involved, gig workers sometimes do skilled jobs with little or no training or prior experience. For example, passengers on online ride-sharing services are often unaware of their driver's skill level, driver's license status, or criminal record.

In addition, convertible drivers are not subject to the same US Department of Transportation limits on the number of hours of continuous driving that traditional commercial vehicle drivers do. While some online travel services now block their drivers after a certain number of hours of driving, drivers often work in multiple services and simply switch back and forth, allowing them to drive for extended hours.

When it comes to the sale and rental of concerts, the old adage "buyer beware" is particularly relevant. Products are often sold without guarantees of quality or authenticity, and rental properties may not be as desirable as they appear on the service's Web site.

Disadvantages of gig work are as follows:

1. Modest Salary: While they can make up to $ 15,000 a year, a study by online lender Earnest found that about 85% of giants make less than $ 500 a month from a single gig. The solution, of course, is to do a few jobs (Cook et al., 2020).
2. No benefits: Very few jobs are associated with any kind of retirement or health benefits. While some long-term contracts may include limited benefits, even this is rare.
3. Taxes and expenses. Because contract workers are not legally classified as "employees," their employers do not withhold income or social security taxes from their salaries. As a result, gig workers must pay tax payments to the IRS on a quarterly basis based on what they have earned. Most freelancers and giants believe that it is necessary to pay between 25 and 30% of each of their salaries in order to avoid paying taxes at the time of filing. In addition, most workers are responsible for purchasing their own work equipment such as cars, computers, and smartphones. Some of these expenses are tax deductible, but not all. Many workers feel that they should also consider the cost of accountants, tax services, or software.
4. Stress: All of the above, along with having to constantly look for your next gig and deal with changes in your current contract, can lead to increased stress—an unwanted compromise with more flexibility in live performance.

Here is some recommendation for specialists on what should they do as not to worry about a career over gig workers:

1. Go beyond the position: Only the lazy did not say that a successful employee is able to give the employer more than he expects. Prepare a report and see

what else the company is able to save or make money on—make comments with suggestions to the report. If you know how to optimize the work of a department, present your idea to the manager. Carefulness will benefit your career as much as professional merit.

2. Maintain uniqueness: Each professional has a unique work experience and a set of knowledge that he can use to complete tasks. Even more interesting is how wide your experience is outside of the professional field. The ability to transfer and use knowledge and skills from the outside and with their help solves work problems, creates new projects or products, and opens up an infinite number of options for the development of your career.
3. Continue learning: The habit of learning in any situation can give you a greater advantage. Nowadays, many perceive business digitalization as a necessary evil. However, this is another opportunity to identify the skills that are in demand and get them as quickly as possible in order to improve while other colleagues just begin to understand them.

Take a new kind of twenty-first-century talent: Companies need to understand open talent—the economy and their needs for different types of workforce and automation over the medium term (the next three to five years) and over the longer term (five to ten) years. The process begins with expanding workforce planning to include "on-bill" and "off-list" talent, as well as combinations of robotics, smart machines, and new labor/technology collaborations.

Identify team leadership blind spots for workforce planning and automation: Workforce planning is a blind spot exercise. The corporate technology, procurement, and strategic planning team must join HR in order to create robust plans for different jobs and technology combinations.

Focus on purchasing—both people and machines: Once companies have identified specific talent needs, they can focus on recruiting and acquiring each type of employee with an overall plan in mind. Technology and machines can complement the "on the list" employees.

Highlight productivity: Productivity and its downside, engagement, are presented in a new way with new workforce opportunities and automation.

These new workforce models and new combinations of talent and technology are critical to improving corporate productivity. New workforce planning approaches the integration of multiple segments of the workforce, and automation and cognitive technologies will improve the productivity and quality of products and services.

Developing new workforce models and automation that focus on engagement and skills is critical to your workforce: Increasing human engagement is one of the most important challenges today. Companies today must learn how to leverage new segments of the workforce and technology to improve the quality, usefulness, and value of your employees.

Main line: the twenty-first century workforce design will present new challenges for HR, technology, and business that require deeper levels of collaboration to develop solutions. Open talent—economics and machines as a workforce are coming to the fore, forcing a rethink of the definition of talent to include the work of people and machines in different fields based on different work contracts.

This is not just a deviation. This is the beginning of the transformation of the twenty-first-century workforce. Leading companies are tackling the questions that need to be answered in order to successfully compete for talent in a new environment. Who and what will make up the workforce? How will it be acquired? How can you measure its performance? How does an organization optimize a new mix of workers from different sources (Cullen et al., 2020)?

Noticed that many segments of the workforce have an impact on products and customers, what are the appropriate ways for all of these segments to interact? And who will direct these efforts?

4 Case Study: Gig Economy Trends in Switzerland

The so-called gig economy is developing at a gigantic pace all over the world, but in Switzerland, until recently, it was treated with distrust. Will the pandemic change attitudes toward the "freelancing economy"?

The Swiss Federal Office of Statistics recently conducted a survey for the first time among individuals who provide services or sell their products through online platforms. The data in Fig. 1 are not very optimistic.

Not only are there very few such workers in the country, but their average income is also minimal. In 2019, only 0.4% of Swiss residents said that in the previous

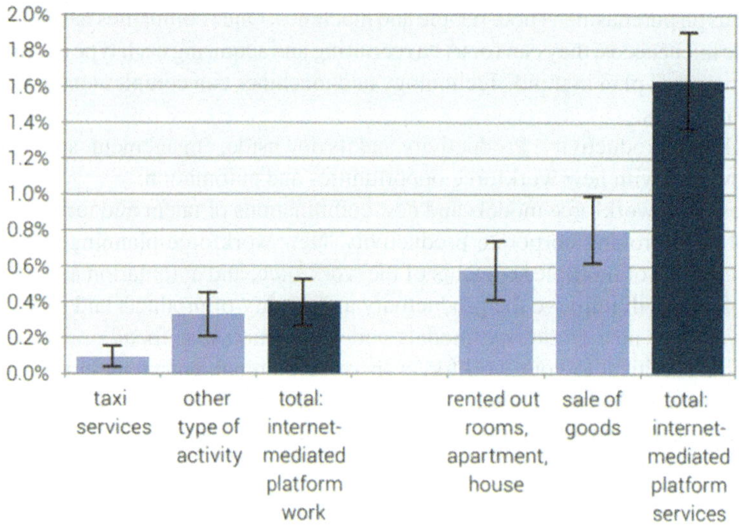

Fig. 1 Internet-mediated platform services by type of activity 2019. 2021 *Source* Swiss Labor Force Survey, ()

12 months they had used online platforms in one form or another to sell their products, to rent housing, organize food delivery, and order a taxi. In comparison, in countries such as India, China, and the USA, a significant proportion of the working-age population has already made the provision of goods and services on demand via the Internet and mobile applications as their main source of income.

In Switzerland, most of those who earn, or are trying to earn, with the help of at least one online platform of the "freelance economy", managed to "dirty," that is, before taxes, earn about 1000 Swiss francs per year. At the same time, the average annual per capita income of Swiss residents who earn money through such online platforms is 5849 francs, that is, only 487 francs per month (Kaine & Josserand, 2021).

Gig economy

In other words, in Switzerland so far in this way you can earn as much per year as the average person earns per month here, working "the old-fashioned way," going to the office every day (or sitting, as now, at a distance). As a reminder, the average monthly salary in Switzerland is now 6538 Swiss francs.

Karin Frick is Senior Research Fellow at the Swiss Institute. She deals with the peculiarities and trends of the country's socioeconomic development. "Switzerland is a rich and prosperous country. So far, there are enough high-paying jobs in the market, and therefore it is very difficult for companies like Uber to gain a foothold here," she said in an interview with the Swiss news site Watson (Açikgöz & Günay, 2020). The results of a survey carried out by the Statistical Office confirm its conclusions. Of all Swiss residents who have become part of the freelancing economy through online platforms, only 1.2% chose this job because they could not find a stable job (Fig. 2).

Marko Kovic, President of the Zurich Research Institute of Contemporary Social Challenges and Threats (ZIPAR, a project of the Forschungsinstitut Öffentlichkeit

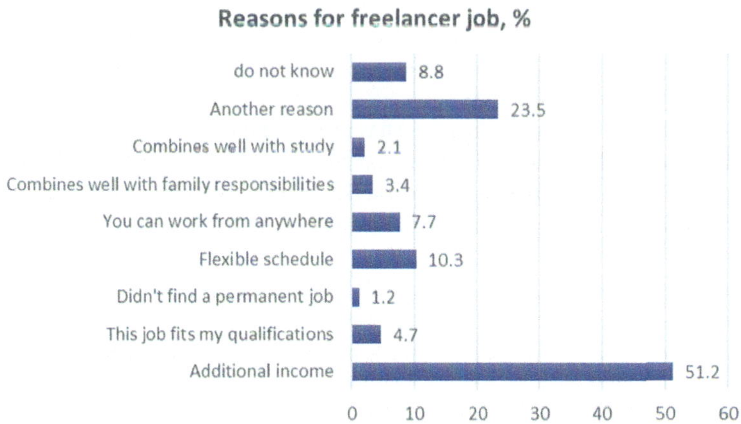

Fig. 2 Results of interview, 2020. Federal Swiss Statistic Homepage (2021 *Source* Federal Swiss Statistics. 2020 https://www.bfs.admin.ch/bfs/de/home.gnpdetail.2020-0505.html)

und Gesellschaft—fög), believes that "compared to the US and China, the freelancing economy in Switzerland is still in early childhood. With such a modest number of professional online platforms, it's still very difficult to make money freelancing here (Al-Awadhi et al., 2020)."

Pandemic as a catalyst?

The pandemic has dealt a blow to the Swiss economy, including the "freelance piece-work economy." Quarantine has forced many freelancers—taxi drivers, apartment cleaners, freelance photographers—to stay home. On the other hand, for many professions from this area, the pandemic has become an unexpectedly beneficial event from the series "there would be no happiness …" (Shvetsova, 2020).

Luisa Elster, Head of public relations at Uber Eats Switzerland (online food delivery service provider), confirms that "Uber Eats, for example, has been very active since mid-March 2020, reaching cities such as Lucerne, St. Gallen, Neuchâtel and Winterthur. We are planning to add significantly to this list in the coming months" (Baker et al., 2020).

Swiss managers believe that in the post-pandemic era, Switzerland will have far more online platforms and mobile applications than it does now to meet consumer demand, so that the country will have much more fertile soil for the growth of the gig economy. There is no doubt about that. The number of people employed in the service sector is expected to continue to increase.

In the face of a decline in employment due to quarantines and a pandemic, many will discover the gig economy as a way to earn some extra money. "I think that this trend will continue in Switzerland and that companies offering jobs within the freelance economy will be able to benefit from the new situation," predicts M. Kovic (Al-Awadhi et al., 2020).

Who benefits from?

At the same time, he emphasizes that, of course, new types of services allowed the Swiss to "keep a safe social distance" during the quarantine period, but a closer look at the situation in this area shows that all these services are prompt delivery of food, which largely replaced closed restaurants, and online taxi orders, which came instead of regular public transport, became possible only due to a noticeable reduction in the palette of guaranteed labor rights.

According to Luisa Elster, Uber Eats has provided the firm's food delivery drivers and employees with all the protective gear they need, including masks, starting in 2018 to pay all of its "independent partners," that is, everyone who works for the company on a freelance basis, financial compensation in case of loss of income due to accidents or illness (Baker et al., 2020).

Freelance Swiss workers are particularly vulnerable when it comes to their position under labor law. The fact is that most of the platforms of the "freelance economy" consider such workers not as hired workers, but as "self-employed persons" who fully take all entrepreneurial risks. They often have to organize their own social security and pension insurance themselves. At the same time, many of them, earning very modestly, do not pay contributions to pension funds, and in the event of an accident, they, losing their income, also lose part of their future pension.

Therefore, in some cantons of Switzerland, the courts intervene in the situation, deciding that freelance employees are salaried employees in a full-time format. For example, in June, a Geneva court ruled that Uber Eats, in accordance with the cantonal Labor Code, is an "employer" obliged to hire its drivers as full-fledged employees who have the right to expect their employer to make the required contributions to funds like social and pension insurance.

5 Conclusion

The gig economy (aka the Internet economy, the economy of digital platforms, the digital economy) is based on the costs of obtaining information and processing it, when, thanks to new methods of extracting and exchanging information, and it became possible to create new business models. The latter, as has happened more than once in history, began to infiltrate traditional sectors and then oust companies with a traditional organization from the markets. This process has both positive and dubious (I do not want to say—negative) consequences.

Until recently, it was impossible to assign risks to digital platforms, including aggregators, for product quality, on the one hand, and for temporary disability of people who worked with the platform, on the other. A sharp decline in the social protection of self-employed people who provide services using the platform (taxi drivers, for example, or any other specialists providing services) can be very painful for them.

For more than 100 years, the employer has assumed the risk of temporary disability of an employee. In the gig economy, aggregators and digital platforms only provide a platform for the buyer of a product or service and its seller to converge on it. But not all governments agree that this is normal. So, about a year ago, the so-called Gig Worker Law was adopted in California—a law according to which self-employed workers for such aggregators as Uber are, in fact, its employees with all the ensuing consequences for the aggregator (Hevia & Neumeyer, 2020).

Hiring the self-employed as workers while disclaiming responsibility for their working conditions has long been considered a successful business model, but only if it is possible to control the quality of the services provided and the goods sold and digital technologies allow you to do this. Quality control is carried out by users who put likes, stars, etc. And the aggregator can always close access to the platform for a company or self-employed, the quality of goods or services of which was rated low by the consumer. The aggregator will not waste time and money on educating the negligent.

The gig economy is now widespread wherever we use mobile phones and devices to exchange information, to receive information about new offers, to order a taxi, to order food, and to buy tickets. In the modern world, it is practically impossible to find a person who would not be involved in the gig economy. True, he may not know about it if the appeal to the platform is hidden from his eyes. The figure you quoted is not entirely correct, because it is incorrect to measure the volume of the gig economy by the number of people employed in it. It will indeed be small, because we are talking about the creators and owners of Internet platforms and aggregator companies.

References

Açikgöz, Ö., & Günay, A. (2020). The early impact of the Covid-19 pandemic on the global and Turkish economy. *Turkish Journal of Medical Sciences, 50*(SI-1), 520–526. https://doi.org/10.3906/sag-2004-6

American College Personnel Association (ACPA) Homepage. Last accessed 10 February 2021. https://www.myacpa.org/

Al-Awadhi, A. M., Alsaifi, K., Al-Awadhi, A., & Alhammadi, S. (2020). Death and contagious infectious diseases: Impact of the COVID-19 virus on stock market returns. *Journal of Behavioral and Experimental Finance, 27*, 100–326.

Baker, S. R., Bloom, N., Davis, S. J., Kost, K., Sammon, M., & Viratyosin, T. (2020). The unprecedented stock market reaction to COVID-19. *The Review of Asset Pricing Studies, 10*(4), 742–758.

Chen, M. K., Chevalier, J. A., Rossi, P. E., & Oehlsen, E. (2019). The value of flexible work: Evidence from Uber drivers. *Journal of Political Economy, 127*(6), 2735–2794.

CIPD annual report Homepage. Last accessed 01 February 2021. https://www.cipd.co.uk/about/who-we-are/annual-report

Cook, C., Diamond, R., Hall, J., List, J. A., & Oyer, P. (2020). The gender earnings gap in the gig economy: Evidence from over a million rideshare drivers NBER Working Paper No. 24732.

Cook, C., Diamond, R., & Oyer, P. (2019). Older workers and the gig economy. *AEA Papers and Proceedings, 109*, 372–376.

Cullen, Z. B., Humphries, J. E., & Pakzad-Hurson, B. (2020). Gender and sorting in the on-demand economy working paper.

Federal Swiss Statistic Homepage. Last accessed 05 January 2021. shttps://www.bfs.admin.ch/bfs/de/home.gnpdetail.2020-0505.html

Harris, S. D., & Krueger, A. B. (2019) A proposal for modernizing labor laws for twenty-first-century work: The "Independent Worker." The Hamilton Project Discussion Paper No. 10.

Hevia, C., & Neumeyer, A. (2020). A conceptual framework for analyzing the economic impact of COVID-19 and its policy implications. COVID19 Policy Document Series.

Horton, J. J. (2017). The effects of algorithmic labor market recommendations: Evidence from a field experiment. *Journal of Labor Economics, 35*(2), 345–385.

Kaine, S., & Josserand, E. (2021). The organization and experience of work in the gig economy. *Journal of Industrial Relations, 9*(3), 23–36. https://doi.org/10.1177/0022185619865480

Katz, L. F., & Krueger, A. B. (2019). The rise and nature of alternative work arrangements in the United States, 1995–2015. *ILR Review, 72*(2), 382–416.

Mas, A., & Pallais, A. (2017). Valuing alternative work arrangements. *American Economic Review, 107*(12), 3722–3759.

MBO Partners, Inc (2018) "The state of independence in America. 2018: The new normal". Herndon: MBO Partners, Inc.

Shvetsova, O. (2020). Technology management in international entrepreneurship: Innovative development and sustainability. Nova Publishing, NY.

Swiss Labor Force Survey (SLFS). Last accessed 21 January 2021. https://www.bfs.admin.ch/bfs/en/home/statistics/work-income/surveys/slfs.html

Thompson Reuters annual report Homepage. Last accessed 21 January 2021. https://www.thomsonreuters.com/en/reports.html

Olga Shvetsova is Assistant Professor at Korea University of Technology and Education (South Korea) since 2016. She graduated from Saint-Petersburg State University of Economics (Russia) in 2004. In 2011, she got Ph.D. there.

She actively provides guest lectures in EU and makes research review for some professional societies (IEEE, IBIMA, EURAM, ISPIM). She published more than 25 research papers and five academic books in the fields of international business, innovation management, and global HRM.

Annually, she develops courses for online MBA in EU and participates in international research projects. She got "Best Teaching" award in 2017 and "Best Young Scientist" award in 2015.

Her major research interests are international business, transferring global technologies and international human resource strategies.

To contact Ms. Olga A. Shvetsova, please send any requests to shvetsova@koreatech.ac.kr.

Critical Success Factors for the Future of Work in Gig Economy: Determinants for Gig Entrepreneurs

Joseph Odhiambo Onyango

1 Introduction

Across the world, the number of independent workers is increasing at a faster rate. For instance, close to 20–30% of the independent workers in the USA make up for the working-age population (McKinsey Global Institute, 2016). Sweden further has close to 55% of self-employed individuals. The increase in independent workers is driven by increased supply and demand factors (Karlsson & Wranne, 2019). Concerning the supply side, the increase is mainly driven by work values and norms among the millennials entering the workforce who prefer flexible work (Deloitte, 2017). About the demand side, organizations want to control the labour force and consider competence in the short run because of increased innovation and digitalization of business processes (Poon, 2018; EY Global, 2018).

In the wave of technological disruptions coupled with the ever-changing market dynamics, technology remains the most significant facilitator of the supply and demand-side factors (Karlsson & Wranne, 2019). The proponents of the gig economy as employment modality contend that workers are seeking work–life balance which can be easily attained through gig scheme of work with flexible. Technology has made it easier for organizations and individuals seeking independent contracting work to match job procedures and skills easier than before (Harris & Krueger, 2015). This connection in the form of "third-party" arrangements gives platforms for employers and employees to interact freely, thus connecting employers with independent workers. As such, the expansion in independent work has resulted from changing values, the need for agile work and the technological developments that influence gig economy.

J. O. Onyango (✉)
Strathmore University Business School, Nairobi, Kenya
e-mail: jonyango@strathmore.edu

A. Gupta et al. (eds.), *Sustainability in the Gig Economy*,
https://doi.org/10.1007/978-981-16-8406-7_3

This type of economy has created a proliferation of public interest as it provides platform upon which companies can engage and contract workers. However, irrespective of technological advancement, there are economic and political factors that hamper the gig economy's growth. The technological platform provides means to bring together employers and freelance workers (Graham & Woodcock, 2018) through software applications (apps), technological infrastructure and algorithms for handling the work. The platform architecture creates an online context in which buyers of services can connect to providers (two-sided market). Through the gig economy, companies can claim themselves as not the sole employers of labour providers.

1.1 *Just-In-Time Workforce*

Even though there has been an exponential growth in the numbers of the gig economy, the impact it creates on labour rights has been overlooked (De Stefano, 2015). The gig type of work economy provides work-on-demand model and crowd work model as the two main emerging strands of models. In as much as the gig economy's forms of work that includes "crowd work model" and "work-on-demand model via apps" provide opportunities to source for jobs and allow adaptable work schedule that allow work modification. Currently, the operations within gig economy are viewed as a split economy alternative to the mainstream economy of work which is not the case in actual sense. This new model of work forms broader casualization and commoditization of work that deviates from formal forms of work within organization (De Stefano, 2015; Williams et al., 2019).

The rapid evolution of gig economy makes it challenging to estimate actual number of people involved in gig economy due to unavailability of data (Singer, 2014). Crowd work platforms utilize different methods for executing work and earning payment for work done (Gol et al., 2019). Both the crowd work and the work-on-demand via apps forms share similar features that make a joint analysis fortune. This allows minimal transaction cost and reduces frictions on markets (Heeks, 2017). The digital platforms provide excellent accessibility for workers to access job opportunities and execute tasks at their convenience (Aloisi, 2015; Irani & Silberman, 2013; McKinsey Global Institute, 2015).

The virtual transaction associated with crowd work contributes to workers executing jobs in a dynamic world of work (Irani, 2015). Essentially, crowd work transactions have limited human interaction that creates invisible workers. Despite the numerous postulated benefits that gig economy offers such as workers flexibility, it does not necessarily mean to say much about the overall sustainability of such arrangements (Ho et al., 2015). Competition between workers expands beyond global dimension through the cyberspace (Gerber & Krzywdzinski, 2019) which has transformed work and pay that has forced people to have alternative work options with flexibility pay over and above routine full-time work (Aloisi, 2015; Margaryan, 2019). Another problem associated with the gig economy is that workers in this model share some challenges of the same nature as of other forms of non-standard workers, for instance with those in "contractual arrangements involving multiple parties" that include but not limited to, temporary agency, subcontracted workers or outsourcing workers (Irani & Silberman, 2013; Prassl, 2015; Waas, et al., 2017; Yin, et al., 2018).

2 Motivational Critical Success Factors for Entrepreneurs in Gig Economy

The gig economy offers individuals to enhance their entrepreneurial activities and skills. However, it provides some differences (Karlsson & Wranne, 2019). For instance, the gig economy is perceived to entail short-term contracting work activities, whereas entrepreneurship is seen as long-term work. Despite the differences, one would need entrepreneurial motivators to succeed as a gig worker in a highly competitive environment and characterized by changing technological developments. Gig workers require a critical mindset that entrepreneurs deploy to succeed in their endeavours (Churchill & Craig, 2019). As a result, this chapter discusses some entrepreneurial motivation factors and connects them to the gig economy.

2.1 Digital Support, Networking and Social Media Enablers

These are online platforms that facilitate social interactions and promot cooperation among various players within an enterprise to allow working and sharing of information. In the past few years, platforms have been created in various organizations to enable communication and social interaction. The platforms have facilitated the growth of independent contracting identification of skills and knowledge to be matched to the available jobs posted on these platforms. It has been established that digital labour platforms impact worker's self-motivation through the ability to find satisfying jobs that meet basic psychological needs. Networking in these platforms brings individuals together, creating referrals, an effective strategy for marketing gig workers.

2.2 Self-Efficacy

Individual efficiency is generally attributed to the self-belief of an individual's capacity to execute the needed output based on the available resources, skills and abilities. Individuals that display a high level of self-efficacy execute the task with innovative effort, set high individual goals and define ideal ways to complete the tasks. There are four sources that an individual needs to compete in entrepreneurial activities and the gig economy that includes mastery experiences (i.e. success of increasing your experiences as a gig worker); culture models (i.e. seeing how individuals succeed in similar roles in the gig economy which motivates one's self-efficacy); social persuasion (i.e. where someone informs the gig worker that he or she can succeed in the same roles—belief) and psychological response (i.e. altering negative response and gaining positive attitude to complete the task Ashford et al., 2018; Hsiao et al., 2018).

Because of ambiguity in most roles in the gig economy, a gig worker must develop a high level of self-efficacy with the proper social and psychological response to succeed. It includes trying, planning and developing persistence to handle every role available. Studies have shown that self-efficacy has a motivational effect on self-employment and entrepreneurial activities (Van den Heuvel et al., 2015). As a result, we can connect these findings to the gig economy. Self-efficacy differentiates individuals in the workforce. Those who know how to plan and try through building a positive attitude may succeed in handling their tasks compared to individuals who do not make an effort at all (Asih et al., 2019).

2.3 *Goal Setting*

Setting higher goals has always been associated with better results than no planning. Individuals who set goals regarding their gig activities as an entrepreneurial approach may develop a tendency of succeeding compared to their counterparts with no goals (Sinicki et al., 2019). Goal setting helps to differentiate long-term and short-term goals, realistic and unrealistic ones. Thus, it provides individuals with practical approaches or strategies to handle their gig roles in a competitive market where most roles are temporary (Su, 2020). Individual-level goals need to be in sync with expected goals of the employer that signifies the expected results. Thus, there is a need for both the gig worker and the employer to match their goals to ensure that the task is not only completed on time but also to ensure expectations are met (Jabagi et al., 2019).

2.4 *Tolerance for Ambiguity*

Two of the gig economy's main characteristics are short-term jobs and ambiguity in roles. Any person who cannot tolerate such attributes of the gig economy cannot be motivated to work (Dubrin, 2018). As a result, one needs tolerance for ambiguity as a motivation factor to succeed in the gig economy. Tolerance for ambiguity is how a person views the environment and situations that circumstances bring, such as uncertain clues and outcomes, and how these unclear instances are confronted. People with low ambiguity tolerance perceive such situations as threatening and may abandon their mission in the gig economy. On the other hand, individuals who are willing to tolerate ambiguity see such situations as attractive and exciting, motivating them to complete their task on time and take the risk (Auditianto et al., 2019).

2.5 *Personal Drive*

The emerging workforce, where the majority are millennials, is driven by the need to succeed in their work roles. They are ambitious, energetic, visionary and persistent in their activities. The drive is the willingness to show forth effort in everyday activities (Allon et al., 2018). Be a critical thinker and show effort in developing ways to realize the ideas put forward. People with ambitions are those willing to create something important when they pursue their goals. They develop high goals with high strategies to achieve them. No matter how unsuccessful they become in achieving their goals, their persistence to try repeatedly gives them the energy to feel motivated and believe that the goal shall be successful. This kind of thinking drives the gig workers to accelerate their value proposition to develop themselves as gig entrepreneurs (Kaine & Josserand, 2019).

2.6 *Desire for Independence*

People want to be free, work at their own time, be the boss and control their working arrangements and time. However, this is highly influenced by entrepreneurial values and behaviours, requiring a high level of responsibility and better judgement. Independence is an essential attribute for gig workers (Mukhopadhyay & Chatwin, 2020). It gives them the willingness to exploit available opportunities in the job market and responsibility for the results of venturing into the gig roles. Results have shown that the desire for independence entrepreneurial activities be linked to the growth within the gig industry (Burtch et al., 2018).

2.7 *Viability and Vitality*

The challenge of gig entrepreneurs have been attributed to creating a balance between viability and vitality (Petriglieri et al., 2018). These two components have become an integral aspect of redefining success in the gig world of work. The gig entrepreneurs peruse a different type of success different from those in employment influenced by viability and vitality from the environmental factors. In this sense, viability is attributed to how busy the industry is and attracts business activities for gig entrepreneurs. However, vitality implies the extent to which the industry attracts continued investments that offers opportunities to gig entrepreneurs. As a critical success factor, the gig entrepreneurs need to gain four connections in the arena where they wish to play and thrive. These connections are the place that is disconnected from the ordinary offices, people who shape their careers, the purpose upon which they strike out their work to find footing in the marketplace and redefine aspects of routine in their lives that improve their workflows. This can be linked to the essential characteristics of business improvement described by Houstoun (2003) including entrepreneurs solving everyday problems and taking advantage of opportunities emerging in their business environment, seeking sustainable funding and providing services within a geographical area. Therefore, the concept of viability and vitality has gotten its application in business improvement (Ratcliffe & Flanagan, 2004). Applied in the gig economy, it conspicuously demonstrates creativity through collaborative thinking and actions of interested groups concern with economic vitality.

2.8 *Career Advancement Skills for Gig Economy Entrepreneurs*

For entrepreneurs to thrive in a gig economy platform, they require advancement skills. These skills range from computer skills, networking skills, financial management skills, marketing skills and the ability to find work (Banwari, 2018; Cho & Cho, 2020). A further complication calling for the advancement of skills arises from the fact that brands and business models adopted in the gig economy vary across economies and industries. These variations come along with new digital platforms that dispatched old platforms into bankruptcy daily (Prassl, 2018). According to Hunt et al., (2019), investments by development partners and the private sector are driving skills in digital skills through impact sourcing. In this regard, it is predicted that up to more than half a billion of the working world population could benefit from online skills development platforms developing their skills by 2025. Consequently, a study released by Mckinsey in 2015 predicted that through digital skills enhancement, more than 50 million would shift their work from formal employment to the gig economy. More recent studies have shown the need to enhance skills against jobs at risk due to automation and increased adoption of digital platforms such as machine learning (Nedelkoska & Quintini, 2018).

3 Emerging Labour Issues

In the recent past, the legal and economic pundits have put much enthusiasm into studying the so-called sharing economy. The most significant is the content of the three-sided contractual relationships between the platform, requester and the worker. It is a fact that virtual avenues in the gig economy have represented the essential source of income for independent freelance gig workers that is now becoming the main source of living (Aloisi, 2015). Besides the fact that gig economy offer more opportunities, many independent workers, including those who prefer to work from their homes comfort or those who only look for opportunities to top-up their income from their formal employment. Nevertheless, incomes are much less predictable. New platforms turn to more-skilled workers that can complete multi-hour task on professional online marketplaces such as desk or work for months to solve research and development challenges on open innovation platforms (Lobel, 2017).

Accordingly, technological advancement is making it possible for most work to be done from sparse geographical locations. Thus, crowd workers are in a global networked labour market, competing with everyone worldwide for business opportunities. Therefore, frontiers may play a much more marginal role, and a vendor can attract and engage short-term contract workers from a different location for a quick or instant work engagement. This phenomenon has raised concerns on the subject of antidiscrimination law, workplace occupational health and safety, and social arbitrage (Adams et al., 2018). The developing debate on this structure influences the polarization of the businesses: on the one hand, there is a global and creative professional who can contract work from specific available online sources, competing with local professionals who act as service providers, delivering work within local jurisdictions, implementing the design and ensuring the relationship with local authorities (Wu et al., 2019).

Gig workers are starting to sue some companies, for instance, the car-hailing apps such as Uber or cleaning platform such as Lyft and Handy for inappropriately classifying them as contractors. However, they do not enjoy the amount of freedom that the level is supposed to entail (Stewart & Stanford, 2017). The current legal tussle may be strenuous but has already reached the goal of raising awareness as from the class-action lawsuit in California over how Uber classified its drivers.

3.1 Challenges and Opportunities Across Various Economies

The first growth of the gig economy varies in characteristics of opportunities and challenges depending on socio-economic developments. This can be seen to be distinctly different in the developed, developing and underdeveloped nations. For instance, in the recent past, India has witnessed an accelerated growth of gig economy (Banwari, 2018). This growth has been attributed to online freelancing, microwork, labour market regulations, demographic changes and digital payments such as blockchain. Across the board, in developed, developing and underdeveloped economies, gig work is being recognized as non-standardized employment. This new form of work brings along with its various opportunities and challenges (Kalleberg, 2000). To a large extent, gig economy opportunities are attributed to the advancement on technological platforms available on internet forums structuring workers mode of communication. The developing literature on opportunities and challenges in the gig economy from the perspective of the developing world from Asia and Sub-Sahara Africa, as documented by Wood et al. (2018), shows that freelance labour is on the rise as accelerated by the development of online platforms creating digital work communities that plays a significant role in developing the future world of work.

In the west, the number of freelance workers that form gig economic has been on the rise. For instance, in America, the number of freelance workers rose by 41% in 2020, 53% are generation z. This growth is attributed to the availability of online freelance platforms such as freelance.com (Warner, 2021). In the USA, most large businesses are embracing the gig economy, thus providing more opportunities for freelancers. Such companies include businesses like Basecamp, Automatic Toptal, among others. This is contrary to the scenario witnessed in the developed economies.

Perspectives witnessed in the developing world show that the expansion of freelance working is on the rise. This is being accelerated with factors like rising middle class in the economies, increased young professional population, increasing urbanization, technological advancement and impact of globalization (Banwari, 2018). On the contrary, in the developing world, the growth of freelance has been hampered by what the emerging gig entrepreneurs worry about; this includes such aspects like unpredictable income, putting enough money into savings, saving for retirement, being paid a fair rate, high taxation, among others (Warner, 2021).

A survey across Sahara Africa and Asia identified a major challenge impeding the development of the gig economy in the work parts. These challenges are characterized by hyper-fragmentation of the online industries, individualized and anonymized nature of microwork being carried out by online freelancer that harbours collective voice (Wood et al., 2018). These factors linked to fragmentation and anonymity of gig workers that constitute online community across occupations and platform lines limit possible scalability of collective action to protect gig worker's rights (Silver, 2003). With most economies classified as underdeveloped in Africa, the employment opportunities and economic development growth have been attributed to the informal sector linked to rising urban youth populations (Ng'weno & Porteous, 2018). However, it is now being recognized that with the emergence of e-commerce and the rising unemployment, a study group on technology and development prospects in Africa points to the informal sector quickly taking up opportunities of future of work through the gig economy. The main challenge again is the protection of gig works associated with young professionals who believe that digital platforms are creating work opportunities.

4 Misclassification of Digital Transformation for Gig Economy

The gig economy is witnessing the disruptive digital transformation of work (Cherry & Aloisi, 2017) due to the surge of computer, mobile phone and technological advancements. The changes observed in various industries are characterized by precarious work. Some of the classic examples are of O'Connor versus Uber, which has received more significant visibility. Other similar cases have been filed on labour standards against other on-demand platforms (Greenwood et al., 2017). Analysis of the ongoing litigation reveals several vital topics, including an emphasis on California's labour laws. Most of the "sharing" companies of the past years have shifted away from "sharing". They are entirely for-profit businesses pursuing a shareholder value maximization model at all costs inspired mainly by their venture capitalist investors (Cherry & Aloisi, 2017).

4.1 Perceptions of Worker Force of the Future

Digital transformation has enabled the gig economy to penetrate the various market through exclusive spatial temporalities associated with the on-demand type of work—often requiring quick performance turnarounds. The nature of gig work continues to take root across industries with shared characteristics of work domains. This drive has pushed the organization to start adopting work-related platforms. These are new labour types that are short-term or one-off jobs type which are commonly remunerated based on outputs and level of involvement (Stewart & Stanford, 2017). Digital platforms facilitated create an ecosystem supported by matching technology and the available job opportunities (Howcroft & Bergvall-Kåreborn, 2019), with analytics being used to manage the performance of the task (Cherry & Aloisi, 2017). Technology diffusion across economies has changed the nature of work and perception of workers opting to be involved in gig work across locations and industries due to access to information (Goods et al., 2019). The changing perception about work by twenty-first-century workers has made gig economies perceived as neo-liberalization of the world of work (Zwick, 2018). Employment is getting dominated by economic forces supplemented by social regulation and deregulation of the current work practices.

The evolving business models represent a new perception of work beyond principles of capitalism on the attitude of worker (Dokko et al., 2015). As a distinct form of resource that is now making itself freely available, the human resource takes advantage of available technological and social networks to acquire work. Consequently, it is creating new online platforms for e-commerce, revolutionizing worker as formally employed, independent contractor and employing enterprise. Effectively, the misclassification of gig works as non-standard work has been associated with the temporary contracting of workers facilitated by digital workforce intermediaries (Johnes, 2019).

Even though digital work platforms present as passive liaisons between individual workers, end-users are compared to traditional types of work. Still yet, many workers worldwide and employers are struggling to fill critical job vacancies while technology is perceived to allow most workers and employers to connect. The development of Fourth Industrial Revolution underplays the active role of harnessing forces shaping socio-economic landscapes (Abraham et al., 2019). For instance, marketing platforms have characterized food delivery platforms, linking various actors in the value chain, including consumers, eateries and workers, to facilitate the purchase and deliver food to the customers (Richardson et al., 2019). These platforms, however, are not similar to short-term staffing by organized staffing companies that provide various labour forces. One of the significant differentiators of the gig economy is the accurate time availability of services in both product and labour markets through their digital infrastructures. Platforms are simultaneously creating and shaping various economies and industries they enable, acting as "active intermediaries".

5 Managing the Future Workforce: What is the Way Forward for an Internal Human Resource?

The gig economy is understood to be a commercial, economic e-exchange where individual workers and organization get most of the work performed through digital platforms as intermediaries. In addition to the rewards reaped by gig workers, they equally face significant risks, such as precarious work conditions (De Stefano, 2016). The world of work is fast changing, and precarious and fractured forms of work are gaining formalization in gig economy workers. Much of the existing literature mainly refer to developed economies (Berg, 2016)—though recent interventions are seen in the emerging economies from developing countries in the low and middle-income countries (LIMC) (Gol et al., 2019). Because most of the gig works happen on various platforms, there is a need to manage the platforms effectively and manage the gig workers. Therefore, this chapter has used the term gig economy to connote independent contracting of work on digital platforms that would also imply freelancing or piece work or temporary work. The future of work is evolving into digitally mediated work through available platforms (Woodcock & Graham, 2019).

5.1 Workforce Planning

The gig economy provides individuals with the opportunity to be their boss. However, organizations seek independent contractors' support to complete their tasks, and planning remains an issue that HR must address. Some of these generic human resource functions include attaining workforce planning purposes and matching skills and jobs through intermediary platforms. This may save time and resource and thus speed up the delivery of various tasks. To this end, many gig economy digital platforms run with limited barriers for workers entry into job markets (Woodcock & Graham, 2019). This brings about new dimensions of workforce forecasting and the acquisition of labour supply as defined by the gig economy. Talent mobility is highly affected, and traditional workforce planning is put at risk.

5.2 *Training and Development*

Because traditional organizations provide training and development opportunities for their employees in the organization, most gig workers may not have the same access to training and services for the organizations they are working for temporarily. For this reason, HR needs to ensure that intermediary platforms provide essential training and development techniques that can equip gig workers with the necessary skills. A recent global survey identified the types of skills that gig workers believe will enable them to progress their careers. The top five crucial skills are found to be networking skills at 40%, marketing skills at 35%, financial management at 33%, project management at 28% and transition skills required to migrate into the future of work at 25% (Warner, 2021).

5.3 *Performance Management*

Because gig workers may get jobs based on the number of referrals and reviews, HR must develop a specific performance management system that takes these concepts into account. HR should provide performance systems that rank independent contractors based on their work to assist other employers to access such information on the platform. Mass technological penetration is turning the relationship of workers and employers on performance measures beyond a simple ranking and reputation system designed to regulate workers performance (Woodcock & Graham, 2020). Digital platforms are now revolutionizing the whole domains of performance management. Some of the emerging developments include scenarios where customers have access to information regarding working conditions that define what it is like to work in the gig economy.

5.4 *Provision of Skills and Networking*

The advent of the gig economy enables skilled labour trade as it allows workers to showcase and sell their skills to a global market. The developing interest in thoroughly examining the nature and experience of gig economy workers is gaining prominence concerning what skills are required and the extent upon which networking and collaboration are stimulating knowledge workers who gig. To this end, the so-called standard employment relationship is being undermined through fragmented work and increased casualization of work (Prassl, 2018). When workers acquire new skill sets that enhance their capability, they positively related these skills to less time and are associated with better performance on the new skill (Huang et al., 2019).

5.5 *Job Design*

The accelerating expansion of the gig economy is altering jobs' design and has become a symbolic way of defining work (Prassl, 2015). There is a need for employers and human resource specialists to redesign their job roles and functions to accommodate the emerging skills in the gig economy. The gig economy's legal traits and regulations are also not apparent, making it difficult to approximate the gig workforce's extent in emerging economies. There is a need to implement laws that promote and protect gig workers against illegal roles or jobs and align the roles to the organizational objectives and market demand. One of the emerging concerns is the extent to which workers can now protect their job through portfolio diversification because their entire jobs are at stake due to the evolution of the world of work and jobs. This development on job design is attributed to the fact that gig workers are spending less time job tasks, delivering exceptional quality output and undertaking more due to the risk of spending time without work or being unpaid while searching for the next tasks or gigs (Woodcock & Graham, 2020).

6 Conclusion

The gig economy is accelerating at a terrific speed sweeping through industries. Several concerns have emerged across practices, such as asserting the benefits and costs as contested in the emerging debates. To this end, this chapter has been structured in five parts that depict the critical success factors for gig workers. This chapter has honed the increasing number of independent workers both in the developed economies, developing and underdeveloped. With the wave of technological disruptions coupled with the ever-changing market dynamics, technology remains the most significant facilitator of the supply, and demand-side factor cannot be underestimated. The development of the economy has created a proliferation of public interest as it provides the platform upon which companies can engage and contract workers. However, irrespective of technological advancement, economic and political factors hamper the gig economy's growth. These challenges are varied according to the levels of economic development. This chapter has recognized the rapid evolution of the gig economy, making it challenging to estimate the number of people involved in the gig economy due to the unavailability of data. Despite the numerous postulated benefits that the gig economy offers, such as workers flexibility, it does not necessarily mean to say much about the overall sustainability of such arrangements.

The motivational critical success factors for entrepreneurs in the gig economy are several. The leading enabler has been identified with digital support networking and social media enablers, personal efficacy that builds on self-beliefs, goal setting, tolerance to ambiguity, personal drive as associated with millennials and generation z, desire for independence, creating a balance between viability and vitality. These factors affect individual motivation levels as attributed to critical success factors.

Career advancement skills for gig economy entrepreneurs are relevant to make gig workers thrive in this volatile, uncertain, complex and ambiguous world. Therefore, gig entrepreneurs must continuously enhance their skill to measure up the emerging skill set required in the gig economy.

Several labour concerns have emerged across the countries that have attracted the attention of legal and economic pundits on the regulation of this economy. Several dimensions of legal imperatives are being put into consideration. Accordingly, technological advancement brings about new perspectives of defining labour market regulations around the precarious nature of employment. This legal imperative takes cognizance of the challenges and opportunities of the gig economy across various economies. The development in the gig economy has significant implication for the existing workforce in formalized standard employment practices. Consequently, there is a need for HR to develop effective policies for managing the gig economies like designing laws and policies, establishing performance measurement and training and development, among others.

References

Abraham, K. G., Haltiwanger, J., Sandusky, K., & Spletzer, J. R. (2016). Measuring the gig economy. *Society of Labor Economists Annual Meetings.*

Abraham, K. G., Haltiwanger, J., Sandusky, K., & Spletzer, J. (2019). The rise of the gig economy: Fact or fiction? *AEA Papers and Proceedings, 109*, 357–361.

Adams, A., Freedman, J., & Prassl, J. (2018). Rethinking legal taxonomies for the gig economy. *Oxford Review of Economic Policy, 34*(3), 475–794.

Allon, G., Cohen, M., & Sinchaisri, W. (2018). The impact of behavioural and economic drivers on gig economy workers. *Available at SSRN 3274628.*

Aloisi, A. (2015). The rising of on-demand work: A case study research on a set of online platforms and apps. *The IV regulating for decent work conference.* Geneva: ILO. Retrieved February 9, 2021, from https://hci.cs.uwaterloo.ca/faculty/elaw/cs889/reading/turkopticon.pdf

Ashford, S. J., Caza, B. B., & Reid, E. M. (2018). From surviving to thriving in the gig economy: A research agenda for individuals in the new world of work. *Research in Organizational Behavior, 38*, 23–41.

Asih, S. N., Sucahyo, Y. G., Gandhi, A., & Ruldeviyani, Y. (2019). Inhibiting motivating factors on online gig economy client in Indonesia. *2019 International conference on advanced computer science and information systems (ICACSIS)* (pp. 349–356). IEEE.

Auditianto, A. S., Gandhi, A., & Ruldeviyani, Y. (2019). Discovering the influencing factors of physical gig economy usage: Quantitative approach on clients9 perception. *2019 International conference on advanced computer science and information systems (ICACSIS)* (pp. 357–362). IEEE.

Banwari, V. (2018). Gig economy: challenges and opportunities in India. *Journal of Emerging Technologies and Innovative Research, 5*(1), 314–420.

Berg, J. (2016). Income security in the on-demand economy: Findings and policy lessons from a survey of crowd workers. *Comparative Laboratory and Policy Journal, 37.*

Burtch, G., Carnahan, S., & Greenwood, B. N. (2018). Can you gig it? An empirical examination of the gig economy and entrepreneurial activity. *Management Science, 64*(12), 5497–5520.

Carr, C., Hall, R., Mason, A., & Varney, E. (2017). Cueing employability in the gig economy: Effects of task-relevant and task-irrelevant information on Fiverr. *Management Communication Quarterly, 31*(3), 409–428.

Cherry, M. A., & Aloisi, A. (2017). Dependent contractors' in the gig economy: A comparative approach. *AM UL Rev, 3*, 635.

Cho, W., & Cho, S.-E. (2020). Entrepreneurial challenges in business model for the gig economy: Agendas for research and business development. *International Journal of Entrepreneurship, 24*(1), 1.

Churchill, B., & Craig, L. (2019). Gender in the gig economy: Men and women using digital platforms to secure work in Australia. *Journal of Sociology, 55*(4), 741–761.

De Stefano, V. (2015). The rise of the just-in-time workforce: On-demand work, crowd work, and labour protections in the gig economy. *Comparative Labor Law and Policy Journal, 37*, 471.

De Stefano, V. (2016). Introduction: Crowdsourcing, the gig economy, and the law. *Comparative Labor Law and Policy, 37*(3).

Deloitte. (2017). *The 2017 Deloitte millennial survey—Apprehensive millennials: Seeking stability and opportunities in an uncertain world.* Deloitte Touche Tohmatsu Limited.

Deng, X., Taylor, J., & Moussawi, S. (2020). Introduction to the minitrack on crowdsourcing and digital workforce in the gig economy. *Proceedings of the 53rd Hawaii international conference on system sciences.*

Dokko, J., Mumford, M., & Schanzenbach, D. W. (2015). Workers and the online gig economy. *The Hamilton Project*, 1–8.

Donovan, S. A., Bradley, D. H., & Shimabukuru, J. O. (2016). What does the gig economy mean for workers?

Dubrin, A. (2018). *Tolerating ambiguity for leadership and professional effectiveness.* Page Publishing Inc.

EY Global. (2018). *The gig economy: A chance to control your costs of accelerating your growth.* EY Global. Retrieved February 8, 2021, from https://www.ey.com/en_gl/growth/the-gig-economy--a-chance-to-control-your-costs-or-accelerate-yo

Gerber, S., & Krzywdzinski, M. (2019). Brave new digital work? New forms of performance in crowd work. *Work and Labor in the Digital Age.* Emerald Publishing Limited.

Gol, E., Stein, M., & Avital, M. (2019). Crowd work platform governance toward organizational value creation. *The Journal of Strategic Information Systems, 28*(2), 175–195.

Goods, C., Veen, A., & Barratt, T. (2019). Is your gig any good? Analyzing job quality in the Australian platform-based food-delivery sector. *Journal of Industrial Relations, 61*(4), 502–527.

Graham, M., & Woodcock, J. (2018). Towards a fairer platform economy: Introducing the fair work foundation. *Alternate Routes, 29*, 242–253.

Greenwood, B., Burtch, G., & Carnahan, S. (2017). Unknowns of the gig economy. *Communications of the ACM, 60*(7), 27–29.

Harris, S., & Krueger, A. (2015). *A proposal for modernizing labour laws for twenty-first-century work: The independent worker.* Retrieved February 8, 2021, from https://books.google.com/books/about/A_Proposal_for_Modernizing_Labor_Laws_fo.html?hl=&id=CrR8jwEACAAJ

Healy, J., Nicholson, D., & Pekarek, A. (2017). Should we take the gig economy seriously? *Labor and Industry: A Journal of the Social and Economic Relations of Work, 27*(3), 232–248. https://doi.org/10.1080/10301763.2017.1377048

Heeks, R. (2017). Decent work and the digital gig economy: A developing country perspective on employment impacts and standards in online outsourcing, crowd work, etc. *Development Informatics Working Paper, 71.*

Ho, C., Slivkins, A., Suri, S., & Vaughan, J. (2015). Incentivizing high-quality crowd work. *Proceedings of the 24 international conference on world wide web*, (pp. 419–429).

Houstoun, L. (2003). *Business improvements districts* (2 ed.). Urban Land Institute.

Howcroft, D., & Bergvall-Kåreborn, B. (2019). A typology of crowd work platforms. *Work, Employment, and Society, 33*(1), 21–38.

Hsiao, J. C., Moser, C., Schoenebeck, S., & Dillahunt, T. R. (2018). The role of demographics, trust, computer self-efficacy, and ease of use in the sharing economy. *Proceedings of the 1st ACM SIGCAS conference on computing and sustainable societies*, (pp. 1–11).

Huang, K., Yao, J., & Yin, M. (2019). Understanding the skill provision in gig economy from a network perspective: A case study of Fiverr. *Proceedings of the ACM on human-computer interaction, 3(CSCW)*, (pp. 1–23).

Hunt, A., Samman, E., Tapfuma, S., & Mwaura, G. (2019). *Women in the gig economy: Paid work, care and flexibility in Kenya.* London: Overseas Development Institute (ODI).

Irani, L., & Silberman, M. (2013). Turkopticon: Interrupting worker invisibility in Amazon mechanical Tuk. *The SIGCHI conference on human factors in computing systems.* Paris.

Irani, L. (2015). Difference and dependence among digital workers: The case of Amazon mechanical Turk. *South Atlantic Quarterly, 114*(1), 225–234.

Jabagi, N., Croteau, A., Audebrand, L., & Marsan, J. (2019). Gig workers' motivation: Thinking beyond carrots and sticks. *Journal of Managerial Psychology.*

Johnes, G. (2019). The gig economy in the UK: A regional perspective. *Journal of Global Responsibility.*

Kaine, S., & Josserand, E. (2019). The organization and experience of work in the gig economy. *Journal of Industrial Relations, 61*(4), 479–501.

Kalleberg, A. (2000). Nonstandard employment relations: Part-time, temporary and contract work. *26*, 341–365. https://doi.org/10.1146/annual.soc.26.1.341

Karlsson, K., & Wranne, J. (2019). *Motivation in the gig economy: A case study of gig workers in the IT and business consulting industry. Master of science THESIS.* KTH Royal Institue of Technology.

Kuhn, K. M. (2016). The rise of the "Gig Economy" and implications for understanding work and workers. *Industrial and Organizational Psychology, 9*(1), 157.

Lehdonvirta, V. (2018). Flexibility in the gig economy: Managing time on three online piecework platforms. *New Technology, Work and Employment, 33*(1), 13–29.

Lobel, O. (2017). The economy and the future of employment and labour law. *USFL Review, 51*, 51.

Mahmod, M., & Hassan, H. (2020). Spatial crowdsourcing: Opportunities and challenges in motivating Malaysian women's participation in gig economy. *2020 IEEE conference on e-learning, e-management and e-services (IC3e)* (pp. 76–81). IEEE.

Margaryan, A. (2019). Workplace learning in crowd work. *Journal of Workplace Learning.*

McKinsey Global Institute. (2015). *A labor market that works. Connecting talent with opportunity in the digital age.* McKinsey Global Institute.

McKinsey Global Institute. (2016). *Independent work: Choice, necessity, and the gig economy.* McKinsey Global Institute.

Mukhopadhyay, B., & Chatwin, C. R. (2020). The significance of Herzberg and taylor for the gig economy of China: Evaluating gigger incentives for Meituan and Ele. Me. *International Journal of Applied Behavioral Economics, 9*(4), 1–17.

Nedelkoska, L., & Quintini, G. (2018). *Automation, skills use and training, OECD social, employment and migration working papers.* OECD Publishing. https://doi.org/10.1787/2e2f4eea-en

Ng'weno, A., & Porteous, D. (2018). *Let's be real: The informal sector and the gig economy are the future, and the present, of work in Africa.* District of Columbia: Center for Global Development. Retrieved from http://hdl.voced.edu.au/10707/509519

Petriglieri, G., Ashford, S. J., & Wrzesniewski, A. (2018). Thriving in the gig economy. (April), (pp. 140–143). Retrieved from https://hbr.org/2018/03/thriving-in-the-gig-economy

Poon, T. S. (2018). Independent workers: Growth, trends, categories, and employee relations implications in the emerging gig economy. *Employee Responsibilities and Rights Journal, 31*(1), 63–69.

Prassl, J. (2015). *The concept of the employer.* Oxford University Press.

Prassl, J. (2018). *Humans as a service: The promise and perils of work in gig economy* (1st ed.). Oxford University Press.

Ratcliffe, J., & Flanagan, S. (2004). Enhancing the vitality and viability of town and city centres; The concept of the business improvement district in the context of tourism enterprise. *Property Management, 22*(5), 377–395. https://doi.org/10.1108/02637470410571210
Richardson, J., Wardale, D., & Lord, L. (2019). The double-edged sword of a seasonal academic career. *Higher Education Research and Development, 38*(3), 623–637.
Silberman, M., & Irani, L. (2016). Operating an employer reputation system: Lessons from Turkopticon 2008–2015. *Comparative Labor Law and Policy Journal, 37*(3), 505–541.
Silver, B. (2003). *Forces of Labor: Workers Movements and Globalisation Since 1870*. Cambridge University Press.
Singer, N. (2014, August 16). In the sharing economy, workers find both freedom and uncertainty. *New York Times*. Retrieved February 9, 2021, from http://www.nytimes.com/2014/08/17/technology/in-the-sharing-economy
Sinicki, A., Sinicki, & Ramachandran. (2019). *Thriving in the gig economy*. Apress.
Stewart, A., & Stanford, J. (2017). Regulating work in the gig economy: What are the options? *The Economic and Labour Relations Review, 28*(3), 420–437.
Su, Y. (2020). Can prosocial incentives within a goal-setting scheme motivate workers?
Van den Heuvel, M., Demerouti, E., & Peeters, M. C. (2015). The job crafting intervention: Effects on job resources, self-efficacy, and affective well-being. *Journal of Occupational and Organizational Psychology, 88*(3), 511–532.
Waas, B., Liebman, W., Lyubarsky, A., & Kezuka, K. (2017). *Crowd work—A comparative law perspective*. Bund Verlag.
Warner, A. (2021). *30+ Freelance Stats—Why the gig economy is growing in 2020*. Retrieved April 23, 2021, from https://www.websiteplanet.com/blog/freelance-stats/
Williams, A., Mark, G., Milland, K., Lank, E., & Law, E. (2019). The perpetual work-life of crowd workers: How tooling practices increase fragmentation in crowd work. *Proceedings of the ACM on human-computer interaction*, (pp. 1–28).
Wood, A. J., Lehdonvirta, V., & Graham, M. (2018). Workers of the Internet unite? *Online Freelancer Organization among Remote Gig Economy Workers in Six Asian and African Countries, 33*(2), 95–112. https://doi.org/10.1111/ntwe.12112
Woodcock, J., & Graham, M. (2019). *The gig economy*. Polity Press.
Woodcock, J., & Graham, M. (2020). *The gig economy; A critical introduction*. Polity Press.
Wu, Q., Zhang, H., Li, Z., & Liu, K. (2019). Labour control in the gig economy: Evidence from Uber in China. *Journal of Industrial Relations, 61*(4), 574–596.
Yin, M., Suri, S., & Gray, M. (2018). Running out of time: the impact and value of flexibility in on-demand crowd work. *Proceedings of the 2018 CH conference on human factors in computing systems*, (pp. 1–11).
Zwick, A. (2018). Welcome to the gig economy: Neoliberal industrial relations and the case of Uber. *GeoJournal, 83*(4), 679–691.

Joseph Odhiambo Onyango Ph.D., is a Senior Lecturer at Strathmore University Business School, Nairobi, Kenya. He is also a management advisory consultant and researcher. His research interest and teaching areas include human resource management, strategic management, organization behaviour and change. His main interest in practice are health system strengthening and institutional development. He has over 15 years of industry practices as a management consultant from leading global professional firms PwC and KPMG, leading multiple advisories across industries. He holds a Doctor of Philosophy in Strategic Management, Master of Science in Human Resource Management, Master Level in Global Health, a Bachelor of Philosophy Degree and numerous Diplomas and Certificates. He is a trained and certified practising expert in strategy (Balanced Scorecard), Change Management (PROSCI), Business edge Trainer of Trainers (World Bank/IMF), among others. He is a published author of professional and academic literature in scholarly books and scientific peer-reviewed journal papers.

Stakeholder Involvement in Sustainable Innovation: Toward an Integrated Conceptual Framework

Jelena Mazaj, Pasquale Massimo Picone, and Arabella Mocciaro Li Destri

1 Introduction

"Globalization changes the power relations" among organizations and "brings with it new dimensions of responsibility" (Jensen and Sandström, 2011, p. 474). Consequently, organizations have increasingly focused on formulating and developing a sustainability strategy (Hall & Vredenburg, 2003). Additionally, the gig economy is imposing a new institutional logic for strategies, fostering new dynamics in actors' behavior and spurring the diffusion of innovative practices (Frenken et al., 2020). We call attention to three elements of the gig economy: (a) "temporary, project-based, and flexible jobs" (Görög, 2018, p. 180); (b) work forms such as "crowd work," "work-on-demand via the app" (De Stefano, 2015); (c) employment of platforms for self-regulating markets (Frenken et al., 2020).

In global and gig economies characterized by "temporary" relations and competitive advantages (Dagnino et al., 2021), almost like an oxymoron, scholars have recognized sustainability as a "core" theme in the strategic management debate (Lüdeke-Freund, 2010). "Concretely identifying to whom they are responsible and how far that obligation extends" (O'Riordan & Fairbrass, 2014, p. 123) represents the hidden challenge for organizations (McGahan, 2020).

Extent literature shows that the quest for sustainability frequently requires combining resources among heterogeneous knowledge actors and developing strategies with a long-term perspective (Schmidthuber & Wiener, 2018; Ketata et al., 2014). Arguably, Boar et al. (2020) underline that the gig economy should positively impact

J. Mazaj (✉) · P. M. Picone · A. Mocciaro Li Destri
Department of Economics, Business and Statistics, University of Palermo, Viale delle Scienze, Building 13, 90128 Palermo, Italy

P. M. Picone
e-mail: pasqualemassimo.picone@unipa.it

A. Mocciaro Li Destri
e-mail: arabella.mocciaro@unipa.it

A. Gupta et al. (eds.), *Sustainability in the Gig Economy*,
https://doi.org/10.1007/978-981-16-8406-7_4

sustainability since it promotes the concepts of the sharing economy. Besides, we have assisted to increased requests for innovation partnerships between organizations (Janssen & Moors, 2013; Manning & Roessler, 2013; Reypens et al., 2016), blending competition and cooperation practices. In this context, each organization may act as a change agent by activating new resource orchestration processes in resolving an existent grand challenge (Ferraro et al., 2015; George et al., 2016).

Overall, prior studies acknowledged that the organizations' dialog with stakeholders facilitates sustainable innovation (Ayuso et al., 2006). With more emphasis, Breukers et al. (2014) argue that innovation can be successful only if supported (or at least accepted) by relevant stakeholders. Nonetheless, sustainable innovation literature is fragmented, and therefore, it is challenging to link and map diverse norms and "global" actions. Additionally, it is not clear how to improve the existing governance and participation gap to leverage diverse expertise and decentralized structures (Bäckstrand, 2006).

This chapter summarizes the existing knowledge on main cooperation objectives and stakeholder involvement within the organizational innovation process. Then, we develop a framework of sustainable innovation practices.

2 Sustainable Innovation: A Closer Look

In 2007, Savitz and Weber (2007) proposed to study sustainability as an issue of "shared value" between financial stakeholders and the publics' interests (or, so called, non-financial stakeholders). After a decade, sustainable development appears to be a crucial point in many organizations' innovation processes (Altenburger, 2018).

Stemming from Kanter's pioneering study (1999) regarding sustainable innovation, the number of conceptual and empirical contributions on sustainability has increased (El-Kassar & Singh, 2019), and arguably, they stress that sustainability depends on innovation (Kusi-Sarpong et al., 2018). From a complementary perspective, innovation literature demonstrates the importance of sustainability on organizational outcomes. Nonetheless, a full agreement on a definition and sphere of sustainable innovation applicability is still missing (Candi et al., 2018; Cillo et al., 2019).

Extent literature provides a wide range of conceptual connections between sustainability and innovation. For example, eco-innovation, sustainability innovation, sustainable development innovation, sustainable innovation, sustainability-driven innovation, environmental innovation, green innovation, partly even, social innovation. All the different related constructs that emerge in sustainable innovation research confirm that "sustainable innovation is a very recent and fragmented topic" (Cillo et al., 2019, p. 1014). Drawing on the multiple views of sustainable innovation, we infer that the definition proposed by Juntunen et al. (2018, p. 331) is the most appropriate for our research because of its inclusiveness: "[*Sustainable*] *innovations are aimed at improving the environmental, social, and economic performance of the innovated solution.*"

Reading existing literature, we build a conceptual framework composed of three main blocks. From right to left, the first block represents the antecedents of sustainable innovation. They include the pressure of external factors, as sustainable innovation is promoted and supported by a wide range of policy instruments adopted in the light of the Sustainable Development Goals (SDGs). Thus, organizational behavior is influenced by policy, technology, society, and the environment. Indeed, according to Juntunen et al. (2018), the challenge of sustainable innovation is related to the framework of ecological or social problems as a driver of input for innovation. Additionally, we recognize a set of organizational drivers of sustainable innovation.

The second block of our conceptual framework is the management of sustainable innovation. We consider both the *organizational resource-based management* of sustainable innovation and the *inter-organizational resource-based management* of sustainable innovation. However, as it is possible to see in Fig. 1, our framework offers substantial attention to the inter-organizational resource-based management of sustainable innovation. Different aspects of the broad theme of sustainable innovation bring a diverse stakeholder focus on collaboration. Summarizing involvement practices, Juntunen et al. (2018) argue that some common work elements are necessary to obtain effective outcomes. These elements correspond to a balanced number of stakeholder groups involved in cooperation activities with an organization and the quality of organizational engagement in maintaining these relationships (Herrera, 2016). Stakeholder integration requires a long time to acquire and the exploitation of external knowledge in product and service development (Graham et al., 2015; Juntunen et al., 2018). For this reason, a large part of our interpretative framework focuses on inter-organizational resource-based management. Specifically, we address the following questions derived from the literature review: (a) with whom to work; (b) when to work; (c) how to work together; (d) what challenges should organizations learn to face. Finally, we disentangle the primary outcomes of sustainable innovation.

3 Drivers of Sustainable Innovation

3.1 The Pressure of External Factors

External factors, such as adopting a sustainability policy framework, strongly impact internal organizational structures and processes, pushing them to adapt to the organizational context (Alves et al., 2017). Extent literature has focused mainly on identifying the external drivers of sustainable innovation. Such drivers include demand-driven and pressure-driven threats (Ketata et al., 2014; Candi et al., 2018). Table 1 presents the most common examples considered in existing literature based on four types of external factors.

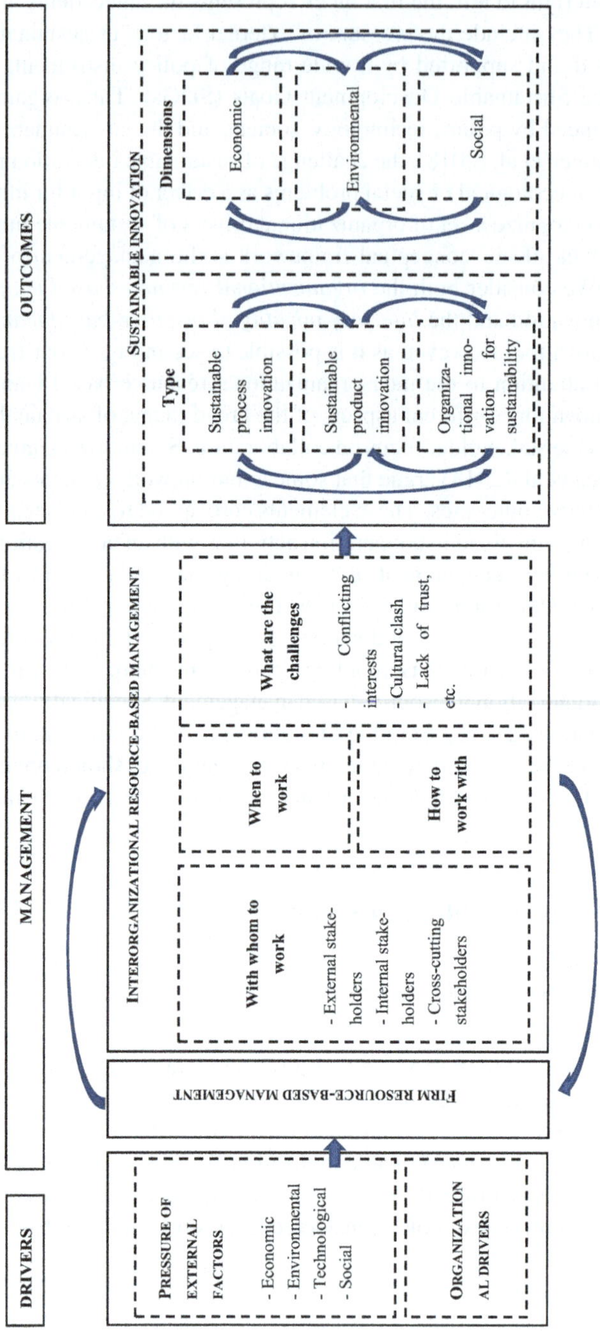

Fig. 1 Framework on stakeholders' involvement in sustainable innovation practice

Table 1 Groups and examples of external drivers presented in the reviewed literature

Type	Drivers	Examples in the literature
Economic	Policy, regulation, fiscal incentives	Candi et al. (2018); Dyck and Silvestre (2018); González-Moreno et al. (2019); Moradi and Vagnoni (2018)
	Legislation	O'Rourke and Strand (2017)
	Market competition	Candi et al. (2018); Vos et al. (2018)
	Financial resource availability	Kusi-Sarpong et al. (2018)
Environmental	Environmental challenges	Albertini (2018); Horng et al. (2018); Olsen et al. 2017; Knowles (2019); Moradi and Vagnoni (2018); Tuni and Rentizelas (2019)
	Inter- and intra-organization collaboration/competition	Candi et al. (2018); Kusi-Sarpong et al. (2018); Lai et al. (2015)
	Designing products to reduce impact on the environment	Kusi-Sarpong et al. (2018); Flammer et al. (2019)
Technological	Technology push/turbulence	Candi et al. (2018); González-Moreno et al. (2019)
	Policy for a change	Hall et al. (2017)
Social	Reducing inequality and local challenges	Andries et al. (2019); Phillips et al. (2017)
	Behavioral change and compliance with customer/pressure/requirements/market demand	Albertini (2018); Candi et al. (2018); Tuni and Rentizelas (2019); El-Kassar and Singh (2019); Alves et al. (2017); González-Moreno et al. (2019); Gronau (2016)
	Implementation of socio-eco-policies in organizations	Kusi-Sarpong et al. (2018); Elzen and Bos (2019)
	Enhancing the social image of the organization and corporate social initiatives	Kusi-Sarpong et al. (2018), Longoni and Cagliano (2016)
	Cultural, social values and norms	Longoni and Cagliano (2016); Kusi-Sarpong et al. (2018); Pancholi et al. (2019)

3.2 *Organizational Drivers*

The first and probably the most essential internal driver of sustainable innovations is related to the quest for competitive advantage (Dibrell et al., 2014; Yu et al., 2017) and reduction in product cost (Kusi-Sarpong et al., 2018).

Furthermore, sustainable innovation is a process of change that entails both employee and organizational involvement. Indeed, the internal drivers of sustainable innovation are linked to multiple stakeholders' actions, such as shareholders, managers, and employees (Watson et al., 2017; Longoni & Cagliano, 2016; Horng et al., 2018; Herrera, 2016). From this perspective, we agree with Flammer et al. (2019), who affirm that social topics help direct managers' attention toward stakeholders' interests. These interests may be less critical in the short-term period, but these become crucial in the long-term perspective. Definitively, a long organizational planning horizon for sustainable innovativeness and acceptance of uncertainty (Longoni & Cagliano, 2016) appear to be at the roots of an organization's long-term economic performance (Vos et al., 2018).

Moreover, employee attention regards negative externalities and plays an essential role in sustainability promotion. So, diverse forms of social interaction support innovativeness in sustainability (Delmas & Pekovic, 2016; Watson et al., 2017). Sustainability epitomizes a part of the formal and regular employee review process in more advanced settings, such as support provided by leaders and senior management, compensation plans, written employee manuals (El-Kassar & Singh, 2019; Watson et al., 2017), and training practices, such as knowledge management/environmental programs (Garriga, 2014).

4 Organizational Resource-Based Management

During the last decades, several policy interventions (e.g., SDGs, EU sustainable development strategy, national tax policy, and green budgeting for circular economy) fostered significant changes in organizational innovation processes, supporting the development and implementation of sustainability strategies. Nonetheless, to exploit sustainable innovation, organizations need resources (physical and financial resources), capabilities, and tactics. Furthermore, learning from the past, increasingly adopting innovative actions and radical innovations is crucial to introduce sustainable innovations (Longoni & Cagliano, 2016). From the organizational side, sustainability requires opening organizational boundaries, strategizing supplier operations transparency, and managing risk (Kusi-Sarpong et al., 2018).

Additionally, since organizations have shown limited capacity to develop sustainable innovations productively (Schmidthuber & Wiener, 2018), it has been argued that a transition pathway and the adoption of multi-actor processes may be beneficial (Quist et al., 2011; Janssen & Moors, 2013; Colvin et al., 2014). Sustainable innovation calls for interactions between heterogeneous stakeholders and understanding cultural differences and work in a specific policy framework (Moradi & Vagnoni, 2018). Consequently, organizations should also acquire operational capabilities that provide instruments to collaborate effectively with stakeholders, such as open innovation tools. Olsen et al. (2017) underline that sustainable innovation requires collaborative efforts. In turn, such efforts foster the existing exchange of expertise and collaborators that can provide efficient communication and coordination capacities. For organizations to co-create value and learn from involvement practices, such capacities should cover: "complex first-order dynamic capabilities to manage the engagement (*engagement management capabilities*); and second-order dynamic capabilities (*engagement learning capabilities*)" (Watson et al., 2017, p. 265).

5 Inter-organizational Resource-Based Management

5.1 Stakeholders Involvement: With Whom to Work

Working with multiple stakeholders helps establish a set of primary incentives to induce and follow sustainability policies (Dyck & Silvestre, 2018). According to Raub and Martin-Rios (2019), a goal of the stakeholder management approach is to ensure that organizations strategically consider the requirements, interests, and values of individuals and/or groups. Interests that may be "affected by or have an effect on any project, initiative, intervention, or effort the organization engages in" (Raub & Martin-Rios, 2019, p. 9). In this debate, we underscore the importance of considering two key contexts. First, the local context impacts a selection of relevant stakeholders (Raub & Martin-Rios, 2019). Thus, there is a strong need to consider local needs by carefully facing their social instances (Dyck & Silvestre, 2018). Local contexts imply that "one size fits all" solutions will not be effective, making the opening of a dialog with local stakeholders a critical issue (Evans et al., 2007). Second, the industry and public contexts influence which actors should be included in the innovation process (Jensen & Sandström, 2011).

In addition to the distinction between local and industry contexts, we acknowledge the importance of developing a more detailed knowledge regarding different stakeholders. Based on Freeman's (1984) stakeholder approach, organizational stakeholders can be divided into external and internal groups based on their interests: institutions/organizations and personal, professional, and/or social interests. Such a division is essential because, although belonging to an institution and following institutional directions, individuals may have their personal, divergent visions, values, and interests. Potentially, there may be hidden conflicts of interest involving the relationship between institutions and stakeholders, as insiders may have different professional and social roles. As a unique stakeholder, we also consider media that strongly influences opinion-making and decision formation, poses pressure on both of the previously mentioned groups, and provides visibility to the topic of sustainability. Consequently, it fills Freeman's stakeholder taxonomy as a separate cross-cutting third group of sustainability actors.

All the aforementioned groups of stakeholders may be categorized based on long- and short-term interests regarding sustainability. They represent public and private interests and values. Finally, each group considered manifests a specific strength due to its nature; depending on the pressure and power, it manages to pose on the topic of interest. Among all the mentioned actors, the policy-level actors take a leading role in promoting sustainability due to their initial power to develop new policy agendas and financial instruments for balancing forces and interests of public and private sectors in this area, for example, based on public-private partnerships.

In sum, to answer the question "*with whom,*" it is necessary to consider the organizations' size and the industry in which it operates; moreover, the degree of organizational openness for collaboration with stakeholders depends on already established processes and practices, as well as the relationships with stakeholder networks (González-Moreno et al., 2019). Dyck and Silvestre (2018) stress that sustainable innovations are more common to be implemented and exploited in contexts in which meta-standardization of local experimentation mechanisms is contextual to local innovation systems. Finally, González-Moreno et al. (2019) posit that collaboration between several organizations and stakeholders should be high for sustainable innovations. Such intensity will help generate trust, reduce the initial distance between knowledge actors, and contribute to the development of a knowledge base for collaboration. Moreover, it supports the development of shared visions to frame priorities and reduce uncertainties (Schmidthuber & Wiener, 2018). In this setting, Juntunen et al. (2018) add that stakeholders can play a catalyst or an obstacle role.

5.2 *Stakeholder Involvement: When to Work Together*

As regards the "*when*", we acknowledge that sustainability could be studied as a transition pathway (Moradi & Vagnoni, 2018) due to the complex multi-level processes implied (Manning & Reinecke, 2016; Gehman et al., 2020). Social learning processes (Smith et al., 2014), social initiatives in education, promotion of smartness in communities, and corporate citizenship strengthen understanding of shared values and co-creation between an organization and stakeholders (Herrera, 2016). Based on a regime change study, Elzen and Bos (2019) provide a list of co-creation activities with stakeholders based on a transition path perspective. These activities include: (a) development and inspiring communication designs with a heterogeneous number of crucial stakeholders; (b) development of sustaining network(s) and establishment of (private/public) links that attempt for follow-up in practice; (c) spaces for experiments, including partnerships and funding; (d) stimulation uptake of "partial innovations," i.e., specific elements from the new designs; € creations of a new production and process system. In some cases, social media and collaboration platforms play a significant role in stakeholder empowerment, develop healthy relationships, and improve understanding of market trends and opportunities (Herrera, 2016). However, physical place-making is essential to support co-creation and knowledge for sustainable growth (Pancholi et al., 2019). Meantime, Fliaster and Kolloch (2017) underline that collaboration with environmental non-governmental organizations is vital for corporate environmental sustainability.

Collaboration strategies and processes are essential in engaging with stakeholders, which create a background to improve risk and reputation management. Such collaboration strategies contribute to solve challenges and reach objectives that are unattainable for single organizations. Furthermore, they provide access to such resources as knowledge, new actors, financial benefits, technology, a better understanding of the environment, and fostering product and process improvements. Overall, context and learning processes play a crucial role in all the processes, supported by organizational policies, infrastructure, and the co-responsibility for collaboration (Colvin et al., 2014).

5.3 Stakeholders Involvement: How to Work

As regards "*how*", Juntunen et al. (2018) state that two stakeholder integration initiatives lead to a high sustainability performance of innovation. The first integration strategy is related to openness and entails including the early integration of external stakeholders (Herrera, 2016). Arguably, an open innovation strategy strongly supports sustainability integration in the innovation process (Ketata et al., 2014; Juntunen et al., 2018; González-Moreno et al., 2019). They learn how to obtain information from outside sources and how many contacts are needed to enhance their efficiency and innovation potential (González-Moreno et al., 2019, p. 53). In these conditions, participatory processes become essential factors for the identity of piloting territories, which is used for external communication and recognition of the pilots (Nielsen et al., 2019). Such cooperation is not feasible without local empowerment that requires changes in the mindset and in the glocal culture, effort from all interested knowledge actors, and the stability of business operations within a societal context (Mena et al., 2009).

The second integration strategy, according to Juntunen et al. (2018), is related to limited openness, in terms of selective integration with only selected stakeholders (or of primary stakeholders) after a fine-tuning phase. Such a particular strategy considers the combination of a specific network of stakeholders and organizational engagement. Following this approach, organizations prefer to refine the solutions' eventual acceptability with stakeholders' help instead of introducing a new product or service fundamentals.

5.4 Stakeholders Involvement: What Are the Challenges

To comprehend the stakeholders' role in sustainable innovation, it is also crucial to investigate the significant challenges that such cooperation faces. This recent literature has outlined several barriers (Hörisch et al., 2014). First, the lack of appropriate cooperation partners is an essential innovation barrier (González-Moreno et al., 2019). We call specific attention to the lack of trust and the role of cultural differences

(Tuni & Rentizelas, 2019). Second, stakeholder interests are so heterogeneous that they may conflict with each other, hindering collaborative practices and preventing envisioning of potential solutions for challenges (Flammer et al., 2019; Fliaster & Kolloch, 2017; Romijn & Caniëls, 2011). Third, the cooperation context is framed by socio-economic and political frames, physical and spatial components, the relationship between actors and conflicting agendas, and power inequalities between them (Romijn & Caniëls, 2011; Nielsen et al., 2019).

6 The Interplay Between Organizational and Inter-Organizational Resource-Based Management

An organization can cover different and diverse phases and sustainability elements through interaction with stakeholders. Indeed, networking is a critical organizational innovation capability, where an organization can play different roles, such as those of the broker, the transformer, the loner, and the augmenter (Phillips et al., 2017). According to Watson et al. (2017), stakeholder involvement for innovation represents a dynamic organizational capability. This is an organizational potential to involve and rearrange internal and external competencies aiming to respond to a changing and dynamic environment. Specifically, organizations need the value-framing capabilities that help minimize these differences between value systems and use them to reorganize problems, distribute capabilities, and co-create innovative products and technologies (Watson et al., 2017). Additionally, organizations need to build structures (including digital ones) and processes that help support "learn to learn" procedures from their stakeholders (Delmas & Pekovic, 2016). Schmidthuber and Wiener (2018) add one more important component to this list: a specific time and space dedicated to reflecting on the differences in value frames among organizations and their stakeholders.

Importantly, innovating with and for stakeholders in the social issue context represents an ongoing social interaction process (Rühli et al., 2015) that requires top management commitment, large-scale data, and human resource practices. Such focus is needed to achieve a competitive advantage and improve an organization's social and environmental performance (El-Kassar & Singh, 2019). While top management plays a crucial role in allocating and re-allocating resources, they create a sustainability philosophy (Herrera, 2016), build capabilities, and help the organization gain a competitive advantage (El-Kassar & Singh, 2019). As such, the intense social interactions between employees improve sustainable innovation performance (Delmas and Pekovic, 2016).

Having stakeholders onboard means increasing innovative capabilities for sustainable innovation based on specific organizational capabilities, such as engagement management capabilities, implementing co-creation actions, and learning from stakeholder engagement activities (Watson et al., 2017). Therefore, stimulating stakeholder dialog and its transformation into knowledge is relevant to integrate sustainability issues into the innovation process. After all, stakeholder involvement means for an organization to find answers to critical questions such as "who, how, and when to work with" (Juntunen et al., 2018), considering stakeholder capabilities. According to Garriga (2014, p. 493), they can be defined "as the stakeholders' effective opportunities to undertake actions and activities with the firm that they want to choose to engage in the value-creation process."

7 Outcomes of Sustainable Innovation

We divide the outcomes of sustainable innovation based on two factors: dimensions and organizational level. We argue that sustainable development may function if all three dimensions are simultaneously pursued (Raub & Martin-Rios, 2019; Nielsen et al., 2019; Manning & Reinecke, 2016): economic sustainability (Fliaster & Kolloch, 2017); environmental sustainability (Vachon & Mao 2008); and social sustainability (Klassen & Vereecke 2012; Candi et al., 2018). Regarding the organizational level, literature distinguishes between process sustainable innovation and product sustainable innovation and sustainable organizational innovation (Vos et al., 2018).

8 Conclusion

Researchers strive to explain how to achieve success in combining sustainability and innovation. There is a general agreement that sustainable innovations reach beyond environmental issues, including all societal challenges and positively related to customer acceptance. Within a global and gig economy, stakeholder involvement regards the organizational activities aimed at stakeholder identification, consultation, communication, dialog exchange, and mutually beneficial collaboration (O'Riordan & Fairbrass, 2014). The latter aspect has a complex nature, requires a multi-stakeholder focus and multiple player interactions, and more intense R&D cooperation (Juntunen et al., 2018).

Altenburger (2018) summarizes several academic works that underline the benefits of stakeholders' involvement in sustainable innovation, including direct access to information linked to social and environmental issues, the renewal of organizational knowledge in changing environments, and the origin of innovations. We call particular attention to the issue of shared vision, stakeholder integration, and organizational learning (Sarpong & Maclean, 2012; Albertini, 2018).

Being an essential process to promote sustainable innovation in organizations, involvement represents a long-term systemic perspective and combination of knowledge actors, technologies, and links in the specific glocal contexts (Breukers et al., 2014; Flammer et al., 2019).

In this study, we contribute to the current understanding of stakeholder involvement elements associated with a context of sustainable innovation. Specifically, we offer a unique overview that overcomes the "snapshot in time" of scholars working in multiple directions (Kusi-Sarpong et al., 2018). Such research will support an understanding of the organizational logics for the gig economy (Frenken et al., 2020), a power relation between employers, workers, and consumers (Healy et al., 2017), and sustainability, which is a primary motive for the use of the sharing economy (Boar et al., 2020).

References

Albertini, E. (2018). The contribution of management control systems to environmental capabilities. *Journal of Business Ethics, 159*(4), 1163–1180.

Altenburger, R. (2018). Corporate social responsibility as a driver of innovation processes. *In Innovation Management and Corporate Social Responsibility* (pp. 1–12). Springer, Cham.

Alves, M. W. F. M., de Sousa Jabbour, A. B. L., D. Kannan, & Jabbour, C. J. C. Contingency theory, climate change, and low-carbon operations management. *Supply Chain Management: An International Journal, 22*(3), 223–236.

Andries, P., Daou, A., & Verheyden, L. (2019). Innovation as a vehicle for improving socially vulnerable groups' access to basic provisions: A research note on the development of a questionnaire module. *Research Policy, 48*(1), 281–288.

Ayuso, S., Rodríguez, A. M., & Ricart, J. E. (2006). Using stakeholder dialogue as a source for new ideas: A dynamic capability underlying sustainable innovation. *Corporate Governance, 6*(4), 475–490.

Bäckstrand, K. (2006). Multi-stakeholder partnerships for sustainable development: Rethinking legitimacy, accountability and effectiveness. *European Environment, 16*(5), 290–306.

Boar, A., Bastida, R., & Marimon, F. (2020). A systematic literature review. Relationships between the sharing economy, sustainability and sustainable development goals. *Sustainability, 12*(17), 6744.

Breukers, S., Hisschemöller, M., Cuppen, E., & Suurs, R. (2014). Analysing the past and exploring the future of sustainable biomass. Participatory stakeholder dialogue and technological innovation systems research. *Technological Forecasting and Social Change, 81*, 227–235.

Candi, M., Melia, M., & Colurcio, M. (2018). Two birds with one stone: The quest for addressing both business goals and social needs with innovation. *Journal of Business Ethics, 160*(4), 1019–1033.

Cillo, V., Petruzzelli, A. M., Ardito, L., & Del Giudice, M. (2019). Understanding sustainable innovation: A systematic literature review. *Corporate Social Responsibility and Environmental Management, 26*(5), 1012–1025.

Colvin, J., Blackmore, C., Chimbuya, S., Collins, K., Dent, M., Goss, J., Ison, R., Roggero, P. P., & Seddaiu, G. (2014). In search of systemic innovation for sustainable development: A design praxis emerging from a decade of social learning inquiry. *Research Policy, 43*(4), 760–771.

Dagnino, G. B., Picone, P. M., & Ferrigno, G. (2021). Temporary competitive advantage: A state-of-the-art literature review and research directions. *International Journal of Management Reviews, 23*(1), 85–115.

De Stefano, V. (2015). The rise of the just-in-time workforce: On-demand work, crowdwork, and labor protection in the gig-economy. *Comparative Labor Law and Policy Journal, 37*(3), 461–471.
Delmas, M. A., & Pekovic, S. (2016). Corporate sustainable innovation and employee behavior. *Journal of Business Ethics, 150*(4), 1071–1088.
Dibrell, C., Craig, J. B., Kim, J., & Johnson, A. J. (2014). Establishing how natural environmental competency, organizational social consciousness, and innovativeness relate. *Journal of Business Ethics, 127*(3), 591–605.
Dyck, B., & Silvestre, B. S. (2018). A novel NGO approach to facilitate the adoption of sustainable innovations in low-income countries: Lessons from small-scale farms in Nicaragua. *Organization Studies, 40*(3), 443–461.
El-Kassar, A. N., & Singh, S. K. (2019). Green innovation and organizational performance: The influence of big data and the moderating role of management commitment and HR practices. *Technological Forecasting and Social Change, 144*, 483–498.
Elzen, B., & Bos, B. (2019). The RIO approach: Design and anchoring of sustainable animal husbandry systems. *Technological Forecasting and Social Change, 145*, 141–152.
Evans, S., Partidário, P. J., & Lambert, J. (2007). Industrialization as a key element of sustainable product-service solutions. *International Journal of Production Research, 45*(18–19), 4225–4246.
Ferraro, F., Etzion, D., & Gehman, J. (2015). Tackling grand challenges pragmatically: Robust action revisited. *Organization Studies, 36*(3), 363–390.
Flammer, C., Hong, B., & Minor, D. (2019). Corporate governance and the rise of integrating corporate social responsibility criteria in executive compensation: Effectiveness and implications for firm outcomes. *Strategic Management Journal, 40*(7), 1097–1122.
Fliaster, A., & Kolloch, M. (2017). Implementation of green innovations—The impact of stakeholders and their network relations. *R&D Management, 47*(5), 689–700.
Freeman, R. E. (1984). *Strategic management: A stakeholder approach*. Ballinger.
Frenken, K., Vaskelainen, T., Fünfschilling, L., & Piscicelli, L. (2020). An institutional logics perspective on the gig economy. In *Theorizing the Sharing Economy: Variety and Trajectories of New Forms of Organizing* (pp. 83–105). Emerald Publishing Limited, Bingley.
Garriga, E. (2014). Beyond stakeholder utility function: Stakeholder capability in the value creation process. *Journal of Business Ethics, 120*(4), 489–507.
Gehman, J., Jarzabkowski, P., Langley, A., Tsoukas, H., Hardy, C., Howard-Grenville, J., & Keller, C. (2020). Call for Papers Twelfth International Symposium on Process Organization Studies.
George, G., Howard-Grenville, J., Joshi, A., & Tihanyi, L. (2016). Understanding and tackling societal grand challenges through management research. *Academy of Management Journal, 59*(6), 1880–1895.
González-Moreno, Á., Triguero, Á., & Sáez-Martínez, F. J. (2019). Many or trusted partners for eco-innovation? The influence of breadth and depth of firms' knowledge network in the food sector. *Technological Forecasting and Social Change, 147*, 51–62.
Görög, G. (2018). The definitions of sharing economy: A systematic literature review. *Management (18544223), 13*(2), 175–198.
Graham, G., Mehmood, R., & Coles, E. (2015). Exploring future cityscapes through urban logistics prototyping: A technical viewpoint. *Supply Chain Management: An International Journal, 2*(3), 341–352.
Gronau, W. (2016). Encouraging behavioural change towards sustainable tourism: A German approach to free public transport for tourists. *Journal of Sustainable Tourism, 25*(2), 265–275.
Hall, J., Matos, S., & Bachor, V. (2017). From green technology development to green innovation: Inducing regulatory adoption of pathogen detection technology for sustainable forestry. *Small Business Economics, 52*(4), 877–889.
Hall, J., & Vredenburg, H. (2003). The challenge of innovating for sustainable development. *MIT Sloan Management Review, 45*(1), 61–68.
Healy, J., Nicholson, D., & Pekarek, A. (2017). Should we take the gig economy seriously? *Labour & Industry: A Journal of the Social and Economic Relations of Work, 27*(3), 232–248.

Herrera, M. E. B. (2016). Innovation for impact: Business innovation for inclusive growth. *Journal of Business Research, 69*(5), 1725–1730.
Hörisch, J., Freeman, R. E., & Schaltegger, S. (2014). Applying stakeholder theory in sustainability management: Links, similarities, dissimilarities, and a conceptual framework. *Organization & Environment, 27*(4), 328–346.
Horng, J. S., Liu, C. H. S., Chou, S. F., Tsai, C. Y., & Hu, D. C. (2018). Developing a sustainable service innovation framework for the hospitality industry. *International Journal of Contemporary Hospitality Management, 30*(1), 455–474.
Janssen, M., & Moors, E. H. (2013). Caring for healthcare entrepreneurs—Towards successful entrepreneurial strategies for sustainable innovations in Dutch healthcare. *Technological Forecasting and Social Change, 80*(7), 1360–1374.
Jensen, T., & Sandström, J. (2011). Stakeholder theory and globalization: The challenges of power and responsibility. *Organization Studies, 32*(4), 473–488.
Juntunen, J. K., Halme, M., Korsunova, A., & Rajala, R. (2018). Strategies for integrating stakeholders into sustainability innovation: A configurational perspective. *Journal of Product Innovation Management, 36*(3), 331–355.
Kanter, R. M. (1999). From spare change to real change: The social sector as beta site for business innovation. *Harvard Business Review, 77*(3), 122–123.
Ketata, I., Sofka, W., & Grimpe, C. (2014). The role of internal capabilities and firms' environment for sustainable innovation: Evidence for Germany. *R&d Management, 45*(1), 60–75.
Klassen, R. D., & Vereecke, A. (2012). Social issues in supply chains: Capabilities link responsibility, risk (opportunity), and performance. *International Journal of Production Economics, 140*(1), 103–115.
Knowles LB, N. (2019). Can the North American ski industry attain climate resiliency? A modified Delphi survey on transformations towards sustainable tourism. *Journal of Sustainable Tourism, 27*(3), 380–397.
Kusi-Sarpong, S., Gupta, H., & Sarkis, J. (2018). A supply chain sustainability innovation framework and evaluation methodology. *International Journal of Production Research, 57*(7), 1990–2008.
Lai, W. H., Lin C. C. & Wang, T. C. (2015). Exploring the interoperability of innovation capability and corporate sustainability. *Journal of Business Research, 68*(4), 867–871.
Longoni, A., & Cagliano, R. (2016). Sustainable innovativeness and the triple bottom line: The role of organizational time perspective. *Journal of Business Ethics, 151*(4), 1097–1120.
Lüdeke-Freund, F. (2010). Towards a conceptual framework of 'business models for sustainability'. Eds. *Knowledge Collaboration & Learning for Sustainable Innovation* (pp. 25–29). Delft.
Manning, S., & Reinecke, J. (2016). A modular governance architecture in-the-making: How transnational standard-setters govern sustainability transitions. *Research Policy, 45*(3), 618–633.
Manning, S., & Roessler, D. (2013). The formation of cross-sector development partnerships: How bridging agents shape project agendas and longer-term alliances. *Journal of Business Ethics, 123*(3), 527–547.
McGahan, A. M. (2020). Where does an organization's responsibility end? Identifying the boundaries on stakeholder claims. *Academy of Management Discoveries, 6*(1), 8–11.
Mena, S., de Leede, M., Baumann, D., Black, N., Lindeman, S., & McShane, L. (2009). Advancing the business and human rights agenda: Dialogue, empowerment, and constructive engagement. *Journal of Business Ethics, 93*(1), 161–188.
Moradi, A., & Vagnoni, E. (2018). A multi-level perspective analysis of urban mobility system dynamics: What are the future transition pathways? *Technological Forecasting and Social Change, 126*, 231–243.
Nielsen, B. F., Baer, D., & Lindkvist, C. (2019). Identifying and supporting exploratory and exploitative models of innovation in municipal urban planning; key challenges from seven Norwegian energy ambitious neighborhood pilots. *Technological Forecasting and Social Change, 142*, 142–153.
O'Riordan, L., & Fairbrass, J. (2014). Managing CSR stakeholder engagement: A new conceptual framework. *Journal of Business Ethics, 125*(1), 121–145.

O'Rourke, D., & Strand, R. (2017). Patagonia: Driving sustainable innovation by embracing tensions. *California Management Review, 60*(1), 102–125.
Olsen, A. Ø., Sofka, W., & Grimpe, C. (2017). Solving environmental problems: Knowledge and coordination in collaborative search. *Long Range Planning, 50*(6), 726–740.
Pancholi, S., Yigitcanlar, T., & Guaralda, M. (2019). Place making for innovation and knowledge-intensive activities: The Australian experience. *Technological Forecasting and Social Change, 146*, 616–625.
Phillips, W., Alexander, E. A., & Lee, H. (2017). Going it alone won't work! The relational imperative for social innovation in social enterprises. *Journal of Business Ethics, 156*(2), 315–331.
Quist, J., Thissen, W., & Vergragt, P. J. (2011). The impact and spin-off of participatory backcasting: From vision to niche. *Technological Forecasting and Social Change, 78*(5), 883–897.
Raub, S. P., & Martin-Rios, C. (2019). Think sustainable, act local"—A stakeholder-filter-model for translating SDGs into sustainability initiatives with local impact. *International Journal of Contemporary Hospitality Management, 31*(6), 2428–2447.
Reypens, C., Lievens, A., & Blazevic, V. (2016). Leveraging value in multi-stakeholder innovation networks: A process framework for value co-creation and capture. *Industrial Marketing Management, 56*, 40–50.
Romijn, H. A., & Caniëls, M. C. (2011). The Jatropha biofuels sector in Tanzania 2005–2009: Evolution towards sustainability? *Research Policy, 40*(4), 618–636.
Rühli, E., Sachs, S., Schmitt, R., & Schneider, T. (2015). Innovation in multi-stakeholder settings: The case of a wicked issue in health care. *Journal of Business Ethics, 43*(2), 289–305.
Sarpong, D., & Maclean, M. (2012). Mobilising differential visions for new product innovation. *Technovation, 32*(12), 694–702.
Savitz, A. W. & Weber, K. (2007). The sustainability sweet spot. *Environmental Quality Management, 17*(2), 17–28.
Schmidthuber, L., & Wiener, M. (2018). Aiming for a sustainable future: Conceptualizing public open foresight. *Public Management Review, 20*(1), 82–107.
Smith, A., Kern, F., Raven, R., & Verhees, B. (2014). Spaces for sustainable innovation: Solar photovoltaic electricity in the UK. *Technological Forecasting and Social Change, 81*, 115–130.
Tuni, A., & Rentizelas, A. (2019). An innovative eco-intensity-based method for assessing extended supply chain environmental sustainability. *International Journal of Production Economics, 217*, 126–142.
Vachon, S., & Mao, Z. (2008). Linking supply chain strength to sustainable development: A country-level analysis. *Journal of Cleaner Production, 16*(15), 1552–1560.
Vos, M. A., Raassens, N., Van der Borgh, M., & Nijssen, E. J. (2018). Balancing modularity and solution space freedom: Effects on organisational learning and sustainable innovation. *International Journal of Production Research, 56*(20), 6658–6677.
Watson, R., Wilson, H. N., Smart, P., & Macdonald, E. K. (2017). Harnessing difference: A capability-based framework for stakeholder engagement in environmental innovation. *Journal of Product Innovation Management, 35*(2), 254–279.
Yu, W., Ramanathan, R., & Nath, P. (2017). Environmental pressures and performance: An analysis of the roles of environmental innovation strategy and marketing capability. *Technological Forecasting and Social Change, 117*, 160–169.

Jelena Mazaj has gained a PhD in Economics and Statistics at the University of Palermo. Her research interests are linked to the area of inter-organizational dynamics within networks with a focus on the interaction between private, public actors, and civil society and dynamics that this collaboration creates for corporate sustainability, sustainable innovation, and business ethics.

Pasquale Massimo Picone is Associate Professor of Management at the University of Palermo. Previously, he worked at the University of Bergamo and at the University of Catania, where he received his Ph.D. in Business Economics & Management. He has held visiting positions at

Texas A&M University and IE Business School. His research work has been published in various outlets, including *Academy of Management Perspectives, Corporate Governance: An International Review, Global Strategy Journal,* and *International Journal of Management Review.*

Arabella Mocciaro Li Destri is Full Professor of Management at the University of Palermo. She has held visiting positions at MIT's Sloan School of Management, Tuck School of Business at Dartmouth, and IAE Business School, Buenos Aires. She earned her Ph.D. from the University of Catania. She has published three books and numerous articles in leading journals, such as *Journal of Managerial Psychology, Advances in Strategic Management, Organization Studies,* and *Long Range Planning.*

Building Credibility in the GiG Economy: The Role of Personal Branding (A Conceptual Framework)

Himanshu Ahuja and Deep Shree

1 Introduction

Post almost ten years of its existence, the platform-based GiG work has become a major contributor to the economies across the globe. The impact created by the popularity of GiG work is wide-ranging and can be observed across businesses belonging to diverse industries. It has completely changed the way an economy functions and has brought novel ways of knowledge sharing, supplying goods, and rendering services as a part of short-term work engagements. This chapter focuses on the challenge of cluttered marketspace in the context of the GiG economy and presents a conceptual framework focused on personal branding and self-marketing. Further, this study also provides implications for the customers (employers) in the GiG economy enabling them to filter out relevant candidates and weed out the irrelevant ones using sound criteria. The study has been carried out using an extensive literature review on the chosen topic and by synthesizing past work already done in this field.

H. Ahuja · D. Shree (✉)
Delhi Technological University, Shahbad Daulatpur, Main Bawana Road, Delhi 110042, India
e-mail: deepshree@dtu.ac.in

H. Ahuja
e-mail: himanshuahuja_2k20phddsm02@dtu.ac.in

A. Gupta et al. (eds.), *Sustainability in the Gig Economy*,
https://doi.org/10.1007/978-981-16-8406-7_5

2 Literature Review

2.1 Background and Evolution of the GiG Economy

In 2008–09, sharing economy came into existence. The sharing platforms are peer-to-peer (P2P) arrangements that organize and leverage idle resources (Frenken & Schor, 2017). The platform economy has witnessed speedy growth since 2008–09, and it now encapsulates a wide range of tech-mediated transactions. Its proliferation has two dimensions. The first is the rampant digitalization that has propelled the established businesses to digitalize their internal workflows as well as the way they transact with other business organizations. Apart from this, the increasing penetration of the Internet and the adoption of smartphones have resulted in a 'platform-like' system for the traditional firms to carry out business operations. The second driver for the growth of the platform economy is the advent of 'digitally native companies.' The platform economy also comprises the social media platforms such as Facebook and Instagram which depend on the revenue streams stemming from the advertising/sale of data. Further, the platform economy also includes Internet service platforms, such as Amazon Web Services (AWS), which provide relevant and sound set-up on which other entities hinge on. The research scholars and management practitioners have already started to frame categories of platform workers based on parameters, including but not limited to the skill sets, the type of work, etc. One of the typologies of these platform workers is the 'GiG workers.' These workers are online platform workers, independent contractors, and on-demand workers. Technology has widened the scope of autonomous work across the globe. All these market trends have led to the proliferation of GiG economy in today's era. According to Gillis (2020), 'GiG economy is a free market system where organizations contract with independent workers for a short-term project or service engagement.' In this economy, the payment to workers is made on a project-to-project basis. A full-time job opportunity was the trend until the recent past; however, with the increasing population, the rising number of the workforce, the stiff competition for limited jobs, the enhanced digitalization and globalization, and the recent economic slowdown owing to the outbreak of COVID-19, this trend has been shifted to the contractual work opportunities, wherein the people work as independent workers, freelancers, or the GiG workers (Manyika, 2016). Further, the increasing 'Millennial' and 'Generation Z' working populace has also been a major contributor to the proliferation of GiG economy (ASSOCHAM, 2020).

2.2 The Cluttered Marketspace—The Core Challenge Within the GiG Economy

The workforce in the GiG economy has to face a plethora of challenges, including but not limited to, low probability of selection due to stiff competition, the necessity of an entrepreneurial mindset, inconsistency of income stream, uneven workload, absence of business rights, and the requirement of networking skills. Further, the absence of a sound regulatory framework for the safety and security of the GiG workers is another prominent challenge. As a consequence of this, the GiG workers are deprived of social security benefits and employment-related rights. Also, the GiG workers are always under constant pressure to up-skill themselves as the needs and demands of skills in the GiG economy are highly dynamic.

Similarly, for the business organizations as well as the staffing organizations, the GiG economy poses a number of challenges making it difficult for the human resource management of the companies to hire the right talent and manage it. Some of the prominent issues faced by the employers when hiring GiG workers include—communicating inappropriate job description owing to the inability to understand the technical requirements of a given job, managing the demand of workers across different seasonal cycles, adhering to numerous compliance requirements in both organized and unorganized sectors, ensuring the safety and security of the GiG workers, especially when they are working from remote locations, ensuring the confidentiality of data through executing the non-disclosure agreements from time to time, and hiring the right talent for the right job at the right time (ASSOCHAM, 2020).

It has been observed that most employers end up hiring subpar workers on a temporary basis and often struggle with the quality of output generated by them. Soriano (2017) highlighted that these companies do not deliberately recruit 'below than average' freelancers. According to Stefano (2016), both the parties, i.e., the employers and the GiG workers, anticipate to create value while entering into any professional engagement. However, in today's scenario, the online job market has become chaotic due to a burgeoning number of false and unauthentic profiles/accounts on GiG platforms. This has resulted in a plethora of applications, including the fake profiles of non-serious candidates, for a single work opportunity posted on the GiG platform. Consequently, a situation of unhealthy and unjustified competition is built up for the prospective workers, and at the same time, it becomes equally challenging for employers to select the best candidate for the job. *Hence, the cluttered marketspace is the central challenge for both the recruiters and the prospective workers within the GiG economy.* Unequivocally, the creation of a personal brand becomes essential in the GiG economy in order to differentiate oneself from the crowd and build credibility. Personal branding is a means to create trust in the GiG economy. According to Zhengyu (2019), the chairman and the founder of Yu Capital, 'A strong personal brand is important in the dynamic GiG economy because it is the only thing that individuals can take with them between jobs. An individual can take control of and actively build their brand so that even if they suffer setbacks in their career, their personal brand can survive.' Hence, personal branding is extremely vital for the GiG workers for ensuring long-term success. Personal branding can be defined as '*A strategic process of creating, positioning, and maintaining a positive impression of oneself, based in a unique combination of individual characteristics, which signal a certain promise to the target audience through a differentiated narrative and imagery*' (Suddaby, 2010). Personal branding is essential in both offline and online environments (Labrecque et al., 2011a, 2011b). However, with the increasing adoption and usage of social media platforms, artificial intelligence, and other novel digital technologies, personal branding on online platforms has taken a lead over the one in an offline environment. As a consequence of the evolving online alternatives, the creation of a personal brand has become a lot convoluted. The GiG workers and freelancers now need more insights about the right content, the right platforms, and the right marketing strategies to create an impactful personal brand. This chapter specifically aims to present a conceptual framework for building a strong personal brand in an online environment.

2.3 *Personal Branding—Theoretical Viewpoint*

The concept of 'personal branding' is cross-disciplinary in nature, and hence, there are multiple theories from different disciplines explaining this concept. To provide a robust conceptual framework as a part of this chapter, the theoretical model presented by Khedher (2015), highlighting the process of personal branding, has been studied and leveraged. This framework provides a broader and more holistic view of the stages involved in creating a personal brand than other extant theories. Many researchers claim that personal branding should be viewed and studied as a process involving some predetermined steps. Just like any other process, personal branding also involves inputs, techniques, strategies, and output. The steps in the process of personal branding are similar to the process of any other type of branding activity (Bendisch et al. 2013). As per the traditional branding model, there are three steps involved in the process of branding ranging from identity construction to communication management to image building (Labrecque et al., 2011a, 2011b). The steps of personal branding process in the chronological order are: creation of 'personal brand identity,' development of 'personal brand positioning,' and assessment of 'personal brand image' (Khedher, 2015).

2.3.1 Personal Brand Identity

According to Khedher (2015), creating a personal brand identity involves investment in building social capital as well as cultural capital. The concepts of social and cultural capital have been propounded by Bourdieu (1983) in his book named 'The Forms of Capital.' Working on building social and cultural capital helps one 'stand out from the crowd' and win opportunities in the competitive marketspace (Khedher, 2015). According to Bourdieu (1983), social capital includes all the lines of contacts, connections, and networks created by an individual. These contacts provide a plethora of benefits to the individual in terms of providing necessary information about work opportunities, career consultancy, earning growth possibilities, etc. This information not only helps an individual in earning better but also helps in his/her career advancement and holistic growth. On the other hand, cultural capital includes the skills, knowledge base, educational qualifications, professional certifications, technical proficiency, etc. that have been learned by the individual through his/her diligence and dedication. The cultural capital enhances the eligibility and proficiency of an individual for a particular work opportunity and thereby increases the employability of an individual (Khedher, 2015).

2.3.2 Personal Brand Positioning

According to Khedher (2015), personal brand positioning refers to the ways in which an individual maintains the personal brand. This step is best explained using the theory, propounded by Goffman (1959), which emphasizes the importance of 'impression management.' According to Khedher (2015), impression management within the personal branding process encompasses verbal maneuvers, artefactual, and non-verbal behavior determined by the individual's communication motivations. This connotes that an individual is required to tactfully present himself/herself before the target audience through upholding idyllic expressions, strategically conceal those facts that are not in tandem with the personal brand, and continuously control the information with respect to the personal brand that others are exposed to (Khedher, 2015). Hence, this step primarily focuses on controlling others' perceptions toward one's personal brand through using tactful means in order to maintain the standards set for the brand in the first place. Some of the prominent techniques of impression management include, but are not limited to, appearance, conduct, and strategic ways of communication, both verbal and non-verbal.

2.3.3 Personal Brand Image

The third step of the personal branding process focuses on the development of best practices of personal branding and on the administration of the already created personal brand (Khedher, 2015). It requires assuming a consciously thoughtful role in constantly improving the personal brand. Without thorough reflection, there cannot be enhancements to the already created personal brand (Khedher, 2015). The consequence of reflective thought process is an 'intelligent action' because all elements of the subject matter have already been thought of rationally by the individual and all the uncertainties or complexities have already been experienced by the individual while thinking of a possible solution to the problem at hand (Dewey, 1933). Reflection not only involves considering the historical actions but also results in the advanced level of knowledge and understanding (Khedher, 2015). Drawing from the implications of the theory propounded by Dewey (1933), Schon (1983) introduced some novel ideas on the process of reflection. Schon (1983) proposed two levels of reflection, namely 'reflection-in-action' and 'reflection-on-action.' 'Reflection-in-action' refers to continuous interpretation and investigation about the problem at hand in one's own capacity while leveraging the information stemming from past experiences in order to govern and direct novel actions (Schon, 1983). This is mostly observed when individuals proactively reach out to people asking for feedback and seek knowledge about how others perceive them (Khedher, 2015). On the other hand, 'reflection-on-action' is a concept focused on looking at the event retrospectively, i.e., it involves looking back after the event has already occurred. According to Schon (1983), 'reflection-on-action' arises when individuals search for information on how their knowledge in the course of action may have impacted the consequence. This level of reflection not only enhances an individual's knowledge but also questions the preconceived notions held by the individual (Bolton, 2001).

The next section proposes the conceptual framework of personal branding based on some aspects of the above-mentioned theoretical perspective of personal branding. The conceptual framework includes the antecedents, mediating variables, moderating variables, and outcomes. The conceptual framework applies to the concept of personal branding in the online context highly relevant for the GiG workers to '*stand out from the crowd.*'

2.4 *Personal Branding—The Conceptual Framework*

See Fig. 1.

2.5 *Antecedents (Building Personal Brand Identity)*

Antecedents include all those factors that help in building the brand identity and are prerequisites for the formation of trust and credibility on the GiG platforms.

2.5.1 Social Capital

According to Bourdieu (1983), social capital is built by the social connections that one establishes over time. In a platform-based GiG economy, the management of social relationships contributes substantially to building a reputation accessible to the professionals and staffing agencies that constitute the network of contacts on online platforms (Granovetter, 1985). Online platforms and tools have necessitated the creation of reputation as a part of marketing oneself and standing out in the cluttered, saturated, and hyper-competitive environment (Ottovordemgentschenfelde, 2017). The role of social capital becomes even more important in the online GiG economy as it has an almost negligible scope of proximity and physical interaction. Social capital is one of the most important prerequisites of securing an employment opportunity, ensuring career advancement and professional growth in the GiG economy (Gandini, 2016).

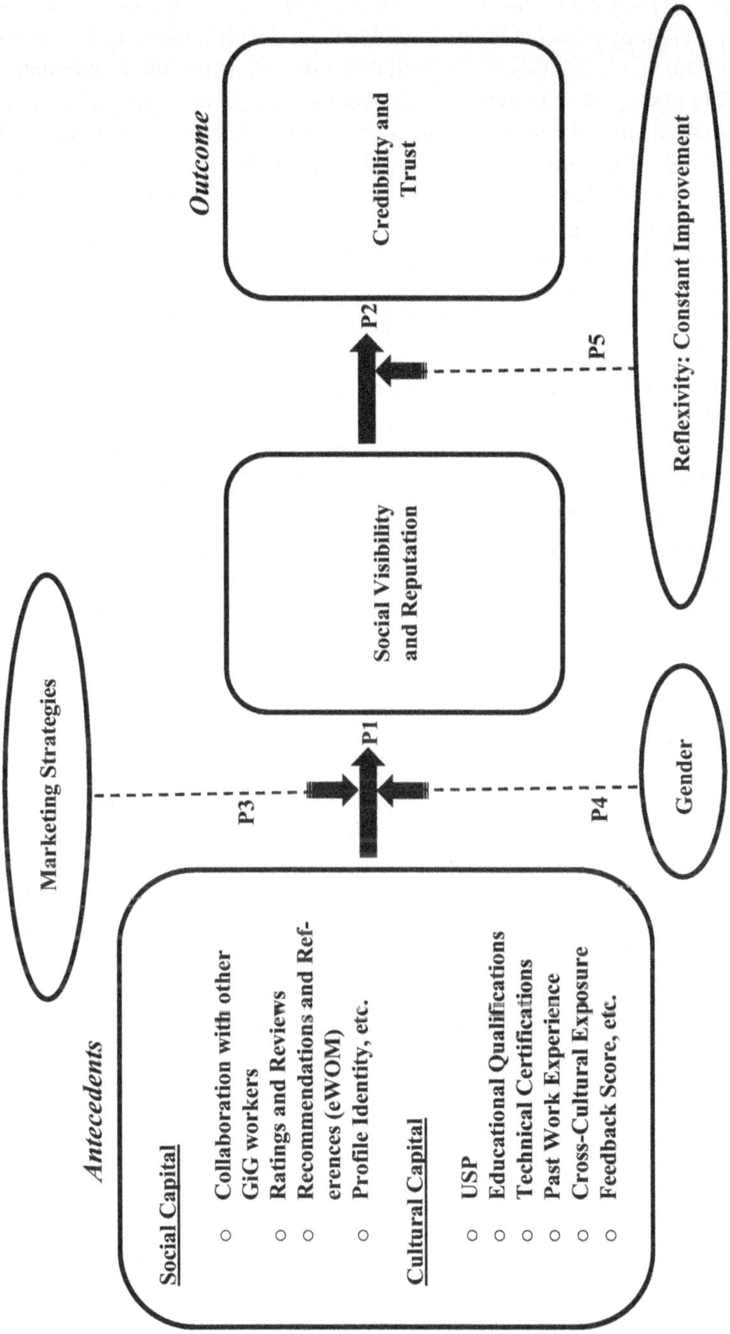

Fig. 1 Personal Branding in the GiG Economy: The Conceptual Framework. Source: Authors' Own

The first step in the personal branding process, propounded by Khedher (2015), is the creation of personal brand identity. The categories of information that are most important for creating personal identity include basic details about self, age, gender, location, occupation, citizenship, residential status, etc. as per the requirement of different GiG platforms (Landberg, 2017). Another important aspect of creating a personal brand identity is having a professional profile image and an authentic bio (Landberg, 2017). According to Bourdieu (1983), social capital is the totality of actual or probable resources that are associated with ownership of a long-lasting network of social relationships built on the grounds of mutual understanding and recognition. Ratings, reviews, positive references, and recommendations, earned from the professionals in the network, add to the overall profile of an individual helping in establishing a reliable reputation on the GiG platform. Such positive references and recommendations help the members of the network in being perceived as reliable, safe, and dependable to work with (Landberg, 2017). Entering into collaborations with other GiG workers plays a pivotal role in the long-term success of a worker in a GiG economy. As most work opportunities emerge from recommendations, references, and electronic word-of-mouth (eWOM), 'collaboration' becomes the key to build reputation and prosper in the GiG economy. 'Collaboration' outclasses 'competition' for the GiG workers and provides them with strategic advantages in numerous ways (Gandini, 2016). Making connections with other relevant target groups such as clients, staffing agencies, and career consultants also benefits a lot in the GiG economy to tap the right opportunities at the right time.

2.5.2 Cultural Capital

Cultural capital is another aspect under the first step of the personal branding process developed by Khedher (2015). Cultural capital includes non-financial resources, such as education, credentials, skills, and knowledge that enable social agility (Raskoff, 2014). Cultural capital constitutes educational qualifications, professional qualifications, skills, knowledge, and other credentials that an individual has earned or has been awarded. Besides this, cultural capital also includes linguistic proficiency, personal flair, technical competence, and specific approaches and attitudes of the individual (Bourdieu & Passeron, 1990). Cultural capital can be classified under two broad heads, namely '*social assets*' and '*symbolic elements.*' 'Social assets' include intellectual capabilities, educational and professional qualifications, certifications, speaking and dressing sense of individuals, etc. On the other hand, 'symbolic elements' include skills, etiquettes, mannerisms, and other credentials that one gets on being a part of a specific culture, group, ethnicity, or social class (Roberts, 2020). Individuals who dedicate significant time, money, and efforts to build a high level of cultural capital are the ones who reap substantial gains as their employability gets improved. Cultural capital becomes a distinguishing factor when selecting the right candidate for an employment opportunity (Bourdieu & Passeron, 1990).

According to Elmore (2010), a strong personal brand created through highlighting the unique selling proposition of an individual helps to create a distinctive image and enhances the visibility in the marketspace. Also, having emotional stability to work within cross-cultural set-ups is indispensable within the GiG economy. Not only this, people from different cultures are put together on several projects making it necessary for them to have prior cross-cultural knowledge and exposure so that resilience at work can be ensured. Some of the other factors under 'cultural capital' include optimized feedback scores and requested fees (Barzilay & Ben-David, 2017). In a nutshell, the cultural capital (qualifications, skills, knowledge, unique selling proposition, cross-cultural understanding, and past work experience), when presented in the form of a compelling story, leads to enhancement of profile visibility, reputation, and employability of an individual on the GiG platforms.

P1: Investment in 'social and cultural capital' positively affects 'social visibility and reputation' underpinning 'credibility and trust' in the GiG economy

2.6 Mediating Variable

2.6.1 Social Visibility and Reputation

The antecedents, i.e., social and cultural capital, lead to building social visibility and reputation of the GiG workers on online platforms among the relevant target audience. According to Zinko and Rubin (2015), reputation is '*a perceptual identity formed from the collective perceptions of others, which is reflective of the complex combination of salient personal characteristics and accomplishments, demonstrated behavior, and intended images presented over some period of time as observed directly and/or reported from secondary sources, which reduces ambiguity about expected future behavior.*' Reputation gets created as a consequence of social relationships when pertinent information with respect to an object is conveyed to others through a robust information system (Granovetter, 1985). According to the '*Law of Visibility*,' which is one of the laws among '*The Eight Unbreakable Laws of Personal Branding*,' the personal brand becomes effective only when it is made visible incessantly and repeatedly (Montoya & Vandehey, 2002). The marketing and communication strategies help in making the antecedents work even better and result in creating better social visibility and stronger reputation. Thus, the 'social and cultural capital' does not directly result in creating trust and credibility on GiG platforms; rather, it leads to the creation of social visibility and reputation, underpinning 'credibility and trust' in the GiG economy.

P2: The extent of 'social visibility and reputation' positively affects the extent of 'credibility and trust' in the GiG economy

2.7 *Outcome*

2.7.1 Credibility and Trust

In the context of the GiG economy, trust refers to the belief that the client/staffing agency (the trusting agent) has on the GiG workers (the trusted agent) with respect to the GiG workers' inclination, keenness, capability, and proficiency to complete a given project (mutually agreed upon service) correctly and in a given time frame (Landberg, 2017). The GiG platforms are virtual platforms, where trust is established between parties virtually and not physically. Hence, this environment is called the '*virtual trust environment*' (Landberg, 2017). The trust between the trusting agent and the trusted agent fluctuates with respect to the noticeable features of individuals within the relationships. These features are perceived as pertinent in deciding whether the party in the relationship is capable of being trusted or not (Austin & Worchel, 1979). This socio-psychological view of trust is based on the characteristics of the trustee. In order to develop credibility and trust, the expertise of the trustee plays an important role in developing trust from the perspective of the trusting agent (Hovland et al., 1953). There are three most important parameters that decide the trustworthiness and credibility of the trustee. These parameters are '*ability*' (capability to discharge a responsibility correctly and within a specified time), '*benevolence*' (the kindness and clear intentions of the trusted party ensuring the benefits for the trusting party), and '*integrity*' (the code of conduct judiciously followed by the trusted party as acceptable by the trusting party) (Mayer et al., 1995). The knowledge about the past record of the trustee plays an important role in the process of building trust (Shapiro et al., 1992). Hence, reputation, formed by the social capital and cultural capital, paves the way toward building trust and credibility in the GiG economy.

2.8 *Moderating Variables (Between Antecedents and Mediating Variables)*

2.8.1 Marketing Strategies (Personal Brand Positioning)

The second step of the personal branding process, propounded by Khedher (2015), is 'personal brand positioning,' fulfilled through the implementation of pertinent and robust marketing strategies. This step primarily deals with managing the personal brand through 'impression management,' which is leveraged to manage how others perceive a particular individual. The use of marketing strategies makes the relationship between antecedents (social and cultural capital) and mediating variable (social visibility and reputation) stronger, thereby acting as a moderating variable. GiG workers have started leveraging word-of-mouth marketing and social media marketing to showcase their projects, relevant experience, and past work to the relevant clients and hiring agencies (Warner, 2021). Recently, most GiG workers have started leveraging digital marketing techniques such as pay per click (PPC) marketing, search engine marketing, paid campaigns on various social media platforms, email marketing, etc. to reach out to the right target audience through boosting profile visibility (Key, 2017). Besides GiG platforms, there are a plethora of online social networks (OSNs) and other forums where they can post their image and a brief bio in order to make their profile accessible to a large number of recruiters. Further, OSNs provide an intertwined network, wherein individuals can share their profiles created on one platform to another platform in order to increase visibility (Landberg, 2017). Another booming technique of self-promotion within the context of the GiG economy is the use of 'artefactual displays' (Khedher, 2015). Personal brand positioning can be done using any one or a combination of criteria based on strategy, capability, performance, audience, and differentiation (Shafiee et al., 2020). Web-based technologies offer an opportunity for individuals to market themselves using autobiographical content through writing impactful posts, using content marketing strategies, creating videos such as 'elevator pitch' (Knouse et al., 1988).

P3: Investment in marketing strategies positively affects the relationship between 'social and cultural capital' and 'social visibility and reputation' in the GiG economy

2.8.2 Gender

There is stark gender inequality in the platform-mediated work arena (Barzilay & Ben-David, 2017). Gender plays a profound role in influencing the attitude and perception of the client toward a worker's personal brand (Roy & Shrivastava, 2020). Research studies show that women work for more hours on the platform than men but are paid less than men. This trend prevails across all the job function categories even when all the factors of social and cultural capital are taken into consideration and are fulfilled. Also, it has been observed that female workers face more difficulty in building and managing online reputation when compared to their male counterparts (Barzilay & Ben-David, 2017). Further, it has been observed that the hourly pay requested by women workers is far below that requested by men workers. Hence, it can be stated that women workers are considered 'devalued' on GiG platforms, and this makes 'gender' a strong moderating variable from the perspective of visibility and reputation management.

P4: The type of gender affects the relationship between 'social and cultural capital' and 'social visibility and reputation' in the GiG economy

2.9 *Moderating Variables (Between Mediating Variables and Outcome)*

2.9.1 Reflexivity (Building Personal Brand Image):

Building personal brand image (based on 'reflexivity') is the third step in the personal branding process given by Khedher (2015). This step is very important to constantly improve the already created brand as well as communication and marketing strategies. It helps individuals in focusing more or less on certain aspects of their profile based on their learnings. It is simply a reflection of an individual to his own efforts in building his personal brand (Khedher, 2015). It is an important technique to ensure personal development and to align the personal brand with the personal goals. 'Reflection-in-action' helps individuals to gather implicit and explicit feedback from others in their environment to constantly know better about themselves and improve accordingly (Wee & Brooks, 2010). On the other hand, 'reflection-on-action' helps in critical self-evaluation and guides in identifying one's latent strengths and weaknesses (Khedher, 2015). It not only helps individuals in improving their performance but also helps in understanding their work roles and associated expectations better (Khedher, 2015). Reflexivity acts as a moderating variable between 'social visibility and reputation' and 'credibility and trust.' Constant adjustment to the personal brand to make it real, authentic, and close to reality helps in building stronger credibility and trust.

P5: Reflexivity on already created personal brand positively affects the relationship between 'social visibility and reputation' and 'credibility and trust' in the GiG economy

3 Implications and Discussion

This chapter explains the concept of 'personal branding' using a conceptual framework developed through conducting an extensive literature review on the topic. This framework is paramount for existing as well as prospective GiG workers in order to stand out from the crowd and create a distinctive image in the minds of clients and staffing agencies.

Implications for existing/prospective GiG workers: The conceptual framework not only helps the existing and prospective GiG workers in building their strong personal brand online but also helps them in knowing the right path to sustain, nurture, grow, and improve their personal brand over time. It is recommended that GiG workers not only concentrate on building their brand through social and cultural capital but also leverage various self-marketing strategies, create strong social networks, and pursue multiple improvement attempts based on external feedback and introspection in order to differentiate themselves from the competition. Through this, they will win credibility and trust on GiG platforms and will be able to '*stand out from the crowd*' in the cluttered marketspace.

Implications for employers/staffing agencies/clients: Once the GiG workers build their strong personal brand online, even clients, staffing agencies, and employers are benefitted from the same, apart from the workers themselves. The trust and credibility established by workers on the GiG platforms help the employers, staffing agencies, and clients in filtering out the right candidates and weeding out the irrelevant ones. This helps in optimizing their recruitment and selection efforts while enhancing the overall productivity. Furthermore, it helps them in mapping the right candidate to the right job at the right time, thereby minimizing the scope of disruption at work. It is recommended that recruiters focus on all social and cultural capital elements to filter out authentic profiles and at the same time focus on strong background verification of the candidates before selecting them.

4 Scope of Future Research and Direction

The need to create brand differentiation is of immense importance in the GiG economy as it has a cluttered marketspace which poses challenges for both the GiG workers and the clients to map the right opportunity to the right candidate at the right time. This chapter presents a set of propositions that can be tested and validated in the future by marketing researchers and scholars. Research studies can be carried out to test and validate the proposed framework with focus on a specific GiG platform. Further, new variables can be identified to make the conceptual framework presented in this chapter more robust.

Statement of Competing Interest *The authors declare that there is no competing interest in the submitted manuscript.*

References

ASSOCHAM. (2020). *GiG economy, aligning consumer preferences: The way forward*. ASSOCHAM.

Austin, W. G., & Worchel, S. (1979). *The Social psychology of intergroup relations*. Monterey, Calif. : Brooks/Cole Pub. Co., ©1979.

Barzilay, A. R., & Ben-David. (2017). Platform Inequality: Gender in the GiG-Economy. *Seton Hall law review*.

Bendisch, F., Larsen, G., & Trueman, M. (2013). Fame and fortune: A conceptual model of CEO brands. *European Journal of Marketing*, 596–614.

Bolton, G. (2001). *Reflective practice: Writing and professional development*. Paul Chapman Publishing.

Bourdieu, P. (1983). *The forms of capital*. Greenwood Press.

Bourdieu, P., & Passeron, J. C. (1990). *Reproduction in education*. Society and Culture.

Dewey, J. (1933). *How we think: A restatement of the relation of reflective thinking to the educative process*. DC Health.

Elmore, L. (2010). Personal branding 2.0. *Women in business, 62*(1), 12–14.

Frenken, K., & Schor, J. (2017). Putting the sharing economy into perspective. *Environmental innovation and societal transitions*, 3–10.

Gandini, A. (2016). Digital work: Self-branding and social capital in the freelance knowledge economy. *Marketing Theory, 16*, 123.

Gillis, A. S. (2020). *GiG economy*. www.whatis.techtarget.com: https://whatis.techtarget.com/definition/gig-economy

Goffman, E. (1959). *The presentation of self in everyday life* (1st ed.). Anchor Books.

Granovetter, M. (1985). Economic action and social structure: The problem of embeddedness. *American Journal of Sociology, 91*(3), 481–510.

Hovland, C. I., Janis, I. L., & Kelley, H. H. (1953). *Communication and persuasion; Psychological studies of opinion change*. Yale University Press.

Key, T. (2017). Domains of digital marketing channels in the sharing economy. *Journal of Marketing Channels, 24*(1–2), 27–38.

Khedher, M. (2015). A Brand for everyone: Guidelines for personal brand managing. *The Journal of Global Business Issues 9*(1)

Knouse, S. B., Giacalone, R. A., & Pollard. (1988). Impression management in the resume and its cover letter. *Journal of Business and Psychology, 3*(2), 242–249.

Labrecque, L. I., Markos, E., & Milne, G. R. (2011a). Online personal branding: Processes, challenges, and implications. *Journal of Interactive Marketing, 25*, 37–50.

Labrecque, L. I., Markos, E., & Milne, G. R. (2011b). Online personal branding: Processes, challenges, and implications. *Journal of Interactive Marketing, 25*(1), 37–50.

Landberg, E. (2017). *A conceptual framework for building trust on a gig platform*. Stockholm.

Manyika, J. (2016). *Independent work: Choice, necessity, and the gig economy*. McKinsey & Company.

Mayer, R. C., Davis, J. H., & Schoorman, F. D. (1995). An Integrative model of organizational trust. *The Academy of Management Review, 20*(3), 709–734.

Montoya, P., & Vandehey, T. (2002). *The personal branding phenomenon*. Personal Branding Press Publishing.

Ottovordemgentschenfelde, S. (2017). Organizational, professional, personal': An exploratory study of political journalists and their hybrid brand on Twitter. *Journalism, 18*, 64–80.

Raskoff, S. (2014). *Social and cultural capital at school*.

Roberts, R. (2020). *Future learning: Gig economies, cultural capital, & new learning pathways*. Medium.

Roy, G., & Shrivastava, A. K. (2020). *Future of GiG economy: Opportunities and challenges*. 14–25.

Schon, D. (1983). *The reflective practitioner: How professionals think in action*. Basic Books. Paperback ed. Arena/Ashgate Publishing.

Shafiee, M., Gheidi, S., Khorrami, M. S., & Asadollah, H. (2020). Proposing a new framework for personal brand positioning. *European Research on Management and Business Economics, 26*(1), 45–54.

Shapiro, D., Sheppard, B. H., & Cheraskin, L. (1992). Business on a handshake. *Negotiation Journal, 8*, 623–658.

Soriano, J. (2017). *Upwork review: Why it's a battle YOU won't win*. Launch A Startup.

Stefano, V. D. (2016). *The rise of the just-in-time workforce, On-demand work, crowdwork and labour protection in the GiG Economy*. International Labour Office.

Suddaby, R. (2010). Editor's comments: Construct clarity in theories of management and organization. *Academy of Management Review, 35*, 346–357.

Warner, A. (2021). *60+ Freelance Stats—Why the gig economy is growing in 2021*.

Wee, & Brooks. (2010). Personal branding and the commodification of reflexivity. *Cultural Sociology, 4* (1), 45–62.

Zhengyu, H. (2019). *Admissions*. Tsinghua University: https://www.tsinghua.edu.cn/en/info/1187/1233.htm

Zinko, R., & Rubin, M. (2015). Personal reputation and the organization. *Journal of Management & Organization*.

Mr. Himanshu Ahuja is currently a 'management research scholar' at Delhi Technological University, New Delhi, India. He is a graduate and post-graduate in Commerce from the University of Delhi. He has also qualified UGC NET Exam and has received a fellowship from UGC for pursuing academic research. He carries with him approximately two years of work experience in the field of 'Market Research - Consumer Insights.' His research interests are in the domain of marketing management with a prime inclination toward consumer behavior, digital marketing, and international marketing. He has achieved several academic awards and accolades for his exemplary performance at the school and college level. He has also received awards for his brilliant performance at several 'National-level Olympiads' in the disciplines of mathematics and accountancy.

Dr. Deep Shree is an assistant professor at Delhi School of Management, Delhi Technological University. She has done Ph.D. in Marketing from the Indian Institute of Technology (IIT) Delhi. Her research interests are public sector marketing, not for profit marketing, brand management, and qualitative research in management. She has published research papers in leading national and international journals. Her research papers were presented and published in several prestigious national and international conferences.

Urban Company Partners: A Status Swivel on the Cards?

Ginni Chawla, Mahrane Hofaidhllaoui, Harrshit M. Kansal, Sagar Venkateshwar Nemani, Padma Priya, Nidhi Divyesh Shah, and Sonali Jindal

1 Introduction

Language has never been as important as it is today in a rapidly changing world. With the advancement of technology, the way of conducting business is changing which in turn has resulted in alteration of human capital associated with the businesses. Indian government has till date enacted a number of labour codes to protect the interests of both workers and non-workers, government and private sector employees, and employees of the organized and unorganized sectors alike since the Indian constitution is worded to stand as a pillar of support for employees/workers of all kinds. But, are these enactments capable of protecting the interests of workers in today's ever-changing world laced with technology?

Technology-enabled platform economy is appreciated for spearheading change from informal employment to formal employment. According to Tracxn, a start-up industry tracker, around 270 service-based "platforms" such as Ola, Uber, and Urban Company (UC), have come up in the past five to six years which has resulted in the formalization of employment (as cited in Anwar, 2018). Prior to their engagement with the platforms, these service providers (or professionals like carpenters,

G. Chawla (✉) · H. M. Kansal · S. V. Nemani · P. Priya · N. D. Shah · S. Jindal
Indian Institute of Foreign Trade (IIFT), New Delhi 110016, India

S. V. Nemani
e-mail: sagar_d20@iift.edu

P. Priya
e-mail: padma_d20@iift.edu

N. D. Shah
e-mail: nidhi_d20@iift.edu

M. Hofaidhllaoui
ESSCA School of Management, 69007 Lyon, France
e-mail: mahrane.hofaidhllaoui@essca.fr

A. Gupta et al. (eds.), *Sustainability in the Gig Economy*,
https://doi.org/10.1007/978-981-16-8406-7_6

beauticians, etc.) used to work on informal terms (Chopra, 2017). These service providers are brought on board by the platforms via contracts, which gives former the access to formal components related to savings and tax assessment. However, this formalization is innately a type of "enlistment" as opposed to "change". Basically, the formalization gives statutory bodies an administrative control over the service providers; the state is able to assess earnings of the service providers which also adds to the banks' monetary resources. However, such contracts do not secure for these professionals the critical provisions underlying any formal contract of employment, such as occupational and income security, or any type of government social security, paid leave, or fixed work timings. Upon eliminating these benefits, professionals' bargaining power is confiscated (Anwar, 2018); consequently, the motivating factors underlying work and the different components of service providers' pay are also set by the platform owners without any dialogue with the workers/employees. For instance, Ola and Uber workers have to work up to 12–16 hrs every day because of the frequently fluctuating incentive designs and asymmetry in data (The Wire, 2018).

An exclusive research on Uber's practices in the USA unearthed the level of mental manipulation going on under the shadows of platforms. The study focused on strategies that manipulate and nudge workers to work against their own interest which mirrors the exploitative capability of the gig economy in dealing with the "freelancing" workforce (Scheiber, 2017). So, the question arises—will companies change their outlook towards this section of the workforce before it is too late?

While professionals/service providers are taking the advantage of standardization of services and better opportunities for marketing themselves, a looming question of worker rights remains as the instances of exploitation by aggregators have been brought to light. The aggregators also are at crossroads now in terms of their implemented policies (with respect to the service providers) owing to the shortage in supply of skilled service providers (Boocock et al., 2020) and an increase in competition among the aggregators to hire the latter (Kuhn & Maleki, 2017). Because the gig workers are known to work for multiple employers at the same time as they lack any commitment to a specific organization due to the contractual nature of their job (Banerjee, 2019), this is expected to lead to lack of sustainable operations for any company (Monga, 2020).

A question thus posed to the management team at UC by the situation is: can UC consider providing employee status to its service providers for maintaining competitive advantage in a rapidly changing environment? It has been identified on the basis of the literature review that there is limited research in the past about non-permanent employees or workers such as the contract or freelancers, collectively called as "gig" workers. Therefore, more research needs to be conducted about the professionals associated with the new age companies who do not have an employee status currently. Particularly, there has been dearth of research on the topic in the Indian context. Hence, UC has been chosen for the present research as an empirical evidence for providing valuable insights into and expanding the knowledge base related to human resource practices followed for the service professionals in gig economy; further, the study throws light on *why* giggers' employment status needs to be changed and *how* it can be changed so that it proves in the best interests of both company and its partners.

2 Urban Company: An Overview

UC is recognized as the fastest-growing start-up in India. It is a mobile marketplace for local services and provides customers a platform to hire competent professionals in various fields. The start-up acts as aggregator for various services like plumbing, wiring, woodworking, cleaning, and pest control and further includes personal services like appliance repairs, grooming, spa, etc.

UC was founded by Abhiraj Bhal, Raghav Chandra, and Varun Khaitan in 2014, and it has quickly become one of the most funded start-ups by 2015 with investors like Tata Group, Vy Capital, SAIF Partners among others. UC was the second attempt of owners to start a venture. Raghav Chandra was previously heading a start-up called Buggy.in, which was an auto-rickshaw rideshare application based out of Noida. Varun Khaitan and Abhiraj Bhal were working on an on-demand movie streaming solution for long-haul travel in buses, trains, and planes. The idea for UC emerged from real-life experiences and the enduring personal pain. The founders had initially taken the idea to senior industry experts but were discouraged from pursuing it. However, they went ahead with it because even in the year as late as 2014 people had to talk to friends or look through yellow pages to find a wedding photographer or a plumber.

UC was started with a vision to build an enduring business model not only for connecting customers to professionals but also for developing a comprehensive environment that encompasses everything right from standardized policies and procedures of hiring, training, to rigorous quality control for providing customers standard services at fixed prices where customers could also view and write reviews relating to the experiences had with service providers listed on the platform. The company has grown steadily over years and currently offers more than 100 services across seven verticals including beauty, spa, grooming, repairs, cleaning, painting, and fitness and yoga. The company has more than 1 lakh trained professionals and has served over 2 million customers so far. Recently, the company expanded its operations abroad to UAE, Australia, and Singapore, and also to 10 more cities in India from initially serving in only eight cities of India including the big metropolitans (Mathur, 2020).

2.1 *The Business Model*

UC follows commission model, wherein upon booking a service the professional (carpenter, beautician, etc.) pays a fixed percentage of the amount earned from a customer to UC. For instance, in the beauty segment, UC charges 20% of the value of services rendered from partners which helps beautician earn three to four times more than what they could when working in a conventional parlour (Terms and Conditions, n.d.).

Further, to foster healthy communication with its customers, a minimal lead fee (or credits) is charged from the professionals for displaying latter's profiles to any customer. This ensures that the customers get responses only from those professionals that are willing to take up the work and have the capability to perform the task. Automation of the platform ensures less biasness towards lead generation for professionals. The matchmaking algorithms and the data insights figure out the likelihood of a probable transaction and accordingly connect a few professionals willing to pay a minimal fee for their introduction to the customer. If the customer does not view a professional's quote or profile, the platform returns the credits used to the professional.

2.2 *Existing Human Resource Policies and Practices at Urban Company*

UC has a comprehensive HR policy with special emphasis on people operations. According to its HR policy, the start-up wants maximum participation and engagement of its employees. The policy thus revolves around understanding the crux of company culture and builds on employees' experience in the organization.

The organization primarily has two categories of employees—partners (professionals who deliver service experiences for the customers) and full-time employees. The HR policies for the two categories of employees have distinct variations which are detailed as under.

2.2.1 Working Environment and Facilities

UC provides employee-friendly working environment that is in sync with the current market trends.

Full-time Employees. The Gurgaon office is filled to the brim with rows of open desks which are surrounded by the meeting rooms and a board room for conducting team meetings, video shoots, and private chats. The office also features a fully furnished gym and two foosball tables for engaging both employees and leaders. The start-up even provides complimentary shuttle services in the morning and evening to take the employees to the nearest metro station. Similarly, complimentary lunch and snacks are provided every day at the office. Further, employees are also given option to work from home for few days in a month.

Each employee is provided with a laptop that suits the demands of his/her job description along with the requisite software such as the Adobe Creative Suite for the creative team which can make the employees' work easier and efficient. Employees are even given the option to purchase a phone for their business communications at the expenses of organization.

To ensure that all employees and teams in the different locations stay connected, Slack an organization common chat is maintained by the HR team.

Partners. Partners are provided with a phone having the UC Partner app so that they can get in touch with the partner side team from the organization for their respective service categories as well as with the customers for each service request.

2.2.2 Training and Learning

A lot of importance is given to providing training to the employees as it is an inherent part of the UC culture. The training focuses around workings of UC and ways of availing different services at the back end.

Full-time Employees. Employees upon first joining the organization are introduced to the company by Mr. Bhal, who considers it to be the most important communication from organization's end because it helps create a lasting impression about the company, its people, and it's work culture on the employees. The session is designed to challenge and inspire the new joinees, introduce them to their leaders, and give them an idea about the vision of UC. Subsequent to this session, the employees are allocated a mentor and are given 7–14 incubation days for thoroughly exploring the organization. Not only are employees made to witness the different teams at work, but also they are given opportunities for informal interaction with their colleagues so that the former can build lasting relationships with latter.

Once the employees have embraced and settled into their job roles completely, they are given multiple opportunities to interact with the founders through Ask Me Anything (AMA) sessions in person or via Slack. Conversations with the top management also take place through a strict open-door policy. In fact, the UC Gurgaon office does not have "rooms" or "cabins" for any of the leaders. Leaders can be found seated in one of the rows of desks, working on their phones or laptops. The office only has meeting rooms for team meetings, interviews, or private chats. The founders and the other top management frequently keep visiting their offices in different locations (Mukherjee, 2017).

On the basis of the performance appraisals of employees and the observations made by their presiding managers or team leaders, employees are given many opportunities to improve their existing skills or learning some new ones. For instance, the digital marketing workshops were organized for the partner side marketing team as they expressed the need for it. Employees are further encouraged to attend workshops and seminars, mainly those conducted by the organizations like Facebook, Twitter, and Google. These enable employees to not only interact with other professionals outside the organization, but also learn about the working processes of other organizations and find ways of getting ahead. The management supports the employees' willingness to learn additional skills by further providing encouragement, mentorship, and the right tools and equipment.

Partners. The supply team of UC has doubled over time to create a training team each for the electricians, plumbers, carpenters, etc., at company. UC has eight beauty specialists on its payroll for training beauticians as this segment is the leading revenue generator constituting up to 20% of the total revenues of the company. Salon partners are trained in the UC offices itself. These training sessions are arranged by the company to ensure that uniform quality is maintained while delivering service to the customers.

2.2.3 Performance Evaluation

The performance assessment system for full-time employees as well as partners is detailed as under:

Full-time Employees. The performance evaluation for employees is conducted semi-annually with their managers and team leaders. The appraisal is based on the employees' performance during preceding 6 months and their orientation with respect to the team goals as well as their progress on their personal goals. On the basis of appraisal ratings received, employees are awarded a suitable increment in their salaries, and if found suitable, they are awarded promotion. Employees are also provided performance bonus depending on their performance review.

Partners are evaluated on the basis of their feedback and ratings given by the customers for the services rendered by them. Factors such as partner's punctuality, level of connectivity with the supply team, and communication skills are additionally taken into account.

2.2.4 Compensation and Benefits

These are outlined in detail as under:

Full-time Employees. The employees are offered a standard pay plan with a healthcare plan and a standard deduction for the Employee Provident Fund (EPF). The pay packages offered to the employees are more than competitive in relation to the market standards as the founders believe that talent deserves to be awarded appropriately, thus giving employees a big incentive to stay. The employees are also provided insurance benefits as part of their pay package.

Employees are also given the option to avail reimbursement of any travelling/dining charges incurred for business purpose; for example, the team leaders can get reimbursed the bills for team dinners up to a predefined limit. Employees can also claim reimbursement for the charges incurred on making any business calls/communications done through their personal cellular devices.

Partners. As explained earlier, UC follows a commission model for its partners. Further, the partners are required to purchase credits in their UC wallets which they utilize to respond to a service request and are often given bonus credits on the completion of a 5-star service.

Additionally, salon professionals are allowed a buy-in of 25,000 INR for purchasing the salon products, carry bags, uniform, and other tools and so on for delivering the "UC salon experience".

2.2.5 Feedback and Grievance Redressal

Full-time Employees. Quarterly Online Surveys (via Google Forms) are floated throughout the organization which allows the employees to anonymously review their managers, supervisors, and the founders. The survey is intended to point out the mistakes made along with the suggestions for improvement. The HR team and the founders review the responses received and devise a suitable plan of action after discussing with the manager or team leader in question.

The open-door policy at the company ensures that the employees can approach anyone in senior positions regarding the issues they may be experiencing.

HR managers are allocated to each department, and they regularly have (at least once every quarter) informal chats with the team members to review the latter's state of mind, satisfaction level with the allocated roles and responsibilities, and level of synchronization with the rest of the team and organization. These chats further help managers get an idea of the individual goals of employees, and a record is maintained to keep track of the changes in the individual goals. Any grievances surfaced during these conversations are shared with the team leadership, and it is ensured that the issue is addressed at the earliest.

Partners. Partners are encouraged to raise the different issues faced by them or give suggestions through their liaison in the UC partner team. However, this process is informal without any proper mechanism for it. Some partners even prefer to approach the founders directly via email.

2.2.6 Contemporary HR Policies and Practices

Full-time Employees. The UC culture encourages employees to express themselves in their own unique manner. To do away with the boredom at the workplace, HR managers often plan days like the Weird Day where employees are encouraged to dress differently from the usual and the two most weirdly dressed male and female employees are awarded at the end of the day; Bring Your Pet To Work Day, where pet owners get a chance to share their workplace with their furry buddies; Traditional Dress Day, where the firm celebrates the traditional Indian manner of dressing, and so on. Small fun-filled activities such as treasure hunt where different teams compete for prizes are also organized to further enhance team cohesion. Major festivals are celebrated with puja, special lunch, and sweets, and cultural events such as Christmas carols for Christmas are organized. All these activities are conducted in the office to encourage employees and to keep them engaged at work.

The organization holds a hackathon once every quarter where employees are encouraged to devise technological innovations related to the existing business processes of the organization. It is needless to say that the tech team participates in each hackathon with immense enthusiasm and is often joined in and supported by the employees from the other departments.

A Brainstorming Week is held twice a year, where people from different departments are clubbed into small teams and asked to evaluate the existing processes of the firm, identify any existing problems or make possible improvements, and design a complete execution plan for the same. This second competition is crucial, as this is also a representation of the basic UC values—hustle, basic, reimagine. Hence, through this competition, not only does the firm improve its processes, but also it lays the seeds of values in their employees and encourages them to embrace those values. Moreover, each employee also gets a break from their regular schedule and duties as well as gets an opportunity to learn and empathize with the problems and timelines associated with the other job roles. At the end of the sprint, the best teams are given recognition and suitable award.

The HR department also runs an employee blog where the role and responsibilities shouldered by an employee are shared along with their motivation for work and personal goals.

UC offered all its initial employees a chance to increase their stake in the fate of the company while it made investments in the stock options available to them. While this is a mandatory practice for an organization before going public, UC took this step in the initial year of its existence, thus showcasing founders' immense belief in the future success of the organization and their desire to share this belief with their partners in this journey. This move not only enhanced the confidence of all the members of the UC family, but by smartly including the employees in the stock options with a clause of staying in the company for a minimum period of 3 years, the management also succeeded in increasing their employee retention. This is especially a significant step, as employee attrition is a major affliction for most start-ups.

Partners. The UC Partner Awards Event is conducted annually where the UC partners from different professions across the country are invited to attend the event. During the event, the partners not only get a chance of mingling with the other partners, the founders, and employees for exchanging some tricks of the trade, but the performances of exceptional UC partners are also awarded and the plan of action for the subsequent year is unveiled with much fanfare. The event is considered to be very crucial for the firm because it brings together all the people involved in fulfilling the vision of Urban Company; hence, it is planned thoroughly with lot of efforts from the business development and the HR teams (Highlights From The Very First UC Partner Awards! 2016). The organization even runs a blog, where the success stories of successful UC partners are shared with the customers, employees, and partners alike.

2.3 The Urban Company Success Story and What Lies Ahead

UC is a marketplace, where talented professionals compete in a healthy environment to capture the interest of customers and grow the business. Each professional acts as a spokesperson for the brand; they are partners in the win upon offering an exemplary service experience to their customer. Similarly, the UC brand is affected if customers experience dissatisfaction in services provided.

From the very beginning, the founders of UC were absolutely certain about delivering quality service experiences to their customers. Their main objective was to provide exemplary experience free from the hassles of hiring a service professional from one's neighbourhood or someone based on the recommendations of relatives. Hence, they employed a security company to verify the backgrounds of each professional who applied to become a UC partner and subsequently ensured that adequate training was provided.

The services offered by UC proved to be highly convenient and hence gained quick recognition among customers. The company was gradually expanding to new cities and was reaching new heights so it started to onboard many professionals for fulfilling the demand which resulted in diminishing quality of services. With increase in the number of complaints on the customer care hotline and Twitter account initially, the management was forced to re-evaluate different aspects to find iniquities within the system.

After thoroughly searching and critically reviewing the business in entirety, it was realized that many awful services had remained unchecked and the service professionals responsible were not properly penalized. Because of the dreadful services, many customers had unpleasant experience, which diminished their satisfaction level and stained the brand image of UC.

Therefore, UC took the harsh decision of summarily removing 3000 of its partners from the platform. Subsequent to this, there was a complete overhaul of the system. Extensive training and learning were undertaken for the partners to ensure better services to customers. Trainings were provided on customer relations and the new methods of delivering services. Furthermore, partners were trained to provide a uniform quality experience throughout the platform. Due care was taken before hiring service providers. The service quality was assessed, and the results were seriously taken, resulting in rejection of approximately 65 per cent of the applications received for becoming a partner. To maintain the trust of customers, UC even started to maintain a black list of service providers—those who had previously flouted the terms of company or broke trust of customers.

This eventually led to an overall increase in the quality of services offered as well as enhanced the levels of customer satisfaction (Vardhan, 2018). Simultaneously, the quality checks undertaken for maintaining standard of services were further improved; the reviews given by the customers were also taken into account when rating partners' services.

This way, service providers' living conditions improved as their pay scale improved when they performed up to the mark. Some of the professionals even emerged as "celebrity" service providers with premium service charges. With time, UC even allowed its partners the freedom to choose which customer(s) to serve once the service request was placed by a customer on the platform. The freedom to choose which customer(s) to serve further ensured overwhelming experience for the former. The company, having opened avenues for its partners to be their own bosses and earn far more than they could in the conventional working arrangements, proved to be one of the biggest selling points for UC adding further to the company's success.

Abhiraj Bhal one of the founders of UC said, "beauticians typically earn 10,000–15,000 INR per month in physical salons, with the bulk of the profits being pocketed by the salon owners. In the business model followed by Urban Company, a beautician is a micro-entrepreneur, getting 80% of the service ticket for each customers. Hence, an average beautician on our platform earns 35,000–40,000 INR per month, and many earn even more than a lac rupees a month. There is no upper ceiling to their earnings now, the more jobs they do, the more the earnings they take home" (Dailyhunt, 2018).

While it cannot be denied that adherence to the contractual form of employment allows some professionals to earn far more than they could ever in a conventional set-up, especially in the categories like salon services, lately a number of partners have de-registered themselves from the company's platform citing UC's policies and practices as the reason for quitting.

On the company reviewing websites such as Glassdoor.com and Google Play Store, partners have put up numerous complaints against UC's arbitrary practices and policies in relation to its service providers. These include random withdrawal of services from the platform without informing partners (Google Play Store, 2019a; Google Play Store, 2020); charging much higher (or lower) prices from the customers without consulting or negotiating the service rates with partners (Google Play Store, 2019b); only hiring on a contractual basis and not offering full-time employee status to its partners (Glassdoor, 2019); UC management being "unsupportive and unprofessional", towards its partners (Google Play Store, 2018a); and so on. In the wake of such issues, some partners have even went to the extent of recommending Google, Justdial (Google Play Store, 2018a; Google Play Store, 2018b; Google Play Store, 2019c), Swisskart (Google Play Store, 2019d), UrbanPro (Google Play Store, 2018c), over UC for better business opportunities.

The foregoing literature thus provides clear evidence to the fact that the partners feel they are at the mercy of the platform owners for allotment of tasks, setting up of prices for services, getting a minimum guarantee, etc. This has led to high dissatisfaction among the partners and consequently poor worker retention and high attrition rates at the company (IWWAGE, 2020).

3 Discussion and Conclusions

It has been clearly brought out in the existing studies on gig workers that highly skilled service providers are limited in supply (Boocock et al., 2020) and the competition among existing home-based service providers to recruit the skilled workers is high (Kuhn & Maleki, 2017); it should thus be a great cause of worry for the platforms when competent professionals quit because "online platforms, like traditional businesses, depend on their workers' performances" for success (Schapers, 2018, p. 3). Since UC is witnessing worker retention issues and attrition rates at the company are high, this could result in lack of sustainable operations for the company in the long run (Monga, 2020). While awarding employee status to its selective partners would be a step in the right direction for UC for retaining its talented service professionals, this will not be easy. UC could face serious internal and external challenges in assimilating its partners into its full-term employees. These challenges are detailed as under:

3.1 Internal Challenges

The first task before the organization would be to figure out which partners would they wish to add to their permanent workforce. Currently, a rating below 4.2 out of 5 is enough to blacklist the partners on the platform (Thakur, 2019). However, before undertaking the process as well as the additional costs of putting the partners on its permanent payroll, the organization would likely want to re-examine its existing quality standards and change them accordingly. For instance, if a service professional after becoming a full-time employee is not able to match the organization's quality standards, what steps would the company take? This would need to be carefully thought through, implemented in the organization and outlined in its employment rules as well.

The current relationship between the employees and the partners is unbalanced, with the employees in the position of job providers and the partners as the hires dependent on the employees' sense of fairness. If this relationship were to change and become truly balanced, this would require the company to carefully undertake change management, beginning from formulating and enacting processes for the same, preparing the existing employees to the transition, as well as instructing the partners on the organization's internal culture and processes. The organization would also need to change the organizational hierarchy accordingly.

Another challenge arising from the assimilation of the partners into the permanent workforce would be the additional costs that the company would have to undertake. As per the recently enacted Labour Codes India, permanent employees in India must be guaranteed benefits such as minimum wages; periodic payment of wages, where the period cannot exceed a month; provident fund; retirement benefits and severance package; and bonus by the employing organization.

The organization would also have to provide time to fixed pay and leave travel concession benefits to its partners too, thus significantly increasing its fixed costs. Additionally, UC may also need to outline a path of career progression, with timely promotions.

3.2 External Challenges

The greatest external challenge facing the organization would be the service professionals themselves. UC has billed its platform as a marketplace for services, where customers, as well as the professionals, can choose the other to create an excellent service experience. In this scenario, the professionals are given the choice to choose the service request they answer and, more importantly, act as entrepreneurs and be their own bosses—which is often one of the biggest selling points for many of them. Some of them also run businesses independent of the platform run by UC, which would no longer be possible if they were to be full-time employees of UC.

Additionally, the professionals may be required to share a greater share of their earnings from each service request with the organization, which may not be palatable to them. Hence, the greatest external challenge facing the organization in this venture may be the unwillingness of the professionals to board the wagon. If pushed, the professionals may choose to be listed on a competitor's platform that offers greater freedom and flexibility instead.

3.3 An Example of Success

After looking at the various internal and external challenges that UC may face if it decides to give employee status to its partners, the authors then looked into the existing literature to find examples of those companies which have successfully undergone this change. An example of an existing aggregator that started giving employee status to its partners is that of Deliv.

Deliv is a leading start-up in the same-day delivery segment in the USA. It has businesses in 1400 cities and 35 markets. The fast-changing regulatory, the legal requirements as well as the needs of the business and retail partners led to Deliv changing its business model.

Deliv had built itself by using independent contractors. In 2019, Deliv announced that it has created a new wholly owned subsidiary that will be hiring the drivers as employees. This subsidiary was based in California. The main changes announced were:

1. The subsidiary, Deliv California Inc., will be first launched in Sacramento and will be then expanded to the rest of the state by August end.
2. The new subsidiary will still offer its employees the option of part-time or full-time roles as well as flexible schedules.
3. The employees will also have access to various benefits like dental, health, vision, pet insurance, 401 k plans, paid sick leaves, etc. Full-time employees can also make use of stock options.

To understand if UC can also act in the same lines of such aggregators and change the status of its partners to employees, the business model of Deliv was studied.

3.3.1 The Business Model

The subsidiary of Deliv licensed Deliv's proprietary platform to now be used by Deliv California's employees instead of the independent contractors. One of the main factors that enabled Deliv to function smoothly despite the change in the employment status of its workers was the unique business model of Deliv which provided the employees with scheduled windows and also allowed multiple stop delivery routes.

Another important differentiator was that the employees were given the same option that the contract workers enjoyed of predictability and the flexibility of choosing their preferred routes on their platform which allowed self-service scheduling. They were also paid at an hourly rate.

The factor that made Deliv agnostic of the classification of the driver is the company's technology. The platform of Deliv could accurately predict as well as balance the demand and supply in real time. It also continuously optimized the routes of the drivers to improve their efficiency.

3.3.2 What It Means for Urban Company

UC can follow in the footsteps of such aggregators as in the USA and adopt a similar business model. However, it will have to make sufficient investments before it can make such drastic changes. Our suggestion would be as follows.

UC should first make its technology robust and improve its ability to predict the demand and supply. It can also form a subsidiary in one state and then expand later as done by Deliv. It should also give the partners an option of whether they would want to be an employee or stay as a contract worker. It should also try to ensure that its employees would continue to enjoy the benefits that they enjoyed as contract workers along with the added benefits of being an employee. This would ensure that the internal challenge of difficulty in the transition of the workers is reduced.

The various benefits enjoyed by the employees will be more expensive to UC in the short run; however, this expense will be paid off, in the long run, owing to the lower churn rate and higher efficiency. The increased benefits to the employees will also reduce the impact of the external challenge of the unwillingness of the workers to get on board with this plan.

However, while implementing a similar business model like Deliv, UC will have to take the following factors into account: the different categories within service providers will have to undergo separate training sessions and must have different employment conditions; the conditions will also have to be changed according to the country in which they are operating. Hence, this model will have to be continuously monitored and optimized as the company grows.

This way, granting employee status to its partners could help UC overcome its sticky problem of partner retention, and it would also ensure sustained competitive advantage for UC. Further, the proposed model would help UC attain job security and/or additional benefits for its partners without compromising with their desire for flexibility.

Interestingly, a number of studies in the gig literature have also suggested awarding "employee status" to the service providers "in part" to ensure consistent quality of work and also to lower their attrition (Dalal & Salman, 2020; Cherry & Aloisi, 2017; Kuhn & Maleki, 2017, p. 196; Weber & Silverman, 2015); still the same has not been considered by the platform owners so far.

The recommendations of this study are also in line with the HR-centred resource-based view (RBV) perspective which postulates that having an "employment relationship" with the human capital resources is necessary for a firm to achieve sustainable competitive advantage (Wright et al., 1994, p. 304). This is more so in the home-based service providers' work context since the former are engaged into work of "interpersonal nature" (Flanagan, 2019, p. 60) which requires maintaining "a reliable team of highly skilled, knowledgeable and well-trained professionals" on the part of company (Sivathanu, 2019, p. 35).

3.4 Conclusions

The case study aims to highlight the challenges and pitfalls faced by the contract workers when working with the online aggregators, and this has been illustrated from the perspective of UC, an online home services provider in India. The differences in the HR policies and practices for full-time employees versus contract workers has helped highlight the differences in the benefits and facilities available to the contract workers vis-à-vis full-time workers as a representation of the prevailing conditions of giggers in the online aggregator industry. The subtle conflict between the contract workers' need for flexibility in working and earnings and the want for proper benefits in the form of health care and pension schemes is drawn to propose possible solution for UC and other similar aggregators to implement. The case study also draws attention towards the rising gig workforce in the country and how the aggregators can deal with the retention issues associated with gig workers to sustain competitive advantages in the face of rising competition among platforms for skilled gig workers. This study can be further extended by using core constructs of HR-based RBV perspective as proposed by Wright et al. (1994) to explore in depth how service providers can contribute towards achieving sustainable competitive advantage for the home-based platform firms.

Acknowledgements Ginni Chawla, Mahrane Hofaidhllaoui, Harrshit M Kansal, Sagar Venkateshwar Nemani, Padma Priya, Nidhi Divyesh Shah, and Sonali Jindal declare that they have no conflict of interest.

References

Anwar, I. A. (2018, Mar 26). *Ola, Uber and the precarious future of blue collar platform workers.* Accessed on Aug 12, 2020 from https://tandemresearch.org/publications/ola-uber-and-the-precarious-future-of-blue-collar-platform-workers

Banerjee, S. (2019, September). Bringing commitment in gig worker would be a challenge. Accessed June 10, 2020 from https://www.businessmanager.in/bringing-commitment-in-gig-worker-would-be-a-challenge.php

Boocock, A., Page-Tickell, R., Yerby, E. (2020). The Dis-evolution of strategic HRM in the Gig economy from talent management to supply chain manager. In: Page-Tickell, R., & Yerby, E. (Eds), *Conflict and shifting boundaries in the gig economy: An interdisciplinary analysis* (pp. 89–105) (The Changing Context of Managing People). Emerald Publishing Limited. https://doi.org/10.1108/978-1-83867-603-220201008

Cherry, M. A., and Aloisi, A. (2017). *Dependent contractors' in the gig economy: A comparative approach.* 66 American Univ. L. Rev. 635, Saint Louis U. Legal Studies Research Paper No. 2016-15. https://ssrn.com/abstract=2847869 or https://doi.org/10.2139/ssrn.2847869

Chopra, A. (2017, March 20). *How UrbanClap grew one on-demand service at a time—Livemint.* Accessed January 10, 2020 from https://www.livemint.com/Companies/ck6h9KKDL9Aw1SCgzvMLRM/The-building-of-UrbanCompany-one-ondemand-service-at-a-time.html

Dailyhunt. (2018, December 17). *Exploring the nooks and crannies behind Urban Company's dominance with Abhiraj Bhal.* Accessed February 1, 2021 from https://m.dailyhunt.in/news/india/english/entrackr+english-epaper-entrackr/exploring+the+nooks+and+crannies+behind+UrbanCompany+s+dominance+with+abhiraj+bhal-newsid-104153053

Dalal, M., & Salman, S. H. (2020). *How the gig economy hurts the small guy.* Mint Website. Accessed January 27, 2021 from https://www.livemint.com/news/india/how-the-gig-economy-hurts-the-small-guy-11585755520304.html

Flanagan, F. (2019). Theorising the gig economy and home-based service work. *Journal of Industrial Relations, 61*(1), 57–78.

Glassdoor. (2019, November 27). *Company Review.* Glassdoor Website, Accessed May 29, 2020 from https://www.glassdoor.co.in/Reviews/Urban-Company-Reviews-E1066580.htm?filter.defaultEmploymentStatuses=false&filter.defaultLocation=false&filter.employmentStatus=FREELANCE&filter.employmentStatus=CONTRACT

Google Playstore. (2018a, July 19). *Shubh Joshi UrbanClap (now Urban Company) partner.* Accessed May 29, 2020 from https://play.google.com/store/apps/details?id=com.urbanclap.provider&hl=en_IN&showAllReviews=true

Google Playstore. (2018b, January 27). *Mahender. UrbanClap (now Urban Company) partner.* Accessed May 29, 2020 from https://play.google.com/store/apps/details?id=com.urbanclap.provider&hl=en_IN&showAllReviews=true

Google Playstore. (2018c, October 15). *Prasad Patil. UrbanClap (now Urban Company) partner.* Accessed May 29, 2020 from https://play.google.com/store/apps/details?id=com.urbanclap.provider&hl=en_IN&showAllReviews=true

Google PlayStore. (2019a, July 11). *Ashok Kumar. UrbanClap (now Urban Company) partner.* Accessed May 29, 2020 from https://play.google.com/store/apps/details?id=com.urbanclap.provider&hl=en_IN&showAllReviews=true

Google PlayStore. (2019b, January 21). *SaurabhMusic UrbanClap (now Urban Company) partner.* Accessed May 29, 2020 from https://play.google.com/store/apps/details?id=com.urbanclap.provider&hl=en_IN&showAllReviews=true

Google Playstore. (2019c, January 14). *Anonymous. UrbanClap (now Urban Company) partner.* Accessed May 29, 2020 from https://play.google.com/store/apps/details?id=com.urbanclap.provider&hl=en_IN&showAllReviews=true

Google Playstore. (2019d, March 22). *Sandeep Patel. UrbanClap (now Urban Company) partner.* Accessed May 29, 2020 https://play.google.com/store/apps/details?id=com.urbanclap.provider&hl=en_IN&showAllReviews=true

Google PlayStore. (2020, May 11). *Mou Sarkar. UrbanClap (now Urban Company) partner.* Accessed May 29, 2020 from https://play.google.com/store/apps/details?id=com.urbanclap.provider&hl=en_IN&showAllReviews=true

Highlights From The Very First Urban Company Partner Awards! (2016, October 10). *Urban company.* Accessed December 10, 2020 from https://www.UrbanCompany.com/blog/trending/highlights-first-UrbanCompany-partner-awards/

IWWAGE. (2020, June). *India's emerging Gig economy the future of work for women workers.* Accessed December 30, 2020 from https://asiafoundation.org/publication/indias-emerging-gig-economy-the-future-of-work-for-women/#:~:text=Through%20surveys%20and%20focus%20group,both%20paid%20and%20unpaid%20work

Kuhn, K. M., & Maleki, A. (2017). Micro-entrepreneurs, dependent contractors, and instaserfs: Understanding online labor platform workforces. *Academy of Management Perspectives, 31*(3), 183–200.

Mathur, N. (2020, January 30). *UrbanClap rebrands itself as Urban company to focus on horizontal gig marketplace.* Mint Website. Accessed January 25, 2021 from https://www.livemint.com/companies/news/urbanclap-rebrands-itself-as-urban-company-to-focus-on-horizontal-gig-marketplace-11580382807868.html

Monga, P. (2020, January 16). *Gig economy —Shaping the future of work.* Invest India. Accessed August 17, 2020 from https://www.investindia.gov.in/team-india-blogs/gig-economy-shaping-future-work

Mukherjee, S. (2017, July 21). *How CEO Abhiraj Bhal looks to lead Urban Company to profitability in the next 12 months.* Inc42.com. Accessed January 12, 2021 from https://inc42.com/buzz/abhiraj-bhal-Urban Company-ama/.

Schapers, V. J. (2018). *Protecting workers in the platform economy, an analysis of tactics used by labor unions. IBA bachelor thesis.* University of Twente, http://essay.utwente.nl/75594/1/Schapers_BA_BMS.pdf

Scheiber, N. (2017, April 2). *How Uber uses psychological tricks to push its drivers' buttons.* The Wire. Accessed 05 Jan 2021 from https://www.nytimes.com/interactive/2017/04/02/technology/uber-drivers-psychological-tricks.html

Sivathanu, B. (2019, October–December). An Empirical study of service quality, value and customer satisfaction for on-demand home services. *International Journal of Information Systems in the Service Sector, 11*(4), 35–57.

Terms and Conditions. (n.d.). *Urban company,* Accessed August 30 2020 from https://www.urbancompany.com/terms

Thakur, A. (2019, September 4). *Are you being served? The UrbanClap success story.* Fortune India. Accessed on February 7, 2021 from https://www.fortuneindia.com/enterprise/are-you-being-served/103554

The Wire (2018, March 26). *Ola, Uber and the precarious future of blue collar platform worker.* The Wire. Accessed January 12, 2021 from https://thewire.in/labour/ola-uber-and-the-precarious-future-of-blue-collar-platform-workers.

Vardhan, J. (2018, December 17). *Exploring the nooks and crannies behind UrbanClap's dominance with Abhiraj Bhal.* Entrackr. Accessed January 02, 2021 from https://entrackr.com/2018/12/urbanclap-dominance-abhiraj-bhal/

Weber, L., & Silverman, R. E. (2015, January 30). On-demand workers: We are not robots. *Wall Street Journal.* https://www.wsj.com/articles/on-demand-workers-we-arenot-robots-1422406524

Wright, P. M., McMahan, G. C., & McWilliams, A. (1994). Human resources and sustained competitive advantage: A resource-based perspective. *The International Journal of Human Resource Management, 5*(2), 301–326.

Ginni Chawla is an Assistant Professor in the HR/OB domain at the Indian Institute of Foreign Trade (IIFT), New Delhi, India. She holds Ph.D. in Industrial Relations from Motilal Nehru National Institute of Technology (MNNIT) Allahabad, Prayagraj. She earned National Scholarship in the domain of labour welfare/personnel management/industrial relations/labour, and social welfare/human resource management from University Grants Commission (UGC), New Delhi, in the year 2010. Her research interests include: trade unions, gig workers, innovative HRM, talent management, and employability.

Articles authored by her have featured in several prestigious refereed national and international journals. She has received various awards and accolades for papers presented at the reputed international conferences both within and outside India. She is the elected National Representative, India (Session 2020–2023), for the European Academy of Management (EURAM). She is also a reviewer with prestigious journals published by Taylor and Francis, Elsevier, Sage, Emerald, IGI Global Journals, etc.

Mahrane Hofaidhllaoui is a doctor in management science, and Professor and Researcher at ESSCA Lyon. His research focuses on employability, dynamics in employer–employee relationships, change management, diversity management and talent management, career development in a changing context, and corporate social responsibility. Member of AGRH, IAS, and ANDRH, he has contributed to the production of collective works and has participated in research work published in high-level French and international professional and scientific journals.

His article titled "Talent retention: Evidence from a multi-national firm in France", published in 2017, received Outstanding Paper Award by Employee Relations and Literati Award for 2018.

He has been practising research intervention in companies and organizations for several years on the topics of change management, managerial skills and posture, and the overall improvement of human and economic performance. He is also Co-author of the book titled "Management des Talents" published in 2017 by Editions Vuibert.

Harrshit M Kansal has completed his MBA from Indian Institute of Foreign Trade (IIFT), Delhi, in 2020. Prior to this, he graduated as an engineer from Birla Institute of Technology and Science (BITS), Pilani. During his MBA, he was a student of a course on HRM under Dr Ginni Chawla, as one of his courses. As a part of academic coursework, he undertook the subject research as a part of a team of students, guided by Dr Ginni.

As a student, Harrshit has always taken a keen interest in research projects during his academic journey; he presented multiple papers on diverse topics in APOGEE, the International Technical Festival of BITS Pilani. He was awarded gold medal by Delhi Public School, Indirapuram, for proficiency in academics for seven consecutive years and won multiple gold medals in national/international Olympiads. He was selected among India's 50 "most employable" MBA graduates, class of 2020 by *InsideIIM*.

Sagar Venkateshwar Nemani A budding marketing and business enthusiast from IIFT and a graduate from NIT Patna, Sagar loves to read and write in his free time. He has won over 17 + B-School and corporate competitions at various levels such as Mahindra WarRoom, Godrej Loud, and Colgate Transcend. He has also penned down two Amazon best-sellers: "The Untold Myths of India" and "Vampire's Vanity".

Padma Priya is a budding marketing professional. She did her MBA from IIFT Delhi where she majored in marketing; prior to her MBA, she did graduation in B.Tech (Mechanical and Automation) from IGDTUW Delhi. She is currently working as Territory Manager, Inside Sales at Medtronic. In her spare time, she likes to read.

Nidhi Divyesh Shah has done masters in International Business from Indian Institute of Foreign Trade as well as studied for a semester at Rennes School of Business, France, on semester exchange programme. She is an avid reader and loves to read fiction books in varying genre in her free time. She has won Mahindra WarRoom competition at international level. She also loves visiting new places and learning about the culture. She has visited over 10 countries across 3 continents.

Sonali Jindal is an avid writer, thinker, and daydreamer. She completed her MBA from Indian Institute of Foreign Trade (IIFT), Delhi, in 2020. She is an avid observer of life around her and plans to learn as many languages as possible (beginning from Japanese). She is Product Manager at a gaming firm currently.

Digital Leadership and the Gig Economy

Mehreen Malik and Muhammad Mustafa Raziq

1 Introduction

With the development of technologies today, the world view in all aspects of life has changed (Yusif et al., 2020). Digitalization has become a global trend, and organizations today are increasingly seeking to adopt digitalization (Gupta, 2018). It is argued that digitalization is the future of this ever-changing world and a requisite for every organization to move toward digital transformation. The two main streams which are changing the digital world are termed as virtual reality (VR) and artificial intelligence (AI) (Brett, 2019). Digitalization has moved the business from basic industrialization to Industry 4.0 which is governed by analogous technologies. This transformation is believed to enhance performance and capabilities through which firms can deliver a modified and an advanced utility service to its customers in a secure, quicker, and more economical way.

As of 2021, the world, specifically advanced countries are moving from industrialization to digitalization. The technologies in digital age are machine learning and artificial intelligence where big amount of data can be processed and analyzed easily and quickly using technology. The use of digital technologies has made the decision-making fast and accurate. Digitalization refers to conversion of objects to digital forms (Solis et al., 2014). In other words, it is the conversion of information from analog to digital form making it understandable by the computer system. Digital change is fast albeit complex in nature (Nwaiwu, 2018).

As stated earlier, digital transformation is omnipresent (Voß & Pawlowski, 2019). Companies such as Kodak, Blackberry, and Nokia, which were once dominant

M. Malik (✉) · M. M. Raziq
NUST Business School, National University of Sciences and Technology (NUST), Islamabad, Pakistan
e-mail: mehreen.phd20nbs@student.nust.edu.pk

M. M. Raziq
e-mail: mustafa.raziq@nbs.nust.edu.pk

A. Gupta et al. (eds.), *Sustainability in the Gig Economy*,
https://doi.org/10.1007/978-981-16-8406-7_7

companies in the industry, were soon replaced by companies such as Amazon, Uber, Netflix, and Google because the latter embraced newer technologies of the digitalization age (Baharuden et al., 2019). To keep up with the changing external environment, it is important for firms to continuously upgrade their capabilities and embrace the emerging trends such as digitalization (Baharuden et al., 2019).

Digitalization of services has brought many advantages bringing ease in the work life. Several tasks once deemed as difficult have been taken over by the automatic machinery, which has significantly increased the production capacity (Heukamp, 2020). However, digitalization also comes with challenges and issues. These include downsizing or unemployment as variety of tasks which were performed once by man are now done by a machine. According to Mckinsey (2017), around 60% of current jobs and 50% work activities are automatable with the use of latest technology available. The second challenge is the loss of privacy and security of data as all data could be available online making access of private data to companies and individuals easier (Heukamp, 2020). Likewise, with regard to poverty reduction, digitalization impact is multifaceted. The impact of digitalization, for example, on 28 European nations (Kwilinski et al., 2020) revealed that for the poorer part of EU, digitalization did not play much a role in lowering poverty. However, in case of wealthy nations, digitalization showed a negative link with poverty.

With regard to work vis-à-vis gig economy, majority of work is performed remotely, via home offices and/or independently as compared to work undertaken in traditional settings. The communication between employees and leadership is impersonal through digital communication as it takes place mostly via emails. To compensate the real loss of face-to-face contacts, personal relationships are created through video link tools such as Microsoft Teams and Zoom. However, despite their benefits, these techniques preclude developing relationships and motivation for the followers (Fest et al., 2019). So, there are issues and challenges there—however, these are easily outweighed by the advantages of digitalization.

While digitalization today is largely a thing of the developed world, firms in the emerging markets are also trying to embrace it to meet their production targets and to compete in the world of digitalization. When it comes to emerging markets, the typical ones are China, India, and Brazil. However, several other emerging markets such as Nigeria and Pakistan also hold great potential (Birkinshaw, 2014; Raziq, 2019). Pakistan, for example, has a large services sector, which is increasingly adopting e-commerce, fintech, and e-government, albeit these technologies there are still in their infancy stage. The growth is slow, and according to WEF's Networked Readiness Index, Pakistan ranks 110th out of the 139 countries in terms of its readiness toward digitalization. This low ranking is mainly because of low adoption of digitalization in operations and processes.

Over the period of last 10 years, scientific research on digitalization and its consequent influence on business models has been growing rapidly (Caputo et al., 2021). Digitalization has gained increasing interest from academic researchers, research institutions, and practitioners. Empirically, existing research on the digitalization, however, has been done mostly in the context of developed countries and developing countries like Pakistan are much ignored. The emerging economy of Pakistan has great potential to grow in digitalization. As per report of McKinsey Global Institute (MGI), digital financial services alone can increase the GDP of Pakistan by 7 points approximately, US$ 36 billion, with creation of new jobs of around 4 million till the year 2025. Likewise, theoretically, digitalization research is lacking in that the actions and roles of leaders and manager remain unclear. The past studies have been emphasizing the need for further empirical and theoretical studies on digitalization vis-à-vis leadership and management aspects (Bondarouk & Ruël, 2009; Marler & Fisher, 2013).

To this end, the purpose of this chapter is to explore the digitalization, gig economy, and digital leadership in the context of an emerging economy of Pakistan. The next sections of this chapter will discuss digitalization and gig economy, and the role of digital leadership in the adoption of digitalization. Thereafter, we will discuss the impact of gig economy on the labor market and on the industrial relations. The last section of this chapter will present the case of Pakistan being an emerging market. Finally, the chapter is concluded with some recommendations.

2 The Gig Economy

The on-demand services, on-demand economy, and on-demand services of employees are the emerging trends of digital economy. The concept of long-term employees in the organizations is being removed from the economy, and the workers are often referred to as self-employed. This new emerging business model is termed as "gig economy" which is characterized as outsourcing of services by the organization. The concept of gig economy started developing over the past forty years (Flanagan, 2019). The process of outsourcing and selecting the right employee is made through online platforms where jobs are advertised by companies through their website or other online media outlets. Thus, the digital platform is a fundamental tool for the functioning of gig economy.

This technological disruption has changed the conventional ways of economic activities globally (Anwar & Graham, 2021). Gig is a hybrid model of doing business in the Fourth Industrial Revolution (Industry 4.0). Gig business model is termed as hybrid because it is a mixture involving traditional hierarchical relationships among the top and lower management and a conduct of business through online platforms.

The worldwide revenue generated in the gig economy is $82.4 billion with 67% annual growth, and this worldwide increasing demand and usage shows a substantial development of the gig economy (Staffing Industry Analysts, 2018). The new major platform-based start-ups like Uber, Airbnb, and Lyft (which are only a decade old) are some examples of the gig economy, having pool of workers digitally mediating economic transactions (Vallas & Schor, 2020). On these shared online platforms, the individuals can share their products and offer their services by offering apartments and homes for rent and cars for driving individuals to their destinations. These services are offered through an online platform by freelancers and businessmen. The turnover gained from the gig economy (B2C) from these three platforms altogether is 75% (Uber = 49%, Didi Chuxing = 23%, Lyft = 9%), while turnover from B2B services is concentrated to 42% (Upwork = 21%, GLG = 8.2%, WorkMarket = 5%, MBO Partners = 3.9%, Axiom = 3.1%) (Dazzi, 2019).

Employment in gig economy is defined as work without workers (Friedman, 2014), and from a jobless future to a bossless future (Daugareilh et al., 2019). The form of doing business in gig economy is different from the traditional forms, which involve sitting in office with a promised salary, vacations, bonuses, and retirement benefits. In the gig economy, the employees work independently. There is no minimum pay, no vacations, no annual or sick leave, and the employees act as contractors or freelancers where they must come up with their own tools and they are subject to provide their services on call (McCann & Murray, 2010). The examples are Uber and Careem services which have emerged recently.

The jobs related to the gig economy can be classified into three categories (Graham & Shaw, 2017). First are the on-demand jobs through apps, through which the individuals can get themselves registered on the app and can perform the on-demand assigned tasks (e.g., Uber and Deliveroo). The second form of job in the gig economy is named as crowd work—in this job, the freelancers, professionals, and IT scientists work from home and offer their services online to different platforms (e.g., Upwork, Freelancer, CrowdFlower, and others). The third form is known as asset renting—the renting of properties using an online medium (e.g., Airbnb).

The contractors and freelancers working in the gig economy have choice to select the working hours as per their availability, and they can offer their services to various online apps at the same time. Thus, it is emphasized in the literature that persons doing business in gig economy are freelancers or independent contractors, but not employees (Bailey, 2016). Perhaps, this division of the platform makes the gig economy most controversial. The benefits which gig economy provides to the organization are that it reduces the costs of companies by reducing direct employment to on-demand employment (Healy et al., 2017).

2.1 Gig Economy and Digital Leadership

It is important to develop the workforce and their skills as eventually, it is the workforce, which leads and shapes the digitalization process of the organization (Elg et al., 2020). Once digitalization has been adopted in the organization, the roles of top-level management, as well as middle managers and employees, change dramatically (Henriette et al., 2016; Parviainen et al., 2017). The use of artificial intelligence technologies creates new opportunities but also poses complex challenges for the leadership responsible for digital transformation (Holmstrom, 2021). Hence, to make full use of digitalization, the organization needs to fill knowledge gaps among the workforces.

Much research has been undertaken in the past on the adoption and working of digitalization (Cocca et al., 2018; Dewa et al., 2018). However, there are still gaps regarding the role of senior management and middle managers in the process of digitalization (Elg et al., 2020; Gastaldi et al., 2018). Singh and Hess (2017) articulate the role of managers in the strategic change process of organizations and suggest that the characteristics of managers influence the organization transformation toward digitalization. Especially, the role of middle manager has been highlighted in the literature during the process of digitalization as they work as a bridge between the top management teams and the lower-level managers. Middle-level managers are first to respond to the changes in technology in organization (Do & Nuth, 2020). Although the middle-level managers are not responsible for making strategies, they are ones who get these implemented in the organization. Middle-level managers develop the culture of workplace and communicate it among the different levels of organization and are the nucleus of digital transformation (Nadkarni & Prügl, 2020).

To achieve successful digital transformation, it is important to make changes at various levels of the organization and the core business (Karimi & Walter, 2015; Yeow et al., 2018), the exchange of resources and capabilities (Cha et al., 2015; Yeow et al., 2018), the reconfiguration of processes and structures (Resca et al., 2013), adjustments in leadership (Hansen & Sia, 2015), and the implementation of digital culture (Llopis et al., 2004). It is argued that digital transformation causes changes in the leadership of the organization in terms of their roles and duties and the overall decision-making process (Mazzei & Noble, 2017), leadership skills (Sia et al., 2016), and communication principles (Bennis, 2013).

In this new form of business termed as the gig economy, the role of middle managers becomes important and optimal also in terms of monitoring of organizations since this transformation expands their monitoring levels. The services are outsourced by the companies, but the needs for controlling and monitoring work of the outsourced companies are there. Thus, to lead this digital wave of gig economy there is need for a digital leader with specific skills to lead the digital economy. Mumford et al. (2007) identify these skills in terms of cognitive, interpersonal, and strategic skills required by the digital leadership.

According to Heukamp (2020), to survive the current digitalization wave, the digital leaders should know the basic AI models such as machine learning. Since digitalization can transform the organization, a digital leader must have the appropriate knowledge, strong decision-making power, a vision to compete in the automatic world, a judgment, and an ability to cope with uncertain situations. Apart from these decision-making skills, the digital leader must possess analytical skills to enhance work performance and quality through the use of AI. Research suggests that although the gig economy has decreased dependency of the hierarchical roles of management due to the self-employed status of workers, the HR managers and digital leaders still have a critical role in the management of digital labors (Wong et al., 2021).

3 Gig Economy and the Labor Market

Empirical evidence suggests that gig economy has an overall positive impact on the employment and productivity of organizations but has a negative (but negligible) impact on the wages of the workers. The self-employed workers have the capacity to earn more by increasing their working hours as per their availability, and it helps in making employees less dependent on their bosses (Hathaway & Muro, 2016). However, as stated earlier, the gig economy is arguably destroying the established structures, norms, and employment relationships (Tassinari & Maccarrone, 2020). The gig economy platforms use digital technology to track the demands for services and provides the services through an online digital platform. These platforms work through developing innovative matching algorithms (Schwellnus et al., 2019).

Two main issues because of the gig economy have been realized: legal issues and policy. The legal issues are concerned with the traditional legal status of employees and whether the new status of employees is still valid with the new way of doing business. The policy issues are concerned with whether the existing legal laws, regulations, and rules for protection of labor rights are still valid in the gig economy or is there a need for the development of new labor laws and policies. In this regard, it is argued that a new legal protection system of labor is needed for the gig economy (Todolí-Signes, 2017).

Previously, the policies and laws for the labor were well defined but the changing work environment of gig economy has changed the status of workers to self-employed workers for which there are no such rules and regulations with regard to the protection of labor rights. Some low-cost companies, such as Ryanair, employ all its pilots as subcontractors, and through this, they deprive the pilots to form a labor union or become members of collective bargaining bodies—hence, following a modern time slavery model. The pilots are paid by an hour flown rule with no insurance, no holidays, and no retirement benefits. Barroso (2005) stresses new forms of control, while controlling and monitoring for work quality remain same. In the traditional form of working, the work quality, working expectations from employees, and certain specific restrictions were well defined to the workers in advance—whereas the gig economy is opposite in that the control and monitoring of work are still there but in new forms. The platform of gig economy offers a proper network through which the performance evaluation of its workers is done. As argued by Barroso (2005), this platform does not give specific instructions for quality assurance while it allows the client to evaluate their performance and take the decisions accordingly, but in reality, those who do follow the pre-specified rules by the companies can lower down their ratings in the case of non-compliance for working protocols (Aloisi, 2015). Thus, the monitoring of workers' performance is under constant surveillance. There is, hence, a need to develop certain rules and regulations for the protection of legal rights of workers.

3.1 Gig Economy and Industrial Relations

The impact of gig economy on the industrial relations depends upon digital platforms through which individuals manage the supply and demand of products. With regard to asset platforms, the efficiency of the network is critical for successful transaction between two parties—the efficient workforce ensures that the transaction is effective and successful. In work dimension as well as online transactions, this hierarchical relationship between the organizations and market also involves the legal formalities and legal status of the organization. Thus, in the digital world of gig economy this hierarchical relation involves costs and organizations are required to make flexible arrangements for the cost optimization for this hybrid system (Dazzi, 2019). The industrial relations in gig economy, therefore, face challenges in the new phase of digital world—the Fourth Industrial Revolution. The new strategies, development of ICT as well as to build the digital economic system require huge capital investment and digital knowledge to lead better and to create better products and services.

Apart from the costs and digital skills requirements to survive in the gig economy, the challenge in the industrial relations between organizations and labor market relates to the trade union matters. The contract of these unions with the organizations will either be less valid or will require new strategies for the protection of labor rights as well as laws. Thus, in the gig economy the labor laws and rights are at great risk. Additionally, the issue of development of industrial relations in the sharing economies, such as gig economy, would need to be addressed.

The industrial relations of the negotiating parties of the contracts that use digital platforms would change dramatically, and hence, there would be a need to develop strategies to survive and secure the relationships between negotiating parties transacting in the digital world. Gig economy platforms are highly popular in the services industry such as transport and personal services involving food item delivery. The existing organizations thus may be lacking in technological advancement that is needed, and there would be high entry barriers and tight rules to operate in the gig economy. Therefore, the application of product market rules will be quite different in the gig economy as compared to the traditional economy.

4 Case of Pakistan

Pakistan is an emerging economy and relatively less advanced with regard to digitalization compared to the developed countries. The ICT development in Pakistan started in the 1990s, and there is steady growth in this sector since the last three decades. Pakistan is facing severe challenges when it comes to digitalization. According to WEF's Networked Readiness Index, Pakistan ranks 110th out of the 139 countries in terms of readiness toward digitalization. Existing research on the digitalization has mostly been done in developed countries and developing countries such as Pakistan are mostly ignored. The emerging economy of Pakistan, however, has great potential in digitalization. As per report of McKinsey Global Institute (MGI), digital financial services alone can increase the GDP of Pakistan by 7 points, which approximately accounts to US$ 36 billion, creating new jobs of up to 4 million till the year 2025. Digitalization requires huge investments in ICT. Knowing the current economic and financial situation in Pakistan, it might be a major hurdle.

Digitalization—gig economy—is an emerging area. The theoretical foundations, for studying the adoption of digitalization, are in their initial phases of development. Similarly, the role of managers remains under-researched. To understand the phenomenon, the researchers have been emphasizing the need for further theoretical and empirical studies (Bondarouk & Ruël, 2009; Marler & Fisher, 2013) in the context of Pakistan (Birkinshaw, 2014; Raziq, 2019). Several studies have been undertaken in the past on the adoption and working of digitalization (Carlsson, 2018; Christiansson et al., 2009; Cocca et al., 2018; Dewa et al., 2018) but according to Gastaldi et al. (2018) and Elg et al. (2020) there is a gap in the literature regarding the role of senior and middle management teams in the process of digitalization. With regard to digital leadership, the leadership literature in general has been studied and developed mainly based on individualistic Western contexts—looking at the context of Pakistan being a collectivistic society may offer alternate perspectives and insights to the leadership research (Raziq et al., 2018).

Although services industry (i.e., e-commerce, fintech, e-government) in Pakistan is moving toward digitalization and the gig economy, the pace is rather slow. According to State Bank of Pakistan Annual Report 2017–18, the Pakistan's industries are supporting IT-related activities by nurturing new enterprises in the digital field. This shows that while Pakistan's gig economy is still in its initial phase of development, there is a great potential of growth in digitalization there. The global giants of gig economy such as Airbnb, Uber, and Careem are successfully operating in Pakistan. Some local outlets, in food delivery segment, have also emerged successfully such as Foodpanda and Cheetah.

The gig economy platforms which consist of self-employed workers may affect the tax collection system because individuals are working independently through an online platform. The self-employed workers typically less contribute toward the tax system as their revenue remains below the bottom line required to pay taxes. Pakistan is already facing chronic challenges in enhancing its taxation revenues, to control tax evasion and to control the corruption in the taxation system (Razzaq et al., 2020). The gig economy platforms may have implications for the tax system and may highly impact the already burdened tax revenue system of Pakistan.

Owing to young, educated, and cheap workforce, gig economy can flourish in Pakistan in the ICT and software industry sectors. However, policies and strategies including laws to regulate gig economy need to be developed to encourage and promote skill development for successful advancement of innovation and technologies (Javed, 2020).

5 Conclusion

The world is rapidly moving toward digitalization. Technologically advanced or developed countries are reaching to the next levels of digitalization with the advancement of services. The developing countries such as Pakistan are in a dire need to reshape the working environment and to compete in the fast-growing trend of digitalization. The modern "platform of capitalism" has emerged and is moving fast. There are advantages and of course disadvantages of the gig economy. It is a complete change and disruption of business. However, it is important for the organizations to recognize the opportunities offered by gig economy. It is imperative to realize the role of top management and middle-level managers in the digitalization process and to instill digitalization culture and prepare the work environment as per the requirements of the modern world. There is a strong need for digital leadership to lead the digitalization of organizations.

Declaration of Interest There are no competing interests to declare.

References

Aloisi, A. (2015). Commoditized workers: Case study research on labor law issues arising from a set of on-demand/gig economy platforms. *Comparative Labor Law & Policy Journal, 37*, 653.

Anwar, M. A., & Graham, M. (2021). Between a rock and a hard place: Freedom, flexibility, precarity and vulnerability in the gig economy in Africa. *Competition & Change, 25*(2), 237–258.

Barroso, M. d. l. R. M. (2005). Trabajo autónomo y trabajo subordinado. Delimitación, análisis y propuestas de reforma. *Estudios financieros. Revista de trabajo y seguridad social: Comentarios, casos prácticos: recursos humanos* (273), 71–144.

Baharuden, A. F., Isaac, O., & Ameen, A. (2019). Factors influencing big data & analytics (BD&A) learning intentions with transformational leadership as moderator variable: Malaysian SME perspective. *International Journal of Management and Human Science (IJMHS), 3*(1), 10–20.

Bailey, M. (2016). Deliveroo boom faces fair work reality check. *Australian Financial Review, 9.*

Bennis, W. (2013). Leadership in a digital world: Embracing transparency and adaptive capacity. *MIS Quarterly, 37*(2), 635–636.

Birkinshaw, J. M. (2014). Subsidiary initiative in the modern multinational corporation. In J. J. Boddewyn (Ed.), *Multidisciplinary insights from new Aib fellows* (*Research in global strategic management*) (Vol. 16, pp. 201–220).

Bondarouk, T. V., & Ruël, H. J. (2009). Electronic human resource management: Challenges in the digital era. *The International Journal of Human Resource Management, 20*(3), 505–514.

Brett, J. (2019). *Evolving digital leadership.* Springer Science, New South Wales.

Caputo, A., Pizzi, S., Pellegrini, M. M., & Dabić, M. (2021). Digitalization and business models: Where are we going? A science map of the field. *Journal of Business Research, 123*, 489–501.

Carlsson, C. (2018). Decision analytics mobilized with digital coaching. *Intelligent Systems in Accounting, Finance and Management, 25*(1), 3–17.

Cha, K. J., Hwang, T., & Gregor, S. (2015). An integrative model of IT-enabled organizational transformation: A multiple case study. *Management Decision.*

Christiansson, P., Svidt, K., & Sørensen, K. B. (2009). Future integrated design environments. *ITcon, 14*, 445–460.

Cocca, P., Marciano, F., Rossi, D., & Alberti, M. (2018). Business software offer for industry 4.0: The SAP case. *IFAC-Papers OnLine, 51*(11), 1200–1205.
Daugareilh, I., Degryse, C., & Pochet, P. (2019). The platform economy and social law: Key issues in comparative perspective. *ETUI Research Paper-Working Paper*.
Dazzi, D. (2019). Gig economy in Europe. *Italian Labour Law e-Journal, 12*(2), 67–122.
Dewa, M. T., Van Der Merwe, A. F., & Matope, S. (2018). Digitalisation of shop-floor operations in the South African tool, die, and mould-making industry. *South African Journal of Industrial Engineering, 29*(2), 153–170.
Do, D. T., & Nuth, A. (2020). Academic library middle managers as leaders: In their own words. *Journal of Library Administration, 60*(1), 41–70.
Elg, M., Birch-Jensen, A., Gremyr, I., Martin, J., & Melin, U. (2020). Digitalisation and quality management: Problems and prospects. *Production Planning & Control*, 1–14.
Fest, S., Kvaloy, O., Nieken, P., & Schöttner, A. (2019). Motivation and incentives in an online labor market.
Flanagan, F. (2019). Theorising the gig economy and home-based service work. *Journal of Industrial Relations, 61*(1), 57–78.
Friedman, G. (2014). Workers without employers: Shadow corporations and the rise of the gig economy. *Review of Keynesian Economics, 2*(2), 171–188.
Gastaldi, L., Appio, F. P., Corso, M., & Pistorio, A. (2018). Managing the exploration-exploitation paradox in healthcare. *Business Process Management Journal*.
Graham, M., & Shaw, J. (2017). *Towards a fairer gig economy.* Meatspace Press.
Gupta, S. (2018). Organizational barriers to digital transformation.
Hansen, R., & Sia, S. K. (2015). Hummel's digital transformation toward Omni channel retailing: Key lessons learned. *MIS Quarterly Executive, 14*(2).
Hathaway, I., & Muro, M. (2016). Tracking the gig economy: New numbers. *Brookings Report, 13*.
Healy, J., Nicholson, D., & Pekarek, A. (2017). Should we take the gig economy seriously? *Labour & Industry: A Journal of the Social and Economic Relations of Work, 27*(3), 232–248.
Henriette, E., Feki, M., & Boughzala, I. (2016). *Digital transformation challenges*. Paper presented at the MCIS.
Heukamp, F. (2020). AI and the leadership development of the future. In *The future of management in an AI world* (pp. 137–148). Springer.
Holmstrom, J. (2021). From AI to digital transformation: The AI readiness framework. *Business Horizons*.
Javed, A. (2020). The scope of information and communication technology enabled services in Promoting Pakistan Economy. *Asian Journal of Economics, Finance and Management*, 1–9.
Karimi, J., & Walter, Z. (2015). The role of dynamic capabilities in responding to digital disruption: A factor-based study of the newspaper industry. *Journal of Management Information Systems, 32*(1), 39–81.
Kwilinski, A., Vyshnevskyi, O., & Dzwigol, H. (2020). Digitalization of the EU economies and people at risk of poverty or social exclusion. *Journal of Risk and Financial Management, 13*(7), 142.
Llopis, J., Gonzalez, M. R., & Gasco, J. L. (2004). Transforming the firm for the digital era: An organizational effort towards an E-culture. *Human Systems Management, 23*(4), 213–225.
McKinsey Global Institute Report. (2017). Jobs lost, jobs gained: What the future of work will mean for jobs, skills and wages.
McKinsey Global Institute. (2016a). Independent work: Choice, necessity, and the gig economy, executive summary.
McKinsey Global Institute. (2016b). Digital finance for all: Powering inclusive growth in emerging economies. https://www.mckinsey.com
Marler, J. H., & Fisher, S. L. (2013). An evidence-based review of e-HRM and strategic human resource management. *Human Resource Management Review, 23*(1), 18–36.
Mazzei, M. J., & Noble, D. (2017). Big data dreams: A framework for corporate strategy. *Business Horizons, 60*(3), 405–414.

McAfee, A., & Brynjolfsson, E. (2017). *Machine, platform, crowd: Harnessing our digital future.* WW Norton & Company.

McCann, D., & Murray, J. (2010). The legal regulation of working time in domestic work. *International Labour Office Conditions of Work and Employment Series* (27).

Mumford, T. V., Campion, M. A., & Morgeson, F. P. (2007). The leadership skills strataplex: Leadership skill requirements across organizational levels. *The Leadership Quarterly, 18*(2), 154–166.

Nadkarni, S., & Prügl, R. (2020). Digital transformation: A review, synthesis and opportunities for future research. *Management Review Quarterly*, 1–109.

Nwaiwu, F. (2018). Review and comparison of conceptual frameworks on digital business transformation. *Journal of Competitiveness.*

OECD. (2019). An Introduction to online platforms and their role in the digital transformation, forthcoming.

Parviainen, P., Tihinen, M., Kääriäinen, J., & Teppola, S. (2017). Tackling the digitalization challenge: How to benefit from digitalization in practice. *International Journal of Information Systems and Project Management, 5*(1), 63–77.

Raziq, M. M. (2019). Examining the foreign multinational enterprises' emergence, strategies, contribution, and sustainability in their operations in Pakistan.

Raziq, M. M., Borini, F. M., Malik, O. F., Ahmad, M., & Shabaz, M. (2018). Leadership styles, goal clarity, and project success. *Leadership & Organization Development Journal.*

Razzaq, A., Nazir, R., & Adil, F. (2020). Dynamic Relationship among tax evasion, control over corruption and political accountability: A case study of Pakistan. *International Journal of Economics and Financial Issues, 10*(5), 256–261.

Resca, A., Za, S., & Spagnoletti, P. (2013). Digital platforms as sources for organizational and strategic transformation: A case study of the Midblue project. *Journal of Theoretical and Applied Electronic Commerce Research, 8*(2), 71–84.

Schwellnus, C., Geva, A., Pak, M., & Veiel, R. (2019). Gig economy platforms: Boon or Bane?

SIA (Staffing Industry Analysts). (2018). The human cloud, the gig economy & the transformations of work.

Sia, S. K., Soh, C., & Weill, P. (2016). How DBS Bank pursued a digital business strategy. *MIS Quarterly Executive, 15*(2).

Singh, A., & Hess, T. (2017). How chief digital officers promote the digital transformation of their companies. *MIS Quarterly Executive, 16*(1).

Solis, B., Li, C., & Szymanski, J. (2014). The 2014 state of digital transformation. *Altimeter Group, 1*(1), 1–33.

State Bank of Pakistan Annual Report 2017–18, Chapter 7, Digitization of Services in Pakistan: Will the Emerging Trends Pave the Way for a Technology Revolution?

Tassinari, A., & Maccarrone, V. (2020). Riders on the storm: Workplace solidarity among gig economy couriers in Italy and the UK. *Work, Employment and Society, 34*(1), 35–54.

Todolí-Signes, A. (2017). The 'gig economy': Employee, self-employed or the need for a special employment regulation? *Transfer: European Review of Labour and Research, 23*(2), 193–205.

Vallas, S., & Schor, J. B. (2020). What do platforms do? Understanding the gig economy. *Annual Review of Sociology, 46*, 273–294.

Voß, F. L., & Pawlowski, J. M. (2019, July). Digital readiness frameworks. In *International Conference on Knowledge Management in Organizations* (pp. 503–514). Springer.

Wong, S. I., Kost, D., & Fieseler, C. (2021). From crafting what you do to building resilience for career commitment in the gig economy. *Human Resource Management Journal.*

Yeow, A., Soh, C., & Hansen, R. (2018). Aligning with new digital strategy: A dynamic capabilities approach. *The Journal of Strategic Information Systems, 27*(1), 43–58.

Yusif, S., Hafeez-Baig, A., & Soar, J. (2020). A model for evaluating eHealth preparedness—A case study approach. *Transforming Government: People, Process and Policy.*

Mehreen Malik is a doctoral candidate at NUST Business School, National University of Science and Technology (NUST) Islamabad, Pakistan. Her research interests are in areas such as digitalization, digital leadership, e-banking, and blockchain technology. She has published in Journal of Internet Banking and Commerce.

Muhammad Mustafa Raziq is currently serving as Associate Professor and Head of Research at the NUST Business School, National University of Sciences and Technology (NUST) Islamabad, Pakistan. He has a Ph.D. in Strategic Management from Massey University, New Zealand. Mustafa is interested in research on strategy, international management, leadership and organization. His work has appeared in reputed journals such as Group & Organization Management, International Journal of Management Reviews, European Management Review, International Business Review, European Journal of Work and Organizational Psychology, Personality and Individual differences, and Journal of Knowledge Management, among others.

Impact of COVID-19 on Gig Workers with Special Reference to Food Delivery Executives

Noonu Mary Jose, David Joseph, Geetanjali Purswani, and S. Girish

1 Introduction

The pandemic COVID-19 has taken a toll on the entire world. Starting from China, it has caught hold around the globe like a wild monster. The pandemic has brought about many surprisingly new ways of living. The earliest response to the pandemic was the introduction of lockdown, business shutdowns, school and university closings, hygiene regulations, social distancing, or restricting movements as a means of slowing down the spread of the pandemic. People were asked to stay at home, learn from home, work from home, eat at home, managing their entire lives from home. All were forcefully locked to a new beginning. Daily life, markets, and economy were all affected, and slowly it became a new normal. All these showed an effect on the work–life of individuals, either in the short run or in the long run. Workers in regular employment were enabled with flexible locations and hours of work. But workers in temporary jobs had to go through a tough time of uncertainty. Temporary employment includes daily wage laborers, delivery executives, and other contract laborers. These are some of the commonly used words in the gig economy.

A gig economy is a general economic framework wherein people are employed temporarily. Organizations recruit accessible specialists for temporary responsibilities. The expression "gig" is a slang word for a work that endures a predefined

N. M. Jose · D. Joseph · G. Purswani (✉) · S. Girish
Department of Commerce, School of Commerce, Finance and Accountancy, CHRIST (Deemed To Be University), Bangalore 560029, India
e-mail: geetanjali.purswani@christuniversity.in

N. M. Jose
e-mail: noonumary.jose@res.christuniversity.in

D. Joseph
e-mail: david.joseph@res.christuniversity.in

S. Girish
e-mail: girish.s@christuniversity.in

A. Gupta et al. (eds.), *Sustainability in the Gig Economy*,
https://doi.org/10.1007/978-981-16-8406-7_8

time frame; performers usually utilize it. Instances of gig representatives in the labor force could include specialists, self-employed entities, project-based laborers, and impermanent or low maintenance enlists.

The gig economy replaced the traditional model of employment in two different forms. A crowd work which works on a global platform with a number of organizations and individuals connected on a global platform accomplishes the task and works on demand via apps where transportations and other services are engaged (De Stefano, 2015).

There has been an ascending pattern toward a gig economy lately. There are many reasons behind increasing interest in contractual/gig working. For one, the labor force is getting more portable, and work should progressively be possible distantly utilizing advanced platforms. Thus, work and area are being decoupled. That implies that consultants can choose among transitory positions and tasks worldwide. In contrast, businesses can choose the best people for explicit activities from a bigger pool than accessible in some random territory.

While the gig economy is famous for the jobs that require high-level skills, there is another set of people who work for not very higher-order thinking tasks, but for routine works like daily wage taxi drivers, delivery executives, construction workers, and other daily wages laborers on a contract basis and so forms part of the gig economy.

Gig work is frequently proclaimed for its adaptability, the opportunity to pick work, its pay age capability, and the self-governance accessible to people performing the work. Exploration as of late has raised worries about low and shaky pay, insufficient admittance to normal work, absence of debilitated leave, just as inferior or no admittance to social insurance, primarily because of the order of laborers as "daily wagers," "temporary or contract laborers" or "self-employed entities" or "consultants." (Berg et al., 2018; Huws et al., 2017; Rosenblat & Stark, 2016).

Gig, being a new form of workforce engagement, remains untested in Indian courts, and with the absence of specific legislation, gig workers cannot claim consequential benefits such as minimum wages, hours of work, overtime, leave, etc. as compared to most traditional long-term employees," said Nishith Upadhyaya, Director—Advisory Services, SHRM (APAC & MENA) (COVID-19 Prompts Workers, Corporates to Adopt Gig Economy, 2020).

The present chapter deals with the people in the food delivery service industry. Here the delivery executives are attached to a delivery service provider who takes orders online from the customers. These orders are placed to the selected restaurants collected by the delivery executives and supplied to the customers.

Figure 1 illustrates the various parties involved in the food delivery sector of the gig economy. In this kind of setup, the essential three-sided market is the conveyance platform. The parties involved are the partners (basic food items or cafés), the conveyance specialist, and the clients—connect. And the trade is encouraged by the platform. These models include a curious administration structure and a bunch of norms and conventions that foster connections between the various parties (customers, clients, and laborers), which are unique concerning conventional business. The links between clients on the platform are fostered by the guidelines and norms laid down in stages'

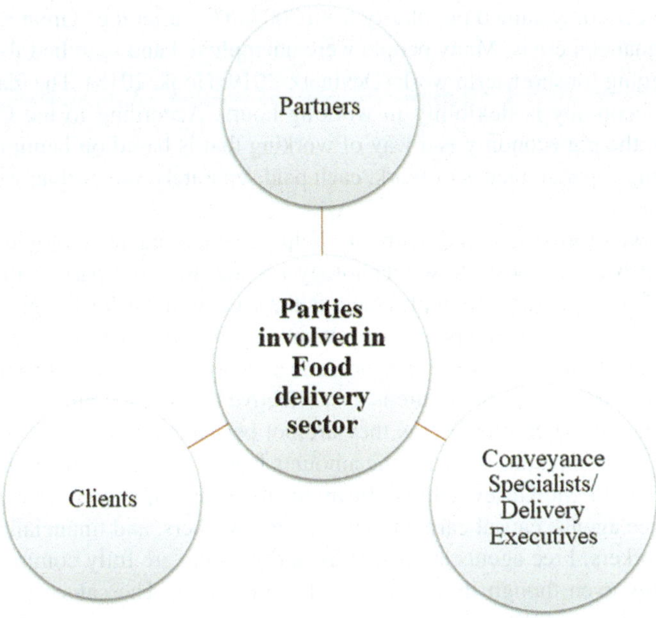

Fig. 1 Parties involved in the food delivery sector. Model created by Jose et al. (2021)

terms of administration arrangements that are singularly controlled by the stages (platform) (Hagel, 2015).

This chapter aims primarily to understand the impact of the COVID-19 pandemic on the employees in the gig economy—gig workers, specifically the delivery executives. Coming sections throw light on the concept of gig economy, the employment categories in the gig economy, and the impact of the COVID-19 pandemic on gig workers. A semi-structured qualitative interview was conducted among delivery executives in Kottayam District in Kerala. This helped in understanding the real-life situations of these executives. The recent initiatives taken by the government in the Union Budget 2021–22 to benefit gig workers have also been included. Finally, the chapter ends with a brief discussion on the journey ahead for the gig workers.

2 Gig Economy—The Concept and the Indian Scenario

The word "gig" was firstly used for music. The gig means the musical performance of a musician or a group of musicians. Usually, these musicians have no particular place for their performance. When they finish performance at one place, they move to the following location. This is why the new working culture got the name "gig economic" because, in the gig economy, workers are flexible in choosing jobs based on their skills, time, and place.

The gig economy gained popularity from 2007 to 09, after the "Great Recession" or global financial crisis. Many people were unemployed and searched for jobs and ended up going for short-term work (Devinatz, 2019; Hook, 2015). The main feature of the gig economy is flexibility in working hours. According to the Cambridge Dictionary, the gig economy is a way of working that is based on being temporary jobs or doing separate pieces of work, each paid separately, rather than working for an employer.

In the twenty-first century, with the help of emerging technologies, the gig economy also got a boost. Now technology became the core part of this sharing economy. The increase in unemployment is the crucial factor for the growth of the gig economy. Because when people do not have a job as per their qualification, they will be forced to do temporary or short-term jobs to earn income. From the view of companies, the emerging culture is cost effective because the employers have no commitments to the employees, as they are not permanent employees of the firm. Therefore, the companies can save the amounts from the pension, insurance, etc.

According to McKinsey Global Institute, there are mainly four independent workers: free agents, causal earners, reluctant gig workers, and financially strapped contract workers. Free agents are active freelancers who are fully committed to the gig economy even though they can work full-time jobs. The causal earners have full-time employment but do the gig work to earn extra income. Those who cannot find traditional jobs and prepare themselves to give up on gig work are called reluctant workers. The financially strapped workers choose gig work due to the necessity of income due to insufficient primary sources of revenue. As per the other classification given by the McKinsey Global Institute, there are mainly two significant gig workers in the economy (McKinsey Global Institute, 2016). The first group of people does work commonly from online platforms. The other group of gig workers are the workers providing transportation services, 'concierge services' including household jobs and workers involved in the delivery of goods and services.

In India, the main sectors in which gig economy culture follows are delivery (e-kart, delivery, etc.), food (Swiggy, Zomato), and transportation (Ola cabs, Uber, etc.). The other sectors looking for gig workers are FMCG- Pharma, Banking, financial services, and insurance, manufacturing, services and technology, and BPO. Out of this, technology and BPO sectors are currently looking for 57% of gig workers to hire ("India Inc Is Going Big on Gig Economy," 2020). The top gig roles available in the gig economy are operational roles like customer support, transactions, operations or processing, and administrative and support roles.

In the gig economy, workers are rewarded for their performance based on different models followed by the respective sectors (India Is Going Big on Gig Economic, 2020). The various models for rewarding the employees include the following:

1. The fixed fee models: In this model, the reward is decided or fixed during contract initiation.
2. Time and effort model: Here, the employee is paid for his effort and time to complete the work.

3. Actual units of work delivered: Employee will be rewarded based on the units of work completed by him.
4. Quality of income: In this model, the reward is purely based on the quality of work done by the employee.
5. Combination models: Here, the organization follows a combined approach by including more than one of the schemes mentioned above.

A recent report by Google and Boston Consulting Group revealed that the Indian online food delivery market would hit $8 billion by 2022 (BCG; Google, 2020). The food delivery segment continues to be the most significant (83%) in the food tech industry (BCG; Google, 2020). In India, there is still immense opportunity for growth. According to the BCG and Google, only 4% of the total food service spend used for online food service. An increase in the online buyer base could become the key growth driver for India's online food delivery business. Internet penetration across rural and urban areas is growing at a CAGR of +20%. Due to a continuous increase in the customer base, the higher-order frequency will be offset by a lower average order value, thus expanding reach in India (BCG; Google, 2020).

In India, Swiggy and Zomato occupy the online food delivery sector. A recent newspaper article reported, "The recent Zomato-Ubereats deal claims to have given Swiggy's closest competitor—Zomato—a 55% market share. But sources told Business Insider that Swiggy still holds 60% revenue share with almost 45 million monthly transactions" (DASH, 2020). Nowadays, companies are paying medical insurance and accidental insurance for the delivery executives.

3 Impact of Pandemic on Gig Economy

The employment style of the gig workers during the pandemic had gone through various phases. At first, it was a stage of uncertainty because everything was shut. During this stage, those gig workers who solemnly depended on gig faced difficulty in earning their livelihood. When the employees outside the gig economy were allowed flexible time and location of work, gig workers were left with neither job nor any benefits to earning their livelihood.

As soon as essential services were allowed, online platforms became active. The gig economy started to accelerate. Gig workers, particularly the delivery executives, played a massive role. For the more significant part of society to endure the "Stay home, Stay safe" serenely, the society depended on them. All the essentials were progressively subject to a huge armada of gig economy laborers working at the forefront, ferrying individuals around, and offering crucial administrations house to house.

Employees in the gig economy who are into services delivery like delivery executives and other taxi drivers occupy the giant pie in the gig economy. Compared to other gig workers, they are in danger because of their work style, as social distancing cannot be guaranteed. There are laborers who rely entirely upon this service delivery

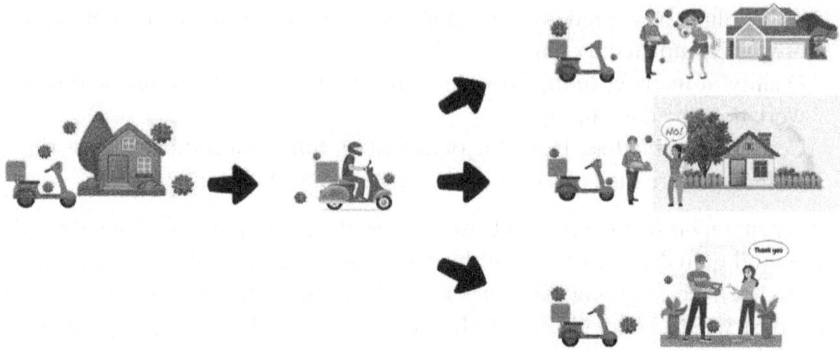

Fig. 2 Food delivery during COVID-19. Model created by Jose et al. (2021)

work for their income. If they do not work, they cannot earn their livelihood. Employment in the gig economy does not provide any sick leaves or other health benefits. They cannot bear to self-isolate regardless of whether COVID-19 protocol was to show up, presenting dangers to both themselves and other people.

With the absence of medical coverage and social assurance, the adherence to COVID-19 protocol becomes challenging for employees in the gig economy. Even though gig workers face health insecurity during a pandemic, they are forced to work to earn their livelihood. Also, there are all chances of the gig workers turning out to be the agents in spreading the infection to the clients or organizations included.

Soon after the initial phase of lockdown, there were relaxations in mobility. Most food delivery apps came out with options like "contactless delivery" to curb the situation. And slowly, the food delivery apps picked their pace. The gig economy also started attracting more people as many were left without jobs in the permanent arrangement. "We have noticed that companies have now started shifting full-time entry-level roles to a gig model," GigIndia Co-founder and CEO Sahil Sharma said, adding that after the lockdown, "we at GigIndia have uploaded around 3500-plus job opportunities for giggers on our platform within six months." There has been a 115% increase in work from home gigs during the lockdown, and the percentage of women giggers grew from 12.07% to 29.34% within six months of the pre/post-lockdown period, Sharma said (COVID-19 Prompts Workers, Corporates to Adopt Gig Economy, 2020) (Fig. 2).

4 Employees Voice

James Thomas Kesterson Jr, a famous musical artist, once said, "Everyone should have the choice of which job they want, instead of that choice being in the hands of employers." Employees are an integral part of every company. If the working culture is not friendly or does not care for employees, that company will eventually suffer. In the gig economy, employees have the freedom to choose their work, working time, and working style. Even though employees have freedom, the company has to monitor the employee activities properly and do performance appraisals. For this chapter, random telephonic interviews with the delivery executives of famous companies, including Swiggy and Zomato from Kottayam, a Kerala district, were conducted. Through this telephone interview, the pulse of delivery executives working in the food delivery sector was checked.

When an employee is opting full time, his working time is from 8 am to 10 pm. If he is ready, he can work for more time. If it is a part-time job, usually people work from 6 to 10 pm. However, if a delivery executive is a full-time delivery or a part-time executive company offers similar incentives and insurance. The delivery executives have to attain specific targets and complete certain hours of work. The targets vary from company to company. If it is based on touchpoints in some companies, the delivery executive has to attain 42 touchpoints in a week to get high incentives. But in other companies, it may be in the form of earnings. If a delivery executive works for more than six months and completes 40 h of work, he will be eligible for insurance. These criteria vary from company to company. This job is a 365 days job, and if a delivery executive works hard, he can easily earn around Rs. 7000 per week. If the delivery executive has good performance, the company will give more orders. According to some delivery executives' comments, the main problems in this job are that sometimes they cannot eat food in time and get only a maximum of six hours to sleep per day with the targets and all. A delivery executive will usually get 19 to 21 orders per day if he works full time. Per order, they will get a minimum of Rs. 20 as commission. The commission may increase if the distance increases. They usually will get orders within a 7 km radius. The interviews with the food delivery executives can be summarized based on the various points that were discussed (Fig. 3).

Figure 3 is a graphical representation of the essence of the discussion with food delivery executives. The employee's opinion and experiences are being discussed and thematically represented based on mode of engagement, requisites for the job, flexibility, health risks associated, freedom, ease of work, and remuneration.

- Mode of engagement

Engaging in the food delivery industry is considered as a temporary or a part-time arrangement by the majority of the employees. Only a few of the delivery executives opted for this job as a full-time engagement. From the conversation, many people have chosen this job as a temporary income cushion to withstand the unexpected loss of employment during the lockdown.

- Requisites for the job

One does not need any skills or need not appear for an interview to get this job. The only requirement is to apply online by a person with a valid driving license. The company will make a call to collect the details about the candidate, and eventually, one can be into the delivery role.

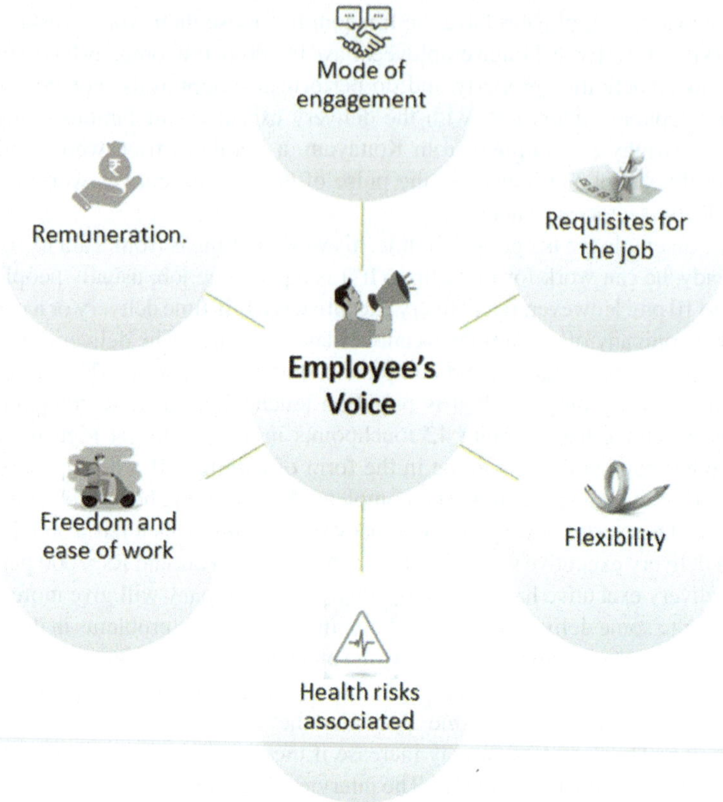

Fig. 3 Food delivery executive's voices. Model created by Jose et al. (2021)

- Flexibility

Employment in the gig economy is known for its flexibility. Employees also agree to this point that their job is very flexible. "Since this job is online, if I do not want to work or need a leave, I go offline. I do not need to inform anyone that I am taking leave." If they need to make an income, they can work. It is up to the employees either to work or not.

- Health risks associated

Food delivery executives agreed that there are many risks associated with this work in the COVID-19 scenario. "No matter what the location is, I have to deliver the foods because I have targets and a touchpoint. There were even situations of delivering orders to hospitalized customers." When people opt for delivery after this lockdown, there might be chances of getting infected. To make the delivery on time, these executives make speedy rides which is also an added health risk.

- Freedom and ease of work

The delivery executives have the freedom to reject the order, but if they reject more than one, the company will deduct some amount from their earnings. In one of the comments of a delivery executive, he opined that there could be some ease if they have a friend circle. Because if they get an emergency during the working time like an accident or vehicle repair, another delivery executive can take over their delivery and complete it on time. It is not official. It is a friendly adjustment among these executives.

- Remuneration

The remuneration was according to the number of "timely deliveries" and "touch-points" from the interviews with the food delivery executives. The better they accomplish these, the better is the remuneration. "I have been doing this job for the last one and half years as my profession. I cannot achieve touchpoints until now." Only half of the interviewed executives could make timely deliveries and meet the "touchpoints" regularly. Hence, there is no guarantee on the remuneration, and the employer does not provide any other benefits to the employees.

In general, the growth prospects in the career for the delivery executives working on this platform are significantly less. The executives are working only for earnings, and the majority of them depend on food delivery jobs as their second source of income. It is clear that from the employee's voice that there should be a regulatory body for safeguarding the interests of the gig workers, including food delivery executives. Government intervention here may help. In addition, the government should implement different schemes for the benefits of the gig workers.

5 Government Initiatives to Protect Gig Workers

The Government of India has been taking initiatives to protect the interest of the gig workers. A very welcoming move is the "Code on Social Security, 2020" passed recently by the Parliament. It aims to shield the interests of the gig workers by giving them government-backed retirement benefits.

- Social Security Funds for unorganized laborers, gig workers, and platform laborers:

The bill of 2019 required that certain funds be kept separate to benefit unorganized laborers, gig workers, and platform laborers. The 2019 Bill insists that the central government set up government-backed retirement funds for unorganized laborers, gig workers, and platform laborers. The 2020 Bill expresses that the central government will set up such funds. Further, state governments will set up and direct separate federal retirement aide funds for temporary/contract laborers. The 2020 Bill likewise makes arrangements for the enlistment of every one of the three classes of laborers—unorganized laborers, gig workers, and platform laborers. This would help get clear statistics regarding the number of people engaged in this area so that appropriate schemes can be framed.

- National Social Security Board for gig workers and platform laborers:

The 2019 Bill expresses the need for a National Social Security Board, which can assist gig workers and platform laborers and suggest and screen plans for gig workers and platform laborers. The board shall contain an alternate arrangement of individuals including:

1. Five delegates of aggregators, designated by the central government.
2. Five agents of gig laborers and stage laborers, selected by the central government.
3. Director-General of the ESIC (Employee State Insurance Corporation).
4. Five agents of state governments.

In the recent Budget Speech, Finance Minister, Ms. Nirmala Sitharaman, made a statement about the launch of a portal to collect information on gig, building, and construction workers to formulate welfare schemes. The aim is to formulate schemes to arrange for the health, insurance, housing, skill, and food requirements of these migrant workers (Portal to Collect Data on Gig Workers in Budget, 2021).

The move is very welcoming for the three million-plus gig workers in the country as it can add new dimensions to the employment structure of the gig worker (Sharma, 2021). Government initiatives will also help curb the uncertainties in the monetary benefits that the gig workers are subjected to.

6 Conclusion

A country like India has an immense scope of opportunities for the online food delivery sector. As per a recent Internet user report, India ranked as the second-largest country of Internet users (41%) after China (Ang, 2020). This growth in Internet users paves the way for growth to the parties involved in the online food delivery sector, especially for the companies and employees working in the gig economy. In respect of companies, the scope of expansion is enormous. Companies are merging to face competition. Zomato and Uber merging is an example of that. Also, the entry of new companies indicates the opportunities in the online food delivery sector. Recently Amazon, the technological giant, announced its entry into the online food delivery sector (Amazon Enters Indian Food Delivery Market, 2020). These all are explaining the potential growth opportunities for the companies in India. The growth of these companies will enhance the requirements for the contract laborers, delivery executives, etc. We would see many people joining the field due to the flexibility it provides. Rising options for on-demand, gig-style employment can take some of the stress out of job searching by offering employees a temporary cushion of income and allowing them to take their time to find the best fit for new employment.

The COVID-19 pandemic has drawn attention toward the much-required need of the economy to look into the requirements of gig workers. Gig workers have demonstrated that they are equivalent to normal workers; they are also fundamental for the economy's survival. Indeed, even before the COVID-19 outbreak, the authorities at the gig platforms were gradually beginning to perceive the requirement for an amendment in labor laws and social security. Now the pandemic has brought a chance for the authorities of gig organizations to uphold and ensure their demand.

Transitory rights and insurances in the wake of the pandemic are the need of the hour. It is important to battle the rising disparity between the workers and the individuals. They are being denied inclusion simply because they choose to work differently and not compulsively with fixed timings and setup. All things being equal, gig workers merit reasonable and straightforward pay structures. This could be cultivated through the enactment of laws, by court choices, or by demonstrations of government. Eventually, common masses would also follow the regime. However, the path forward relies upon assuring assurances for all laborers, irrespective of their type of work. Pay security for gig workers will be needed to make the gig workers part of the mainstream. As organizations, controllers, and policymakers start thinking about the result of the pandemic, they ought to be careful not to consign gig workers to the dead zone or dim region where they will be denied representative assurances. Gig workers have substantiated themselves deserving of similar work market insurances that different laborers get under the law.

References

Journals and Articles

Alvarez-Palau, E., Viu-Roig, M., & Reixach Molet, J. (2020) How do food delivery platforms affect urban logistics? The case of Glovo in Barcelona as a preliminary Study. In I. Ramos de Luna, À. Fitó-Bertran, J. Lladós-Masllorens, & F. Liébana-Cabanillas (Eds.), *Sharing economy and the impact of collaborative consumption* (pp. 221–236.). IGI Global.

BCG; Google. (2020). *Demystifying the online food customer: An $8 Billion opportunity*. The Boston Consulting Group.

Berg, J., Rani, U., Furrer, M., Harmon, E., & Six Silberman, M. (2018). *Digital labour platforms and the future of work*. International Labour Organization.

De Araujo Leão, A., Dos Santos Cabral, L., Pereira Gomes, R., Pereira Gonçalves, B., Lobo de Oliveira, J. M., & Barbosa de Alencar, D. (2019). Shared economy: A Uber-Eats case study in Manaus City. *International Journal for Innovation Education and Research, 7*(11), 450–466.

De Groen, W. P., Kilhoffer, Z., Lenaerts, K., & Mandl, I. (2018). *Employment and working conditions of selected types of platform work*. Publications Office of the European Union.

De Stefano, V. (2015). The rise of the just-in-time workforce: On-demand work, crowdwork, and labor protection in the gig-economy. *Comparative Labor Law and Policy Journal, 37*, 471.

Devinatz, V. G. (2019). Introduction to "Independent workers: Growth trends, categories, and employee relations implications in the emerging gig economy." *Employee Responsibilities and Rights Journal, 31*(1), 61–62. https://doi.org/10.1007/s10672-018-9328-6

Drahokoupil, J., & Piasna, A. (2019). Work in the platform economy: Deliveroo riders in Belgium and the SMart arrangement. ETUI Working Paper 2019.01, Brussels: ETUI.

Glaser, B., & Strauss, A. (2017). *The discovery of grounded theory: Strategies for qualitative research.* Routledge.

Hagel, J. (2015). *The power of platforms. Business trends series.* Deloitte University Press.

Huws, U., Spencer, N., & Joyce, S. (2016). Crowd work in Europe. *Foundation for European Progressive Studies, 58.*

Huws, U., Spencer, N., Syrdal, D., & Holts, K. (2017). *Work in the European gig economy: Research results from the UK, Sweden, Germany, Austria, The Netherlands, Switzerland and Italy.* FEPS, UniGlobal and University of Hertfordshire.

Institute, M. G. (2016). *Independent work: Choice, necessity, and the gig economy.* https://www.mckinsey.com/featured-insights/employment-and-growth/independent-work-choice-necessity-and-the-gig-economy

Ivanova, M., Bronowicka, J., Kocher, E., & Degner, A. (2018). The App as a Boss? Control and autonomy in application-based management. Work in Progress interdisziplinärer Arbeitsforschung, 2, Frankfurt (Oder): Viadrina. https://doi.org/10.11584/Arbeit-Grenze-Fluss.2

Izakowski, Ł. (2020). Milion pobrań aplikacji Glovo. Ponad 2, 7 tys. Partnerów. https://retailnet.pl/pl/2020/06/01/59144-milion-pobran-aplikacji-glovo-ponad-27-tys-partnerow/

Jacob, A. M., Sreedharan, N. V., & Sreena, K. (2019). Consumer perception of online food delivery apps in Kochi. *International Journal of Innovative Technology and Exploring Engineering, 8*(7), 302–305.

Joyce, S., Neumann, D., Trappmann, V., & Umney, C. (2020). A global struggle: Worker protest in the platform economy. *ETUI Policy Brief, 2*, 1–6.

Martínez, A. D. (2019). App capitalism. *NACLA Report on the Americas, 51*(3), 236–241.

Monty, R. (2018). Creative economy: How the interface of Uber Eats and ifood could change your menu. *Brazilian Journal of Operations & Production Management, 15*(3), 413–419.

Myck, M., Oczkowska, M., & Trzciński, K. (2020). Skala Ryzyka Finansowego dla Gospodarstw Domowych: Pierwsza Fala Konsekwencji Gospodarczych Pandemii COVID-19 , Szczecin: CenEA, Centrum Analiz Ekonomicznych.

Polkowska, D. (2019). Does the app contribute to the precarization of work? A case of Uber drivers in Poland. *Partecipazione e Conflitto, 12*(3), 717–741.

Raina, A., Rana, V. S., & Thakur, A. S. (2018). Popularity of online food ordering and delivery services—A comparative study between Zomato, Swiggy and Uber Eats in Ludhiana. *International Journal of Management, Technology and Engineering, 8*(3), 350–355.

Raj, M., Sundararajan, A., & You, C. (2020). COVID-19 and digital resilience: Evidence from Uber Eats (June 12, 2020). Available from: SSRN June 30, 2020. https://ssrn.com/abstract=3625638 or https://doi.org/10.2139/ssrn.3625638

Rani, U., & Dhir, R. K. (2020). Platform work and the COVID-19 pandemic. *The Indian Journal of Labour Economics, 63*(1), 163–171.

Rosenblat, A., & Stark, L. (2016). Algorithmic labor and information asymmetries: A case study of Uber's drivers. *International Journal of Communication, 10*, 3758–3784.

Scheiber, N. (2020). Jobless claims by Uber and Lyft drivers revive fight over labor status. *The New York Times.* April, Available from www.nytimes.com, August 12, 2020.

Schilling, B., Krader, K., Jennings, L., Deschamps, T., Newswire, C., Suhartanto, D., & Jennings, L. (2019). Uber Eats team opens up about the future of the service in Canada. *Restaurant Hospitality, 35*(1), 81–97.

Spurk, D., & Straub, C. (2020). Flexible employment relationships and careers in times of the COVID-19 pandemic. *Journal of Vocational Behavior.* https://doi.org/10.1016/j.jvb.2020.103435

Stephany, F., Dunn, M., Sawyer, S., & Lehdonvirta, V. (2020). Distancing bonus or downscaling loss? The changing livelihood of US online workers in times of COVID-19. *Tijdschrift Voor Economische En Sociale Geografie, 111*(3), 561–573.

Tassinari, A., & Maccarrone, V. (2020). Riders on the storm: Workplace solidarity among gig economy couriers in Italy and the UK. *Work, Employment and Society, 34*(1), 35–54.

Taylor, M., Marsh, G., Nicole, D., & Broadbent, P. (2017). Good work: The Taylor review of modern working practices. https://www.gov.uk/government/publications/good-work-the-taylor-review-of-modern-working-practices

Vandaele, K. (2018). Will trade unions survive in the platform economy? Emerging patterns of platform workers. Collective Voice and Representation in Europe', ETUI Working Paper 2018.05, Brussels: ETUI.

Wood, A. J., Graham, M., Lehdonvirta, V., & Hjorth, I. (2019). Good gig, bad gig: Autonomy and algorithmic control in the global gig economy. *Work, Employment and Society, 33*(1), 56–75.

Yin, R. K. (2013). *Case study research: Design and methods.* SAGE.

Books and Chapters

Sinicki, A. (2019). *Thriving in the Gig Economy—Freelancing online for tech professionals and entrepreneurs.* In *Harvard business review.*

Newspaper Articles

Amazon enters Indian food delivery market. (2020, May 21). The Hindu. https://www.thehindu.com/business/Industry/amazon-enters-indian-food-delivery-market/article31641025.ece

Ang, C. (2020, November). *Which countries have the most internet users?* Datastream. https://www.visualcapitalist.com/countries-with-most-internet-users/

COVID-19 Prompts Workers, Corporates to Adopt Gig Economy. (2020, October 18). *The Economic Times.* https://auto.economictimes.indiatimes.com/news/industry/covid-19-prompts-workers-corporates-to-adopt-gig-economy/78732889

DASH, S. (2020, January 24). Swiggy says it's the most loved brand and doesn't need discounts. *Business Insider.* https://www.businessinsider.in/business/startups/news/swiggy-top-executive-says-it-doesnt-need-discounts/articleshow/73575887.cms#:~:text=While the recent Zomato-Ubereats,transactions%2C sources told Business Insider

Hook, L. (2015). Year in a word: Gig economy. *Financial Times.* https://www.ft.com/content/b5a2b122-a41b-11e5-8218-6b8ff73aae15

India Inc is going big on Gig economy. (2020, September 27). The Economic Times. https://economictimes.indiatimes.com/jobs/india-inc-is-going-big-on-gig-economy/articleshow/78348386.cms

Portal to collect data on gig workers in Budget. (2021, February 1). The Hindu. https://www.thehindu.com/news/national/portal-to-collect-data-on-gig-workers-in-budget/article33717552.ece

Sharma, S. (2021, January 31). Gig economy: In competitive times, gig workers can make the difference between leaders and also-rans. Financial Express. https://www.financialexpress.com/industry/gig-economy-in-competitive-times-gig-workers-can-make-the-difference-between-leaders-and-also-rans/2183191/

Noonu Mary Jose is Research Scholar in the Department of Commerce, School of Commerce, Finance and Accountancy at CHRIST (Deemed to be University) Bangalore, India. She holds a degree in Master of Philosophy in the Commerce and Management discipline and has two years of teaching experience. Her area of interest is human resource management and pursuing qualitative studies in this field. She also has a few peer-reviewed refereed journals to her credit.

David Joseph is Research Scholar in the Department of Commerce, School of Commerce, Finance and Accountancy at CHRIST (Deemed to be University) Bangalore, India. He holds a degree in Master of Commerce and has three years of teaching experience. His area of interest is financial technologies and currently pursuing research in the different subsets of financial technologies.

Geetanjali Purswani is Assistant Professor in Department of Commerce, School of Commerce, Finance and Accountancy at CHRIST (Deemed to be University) Bangalore, India. She holds a Ph.D. in the Commerce discipline. She has eleven years of teaching experience. Her area of specialization is accounting and finance. She has presented her research in various conferences, has her paper published in various journals, and has been a spokesperson on different occasions.

S. Girish did his M.com in Advanced Management Accounting and Finance, University of Mysore. Later on, he completed P.G Diploma in Marketing Management, Bahadur Institute of Management Sciences, University of Mysore, Master of Philosophy in Accounting from Sri Ventakeshwara University, Thirupati, MBA in Finance from IGNOU, New Delhi, and Ph.D. from Rayalaseema University, Kurnool, in Finance specialization. He has blend of experience in corporate and academic. Currently, he is Assistant Professor, Department of studies in Commerce, CHRIST (Deemed to be University), Bangalore. His academic interest includes banking and insurance, accounting and taxation and investments and finance. He has also presented and participated in various states, national, and international seminars and conferences organized by UGC and other bodies. He has published many articles in national and international refereed journals and also published international monograph, textbooks for Bangalore University syllabus and working paper. He was the youngest and recognized resource candidate to be selected by Government of Karnataka to convert from Single entry system of book keeping to double entry system of book keeping in various Municipalities and Urban Local Bodies in Karnataka state. He has completed the Government of Karnataka, Labor Department project on Effective Cess Collection Mechanism. He is also Member of Board of Studies and Board of Examination at various universities and autonomous colleges in India. His interest includes drawing, painting, playing chess, carom, football, cricket, traveling, and trekking.

Sustainability of Gig Era and Industry 4.0

Can Labour Productivity Impact India's Gig Economy?

Isha Jaswal and Upasana Singh

1 Introduction

A huge inclination towards smartphone usage and increased digitalization has led to rapid emergence of gig professionals in the past few years who are rendering their freelance services via tech-based mediums. The flip side of COVID-19 health pandemic has been the exponential boost to digitalization which has unleashed increased preference towards flexible jobs or working hours. This in turn is driven by an array of factors like choice autonomy, technology upgradation, skill focus and alternate source of income.

In consonance with the gig economy which also gives way to assignment ownership, flexibility and handiness, one can decide and ascertain the variety and volume of assignments to take up given the reciprocal earnings and hence strike a work—life balance as per one's preferences. Likewise, and in contrast to the traditional working system, it gives flexibility to keep out of a task or decline servicing for a particular work. In other words, gig freelancers can opt for work opportunities in which they are best suited or are relatively skilled. Moreover, the rising costs of living is also inducing the search for gig work as an alternative source of income.

Digitalization and related awareness and literacy has further boosted this form of economy. In fact, organizations which are constituents of gig economy will soon take over the traditional economy working patterns. From a cab driver to an educator, from a photographer to a software developer, from a musician to a therapist, the concept of working is being shaped by gig economy. Even though this concept is seemingly an old wine in new bottle, the technological advancements and its rapid adoption and usage have led of widespread diversion towards gig jobs.

With regard to its growth, industries and sectors have witnessed exponential rise in gig work. For instance, in 2017, the Bureau of Labor Statistics found that nearly 34% (55 million) of America's workforce was engaged in gig work and this was

I. Jaswal (✉) · U. Singh
Delhi Metropolitan Education (GGSIPU), New Delhi, India

A. Gupta et al. (eds.), *Sustainability in the Gig Economy*,
https://doi.org/10.1007/978-981-16-8406-7_9

then expected to grow over the years in future. Thus, the role and importance of gig economy are assumed to hold high stakes in various economies of the world. Nevertheless, it is equally important to highlight the downside of this nature of work especially if it is envisioned to overthrow the traditional economy. The gig workers replacing the full-time workers are not protected by labour laws and cannot avail social security and other benefits as well.

2 Impact of Digitalization on Gig Economy

'Digitization', 'digitalization' and 'digital transformation' are sometimes mistakenly used interchangeably. 'Digitization' means conversion of analog material into digital format. 'Digitalization' means a process where use of digital technology is increased/adopted by the user. 'Digital transformation' signifies organizational change besides only implementation of digital technologies (Feldman, 1997). Thus 'digitalization' and 'digital transformation' are the terms relevant in the context of impact that technology has on society and employment.

Gig economy employment model can be characterized with high job autonomy, flexible working hours, easy access to employer, extra source of income, lesser rigidity in hierarchy, wider customer reach and probably more scope to innovate. These characteristics make gig economy model adaptable to digitalization. Impact of digitalization on gig economy has become even more relevant because of the COVID-19 pandemic that the world is battling with. Digitalization of businesses is not an aspiration anymore and has become a pressing need. The digital economy has been growing 2.5 times faster than the legacy economy, thereby contributing +35% to GDP of leading nations (Dhaini, 2021). And digital platforms act as gig marketplaces, connecting gig service providers with consumers (Dhaini, 2021), for example, Uber, Deliveroo or Fieverr.

Internet/digitalization has enabled 'gig economy' service providers to find work that they could not engage into earlier. Online labour platform removes the limitation of time and distance between the client and the labour. The evident success of this business model has led some proclaim that 'traditional job' will come to an end (Stanford, 2017). Instead being in regular job, the workers will prefer keeping themselves as independent, free and flexible workers moving seamlessly from one job ('gig') to another, using digital technology to find suitable market for their services (Stanford, 2017). While some welcome this change, others fear this might increase instability in market and adversely affect the quality of work. However, most see this change as 'a process driven primarily by technology and consider it largely 'inevitable': opposing gig economy is as fruitless as the efforts of Luddites to stop the steam engine and the spinning jenny' (Stanford, 2017).

Interestingly, the standard employment relationship (SER) gained impetus with the growth of centralized production in larger factories beginning in the nineteenth century. Technological advancement related to bulk production and Industrial Revolution encourages SER in nineteenth–twentieth century. This was the time when capitalism was establishing itself and free market was getting bigger. The major defining features of SER are: workers would work with one employer, for longer durations, usually on a full-time basis; they use the employer's equipment and work on their premises (Cranford et al., 2003). Slowly, SER was associated with job security, labour laws defining rights and responsibilities of employer and employee, expectations of fairness and stability, trade unions and collective bargaining, employment benefit schemes, pensions, provident fund and other features which bring SER closer to social security.

In the wake of advancement in information and communication technology, the work is getting more decentralized. Now due to increasing availability of high-speed Internet, job (gig) opportunities are getting available even outside of one's local territory. Gig worker can train remotely and also work remotely. Also, the growing importance of service sector, characterized with smaller scale of production, is disenchanting the people with the idea of SER. Also with the development of surveillance technology and performance monitoring, the employers do not need positive inducements like permanent work or superior wages to elicit performance (Stanford, 2017).

Rise in gig economy is primarily attributed to globalization, the great recession of 2008 and digitalization. Freelance work arrangements are getting popular because of many reasons like disenchantment from 9 to 5 routine, sudden firings because of retrenchment efforts of employers, difficulty in finding jobs in the competitive labour market and other reasons. Whatever the motivation for this shift is, it is undeniable that this model of employment is rapidly alongside the emergence of digital platforms/marketplaces. The digital gig economy (DGE) generated approximately $204 bn from worldwide customers in 2018. Transportation-based services contributed to over 50% of this value. The size of the gig economy is projected to grow by a 17% CAGR and generate a gross volume of ~$455 bn by 2023 (Monga, 2019). In a report by Mckinsey, it is observed that by 2025 online talent platforms could raise global GDP by up to 2.7 trillion dollars and employment by 72 million full-time equivalent positions. There are approximately 40 million platform workers in the Global South alone, and it is estimated that digital labour platforms currently earn at least 50 billion USD per year (Graham et al., 2019).

The expansion of digital labour platforms can be attributed to the benefits it offers to the clients, new economic opportunities offered to workers, cutting of transactional and infrastructural cost, flexibility, access to wide range of skills, etc. Due to the rapid technological development, the transaction cost for outsourcing non-core activities is reducing and aiding in an increase in the number of tasks which can be performed by each worker. This is resulting in shrinking of firms in size and a rise in start-ups which are outsourcing many activities to expert service providers on a contractual basis (Monga, 2019). Figure 1 depicts the diversity of digital labour platforms, from micro-tasking to highly specialized projects.

Technological developments during the twentieth century impacted the course of labour market in twenty-first century and will continue to impact and develop (Larson, 2020). For instance, agricultural revolution of the 1950–60 increased agricultural

Fig. 1 Diversification of digital platform workers. *Image source* Cañigueral (2019)

production; this was followed by scientific–technical revolution of the 1970s and this was followed by digital/information and telecommunications revolution, also known as 'Third Industrial Revolution' (1975–2010) (Melnikov & Semenyuk, 2014). These eras impacted both, the way of life of people and the economics of society and the way in which labour market operated. Progressing ahead of the 'Third Industrial Revolution' is the 'Information Age' or the 'Fourth Industrial Revolution' or 'Industry 4.0' characterized by technological breakthroughs and developments in fields such as robotics, artificial intelligence (AI), blockchain and 3D printing (Walwei, 2016). Information Age is more importantly about new means of communication and connectivity than technological advancements (Schwab & Davis, 2018). These new forms of communication technologies connect people worldwide via Internet, thus significantly improving the efficiency of business and organizations.

2.1 *Gig Economy and India*

Developed countries are early adopters of the gig economy model due to earlier digitalization, higher economic growth and available investment. It is perhaps because of these factors that leading global companies using digital platforms like Uber, Airbnb, Deliveroo, Upwork are founded in countries like USA and UK. USA is currently a leader in the global gig economy. Developing countries like India have great potential in terms of availability of freelancers and skilled labour. With technology penetration in its interiors, India can study trends in developed countries like USA and its gig economy to build its own gig economy. For example, for Uber, Airbnb, Amazon and Venmo in the USA, there are Ola, OYO, Flipkart and Paytym in India, respectively.

India is emerging as leading country for flexi-staffing or gig and platform according to the Economic Survey, 2020–21, launched by Government of India

(India emerges as leading country for flexi-staffing, 2021). E-commerce industry created gig opportunities in the market during pandemic. Technology made remote working the new normal, and along with growth of gig economy, lockdown period also saw increasing work from home in the organized sector as well (India emerges as leading country for flexi-staffing, 2021). The economic survey stated that due to technological advancement the nature of work has been changing and along with innovation in organization structures new business models are evolving. Digital platforms emerged as one of these new business models of employment creation with the power to connect job seekers and job providers. India has emerged as the 5th largest country for flexi-staffing after USA, China, Brazil and Japan.

While the gig economy is popular among the blue-collar workers in India—Uber/Ola drivers, there is now huge potential for the white-collar workers as well, due to increasing demand in industries—project-specific consultants, logo/content design, Web design, etc. (e.g. TapChief in India). The gig economy is expanding from less skilled services (e.g. domestic chores at BookMyChotu in India and TaskRabbit in USA) to more skilled jobs (e.g. Guru in India and Upwork in US).

In the gig economy business model if the organizations manage to fit contingent workers in their holistic talent strategy, then such workers will be utilized to fill gaps, meet project needs and spearhead change. The companies will have to work hard to find out the right technology and a clear strategy to engage with non-payroll workers.

3 Total Factor Productivity (TFP) and Gig Economy

The basic economic theory of production propagates that total product or output is the function of factor inputs, meaning that a change in factor inputs leads to a change in output produced. Economic growth which is generally quantified in terms of gross domestic product (GDP) can thus be viewed as function of factor inputs employed, like labour and capital. The trickle-down theory professes that rise in GDP will have a positive effect on employment. As economy grows, more employment is generated and labour is seen to shift from agriculture sector to manufacturing and then to services.

Moreover, economic growth also boosts technological advancements and innovations in production processes. This in turn gives impetus to productivity of factor inputs. Productivity or factor inputs' capacity to produce rather affects the level of production without any change in the number or amount of labour and or capital employed. Importantly, rise in productivity speeds up the growth process of an economy.

At this juncture, it is imperative to highlight the important concept of total factor productivity (TFP) which evaluates the growth of output in real terms. Thus, if TFP increases, it indicates towards rise in economic growth keeping labour and capital employed constant. TFP is hence a crucial concept with respect to productivity of factor inputs.

In fact, Samiran Chakraborty, Citigroup's Chief Economist for India, reported in Financial Express in 2018 that rise in production is dependent not only upon increase in labour pool but also in growth of labour productivity. In order to undertake the analysis, data of annual growth from 1950 was studied for 26 nations. The results of the study showed that where growth of labour productivity was more than 6%, GDP was more than 8% in three-fourth of panel countries data. And for labour productivity ranging between 4 and 6%, growth of GDP was majorly found to range between 5 and 8%. For three decades post-1950, India's growth of labour productivity averaged a pretty low percentage of 1.7. It fared well with the average value above 3% for the next two decades and with the average value reaching 8% between the years 2005 and 2011 which also witnessed the best economic growth years of India. The study highlighted that growth in productivity of labour via investment in human and capital formation will ultimately enhance total production efficiency which in turn is engulfed in TFP.

Further, Fig. 2 depicts the criticality of the concept of TFP.

An article in Livemint (2020) highlighted total economy database (TED) findings which indicated that economies which experienced TFP above 3% had GDP growth rate equivalent to or higher than 8%. With regard to India, TED indicated that for the years 2005, 2006 and 2007, adjusted GDP growth was 9%, 9.3% and 10.1%, respectively. Importantly, for all these year, India's TFP ranged between 3.1 and 3.5%.

The relation between a country's growth and TFP is quite intricate. Thus, TFP is an important factor to accelerate economic growth especially to pull the nations out from the current slowdown. However, if one goes by the notion of capital and technology-induced productivity growth, then the stance of employment becomes worrisome. Though literature also talks about an amicable correlation between productivity and

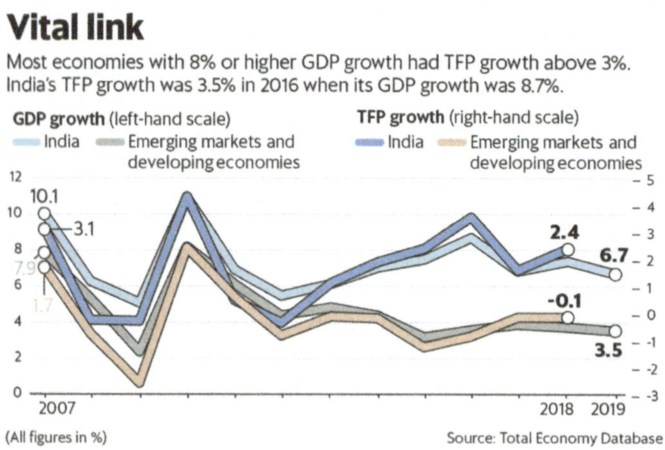

Fig. 2 TFP and related GDP growth. *Source* Bhasin (2020)

employment, but it is important to reason out if employment and growth enhancement are inimical to each other especially in this age of digitalization and artificial intelligence.

An important study in this regard was conducted by Autor and Salomons (2017). They explored the relationship between the two by employing more than 35 years of data at country and industry level from 19 nations. Interestingly, there were two noteworthy findings. Firstly, the employment at industry level was found to decline rapidly with the rise in industry's productivity. Secondly, the results also reported that with rise in total productivity, employment at country level also rises. Strikingly, it was also reported that growth in productivity in primary and secondary sector's industries led to huge reallocation of labourers towards service sector. Importantly, the study concluded that rise in productivity did not reduce demand for labour at aggregate level, but it definitely brought about shifts in factor demand based on skills.

Fall in demand of labour industry-wise and a shift towards skill-biased demand might be seen to indicate to the changing dynamics of work culture in the near future. Rather, according to Forbes Councils Member, Mike Volkin (2020), 'companies that aren't embracing gig workers will soon be left behind'.

4 Rise in Productivity and India's Gig Economy: A GTAP Evaluation

India's productivity level experienced a hit after the global recession of 2007–08 and so did its growth rate. And now, like any other economy of the world there is an economic slowdown owing to the pandemic unleashed by COVID-19. Along with this, it is felt that the nature of work culture has changed permanently and will be skewed towards digitalization after the pandemic. With the changing work culture, India is currently struggling to find its way back to a reasonable growth trajectory. The Economic Times (2020) reported that according to India Ratings and Research, productivity of labour in India needs to be raised by 6.3% in order to achieve an 8% growth in GDP.

Given these figures, the authors have attempted to analyse the rise in factor productivity on the Indian economy by general equilibrium analysis. For this, the Global Trade Analysis Project (GTAP), GTAPv10 database is employed to evaluate the impact on Indian economy due to a productivity shock. GTAP is a worldwide network encompassing researchers and policy analysts engaged in quantitative research in global policy issues. The prominence of this framework is highlighted by the fact that two conferences cosponsored by the WTO and the World Bank (Millenium Round of Multilateral Trade, Geneva) witnessed nearly all quantitative studies based in GTAP. 'Innovative aspects of this model include: (i) the treatment of private household preferences using the non-homothetic CDE functional form, (ii) the explicit treatment of international trade and transport margins; bilateral trade is handled via the Armington assumption, (iii) a global banking sector which intermediates between global savings and consumption'.

Standard static GTAP model which is multi-region, multi-sectoral, CGE model with the assumption of perfect competition and constant returns to scale has been used in this research study. The model consists of 57 sectors clustered in 15 sectors for the study. Not being too ambitious and noting a reasonable figure from the preceding sections, a shock of 3% rise in productivity of factor inputs has introduced in the model.

As a result of rise in productivity by 3%, India's GDP is predicted to rise by 3%. Thus, a productivity rise more than 3% is necessary to attain higher levels of growth, as claimed by India Ratings and Research. Further, it was found that production or output in all sectors would witness a rise as depicted in Table 1.

However, the results simultaneously depicted that demand for labour will reduce in all sectors except trade, utility and construction, and other services. Further, in percentage terms, a substantial fall in demand for labour was observed in sectors like transport and communication, recreation, trade and other businesses (Table 2).

It can thus be inferred that rise in productivity can potentially reallocate India's labour force and can simultaneously give a boost to the gig economy framework.

Table 1 Percentage change in output production (India)

Sectors	% Change
Recreation	2.03
Other businesses	1.05
Trade	3.58
Other transport	2.92
Communication	2.48
Grains and crops	2.37
Livestock and meat products	2.76
Extraction	2.79
Processed food	2.4
Textile and clothing	1.39
Light manufacturing	2.21
Heavy manufacturing	2.28
Utilities and construction	4.07
Transport	0.41
Other services	3.61

Author's calculation

Table 2 Percentage change in demand for labour, sectorwise (India)

Sectors	Unskilled labour	Skilled labour
Recreation	−0.7	−1.12
Other businesses	−1.65	−2.06
Trade	0.81	0.26
Other transport	0.06	−0.49
Communication	−0.37	−0.79
Grains and crops	−0.94	−1.04
Livestock and meat products	−0.7	−0.87
Extraction	−0.25	−0.32
Processed food	−0.49	−0.86
Textile and clothing	−1.5	−1.92
Light manufacturing	−0.68	−1.09
Heavy manufacturing	−0.58	−1
Utilities and construction	1.26	0.81
Transport	−2.45	−3
Other services	0.88	0.46

Author's calculation

5 Conclusion

India is increasingly emerging as a gig economy in the global economy. Like any other economy of the world, India's economic growth also experienced a setback in wake of COVID-19. Rise in productivity plays an important role in enhancing the GDP growth rate of an economy. As indicated by India Ratings and Research, a 6.3% rise in labour productivity is required to enhance India's GDP growth by 8%. When GTAPv10 model was employed to simulate for rise in productivity by 3%, GDP of India was seen to rise though not by a substantial percentage. In fact, all 57 sectors experienced a rise in output in simulation result. Strikingly, demand for labour in majority of the sectors was found to decline, thus indicating that India's gig economy might experience a potential boost.

References

Bhasin, K. (January, 2020). Productivity has big role in India's $5 tn GDP dream. *Mint*. https://www.livemint.com/news/india/productivity-has-big-role-in-india-s-5-tn-gdp-dream-11578424261604.html

Cañigueral, A (June 29, 2019). How can tech meet the needs of platform workers? RSA. https://www.thersa.org/blog/2019/06/tech-platform-workers

Cranford, C. J., Vosko, L.F., & Zukewich, N. (2003). Precarious employment in the Canadian labour. *Just Labour, 3*(Fall), 6–22.

Dhaini, A. (2021). Covid-19 as accelerator for digital transformation and the rise of the gig economy. In *KPMG*. https://assets.kpmg/content/dam/kpmg/sa/pdf/2020/covid-19-as-accelerator-of-digital-transformation-and-the-gig-economy.pdf. Accessed February 24, 2021.

Drivers opt for Uber to offer their driving services and customers connect with drivers using Uber.

Feldman, T. (1997). *An introduction to digital media*, 1st ed. Routledge.

Graham, M. et al. (2019). The Fairwork Foundation: Strategies for improving platform work. In *Proceedings of the Weizenbaum Conference on Challenges of Digital Inequality – Digital Education, Digital Work, Digital Life*, Berlin (pp. 1–8).

India emerges as leading country for flexi-staffing, Eco Survey. *Business Standards*. https://www.business-standard.com/article/economy-policy/india-emerges-as-leading-country-for-flexi-staffing-eco-survey-121012901532_1.html. Accessed on February 24, 2021.

Larson, A (2020). A journey of a thousand miles: An introduction to the digitalization of labour. In A. Larsson, & T. Robin (Eds.), *The digital transformation of labor: Automation, the gig economy and welfare* (pp. 1–13). Routledge.

McKinsey & Company. (2015). A labour market that works: Connecting talent with opportunity in the digital age. https://www.mckinsey.com/~/media/McKinsey/Featured%20Insights/Employment%20and%20Growth/Connecting%20talent%20with%20opportunity%20in%20the%20digital%20age/MGI%20Online%20talent_A_Labor_Market_That_Works_Executive_%20summary_June%202015.pdf. Accessed February 24, 2021.

Melnikov, A. V., & Semenyuk, E. P. (2014). The information revolution and the modern printing industry. *Scientific and Technical Information Processing, 41*(1), 1–11.

Monga, P. (2019). Gig Economy—Shaping the future of Work. In *Invest India: National Investment Promotion & Facilitation Agency*. Available via https://www.investindia.gov.in/team-india-blogs/gig-economy-shaping-future-work. Accessed on February 23, 2021.

Schwab, K., & Davis, N. (2018). *Shaping the future of the fourth industrial revolution: A guide to building a better world*. Penguin.

Stanford, J. (2017). The resurgence of gig work: Historical and theoretical perspectives. *The Economic and Labour Relations Review, 28*(3), 382–401.

Walwei, U. (2016). Digitalization and structural labour market problems. In *The case of Germany*. ILO Research paper No. 17. Available at: https://www.ilo.org/wcmsp5/groups/public/---dgreports/---inst/documents/publication/wcms_522355.pdf. Accessed on February 24, 2021.

Impact of Gig Economy on Unethical Work Practices and Work Culture Adopted by Gig Organizations—Sustainability Concerns for the Future

Komal Kapoor and Alpana Agarwal

1 Introduction

Amalgamation of globalization with technology has created unique and innovative business opportunities for organizations and workforce alike. Among all the business changes and transformations, development of gig economy has been one of the most prominent one. As per Tassinari and Maccarrone (2020), gig economy is referred to the free market system of business working where contractual agreements of working between the organizations and employees are common as major employment is based on independent hiring that is time bound. As the world undergoes structural changes, it has transformed the working practices in existing organizations and even given birth to gig economy-driven organizations like food delivery and taxi aggregators. The term gig may not be an official language word but has its origin from the musician fraternity. In the current scenario, it has come to stand for everything which is temporary, contractual, freelance or even part-time working.

The changing nature of businesses and jobs based on digitization has led to higher demand for flexibility and customer-driven working. Also, the financial pressures on the bottom line of organizations have created many such opportunities where through remote contracting the work can be attained even without long-term contracts with employees. Many industries have seen this change and flux of such gig workers like IT, software, project management, education, content creation, designing, transportation, aggregators, etc. that has created a different kind of HR working in these sectors. As these are freelancers and project driven, there is a lack of the proper safety net for such workers from the HR practices point of view. Many concerns linked to protection of job, long-term security, perks and benefits have been raised on such companies showcasing the dark side of the gig economy (Karmakar & Hammer,

K. Kapoor
IMSUC, Ghaziabad, India

A. Agarwal (✉)
Amity University, Noida, U.P., India

A. Gupta et al. (eds.), *Sustainability in the Gig Economy*,
https://doi.org/10.1007/978-981-16-8406-7_10

2019). The future of such gig workers is uncertain due to many issues like irregular income, lack of insurance, low wages as they are independent workers, poor work life balance, long-term insecurity, environmental impact on job like COVID-19 impact, etc. Due to this concern, the gig workers are exposed to poor HR and work practices along with toxic culture in many of the companies that are reluctant to take the ownership of these employees.

Many such cases linked to Uber in USA, Swiggy in India, construction companies in UK and many other have been criticized for their anti-employees policies and culture that has further raised question on the longevity of this gig culture. It is thus critical to understand the impact such working practices and culture on unethical concerns that are being raised on companies in the gig economy (Agarwal et al, 2019).

2 Impact of Gig Economy on Workforce Management

Businesses today are trying to increase the productivity at minimum cost for sustenance. Unfortunately, when it comes to cost cutting, employees are the softest target. Nevertheless, businesses have adopted an alternate way of cost cutting. Instead of hiring full-time employees, they prefer an alternative arrangement, i.e. hiring people on contract for finishing the task and 'hiring people for finishing the task', which means they are not hiring as employees. Companies prefer somebody to come, finish the task and leave. Such workers are named as 'gig workers/employees'. This arrangement is not only reducing the cost of the employees when not working but also giving them better skilled employees to do the work. However, apart from the immediate benefits of hiring temporary staff, there are some drawbacks as well. Hiring gig workers require human resource management department to meet certain preconditions to accommodate varied requirements of such alternative arrangement. These preconditions involve 'technological infrastructure', 'digital legibility of work', 'mass connectivity', optimal flexibility, special regulatory policies, 'worker power' etc. (Woodcock, 2021). Information from the companies adopting 'gig' option shows following challenges:

1. **Hiring contractual staff also require HR department to address the skill gap**. Present training models do not consider gig workers need. In fact most of the time, they are not at all accessible to them. Although there are platforms like Upworks and Fiverr that provide services to fill such gap (Mukerjee, 2020). But in order to utilize such offered services, HR professionals shall incorporate a gig worker training budget in their strategy. In fact a vital element to enable gig workers acquires relevant skill, and the concept of 'last mile training' would play a significant role. This can be justified by Amazon's recent announcement of spending $700 million for next six years to upskill 100,000 of its low-wage fulfilment centre contractual (Mukerjee, 2020). Addressing the skill gap will ensure expected productivity levels.

2. **Another challenge with gig workers is because of their short stay with the company**. This includes difficulty in encouraging team spirit, leadership and commitment. The HR professionals, who strategize to take leverage by hiring temporary staff, need to do appropriate workforce planning to boost their morale and integrate them in the company's culture (Petersen, 2019). Understanding and cultivating a unique cultural value proposition from the inside out will attract (and keep) the employees that are right for the company.
3. **Much of the gig worker related challenges can be addressed by hiring right people**, which further require HR to be cognizant of the internal gig network or specialized agencies to source them.
4. **HR professional shall also understand that contract work is not suitable for all roles and projects** and therefore consider which specific jobs they need freelancers to perform and make sure the contractors clearly understand what they are expected to deliver (Dyson, 2021).
5. **For leveraging through gig worker, HR department must coordinate with legal teams**. Such coordination is important in order to understand the legal obligations in hiring contractual employees, safeguarding their rights and avoid the hassle of getting into a legal conflict with them. This will also help HR professional in setting some ground rules to avoid events like discrimination (Deloitte, 2016).
6. **Activities involved in hiring temporary staff like sourcing, vetting, contracting also** increases the administrative burden of the HR department. In order to effectively manage the administrative needs, organization shall equip themselves with right technology like artificial intelligence (Dyson, 2021).
7. **Before building any contractual relationship, HR professionals are also required to assess the risks involved and governance related issues in hiring gig workers** (Petersen, 2019).
8. **Difficulty in retaining corporate culture and worker engagement is high with people** staying for a short span with the company. HR needs to develop best practices to develop right skill and attitude towards the task and company's goal (Morley, 2021).
9. **Contractual relationship also requires HR professionals to rethink** on the ways to measure the impact of the hired staff on achievement of business goals. They need to update their appraisal policies to incorporate freelances as well (Visier team, 2020).
10. **Above all, getting task with gig employees also requires the HR department** to incorporate certain modifications in the communication policy. It needs to see the things from their perspective also and encourage transparency to build mutual trust and relationship (Gigonomy, 2020).

3 Regulatory Framework for Workforce Well-Being

This section discusses a comparative analysis on the information and advancements in the law pertaining to gig economy in the USA, Canada, UK, New Zealand, Australia and India.

Considering the rising gig economy in India, the Indian legislature has also introduced draft labour code bill, i.e. the Code on Social Security, 2019 (the 'Code'), to safeguard the rights of gig workers (Pathak & Sahni, 2020) (Table 1).

4 Work Practices and Culture in Gig Economy

Gig work is a non-standard form of employment, available in many forms like temporary, contractual, freelance, independent contractor, platform worker, unorganized worker, etc. The platform sourcing gig employee are termed as 'intermediary' (De Stefano, 2015). Gig form of relationship offers certain benefits but question others. Gig employees are free from many liabilities and obligations because of temporary nature of employment. However, these results in several disadvantages like unstable income, social insecurity, limited power and authority, etc. This section is pointing out work practices prevalent in gig economy. Key unethical practices are also touched.

Legal regulations of most countries are based on the type of employment relationship. And, organizations follow different classification for the gig workers. This complicates the situation and makes it difficult for the gig employee to claim anything. Nevertheless, some organizations have created a new category of employment—termed 'dependent contractors' or 'flexible workers'. The term appraises it as a form of employment which recognizes those workers not considered employees of a company who nonetheless are not fully independent in their choices of when, where, and how to work. Many times the gig employees are excluded from important meetings and discussions significant for them to perform the job (Younger & Smallwood, 2016).

The businesses denying having an employment relationship with the gig worker are eventually denying the responsibility to comply labour laws. Hence, employee's independent workers have limited access to income security protections, such as unemployment insurance, workers' compensation, and disability insurance. Minimum wage, retirement security, and anti-discrimination laws are not applicable for them (Manyika, 2016). The delivery of benefits is another concern in the relationships, wherein contracts promise some benefits. Unlike traditional employees, gig workers do not have the right to form unions and bargain collectively under labour laws in most places.

This is mainly because the gig employees are paid for the job that they do. A significant impact of this is need to be on-call all the time (Mukhopadhyay, 2020). Another potential hurdles include reduced access to credit, the risk of not being paid

Table 1 Comparative analysis of legal advancements in different countries

	USA	Canada	United Kingdom	New Zealand	Australia	India
Employee/worker classification	Employee, worker and independent contractor (Assocham, 2020)	Employee and self-employed individual/independent contractors 'dependent contractors'	Same as that of USA (Assocham, 2020)	Same as that of USA (Assocham, 2020)	'Employees' or 'independent contractors' (Fullbright, 2021)	Gig workers, platform workers and unorganized workers
Regulatory schemes	In September 2019, a bill was passed titled ('AB5') to address the 'employment status' of workers who are called independent contractor instead of employees. It became effective from 1st January, 2020 (Pathak & Sahni, 2020)	The issue of gig workers have been taken up by federal court, and an expert panel on modern federal labour standards has been created in February 2019 to examine the issue of protection related to non-standard workers (Fullbright, 2021)	Courts and tribunals will look into content of the relationship rather any labels that the parties have given to the relationship when interpreting gig workers (Fullbright, 2021)	Employment Relations Act 2000 and Deregulation Assessment of Employment Relations Act (DBA Act)	The Fair Work Act 2009, the Independent Contractors Act 2006, Competition and Consumer Act 2010, Australian Competition and Consumer Commission 2016	Employees' Provident Fund Act, 1952, the Maternity Benefit Act, 1961, and the Unorganized Workers' Social Security Act, 2008 (Pathak & Sahni, 2020). The Social Security Code 2019, (Pathak & Sahni, 2020)

(continued)

Table 1 (continued)

	USA	Canada	United Kingdom	New Zealand	Australia	India
Entitled benefits		Dependent contractors have the right to unionize under labour laws in the same way employees do. Some also enjoy entitlements upon termination as well	'Establishing the nature of the employment relationship will determine the employment rights to which an individual is entitled' (Fullbright, 2021)	NA	Contractor is not provided with the same entitlements and does not have the right to make the same claims as an employee post assignment (Fullbright, 2021)	'Social security schemes like employees' provident fund scheme, an employees' pension scheme, and an employees' deposit linked insurance scheme, life and disability cover'
Weak area	The bill has been challenged on grounds of 'violation of equal protection', the bill seeks to classify few of the 'independent contractors' as employees thereby reducing their present freedom and flexibility (Pathak & Sahni, 2020)	Lack of guidance from lawmakers. No new law to be framed in near future (Fullbright, 2021)	Status is unambiguous The traditional laws are incompatible with the new changing work environment. Brexit has added to this confusion as it is not clear whether the laws will be amended to give the works rights and privileges of the EU workers (Fullbright, 2021)	NA	The status of gig worker is lucid. Cross border and geographical location is adding weight to this ambiguity (Stewart & Stanford, 2017)	Absence of government database for tracking the beneficiaries of social security measure

(continued)

Table 1 (continued)

	USA	Canada	United Kingdom	New Zealand	Australia	India
Popular cases	Uber and Lyft	NA	The Uber case	LSG Sky Chefs	'Joshua Klooger versus Foodora Australia Pty Ltd'	'Ram Singh and Ors.versus Union Territory, Chandigarh and Ors 2004'

Source Author's

for work that is already performed, and complex tax filing, licencing, and regulatory compliance requirements (Manyika, 2016).

Nevertheless hiring trend for independent contractors is unlike. They cannot negotiate the compensation in most cases. They can only electronically accept the platform's terms in order to get the project (Tran et al., 2017). However, because of increasing demand of gig employees these days, there is healthy competition for this workers. Also, though most gig accepts a project by choice they can be fired for any reason. Aloisi (2016) notes, 'uncertainty and insecurity are the price for extreme flexibility'. Since gig workers do not have a contract, they are left with no choice letting it go (Weil, 2014).

Another concern with gig employees is the unanticipated health and safety risks. This is because of improper training; in fact many times gig workers continue doing the job in absence of training due to fear of job loss (Foley et al, 2014). The quality of work may also get compromised in such situation (Mukhopadhyay, 2020).

As the independent workforce is growing, there has been a pressure to offer benefits comparable to conventional employees, separate policies to use these benefits.

5 Gig Economy Organizations: Select Examples

The transformations taking place around the globe are fuelling the growth of gig workers but not towards safeguarding of the rights of gig workers. As the work is contractual in nature, many issues pertaining to pay, over time wages, perks, benefits, security and safety of work, flexibility in work are missing leading to many unethical cases being filed against the top gig recruiters. Lawsuits filed against big companies like Uber, Lyft, Deliveroo, and Amazon for their bad HR practices and non-worker orientation (Ethical Unicorn, 2019). The gig economy has helped semi and unskilled people become employable but have also raised doubts on the long-term stability of such gig economy companies.

1. **Uber and Lyft lawsuit**: The workers employed by the two companies filed a lawsuit against the companies as they were classified as independent contractual workers not covered under the rules for the permanent employees. This created much job problems during the pandemic caused by COVID-19 as the source of income dried up and the workers were not covered under the employment policies like the other regular workers. The lawsuit enforced the companies to term them as employees and not as contractual workers while safeguarding the interest of the workers. With the transformation in the digital economy, many such organizations have been benefitted through the sharing economy and have given employment to large pool of employees but not with the same kind of security and benefits (The Guardian, 2020). The app-based collaborative economy working of companies like the ride sharing ones have continuously been questioned on their practices in the court of law. The gig economy

may also be considered similar to zero hour contracts as both of them do not provide guarantee of minimum pay or working hours or any kind of job security. The difference comes when zero hour contracts are technically considered as employees and they are eligible for holiday pay, however neither is entitled to sick pay (CNBC, 2020). Even when a large pool of workers are self-employed in such companies, in percentage wise around 15% of the workforce in USA falls in this category. Looking further afield, in 2017, the gig economy in the USA was estimated to have around 34% of the workforce that was expected to increase to 43% in 2020 when the pandemic hit the world. Even as per Harvard Business Review, 150 million workers in North America and Western Europe would be in the category of independent contractors that is very risky for a stable future. A five-year long running case between Uber and its drivers for the right nomenclature of self-employed workers (Business Human Rights, 2020a; b). The company has been appealing in many of the UK courts to overturn the verdict given by the judges so that there is no obligation to give the minimum wages to the workers as that would put a burden on the company.

2. **Deliveroo Pay Issues**: In many of the countries, food delivery App Company has been questioned on its pay structure for the workers and working conditions. The workers of Deliveroo called for a strike to protest against the reduction in the pay structure per delivery as well as demand for improving working condition in England as they did not agree with the same. The new payment system reduced their payment of £7 for each delivery to £3.75 for each delivery (Black, 2020). The striking workers have also protested for the government intervention as to develop some practices against these dodgy employment practices that has further reduced the stability and security of jobs.
3. **Uber Eats and Foodora in France**: The workers and delivery agents protested strike and concerns during the World Cup to raise the concerns on pay structure and reduced wages and also the demeaning working conditions. The Independent Deliverymen's Collective in Paris has portrayed itself as the body standing for the human rights of the delivery agents. Strike was to protest against what it deems to be dangerous working conditions, an aggressive recruitment strategy, a rise in the number of available workers, which has depressed wages, and other concerns. Workers for delivery platforms Stuart and Glovo also participated leading to complete pause or orders and deliveries during a very high peak demand of World Cup week (SHRM, 2020).
4. **Swiggy workers on strike in India**: Online food delivery app Swiggy witnessed strike by its nearly 300 delivery executives over the issue of reduction in their payments. This was preceded by two more strikes in the same week in which workers did not receive the order nor they went to deliver at customers' doorstep.
5. **OLA and Uber taxi drivers**: These taxi drivers are unsatisfied with the commissions charged by the companies. They are also demanding hire in fare as well as relaxation in paying monthly instalment of their vehicles. They are also expecting rollback of e-challans (DeBruyne, 2017).

6 Conclusions and Managerial Implications

After the great crisis of 2008–09 that forced many semi and unskilled labour out of job, the gig working opportunities provided these workers with a source of income. This clubbed with the disruption in technology lead to emergence of technology-driven companies like Uber, AirBnB, Amazon, Deliveroo and many such aggregators that provided easy and quick restart of the working life. With limited professional knowledge needed for performing the task, an easy absorbing HR strategy adopted by these tech giants gave employment to millions of workers leading to build up of daily source of income. This came to be known as the gig economy with gig workers and gig working practices. Few initial years witnessed tremendous growth for these gig companies either in the business of ride sharing or even food delivery apps. This created a good pay structure and incentives for the workers but still these companies have been questioned for their HR practices of not treating these workers as permanent employees and giving them the desired benefits. Gradually, this problem of poor income levels, stature of being an independent worker, lack of sick and other leaves, security and medical coverage brought to light many such poor working practices adopted by these companies.

This further led to many protests and strikes by the drivers and the delivery agents that were filed in the form of lawsuits in the courts of UK and USA. The same was witnessed in Asian nations also as the poor working practices and toxic culture played its role in creating this uproar. Most of the concerns raised lead to identification of the work practices that is adopted by such companies and what kind of managerial implications it has for the future of gig economy. As gig word has been there for very long in the form of musicians, freelance writers, contractual labour, etc., the real meaning came to front only after the tech-based companies started their businesses. This leads to jobs for such drivers, delivery agents who could make a living out of it. But the HR implication for the same is that these cannot be neglected as contractual labour that needs no security and safety net. As they have not been counted as full-time employees, they have faced many corrupt and unethical HR practices leading to instability in the way work was done.

7 Future Research Opportunities

Gig economy and gig working are here to stay and would further see an upswing in the number of companies joining the gig economy and also the number of people who are employed in these sectors. As the economies move more towards digitalization and technology based working, it has become pertinent for all the stakeholders like companies, workers, government, regulatory bodies, etc. Currently, the study is limited and only focussed on the problems of pay structure, wages, overtime pay, leaves, and compensation issues, but over time, these concerns with respect to HR practices that are directed towards the workers. The future may also witness more unethical practices linked to job security and benefits being provided to these contractual workers as more companies are preferring this route of undertaking the business. The number of studies on the dark side of gig economy and its sustainability in the future are limited and hence require a more in-depth research to be taken that can act as the benchmark for the future. With respect to working procedures, work practices, culture building, HR policies, and practices for workers who may be contractual but work like full time and many long-term benefits that are given to full-time employees. Researchers need to understand the main ecosystem of the gig economy and on the basis of which it works so that the main internal and human resource issues can be sorted. The current chapter has covered limited aspect of work practices and pay systems that have been termed as unethical for such companies. But this gig economy culture and the future scope of creating such practices that are specific to this kind of working require more research to be undertaken.

Detailed studies and empirical studies can be undertaken on the recruitment and selection methods adopted for gig workers, methods of induction and training given so as to develop the sense of ownership among the contractual workers, developing the right mix of benefits and relaxations that should be offered to them, appraisal methods to compensate for the loss of long-term benefits and growth opportunities. These need to be taken up both for conceptual and empirical studies so that a linear relationship can be created for gig economy working that can pave the way for future development of strategies. Each change and transformation in the world build up the path to undertake new research that is needed to build upon future academic output. Concerns about the unethical practices have highlighted the dark side of the gig economy putting a question mark on the sustainability concerns of this kind of working. Over the years, as more companies have entered the gig working, it has become relevant for the researchers to consider each company as one case study whether it is Amazon, Uber, Lyft, or Deliveroo as the business model and the sector differ significantly. This would further help in delving deep into the issues pertaining to each company, business, leadership, questions raised, lawsuit filed, HR practices, etc. that can build upon premises for further studies to be undertaken.

References

Agarwal, S., Mani, D., & Telang, R. (2019). The impact of ride-hailing services on congestion: Evidence from Indian cities. *Indian School of Business.*

Aloisi, A. (2016). Commoditized workers. Case study research on labour law issues arising from a set of 'On-Demand/Gig Economy' platforms. *Comp Labor Law Policy J* 37:38.

Assocham. (2020, January 24). *Proceedings of national conference on gig economy*. Retrieved on January 26, 2021, from https://www.assocham.org/userfiles/GIG%20REPORT_2020.pdf

Business Human Rights. (2020). Deliveroo riders strike. Retrieved on February 4, 2021, from https://www.business-humanrights.org/en/latest-news/uk-deliveroo-riders-strike-over-changes-in-pay-structure-working-conditions-includes-comments-from-deliveroo/

Business Human Rights. (2020). Uber loses the appeal against the ruling. Retrieved on February 6, 2021, from: https://www.business-humanrights.org/en/latest-news/uk-uber-loses-appeal-against-ruling-that-its-drivers-are-workers-with-minimum-wage-rights/

Chen, M. K., Rossi, P. E., Chevalier, J. A., & Oehlsen, E. (2019). The value of flexible work: Evidence from uber drivers. *Journal of Political Economy, 127*(6), 2735–2794.

CNBC. (2020). Uber and Lyft lose appeal in cases to reclassify workers. Retrieved on February 6, 2021, from https://www.cnbc.com/2020/10/22/uber-and-lyft-lose-appeal-in-case-to-reclassify-workers.html

Crank, A. L. (2015). O'Connor v. Uber Technologies, Inc.: The dispute lingers-are workers in the on-demand economy employees or independent contractors. *American Journal Trial Advocate, 39*, 609.

De Stefano, V. (2015). Non-standard workers and freedom of association: a critical analysis of restrictions to collective rights from a human rights perspective, working papers del Centro Studi di Diritto del LavoroEuropeo Massimo D'Antona. INT—123/2015.

DeBruyne, N. L. (2017). Uber drivers: A disputed employment relationship in light of the sharing economy. *The Chicago-Kent Law Review, 92*, 289.

Deloitte. (2016). The future of workforce: Critical drivers and challenges, Deloitte Report. Retrieved on March 15, 2020, from https://www2.deloitte.com/content/dam/Deloitte/global/Documents/HumanCapital/gx-hc-future-workforce.pdfon

Dyson, E. (2021) A look into the gig economy, People Scout. Retrieved on March 15, 2020, from https://www.peoplescout.com/insights/gig-economy-effect-on-hiring-talent/on

Ethical Unicorn. (2019). What is gig economy is it hurting workers. Retrieved February 8, 2021, from https://ethicalunicorn.com/2019/05/26/what-is-the-gig-economy-is-it-hurting-workers/

Foley, M., Ruser, J., Shor, G., Shuford, H., & Sygnatur, E. (2014). Contingent workers: Workers' compensation data analysis strategies and limitations. *American Journal of Industrial Medicine, 57*, 764–775.

France 24. (2016). Deliveroo cyclists boycott work on pay dispute. Retrieved on February 6, 2021, from: https://www.france24.com/en/20190808-deliveroo-cyclists-freelancers-strike-boycott-pay-dispute-delivery

Fulbright, N. R. (2021). Worldwide: Doing business in the gig economy: A global guide for employers. https://www.mondaq.com/canada/employee-benefits-compensation/1026496/doing-business-in-the-gig-economy-a-global-guide-for-employers

In the Black. (2020). Protecting the workers in gig economy. Retrieved on February 5, 2021, from: https://www.intheblack.com/articles/2020/10/01/protecting-workers-gig-economy

Karmakar, S., & Hammer, A. (2019). Work and employment in the times of automation 12 and artificial intelligence: The Indian case. *The Political Economy of Work in the Global South*, 241.

Manyika, J., Lund, S., Bughin, J., Robinson, K., Mischke, J., & Mahajan, D. (2016). Independent work: Choice, necessity, and the gig economy, McKinsey Global Institute Report. Retrieved on March 15, 2020, from https://www.mckinsey.com/~/media/mckinsey/featured%20insights/employment%20and%20growth/independent%20work%20choice%20necessity%20and%20the%20gig%20economy/independent-work-choice-necessity-and-the-gig-economy-executive-summary.ashx

Meenakshi, N., & Sinha, A. (2019). Food delivery apps in India: Wherein lies the success strategy? *Strategic Direction.*

Mehta, B. S., & Kumar, A. Future of work: The emerging gig economy. *Journal of Development Policy Review, 1*(1), 10–16.

Morley, I. (2021). How the gig economy is impacting the corporate workplace, serraview. https://serraview.com/gig-economy-impacting-corporate-workplace/

Mukerjee, D. (2020). How the advent of the gig economy is reshaping the future of HR, People Matters. Retrieved on Mach 25, 2020, from http://www.peoplematters.in/article/strategic-hr/how-the-advent-of-the-gig-economy-is-reshaping-the-future-of-hr-24543

Mukhopadhyay, B. K. (2020, August 19), What's your workplace culture in gig economy? The Sentinel. https://www.sentinelassam.com/editorial/smoking-is-injurious-to-health-523701?infinitescroll=1

N.d. (2020). Workforce management in the gig economy, Gigonomy. https://gigonomy.info/workforce-management-in-the-gig-economy/

Pathak, M., & Sahni, N. (2020) India: Gig economy—Legal development. Retrieved on February 12, 2020, from https://www.mondaq.com/india/employment-and-workforce-wellbeing/955662/gig-economy-legal-developmentson

Petersen, G. (2019). HR leaders—Are you at peace with the gig economy? HR trends. Retrieved on January 20, 2020, from https://www.ajoconnor.com/blog/gig-economy

Poon, T. S. C. (2019). Independent workers: Growth trends, categories, and employee relations implications in the emerging gig economy. *Employee Responsibilities and Rights Journal, 31*(1), 63–69.

SHRM. (2020). What unethical practices are present in gig working. Retrieved on February 5, 2021, from https://www.shrm.org/resourcesandtools/hr-topics/technology/pages/what-are-employers-ethical-obligations-to-gig-workers.aspx

Stewart, A., & Stanford, J. (2017). Regulating work in the gig economy: What are the options? *Economic and Labour Relations Review, 28*(3), 382–401.

Surie, A. (2018). Are Ola and Uber drivers entrepreneurs or exploited workers. *Economic and Political Weekly, 53*(24), 1–7.

Tassinari, A., & Maccarrone, V. (2020). Riders on the storm: Workplace solidarity among gig economy couriers in Italy and the UK. *Work, Employment and Society, 34*(1), 35–54.

The Guardian. (2016). Deliveroo workers strike again. Retrieved on February 5, 2021, from https://www.theguardian.com/business/2016/aug/15/deliveroo-workers-strike-again-over-new-pay-structure

The Guardian. (2020). Uber drivers fight for workers rights. Retrieved on February 7, 2021, from https://www.theguardian.com/technology/2020/jul/21/uber-drivers-fight-for-workers-rights-reaches-supreme-court

Tran M., & Sokas R. K. (2017, April). The gig economy and contingent work. *Journal of Occupational and Environmental Medicine, 59*(4), e63–e66

Visier team. (2020). Gig work transforms hourly work, HR Trends 2020 report. https://www.visier.com/clarity/how-gig-economy-will-impact-hr-in-2020-and-beyond/

Weil, D. (2014). *The fissured workplace: Why work became so bad for so many and what can be done to improve it*. Harvard University Press.

Woodcock, J. (2021). The impact of the gig economy, Open Mind BBVA. https://www.bbvaopenmind.com/en/articles/the-impact-of-the-gig-economy/

Younger, J., & Smallwood, N. (2016). Performance management in the gig economy, Harvard Business Review. https://hbr.org/2016/01/performance-management-in-the-gig-economy

The Open Manufacturer. How Industry 4.0, Open-Source, and the Gig and Sharing Economy Shape the Post-COVID Manufacturer?

Harinderpal Hanspal

1 Introduction

COVID-19 brought business to a standstill (Okorie, et al., 2020) for many manufacturers. In a survey (NAM, 2020), more than half anticipated a change in their operations, and over one-third were facing supply chain disruptions. COVID amplified problems across their entire business operations due to shelter-in-place orders and social distancing guidelines:

- **Designing and Building Products**. Closure of laboratories, workshops, and maker spaces halted researchers' and engineers' ability to work as they needed physical access to equipment and tools to perform their jobs.
- **Finding and Keeping Customers**. Social distancing and customers' refusal to allow visitors into facilities made it difficult for sales to meet with customers and for field technicians to install and service equipment. Where customers allowed visitors, there were strict policies to keep the technicians and customers safe.
- **Managing Ecosystem**. International travel bans, delays in cross-border traffic, and lack of air or ocean freight capacity created shortages of raw materials, components, finished products, and spare parts. (Buxbaum, 2020) With suppliers shutting down due to COVID, there was no visibility for manufacturers into the availability of goods, forcing manufacturers to look for alternative suppliers.
- **Accessing Talent and Skills**. Unemployment in manufacturing spiked to historically high levels as manufacturers shut down their businesses for quarantine. (Sleger, 2020) Essential manufacturing businesses that remained open had to address employee concerns around safety and employee well-being, many of whom the pandemic impacted materially (CDC, 2021).
- **Controlling Revenue and Costs**. Eight out of ten manufacturers expected financial losses from COVID's abrupt and massive disruptions (NAM, 2020).

H. Hanspal (✉)
Thing Company LLC, Mercer Island, WA 98040, USA
e-mail: hans@thing.company

A. Gupta et al. (eds.), *Sustainability in the Gig Economy*,
https://doi.org/10.1007/978-981-16-8406-7_11

As guidelines for opening manufacturing plants safely came out (CDC, 2021), manufacturing companies repurposed their production lines to pivot their businesses to high-demand products such as respirators, respirator parts, medical PPE, and hand sanitizers (Okorie et al., 2020). Pivoting, where companies shift their business models to entirely new product lines, sales channels, suppliers, or customer segments, is commonplace in the technology start-up community. Manufacturers that successfully pivoted identified three key areas that enabled them to pivot (Okorie et al., 2020):

- **Rapid decision making and organizational flexibility**. Pivoting the entire business needed quick decision making and organization flexibility for actions such as setting up work from home capabilities, redesigning office and manufacturing spaces, and expanding sourcing partners.
- **Employee skills and know-how**. With reduced capacity and staffing levels, employees needed to wear many hats, requiring diverse skill sets.
- **Digital technological ability and capacity**. Firms with a high digitization level were more technically adaptable and resilient than manufacturers with lower digital adoption in pivoting.

A recent Global Risks Report (WEF, 2021) has identified environmental issues—extreme weather, natural disasters, and climate action failure—as the highest risks, both in terms of the events' likelihood and global impact. In recent years, manufacturers have seen an increase in the number and frequency of supply chain disruptions due to trade wars, epidemics, and material shortages.

With COVID-19 taking hold of the world in 2020 and the continued risk of future disruptions (Ma, 2020), manufacturers are looking to reshore production, change training and hiring practices, and invest in digital technologies.

This paper examines the following:

- The business and operational challenges faced by manufacturers,
- Business models and technology from digital consumer and software industries are helping address these challenges, and
- How these echnologies and business models enable an "Open Manufacturer" that is lean, flexible, productive, and resilient.

2 Life of a Manufacturer

As the pace of consumer and business technology innovation increases, so do buyer expectations of finished products targeting consumer, business, and industrial markets. In the digital age, buyers, armed with smartphones and the Internet, can access products, services, and experiences anywhere, anytime, and on demand (WEF, 2021). They expect all physical products to have the same experience as their smartphone—seamless, from purchase to ownership and disposal. (Thales Group, n.d.). It does not matter whether the buyer is a business or a consumer; both expect similar capabilities (Gandhi et al., 2019). This behavior change applies to buyers in developing and developed markets around the globe. (WEF, 2021).

With the shift in buyer expectations combined with the increased risk of future disruptions, manufacturers must rethink their business and operating models while investing in new products and customer experiences that are engaging. In making this shift, they will need to consider the complexity of existing manufacturing value chains and challenges as follows:

- **Majority Small–Mid-sized Firms**. The vast majority of manufacturers in most countries are small–mid-sized enterprises. In the USA, for example, ninety-eight percent of manufacturers have five hundred employees or less, while seventy-five percent firms have fewer than twenty employees. (NAM, n.d.)
- **Outsourced Production**. Increasingly production is outsourced to contract manufacturers as manufacturers focus on product innovation and customer experience to align with buyer needs and expectations.
- **Offshore Production**. Only a few countries can cost efficiently manufacture high-volume products assembled with significant manual labor. Half of the USA and European hardware start-ups, for example, manufacture in China (Romand-Monnier, 2019)
- **Global Supply Chains**. Vertical integration, where the manufacturer makes most of the components and sub-assemblies needed for the finished product, is difficult and expensive due to the highly specialized skills and technologies needed for modern products. (Shih, 2020) As product complexity increases (Porter & Heppelmann, 2014), so does the manufacturer's third-party supplier network of specialists, which frequently crisscrosses the globe (Apple Inc, 2019) and is multi-tiered (Celo et al., 2018).
- **Hiring and Training Talent**. There is an increasing need for digital skills in advanced technologies and automation as manufacturers shift to adopting digital technologies. (Deloitte, 2018) An aging workforce, declining birth rates, lack of vocational education and apprenticeships, and manufacturing perceptions as a "dirty and dangerous" career have led to fewer younger workers entering the manufacturing profession. (Manufacturing Institute, 2019) Over two million manufacturing positions will be unfilled in the USA due to a lack of skilled talent by 2028, a potential impact of $2.5 trillion on the manufacturing GDP.
- **Reshoring Costs**. Manufacturers and their suppliers must add and update production capacity and infrastructure, outfitting factories and warehouses with state-of-the-art automation equipment. A single factory can cost hundreds of millions or more to build (Yu & Plume, 2019). Manufacturers also need access to maker spaces, laboratories, fabrication machines, robots, assembly tools, warehouses, logistics infrastructure, and more. The CAPEX cost to reshore the world's supply chains is estimated to be $1 trillion over five years to shift all foreign manufacturing in China, not consumed domestically in China. (Bank of America Securities, 2020)
- **Digital Laggards**. Industry 4.0 technologies such as the IoT, artificial intelligence, cloud computing, robotics, computer vision, and 3D printing are changing how companies design, build, sell, distribute, and service their manufactured products. However, the manufacturing industry is behind many other industries in adopting digital and automation technologies, with only twenty percent claiming to be

"prepared" to address digital technologies' opportunities. (Wellener et al., 2018) Although there are many examples of Industry 4.0 technologies in use creating value (Betti & Boer, 2020), the reality is that success is limited to a small number of industry leaders (Prising et al., 2018).

Whether they are manufacturing a pharmaceutical drug or an airplane, manufacturers must meet buyer expectations by turning raw materials and components into finished products that can be distributed and sold through direct and indirect channels. To become profitable, they must improve output, productivity, and costs in innovating, producing, marketing, and servicing their products. (WEF, 2021) They have learned from their COVID experience that they need new tools and business models to pivot quickly.

3 Lessons from the Technology Industry

Technology companies, from start-ups to enterprises, have overcome many of the same resource constraints as manufacturers by use of new tools and business models, allowing companies to build more innovative products and to pivot quickly and efficiently as business conditions change:

- **Gig Economy**. Freelance marketplaces give technology companies on-demand access to a global talent pool of skilled "gig" workers—from user interface designers and software developers to product managers and documentation writers.
- **Sharing Economy**. Cloud services provide technology companies on-demand access to expensive compute, storage, and network assets by sharing access to these resources. Idle capacity on the assets is "shared," on demand with others.
- **Digital Technologies**. A World Economic Forum report on the GDP impact of investing in digital technologies showed that GDP increased by twenty dollars for every US dollar invested. It is estimated that twenty-four percent of global GDP will come from Industry 4.0 technologies by 2025. (Prising et al., 2018)
- **Open-Source Models**. A security scan of commercial software code found that over ninety percent of them had an average of 257 open-source components and rapidly growing (Zorz, 2018). Technology companies cite (Blind et al., 2020) many benefits from open source, including open standards and interoperability, independence from proprietary providers, access to source code, active community, and cost savings, and improved developer productivity. Adopting open-source software and hardware could translate into €95 billion per year to the E.U.'s GDP (Blind et al., 2020) while having three times the impact on innovation than companies using proprietary technologies (Srivastava et al., 2020).

3.1 Gig Economy

Uber and Lyft connect passengers who need to travel between locations with drivers who will drive them there. TaskRabbit connects homeowners, among others, to people who can help them with handy work around the house. Fiverr connects businesses to graphics designers, content writers, and marketing experts who can help them design logos, create blogs, and manage their social media marketing. Turing connects companies with remote software developers.

The driver, handyman, designer, writer, marketer, and developer are examples of "Gig" workers with specialized skills. Pay for gig workers is by the hour, day, unit of time, task (or microtask), or project on a short-term or long-term basis. This model provides on-demand talent with specialized skills and knowledge for the passengers, homeowners, families, and businesses. Uber, Lyft, TaskRabbit, Fiverr, and Turing act as gig economy platforms, helping connect the two or more groups and facilitating payments between them through online and mobile apps. Together, the gig workers, the talent seekers, and platforms make up the gig economy.

The gig economy provides one mechanism for manufacturers to address the skills gap at all levels to meet their needs. Manufacturers can tap into a global talent pool with the gig economy model, on demand, for partial or whole projects. Experts from industrial designers and fabrication specialists to digital marketing and field service representatives, paid for by the hour or fix-fee project for a short or long period. (Wilgus, 2018) Examples of gig economy platforms that help manufacturers to connect on demand to the right talent include

- **Designers**. GrabCAD connects manufacturers with one of the largest communities of professional designers, engineers, manufacturers, and students. (GrabCAD, 2021)
- **Field Service**. Workrise connects manufacturers to skilled workers across solar, wind, construction, defense, and oil and gas industries. (Workrise, 2021)
- **Mobile Service**. Wrench connects car owners with mechanics for mobile auto repairs and maintenance. (Wrench, n.d.)
- **Delivery, Collections, and Payments**. Mimo Technologies connects companies in India to local agents, available on demand for last-mile delivery of products, invoice collections, and payments. (Mimo Technologies, n.d.) TraqIQ, MIMO's parent company, helps companies set up similar "gig economy" networks for public and private institutions. (TraqIQ, 2021)

3.2 Sharing Economy

Airbnb enables homeowners to rent out their unused bedrooms or whole homes directly and on demand to temporary visitors. Turo allows car owners to rent out their cars when not in use directly to others on demand. WeWork shares office space, from a single desk to whole offices, with individuals and businesses. Amazon Web

Services started by sharing Amazon.Com's spare compute, storage, and networking capacity with software developers. The renters, developers, asset owners, shared assets, and platforms that enable the transactions are the sharing economy.

In the sharing economy, idle capacity on physical assets owned by individuals or businesses is "shared," on demand with others who need access to the physical asset. Access can be for a short or long period, depending on the asset's available idle capacity, paid for by subscription, pay-per-usage of the asset, or pay-per-outcome delivered by the asset. Online marketplaces and mobile applications, frequently operated by third parties, connect users to the asset owners. Like the gig economy, users can locate, book, and pay for the asset from the marketplace or app. Upgrading, maintaining, and operating the shared assets are the asset owner's responsibility, freeing the users to focus on their customers, products, and business. Economies of scale give shared asset owners and sharing economy platforms a considerable cost advantage and are among the main reasons for their success. (Osztovits et al., 2015).

For manufacturers, many of whom are small and mid-sized enterprises. (NAM, n.d.), the sharing economy model can provide on-demand shared access to expensive resources paid for by subscription, usage, or outcome. Examples of shared equipment and spaces for manufacturers include the following:

- **Shared Workshops**. Designers and engineers can join "Maker Spaces," paid monthly, where they have access to a shared physical space with the equipment and tools they need to design and engineer.
- **Shared Trucks**. Shippers can connect to freight carriers' networks to locate them, book a partial or full truck, pay for the shipment, and monitor their freight from a single platform.
- **Shared Robots**. Robots can be expensive to buy, maintain, repair, and upgrade. Manufacturers can add robots to their toolset, on demand for as long as they need, and paid for by the use. Robots are upgraded, maintained, and repaired by the company providing the robots.
- **Shared Factories**. Manufacturers can locate, select, submit, and pay fabrication and assembly jobs using manufacturing shared economy platforms. Products can be fabricated using various materials and fabrication methods.
- **Shared Logistics**. Finished products do not need to sit in manufacturer warehouses. Retailers have existing infrastructure for storing, picking, packing, shipping, and providing customer service for finished products. For a fee, retailers now share that infrastructure with manufacturers.

3.3 Digital (Industry 4.0) Technology

Since the late eighteenth century, we have seen three significant industrial revolutions and are in the midst of the Fourth Industrial Revolution (Tay et al., 2018). Each industrial revolution has led to substantial improvements in productivity, efficiency, production techniques, and business processes:

- **First Industrial Revolution**: the shift from our reliance on animals, human effort, and biomass as primary energy sources to using water and steam as energy sources for mechanized tools and equipment.
- **Second Industrial Revolution**: shift to electricity, gas, and oil as sources of energy, leading to creating the mass production assembly line.
- **Third Industrial Revolution**: shift to the increased usage of computerized systems to automate production and business processes.
- **Fourth Industrial Revolution**: Also known as Industry 4.0, this shift optimizes existing computer systems and automation tasks using technologies such as the Internet of Things, artificial intelligence (AI), cloud computing, big data, robotics, and 3D printing to build autonomous products and business operations.

The Fourth Industrial Revolution places great importance on a decentralized approach with independent management of processes and objects in the network. (Erboz, 2017) Industry 4.0 technologies enable innovation, industrial, and commercial processes to be more efficient, flexible, and productive (Tay et al., 2018). Robotics, for example, has the most significant impact in asset-heavy industries, while IoT, AI, and big data analytics have the most impact on asset-light industries. (Prising et al., 2018).

Industry 4.0 technologies have been available for several years and continue to develop and advance quickly. There are several examples of how one or more of these technologies deliver outcomes for manufacturers:

- **Autonomous Products**. PACCAR, a manufacturer of the Peterbilt and Kenworth heavy-duty trucks, uses IoT, cloud, and AI to build self-driving trucks to improve safety and freight efficiency for its customers (PACCAR, 2021).
- **Custom Products**. Ford Motor Company uses 3D printing for several production polymer parts: Ford Focus HVAC Lever Arm, Ford Raptor Auxiliary Plugs, and Ford Mustang GT500 Electric parking brake brackets (Carbon, 2019).
- **Product Quality and Capability**. G.E.'s GE9X engines for the Boeing 777X include 300 3D printed parts, including titanium aluminide blades and fuel nozzles (GE, 2020).
- **Collaborative Design**. 3D printer manufacturer, FormLabs, uses a cloud-based computer-aided design (CAD) tool to allow product designers and engineers to connect, collaborate, and design products online from anywhere. It also allows them to connect and share their designs with their third-party suppliers and contract manufacturers in real time (Onshape, 2020).
- **Digital Marketplaces**. There are several digital marketplaces available for users to buy and download CAD models. Sellers of the CAD models can be individuals or businesses. CAD models available for purchase include prosthetic limbs, surgical instruments, homes, supplier-certified parts, electronics, and more. For finished products, sellers can list their products on various e-commerce marketplaces, including Amazon, eBay, and Alibaba.

- **Engineering Simulation.** Volkswagen Motorsport uses engineering simulation software that leverages big data, cloud, IoT, digital twins, and AI to investigate component and system-level performance, safety, and cost of thermal management of electric vehicle batteries (Ansys, 2019).
- **Production Automation.** Flex is deploying "micro-factories" built with robotics, computer vision, and AI to eliminate manual labor on their production line. The machines automate repetitive assembly and inspection tasks such as assembly, fastening, pressing, and labeling (Bright Machines, 2020),
- **Supply Chain and Logistics.** Rwanda and Ghana's governments use an autonomous drone service to deliver medical supplies to thousands of health facilities, many of which are remote (IoT Hub Meetup, 2020).
- **Employee Training, Sales, and Service.** Augmented reality, combined with IoT, is changing how products are manufactured, serviced, and sold. Rockwell automation is using A.R. to train employees to wire effectively (PTC, 2021). BID group uses A.R. to improve communications during service calls to provide technicians with accurate and precise service and repair instructions (PTC, n.d.). The automotive manufacturer INFINITI uses A.R. to create an in-store sales experience for customers (PTC, 2021).

3.4 Open-Source Industry 4.0

Apple's first commercial phone, the iPhone running its proprietary iOS, was launched in June 2007. The first commercial Android-based smartphone was launched in October 2008. Android is an open-source and freely available mobile operating system. Anyone looking to build a smartphone can download the source code, modify it, and distribute it as part of their phone. Android beat out then leaders Symbian and Blackberry O.S., both proprietary mobile operating systems, to become the leader three years later. Symbian was discontinued in 2013, while Blackberry replaced Blackberry O.S. with Android in 2015. Today, Android-based smartphones represent more than eighty percent share of the smartphone market and likely to maintain that lead in the future. (Statista, 2021)The market share for Apple's proprietary operating system, iOS, has hovered between 14 and 21%. An open-source mobile operating system had gone from nothing to dominating the smartphone industry in less than a decade while driving rapid innovation in the smartphone market.

Manufacturers have to invest in hardware and software technologies to improve their products and business and customer operations. They can choose to build it themselves, source proprietary technology from a vendor, or join an open-source community to build it with others who also require the technology. Several open-source communities and non-profit foundations already create Industry 4.0 open-source hardware and software for manufacturers, allowing manufacturers to enjoy the same benefits from open-source adoption as technology companies.

As with the Android community, several open-source communities and non-profit foundations are focused on jointly building open-source hardware and software for

Industry 4.0, including Arduino, The Linux Foundation, The Eclipse Foundation, and Open Robotics. Examples of open-source projects to support Industry 4.0 include the following:

- **Arduino** is an open-source hardware and software platform that provides building blocks for "smart" hardware products (Teja, 2021).
- **Robotics Operating Systems** (ROS) and **ROS Industrial** are open-source operating systems to control and manage robots, drones, and other autonomous vehicles and devices (ROS Industrial, 2021).
- **Linux Foundation's EdgeX Foundry** provides the building blocks for "smart" products to collect, send, and receive data (LF Edge, 2021).
- **Eclipse Ditto** is an open-source framework for creating digital twins. Digital twins are virtual representations of physical objects (Eclipse IoT, 2021).
- Several open-source **3D printer** designs are available to download for building 3D printers. Each design comes with CAD drawings, bill of materials, "how-to" instructions, firmware and software, contributed by community members (Bhavnagarwala, 2020).

4 Open Manufacturing: The Future of Manufacturing

As COVID-19 cases increased, patients inundated hospitals in every country, overwhelming hospital systems. It became clear that there was a dire need for respirators to help patients with their breathing and personal protective equipment (PPE) for frontline doctors and nurses. The World Health Organization estimated that 89 million medical masks, 76 million examination gloves, and 1.6 million medical goggles would be required for the COVID-19 response each month. It would take time for manufacturers of respirators and PPE to ramp up manufacturing and distribute PPE to every country. It did not help that only a handful of countries produce the vast majority of PPE, with China accounting for half the masks' global supply. With each country dealing with the pandemic, many banned exports of PPE, limiting the supply in countries that depend on importing PPE. Quarantine in each country also limited PPE production due to staff shortages, impacting shipping and logistics. The global PPE supply chain had ground to a halt (Park et al., 2020).

Communities such as Open-Source Medical Supplies, Nation of Makers, We The Builders, and Make4Covid responded by bringing together a global group of thousand industrial designers, engineers, software developers, manufacturers, medical experts, and government institutions (Bowser et al., 2021):

- OSMS and others provided "gig economy platforms" to connect communities with experts.
- The communities acted as "sharing economy platforms" to track manufacturing capacity across locations and connect communities to local resources that could fabricate, assemble, and deliver PPE based on their local needs. Resources

included individual and business owners of 3D printers and CNC machines sharing access to their equipment, workshops, and factories.
- Cloud-based design tools enabled designers to collaborate worldwide to create open-source PPE, respirator, and respirator part designs.
- Medical experts guided designers through the intricacies and unique requirements for medical devices.
- Digital marketplaces such as the NIH 3D Print Exchange allowed individuals and businesses anywhere to download and, if needed, modify PPE designs and manufacturing instructions based on local needs.
- Use of software development practices such as time-bound sprints and "huddles" to refine and scale everything from PPE design to distribution in an agile and iterative manner.

The gig economy, sharing economy, and open-source models allowed communities to connect globally, share knowledge, and jointly design and freely distribute the designs. The freely available open-source designs made it cost effective and easy for designers, fabricators, and volunteers anywhere in the world to download, modify, build, and distribute equipment for their local needs. Connecting local communities in need of PPE with a pool of skilled talent, shared equipment, and factories in multiple locations added resiliency by eliminating a single source for production. Industry 4.0 technologies enabled an agile and lean process with continuous improvement and just-in-time production. This model of manufacturing is referred to as "Open Manufacturing." (P2PF, 2010).

COVID highlighted several problems across every manufacturer's business. The approach used by the PPE communities addresses many of these challenges. It gives small and large manufacturers alike the same abilities as manufacturers who successfully pivoted during COVID: rapid decision making, organization flexibility, employee skills and know-how, and digital technologies (Okorie et al., 2020).

Has PPE manufacturing given us a glimpse of a post-COVID "Open Manufacturer" that is lean, flexible, and resilient to shifts in buyer expectations and supply chain disruptions?

References

Ansys. (2019). *VW motorsport presents: Battery simulation—An essential technology for the ID. R at Nürburgring and the record at pikes peak*. Retrieved from Ansys: https://www.ansys.com/resource-center/webinar/battery-simulation-vw-motorsports

Apple Inc. (2019). *Apple supplier list*. (Apple) Retrieved from Apple: https://www.apple.com/supplier-responsibility/pdf/Apple-Supplier-List.pdf

Bank of America Securities. (2020, July 26). *How much will it cost to reshore the world's supply chains?* (Bank of America Global Research) Retrieved from https://www.bofaml.com/content/dam/boamlimages/documents/articles/ID20_0734/cost_of_remaking_supply_chains.pdf

Betti, F., & Boer, E. D. (2020, January 10). *Global lighthouse network: Insights from the forefront of the fourth industrial revolution*. (World Economic Forum) Retrieved on Febrauary

1, 2021, from https://www.weforum.org/whitepapers/global-lighthouse-network-insights-from-the-forefront-of-the-fourth-industrial-revolution
Bhavnagarwala, H. (2020). *3D printer plans: 10 great 3D printer blueprints to DIY*. (All3DP) Retrieved from All3DP: https://all3dp.com/2/3d-printer-plans-3d-printer-blueprints/
Blind, K., Nagle, F., Böhm, M., Katz, A., & Pätsch, S. (2020, November). *European Commission open source study*. (Fraunhofer ISI) Retrieved from https://www.openforumeurope.org/wp-content/uploads/2020/11/OFE_Fraunhofer_OS_impact_study_5_Nov.pdf
Bowser, A., Long, A., Novak, A., Parker, A., & Weinberg, M. (2021, February). *Stitching together a solution: Lessons from the open source hardware response to COVID-19*. (Wilson Center) Retrieved from https://www.wilsoncenter.org/publication/stitching-together-solution-lessons-open-source-hardware-response-covid-19
Bright Machines. (2020). *Flex partners with Bright machines to innovate today and into the future*. (Bright Machines) Retrieved on April 29, 2021, from Bright Machines: https://www.brightmachines.com/customers/
Buxbaum, P. (2020, March 17). *Coronavirus and manufacturing: Shipping and logistics*. (Industry Today) Retrieved February 1, 2021, from https://industrytoday.com/coronavirus-and-manufacturing-shipping-and-logistics/
Carbon. (2019, January 16). *Carbon and ford expand collaboration to digitally manufacture new durable, end-use parts*. (Carbon) Retrieved from https://www.carbon3d.com/news/press-releases/carbon-and-ford-expand-collaboration/
CDC. (2021, April 16). *COVID-19 manufacturing workers and employers interim guidance*. (Centers for Disease Control and Prevention) Retrieved on April 29, 2021, from https://www.cdc.gov/coronavirus/2019-ncov/community/guidance-manufacturing-workers-employers.html
Celo, S., Nebus, J., & Wang, K. (2018, March). The role of internal and external complexity in global factory performance: An NKC application. *Journal of International Management, 24*(1), 65–83. Retrieved from https://www.sciencedirect.com/science/article/abs/pii/S1075425317300030
Deloitte. (2018). *2018 Deloitte and The Manufacturing Institute skills gap and future of work study*. (Deloitte) Retrieved from https://www2.deloitte.com/us/en/pages/manufacturing/articles/future-of-manufacturing-skills-gap-study.html
Eclipse IoT. (2021). *Open source for IoT*. Retrieved from Eclipse Foundation: https://iot.eclipse.org/
Erboz, G. (2017). How to define industry 4.0: Main pillars of industry 4.0. In *Managerial trends in the development of enterprises in globalization era*. Nitria. Retrieved from https://www.researchgate.net/publication/326557388_How_To_Define_Industry_40_Main_Pillars_Of_Industry_40
Gandhi, S., Jamjoum, A. K., & Heider, C. (2019, February 1). *Why customer experience matters for B2B*. (MIT Sloan Management Review) Retrieved from https://sloanreview.mit.edu/article/why-customer-experience-matters-for-b2b/
GE. (2020, January 26). *3D printed jet engine: Meet the team of young engineers that brought 3D printing inside the GE9X—The world's largest jet engine*. (3D Printing Industry) Retrieved on February 6, 2021, from General Electric: https://www.ge.com/additive/stories/3d-printed-jet-engine-meet-team-young-engineers-brought-3d-printing-inside-ge9x-worlds-largest
GrabCAD. (2021). *GrabCAD*. (GrabCAD) Retrieved on April 29, 2021, from GrabCAD: https://resources.grabcad.com/company/
IoT Hub Meetup. (2020, November 8). *Autonomous drones delivering medical supplies and saving lives with Keenan Wyrobek (Zipline)*. Retrieved from IoT Hub Meetup: https://www.youtube.com/watch?v=QMLcSElQRNk&t=23s
LF Edge. (2021). *Building a open source framework for the edge*. Retrieved from Linux Foundation LF Edge: https://www.lfedge.org/
Ma, C. (2020, July 14). *Manufacturer interest in reshoring, hiring, and apprenticeships increasing during COVID-19 pandemic [Report]*. (Thomas.Net) Retrieved February 1, 2021, from https://www.thomasnet.com/insights/manufacturer-interest-in-reshoring-hiring-and-apprenticeships-increasing-during-covid-19-pandemic-report/

Manufacturing Institute. (2019, July). *The aging of the manufacturing workforce.* (Manufacturing Institute) Retrieved from Manufacturing Institute: https://www.themanufacturinginstitute.org/wp-content/uploads/2020/03/MI-Sloan-Aging-in-the-MFG-Workforce-Report.pdf

Mimo Technologies. (n.d.). *Mimo technologies home page.* (Mimo Technologies) Retrieved April 29, 2021, from https://mimo-technologies.com/

NAM. (2020, March 9). *Economic and operational impacts of COVID-19 to manufacturers.* Retrieved from National Association of Manufacturers: https://www.nam.org/coronasurvey/

NAM. (n.d.). *Facts about manufacturing.* (National Association of Manufacturers) Retrieved from National Association of Manufacturers: https://www.nam.org/facts-about-manufacturing/

Okorie, O., Subramoniam, R., Charnley, F., Patsavellas, J., Widdifield, D., & Salonitis, K. (2020, September 1). Manufacturing in the time of COVID-19: An assessment of barriers and enablers. *IEEE Engineering Management Review, 48*(3), 167–175. https://doi.org/10.1109/EMR.2020.3012112

Onshape. (2020, November 23). *Formlabs uses onshape CAD and AWS to shave weeks or months off design cycles.* (OnShape) Retrieved from Onshape: https://www.onshape.com/en/resource-center/user-stories/formlabs-uses-onshape-cad-and-aws-to-shave-weeks-or-months-off-design-cycles

Osztovits, Á., Kőszegi, Á., Nagy, B., & Damjanovics, B. (2015). *Sharing or paring? Growth of the sharing economy.* (PwC) Retrieved from https://www.pwc.com/hu/en/kiadvanyok/assets/pdf/sharing-economy-en.pdf

P2PF. (2010, May 31). *Open manufacturing value stream.* Retrieved from P2P Foundation: https://wiki.p2pfoundation.net/Open_Manufacturing_Value_Stream

PACCAR. (2021, January 19). *PACCAR and aurora form strategic partnership to develop autonomous trucks.* Retrieved from Paccar News: https://www.paccar.com/news/current-news/2021/paccar-and-aurora-form-strategic-partnership-to-develop-autonomous-trucks/

Park, C.-Y., Kim, K., Roth, S., Beck, S., Kang, J. W., Tayag, M. C., & Griffin, M. (2020, April). *Global shortage of personal protective equipment amid COVID-19: Supply chains, bottlenecks, and policy implications.* (Asian Development Bank) Retrieved February 1, 2021, from https://www.adb.org/sites/default/files/publication/579121/ppe-covid-19-supply-chains-bottlenecks-policy.pdf

Porter, M. E., & Heppelmann, J. E. (2014, November 1). *How smart, connected products are transforming competition.* (Harvard Business Review) Retrieved on February 6, 2021, from Harvard Business Review: https://hbr.org/2014/11/how-smart-connected-products-are-transforming-competition

Prising, J., Sorenson, A., & Weinelt, B. (2018, May 3). *Maximizing the return on digital investments.* (World Economic Forum) Retrieved on February 1, 2021, from https://www.weforum.org/whitepapers/maximizing-the-return-on-digital-investments

PTC. (2021). *Digital transformation: continuously optimizing manufacturing operations.* (PTC) Retrieved from https://www.ptc.com/en/case-studies/rockwell-automation

PTC. (2021, February 1). *INFINITI creates augmented reality in-store experience.* (PTC) Retrieved on February 1, 2021, from https://www.ptc.com/en/case-studies/infiniti-augmented-reality-in-store-experience

PTC. (n.d.). *BID group streamlines service and improves customer experience with vuforia chalk.* (PTC) Retrieved on April 29, 2021, from PTC: https://www.ptc.com/en/case-studies/bid-group-streamlines-service-with-vuforia-chalk

Romand-Monnier, P. (2019, July 19). *5 things you didn't know about hardware startups.* (Hardware Club) Retrieved on February 6, 2021, from https://blog.hardwareclub.co/5-things-you-didnt-know-about-hardware-startups-28291bb2da16

ROS Industrial. (2021). *ROS industrial.* Retrieved from ROS Industrial: https://rosindustrial.org

Shih, W. (2020, April 15). *Bringing manufacturing back to the U.S. is easier said than done*. (Harvard Business Review) Retrieved on February 1, 2021, from Harvard Business Review: https://hbr.org/2020/04/bringing-manufacturing-back-to-the-u-s-is-easier-said-than-done

Sleger, G. (2020, April 6). *Manufacturing supply chains, jobs reports show obvious downturn amid COVID-19 crisis*. (The Fabricator) Retrieved from https://www.thefabricator.com/thefabricator/blog/covid19/manufacturing-supply-chains-jobs-reports-show-obvious-downturn-amid-covid-19-crisis

Srivastava, S., Trehan, K., Wagle, D., & Wang, J. (2020, April 20). *Developer Velocity: How software excellence fuels business performance*. (Mckinsey) Retrieved from Mckinsey & Company: https://www.mckinsey.com/industries/technology-media-and-telecommunications/our-insights/developer-velocity-how-software-excellence-fuels-business-performance

Statista. (2021). *Mobile Android operating system market share by version worldwide from January 2018 to January 2021*. Retrieved from Statista: https://www.statista.com/statistics/921152/mobile-android-version-share-worldwide/

Tay, S. I., Chuan, L. T., Aziati, A. N., & Ahmad, A. A. (2018). An overview of industry 4.0: Definition, components, and government initiatives. *Journal of Advanced Research in Dynamical and Control Systems, 10*(14), 1. Retrieved from https://www.researchgate.net/publication/332440369_An_Overview_of_Industry_40_Definition_Components_and_Government_Initiatives

Teja, R. (2021, April 5). *What are the differences between Raspberry Pi and Arduino?* Retrieved from Electronics Hub: https://www.electronicshub.org/raspberry-pi-vs-arduino/

Thales Group. (n.d.). *Exploring consumer expectations of IoT in 2030 (Connected Living III)*. (Thales Group) Retrieved on April 29, 2021, from Thales Group: https://www.thalesgroup.com/en/markets/digital-identity-and-security/iot/documents/connected-living-2030

TraqIQ . (2021, January 19). *Has the last mile revolution changed the supply chain forever?* (TraqIQ) Retrieved from TraqIQ: https://www.traqiq.com/blog/last-mile/has-the-last-mile-revolution-changed-the-supply-chain-forever/

WEF. (2021). *How companies can win the race to meet customer expectations*. Geneva: World Economic Forum. Retrieved from http://reports.weforum.org/digital-transformation/the-race-to-meet-customer-expectations/

WEF. (2021). *The global risks report 2021*. World Economic Forum. Retrieved from https://www.weforum.org/reports/the-global-risks-report-2021

Wellener, P., Ashton, H., & Lapper, S. (2018, August 23). *Distinctive traits of digital frontrunners in manufacturing*. Retrieved on February 1, 2021, from Deloitte: https://www2.deloitte.com/us/en/insights/focus/industry-4-0/digital-leaders-in-manufacturing-fourth-industrial-revolution.html

Wilgus, C. (2018, December 12). *Manufacturing jobs in the gig economy*. (Manufacturing Tomorrow) Retrieved from https://www.manufacturingtomorrow.com/article/2018/11/manufacturing-jobs-in-the-gig-economy/12579/

Workrise. (2021, April 29). *RigUp announces new corporate brand—Workrise—To align with expanded mission, new verticals*. (Workrise) Retrieved from Workrise: https://www.workrise.com/hub/introducing-workrise/

Wrench. (n.d.). *Frequently asked questions*. (Wrench) Retrieved on April 29, 2021, from Wrench: https://wrench.com/faq/

Yu, J. M., & Plume, K. (2019, January 29). *Exclusive: Foxconn reconsidering plans to make LCD panels at Wisconsin plant*. (Reuters) Retrieved from Reuters: https://www.reuters.com/article/us-foxconn-wisconsin-exclusive-idUSKCN1PO0FV

Zorz, Z. (2018, May 22). *The percentage of open source code in proprietary apps is rising*. (Help Net Security) Retrieved from https://www.helpnetsecurity.com/2018/05/22/open-source-code-security-risk/

Harinderpal (Hans) Hanspal is a Venture Partner with Momenta Ventures, a venture capital firm investing in industrial startups at the intersection of industry and digital. He is also the founder of Thing Company LLC, an advisory firm helping organizations across industries craft product, customer, and revenue strategies for "Everything-As-A-Service" (XaaS) business models. He is a technology industry veteran and start-up entrepreneur who has helped create and grow several global technology-enabled businesses in industrial, technology, and telecom industries, including a successful start-up exit as a founder. In his spare time, he leads Seattle's 4200+ member IoT Hub Meetup group.

Exploring the Dark Side of Gig Economy, Markets and Jobs

Hergovind Singh, K. Pallavi, and Harsh Vardhan Samalia

1 About Gig Economy

During early period of industrialization in the nineteenth century, it was fairly an uncommon sight for people to engage in short-term multiple jobs. However, due to the emergence of a recent trend, namely "Gig economy", the same has become quite ubiquitous in current era (Angela, 2019). The Gig economy is defined as a way of working that involves workers being paid on the basis of piece(s) of work carried out by them rather than the fixed monthly salary. Therefore Gig economy involves a flexible and temporary workplace where workers can associate themselves with companies for shorter periods and work can also engage via online platforms (Yu, 2019). The people engaging in such type of economic activities are commonly termed as 'Gig workers'. These Gig workers primarily work on freelance basis, majority primarily connecting to clients/customers, through an online platform (Mukhopadhyay & Mukhopadhyay, 2020). Gig workers vary from conventional independent workers to freelancers to temporary employees who work for selected hours in a week. Few platform-based business firms that use the concept of Gig workers/work for their advantage include Ola, Swiggy, Oyo and Zomato in India and TaskRabbit, Lyft in the USA to name a few, where work is broken down into components that allow tasks to be tailored and allocated as required. As per a study carried out research in US context, it is was found that nearly one-third of 33 percent of their total workforce depends on Gig work to supplement their primary source of income.

The main major reasons behind companies in engaging in freelance workers are because it provides these firms with the requisite amount of tradition is that (a) flexibility, (b) access to expertise, (c) speed responsiveness and (d) cost savings

H. Singh (✉) · K. Pallavi
Maulana Azad National Institute of Technology, Bhopal, India
e-mail: hgs@manit.ac.in

H. V. Samalia
National Institute of Technical Teachers Training & Research, Chandigarh, India

A. Gupta et al. (eds.), *Sustainability in the Gig Economy*,
https://doi.org/10.1007/978-981-16-8406-7_12

(Kässi, 2018). However, in-spite of having number of advantages Gig economy, is remains quite challenging for small and medium enterprises to obtain access to these part-time workers (or Gig workers as commonly referred here), as there are plenty of options available for these such Gig workers. As per a survey carried out by Deloitte in 2014, it was found that 51% of the population expects a sharp hike in the use of contingent talent in upcoming years. This kind of temporary or irregular work modules are suitable for those who are looking for some extra income or for those who opt for ad hoc work schedule. Nonetheless, a big portion of India's economy relies upon Gig work, although it fails to provide them with the required stability and they end up being paid less for the work they do. For a longer period as of now, the state legislation and government regulation policies have been looking toward making the aforementioned Gig environment more compatible.

The key claim by many of the platform providers regarding is that their Gig workers should be considered as independent contractors and not as an 'employees' which has left lot to be desired (Polzin, 2016). The goodwill accrues to the platform provider, leaving the worker with fewer options. Gig workers take up much of the risk involved in many of these platform-based businesses which not only relate to their labor but also to their own amount of capital involved in these platform-based businesses (Mehta, 2020). Gig worker's risk exposure mitigation further increases when continued ownership of the assets used in work is dependent on a set of circumstances outside the control of the concerned worker. For example, Uber or Ola drivers use their own money, or borrow/avail loans in order to, buy their cars. This can be due to few circumstances, such as; (a) when the company changes significantly decreases the amount it pays to drivers or, (b) when the ride-hailing industry experiences higher competition or, (c) when the company gets flooded with new Uber drivers due to low barriers of entry and / or firm's growing popularity among users –the firm might take a decision to 'decommission' certain drivers either due to one or more of the above reasons or may be also for securing low user ratings, now, the driver becomes burdened with debt and, with no ready means to pay it back the same (Bieber, 2020).

The fluctuations that are caused in this kind of earnings can be highly stressful and even can be difficult for the survival of such workers. Added to this, this kind of freelance work doesn't provide the Gig worker with any retirement or pension plan benefit. Also, the worker in question has no advantage of availing sick or any type of leaves which are like there available to all the workers employed in permanent jobs. Further, to complicate the matter more, a Gig worker is unable to earn during the time if she/he falls sick, simply does not earn.

The only two key ways to overcome such situations are self-organization and self-motivation and to maintain a solid reputation by ensuring continuity in fulfilling the said commitments given orders within time. However, the tact with which emerging economies manage this trend should carefully curb the balance of externalities on the Gig workers and platform providers. Simultaneously, we need to adapt our ideas of fixed employment to suit and evolving digital age with a small portion of the market to work and earn as they wish.

1.1 Emergence of Gig economy—Beating the Stereotypes

As per some HR experts, the word 'Gig' was first used by Jazz musicians in 1915, which meant 'Job'. In 1940, the first temp agency was established which provided jobs to typists and other clerical staff workers on temporary basis. The trend of Gig economy started taking hike in the late 90s along with the digital era. During 1990s, nearly 10% of US workers worked on freelance basis, according to the increasing demand of Gig work. In the year 1995, Craigslist was introduced, which provided different jobs to local San Francisco-based online classifieds for sale, Gigs, services, housing, etc. This was followed by Upwork in 1999, which permitted Gig workers with Internet services to find new projects and clients. Gig economy gained much popularity around 2008, when the world was hit by the Great Recession due to which people had limited work and less security toward job and stable work. This Gig trend hit the world even harder during recent times in year 2020 due to because of the **Covid-19** scenario, which reinforced the dependency of the number of organizations on these as most of the companies are depending upon Gig workers.

1.2 Gig Economy in Indian Context

People in India are adopting and accepting the current trend of Gig economy with an increasing pace. The concept of retiring with a work life under a single employer is quite outdated now (Bansal, 2020). The latest trend of Gig work calls out for 'work on your own terms'. As the recent data trend suggests, India is one of the biggest demographic unit where a large number of people are involved work as freelancers or as 'On-demand' workers. Various advanced economies countries such as USA, Australia, Canada and UK along with number of middle-east economies, etc. opt maximum for Indian freelancers. This goes well for a highly populated country like India where providing employment to the large number of qualified and eligible work force is a serious concern. Gig economy is basically includes consulting and contractor arrangements, part-time jobs, temporary assignments, freelancing, side Gigs and on-demand work.

While demographically diverse, independent workers largely fit into four segments (exhibit): free agents- who actively choose independent work and derive their primary income from it; casual earners, who use independent work for supplemental income and do so by choice; reluctant, who make their primary living from independent work but would prefer traditional jobs; and the financially strapped, who do supplemental independent work out of necessity.

2 Dimensions of Gig Economy

2.1 Behavioural Dimensions of Gig Economy

The pace of which Gig economy is growing is quite fast, and as conditions of employment are changing very rapidly. Shifting of employment from traditional payroll to contingent system is further providing the thrust to this transition. Different dimensions below of Gig economy provides better understanding about challenges and opportunities posed by the Gig economy in today's time:.

It has been agreed worldwide that there are basically two different perspectives that are centered around the work agility. The traditional model of work culture follows the principle of more work against more wages. The workers are expected to devote more hours of work if they are paid high. However, this imbalances their work–life state. On the other hand, the modern (behavioral) model follows reverse approach that to the traditional one. It says, workers in Gig economy can freely decide their schedule accordingly switching comfortably between different providers and in the process can even earn more depending upon their case situation. This new and behavioral model includes 'the stop working once the income target is increased' thought process based on the daily earning basis. These findings result into a realistic behavioral explanation of a Gig worker.

It's a good idea if one chooses a Gig lifestyle as it provides lots of freedom to the concerned Gig worker (Keith, 2020). This is due to the reason, that a Gig worker has liberty to choose work location, work hours and can also choose various projects to work on. She/he can be called no less than an analyst if she/he analyze among from the given various options, number of projects in order to work on, which project will provide the maximum payoff at the end. This will help her/him to make calculations based on overall income, depending upon priorities of work–life balance. This way he can maximize his profit via choosing project to work on. A Gig worker can sharpen her/his skills while working as one day she/he can choose to work in a finance project and on the other day she/he can choose to work on as a marketing personnel. The only negative side of Gig work is that, the Gig workers till date largely remains underpaid and undervalued. This can be understood better by supposing that, one fine day, (suppose), you met a work contractor who can carve out a sofa set, can fix the running tap in your kitchen or can paint your house. But she/he will be paid below average for most of the work carried out by her or him as they are what if you pay less for his work. He is undervalued for their multiple skills.

This can also understood the other way. Suppose, an architect hires a chef as her/his assistant and expects her/him to work with as an architect. How the architect will use chef's cooking skills into building a house remains questionable. Thus, companies should thrive to hire the right talented minds at the right place and should offer them fair pay for their work.

2.2 *Gender-Specific Dimension and Gig Economy*

Gig and non-traditional workers are men and women, young and old, live across the country and reflect the racial, ethnic and socioeconomic diversity of the country. The men and women be it of any age group, any origin are the participants of Gig economy. A few researches show that men engage more than women in Gig work whereas a few more researches claim that women are more likely to engage in part-time work and also involve in direct marketing via online platforms (Kasliwal, 2020). The Gig platforms have attracted female workers over years due to flexibility it offers (Brendan, 2019). The first and foremost barrier for inability for female inclusion in regular workforce was due to their imbalance between their household work and their jobs. Thus, working via Gig platforms helps them manage both well. This benefit may attract more female workers toward Gig work. Secondly, women feel much more secure and comfortable working from their home at their own ease. Females as regular workers were quite uncomfortable if they work in night shifts or may be if they get some late from their office. They had a threat to their security at odd hours, reaching back their home. But, due to Gig work, a women worker can comfortably work at late night hours. Thirdly, there are less chances of harassment at workplace with women as the work is totally based on virtual platforms. Still, there needs to proper law making and its implementation in order to make women more comfortable at work and to encourage more to step into Gig world.

3 Murkiness of Gig Economy

Gig economy is of course a boon to the fast-moving world, but we cannot ignore the hard reality in it. Gig workers are in happy-not-happy situation. A part of people vote yes for the Gig work as they can work easily and earn more, whereas the other part unwelcome Gig work as they have lost their work–life balance (Graham et al., 2017). Families where there is only one person earning and rest are dependent upon him are unhappy and families where more number of people in the family are working from home and at part-time basis sitting at their home are happy. Workers say IT professionals find it easy to have regular work lifestyle which even paid them high than Gig work. These realities divert us to understand what Gig economy offers.

3.1 The Perception and Reality

The interest on Gig workers is on rise worldwide. 61% of organizations show their interest toward engaging with Gig workers. The Gig economy is often discussed in context with other working and economic practices enabled by digital technology, including the sharing economy and the platform based economy besides both having their own similarities and differences. The lack of a specified framework for Gig economy has led companies to exercise Gig economy on their own with understanding and their own terms. This makes varying of size and rate of expansion of Gig economy. This kind of evolving work practices led the policy-makers and regulators to understand about this new found reality and defining legislation for Gig economy.

Basically, a Gig platform enables the social rating of a Gig worker based on which it is decided for a worker that how much work he gets or how much does he gets paid. As per the PayPal's India freelancer report, most of the freelance work comes to Indian freelances is from USA, UK and Australia.

We are to understand each of these elements in brief:

(i) ***The impact on employment***—The Gig trend is surging in employment sector towards creating opportunities for employment. This platform even created opportunities for self-employment which were not accessible previously. As per World Bank report of April 2018, India would need 8 million jobs as the unemployment number is increasing by 1.3 million every year. Of course then, the economy would depend upon Gig economy with an estimated employment generation of 565 through it and an estimated growth rate of 25–30% per annum.

(ii) ***Improving organizational competitiveness***—Organizations worldwide believe that the trend of Gig economy helps them hire the right talent in short period. It is also believed that companies can save precious time and resources by engaging with Gig workers and have the ability to pivot their approach quickly if something does not work. This grows with the concept of hiring 'on-demand' workers.

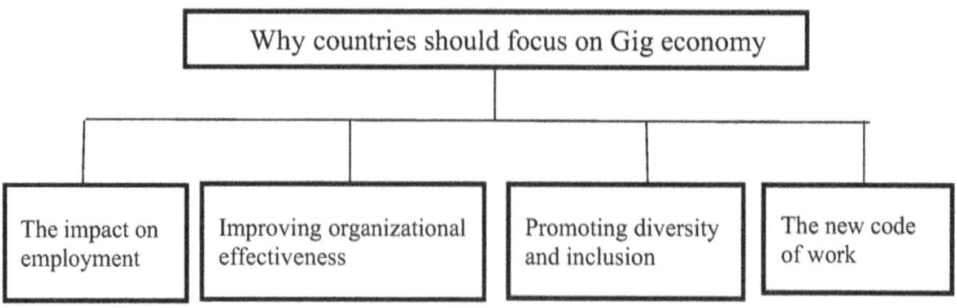

Fig. 1 Why countries should focus on Gig economy. *Source* GigEconomy-What We Know and What We Don't (Amol Pawar; Khushboo Dahiya; Kamakshi Pant, 2018)

(iii) ***Promoting diversity and inclusion***—Gig economy encourages the concept of promoting diversity and inclusion for all which means that the pool of Gig minds can reach to numerous Gig opportunities right from the comfort of their house using simple technology tools.
(iv) ***The new code of work***—The progressing Gig trend drives us to the new code of work as the upcoming talented brains are finding it easy and cozy to interact with the organizations via digital platforms and social media. This even simplifies the burden of such organizations who are in hunt of such right and talented Gig brains.

But not only discussing about the pros of Gig trend but also understanding the cons of it makes it a complete analysis of the perception versus reality that is faced in Gig work. As every coin has two sides, this was the attractive perception of Gig economy, now we shall discuss the grounded reality/challenges with it.

The challenges highlights:

(a) *Missing social benefits*—The Gig worker works for a fixed amount of salary based on the predefined contractual work which limits the benefits (like, PF, ESIC, employee stock option plans (ESOP)), he could avail while as a regular worker.
(b) *Unclear legal framework*—The labor laws presently functional worldwide do not consider Gig workers. The acts like maternity benefit, sexual harassment at workplace, etc. are ambiguous whether they are applicable to Gig workers or not.
(c) *Talent management*—The Gig economy brought in a situation of people working from different geographical locations connected via online platforms like Skype, Webex, etc. Thus, it becomes quite challenging for the organizations to manage, supervise and control these Gig workers than their regular workers.

3.2 Gig Versus Jig

So, as per the ongoing discussion so far, Gig economy has got all good things in store. Gig workers are happy and contended and are leading a cozy life earning sufficient to feed their tummies with less work hours as per their convenience, Right? Unfortunately, NO!!!

Why? The reason is things aren't all that rosy as seem to be. There are several pitfalls to it. The first and the foremost thing is the run race associated with the daily earning system. The Gig worker has to make sure he catches another project as soon as the current one ends. Suppose, a taxi driver is serving a customer but he has to find another customer while he drops the current one to his destination. If in case, he does not get any such customer at the right time and same place, he may be loosing his time and wage for that particular hour (Allon et al., 2018). And in case, he gets customers in excess on someday, he may have to run throughout the city ending up tired and lack in resting hours. In some metro cities like Mumbai, taxi drivers spend their nights in their own taxis in order to adjust to their hectic schedule.

A few more things which can be looked upon in relation to this are:

(a) *Job insecurity*—This Gig economy gave birth to job insecurity as companies on regular basis are hunting for fresh and agile talented minds. Thus, a Gig worker working with an organization today isn't sure to be kept or be replaced by some other by tomorrow.
(b) *Unclear status and out of pocket expenses*—Gig workers somewhere are treated as regular employees, whereas in some other places they aren't treated so. This keeps their status as unclear. Plus, due to the monetary benefits received by a regular employee like insurance, healthcare, etc., any sudden out-of-pocket expense can be recoverable for him, whereas the same is not for a Gig worker.
(c) *Crowd-work and race to the bottom*—A freelancer platform offers various jobs at lower and higher rates; thus, it becomes a rat race for Gig workers that over deserving talented minds are fighting for smaller and less paying jobs. This gives an advantage to companies to auction job offers at lesser and lesser pay.
(d) *Employer double-standards*—Due to lack of proper legislations and laws for Gig workers, the companies try to suck maximum work from workers in less pay and without even providing the minimum basic allowances to them from their company. This calls for proper laws to be put into the constitutional system to protect such contract workers.
(e) *Dishonest clients (a.k.a. Not Being Paid for Work)*—Many companies often ditch the Gig workers by taking them into short-term projects on part-time basis and end up making them work for more and more hours. Workers not only are exploited against work but also are threatened of termination and are forced to work for longer hours starving them for pay.
(f) *The time suck*—Companies and Gig workers are often looking for various opportunities while experience little or actually no time to respond to their existing clients. This implies the fact that Gig workers' maximum time is wasted on marketing in the early stages. For companies also, this hunt restricts the appropriate time to invest in long-term working relationships with workers.
(g) *No ladder*—By working on contract terms, a worker loses the prospect of working their way up within a company for a long run. Having no promotion ladder up in the company, a Gig worker is stagnated at one position in a company. Also, in time of crisis in a company, the company may first chose these contract workers to cut the corners. This leads such Gig workers stand at stake of their job.
(h) *Mental health*—Having financial insecurity in a Gig work obviously will lead to mental stress, anxiety, depression causing disturbed health. Many workers suicide due to such extreme stress and depression ending up their life.

3.3 Resistance and Change Undecided

Resistance in work life can include misbehavior and counterproductive practices toward work and the use of work material for non-work purposes. Work actions like strikes, demonstrations are termed as direct resistance practices, whereas indirect resistance may include wage negotiations. These resistance forms are seen by regular workers (Roy & Avinash, 2020). Thus, Gig work is seen as a substitute for the one who is dysfunctional. The organizations are at an advantage as they have few more workers waiting to work for them that too at a lesser pay.

But is this trend adaptable enough for future? Will the economy accept this change? Undecided!! Well why… because, there are also a few issues associated to Gig trend. The Gig workers also show their resistance at work by partially being present in meeting through online platforms, using office hours as their own personal time, not finishing up work on time. Then who would monitor. There is no proper control system to monitor such Gig workers. On the very side of a worker, who was paid smartly by his company, got his salary cut to half and asked to work as a Gig worker (Friedman, 2014). He is to work from home. The company even cuts the hours to travel to office and back to home stating the reason that he receives a few more extra hours to work due to not traveling. Instead of this, the companies ask the workers to work more than the office hours. This results in a regular well-paid worker is converted to a part-time Gig worker, working more and earn less. This is all due to the present pandemic of Covid-19 that the world is facing.

This less pay and more work hours creates tension among workers, and they are reluctant to accept this trend of Gig economy. They want to return back to regular work.

References

Allon, G., Cohen, M., & Sinchaisri, W. (2018). The impact of behavioral and economic drivers on gig economy workers. *SSRN Electronic Journal*. https://doi.org/10.2139/ssrn.3274628

Angela, S. (2019, August). Leveraging the gig economy: A novel solution to improve health care costs. *Nurse Leader, 17*(4), 356–359.

Bansal, R. (2020, February). *The emergence of gig economy in India: A paradigm shift Parishodh Journal, IX*(II). ISSN NO:2347-6648.

Bieber, F. (2020). Risk shifts in the gig economy: The Normative case for an insurance scheme against the effects of precarious work. *The Journal of Political Philosophy* 1–24.

Brendan, C. (2019, December 16). Gender in the gig economy: Men and women using digital platforms to secure work in Australia. *Journal of Sociology*, SAGE Publication.

Friedman, G. (2014). Workers without employers: Shadow corporations and the rise of the gig economy. *Review of Keynesian Economics, 2*(2), 171–188. https://doi.org/10.4337/roke.2014.02.03

Gig economy platforms: Boon or bane? (2019). OECD Economics Department Working Papers. https://doi.org/10.1787/fdb0570b-en

Graham, M., Hjorth, I., & Lehdonvirta, V. (2017). Digital labour and development: impacts of global digital labour platforms and the gig economy on worker livelihoods. *Transfer: European Review of Labour and Research, 23*(2), 135–162. https://doi.org/10.1177/1024258916687250
https://smarttribe.io/the-gig-economy-lifestyle-for-data-scientists/
https://sanam-akram.medium.com/the-dark-side-of-the-gig-economy-e60b91e00535
https://www.bbvaopenmind.com/en/articles/the-impact-of-the-gig-economy/
https://www.convinceandconvert.com/digital-marketing/gig-economy/
Kasliwal, R. (2020, May). Gender and the gig economy: A qualitative study of gig platforms for women workers. ORF Issue Brief No. 359, Observer Research Foundation.
Kässi, O. (2018, December). Online labour index: Measuring the online gig economy for policy and research, technological. *Forecasting and Social Change, 137*, 241–248.
Keith, M. G. (2020). Worker health and well-being in the gig economy: A proposed framework and research agenda. In P. L. Perrewé, P. D. Harms, & C.-H. Chang (Eds.), *Research in occupational stress and well-being* (Vol. 18, pp. 1–34). Emerald Publishing.
Polzin, F. (2016, July). What encourages local authorities to engage with energy performance contracting for retrofitting? Evidence from German municipalities. *Energy Policy, 94*, 317–330.
Mehta, B. S. (2020). Changing nature of work and the gig economy: Theory and debate. *FIIB Business Review*, 231971452096829. https://doi.org/10.1177/2319714520968294
Mukhopadhyay, B., & Mukhopadhyay, B. K. (2020). What is the gig economy? Tripura Times, Post-Editorial.
Roy, G., & Shrivastava, A. (2020). Future of gig economy: Opportunities and challenges. *IMI Konnect, 9*, 14–25.
Yu, R. (2019, December). Exploring impact of future flexible working model evolution on urban environment, economy and planning. *Journal of Urban Management*, 8(3), 447–457.

Dr. Singh competed his bachelor of engineering (electrical engineering) from Jiwaji University, Gwalior, India, and MBA and Ph.D. from Indian Institute of Information Technology and Management, Gwalior, India. He is presently working as 'Asst. Professor' in the Department of Management Studies, Maulana Azad National Institute of Technology, Bhopal, India. Work experience is about 14 years which includes industry, academia and research. Areas of interest include technology and innovation management (strategic management) and information management (e-governance).

K. Pallavi is an MBA (finance and HR) graduate from MANIT, Bhopal. She worked in ICICI bank at Bhopal (Central India) location managing retail banking and business loans operations. She is taking up some voluntary research works under the able guidance of Dr. Hergovind Singh (Prof. In MANIT).

Dr. Harsh Vardhan Samalia is an associate professor in the EDIC Department at NITTTR, Chandigarh. Dr. Samalia has a rich experience of 17+ years in corporate, teaching, research and consultancy domains. Prior to joining NITTTR, Chandigarh, he has been associated with IIM Shillong for 7+ years (as associate professor) and Thapar University, Patiala (as assistant professor) for 5+ years at IIM Shillong. He had completed both his MBA and Ph.D from Indian Institute of Information Technology and Management (IIITM), Gwalior as well as postgraduate diploma in patent law from NALSAR, Hyderabad. He has been a visiting faculty at number of reputed B-schools including IIM Kashipur.

Gig Economy: Is It a Poisonous Apple? an Empirical Study of Uber Drivers

Walid Chaouali, Mohamed Mousa, and Samiha Mjahed

1 Introduction

The development of digital peer-to-peer platforms and applications, known as the gig economy, is radically reshaping the economy, management, information systems, and marketing thoughts and practices, and shaking up traditional business models and the expectations of the stakeholders, such as consumers, employees, and policy-makers (Duggan et al., 2020; Kost et al., 2020). For example, applications, such as Airbnb, have disrupted the business models of traditional hotels and the accommodation industry (Lee et al., 2021; Ossig et al., 2021). These new business models are spreading exponentially and are now generating enormous profits that were, generally, unexpected at the time of their launch (Cheng & Jin, 2019). Experts and scholars anticipate that these businesses will continue to rise even more and will account for a significant proportion of the economy, with considerable global economic consequences (Bengler; Barile et al., 2016; Burtch et al., 2018, p. 5461).

From the perspective of research on the gig economy, the majority of studies focus on the motivations (bright side of the gig economy) of partners to adopt this new business model. Despite the fact that the gig economy accounts for a limited proportion of overall jobs, it is becoming a more common aspect of employment (Berger et al., 2019). In this vein, management and information system research assumes that these businesses are very well appreciated and accepted by independent contractors and

W. Chaouali (✉)
Carthage Business School, University of Tunis Carthage, Member of ARBRE, Higher Institute of Management of Tunis, Tunis, Tunisia
e-mail: wchaouali@utctunisie.com

M. Mousa
Department of Management Sciences, Pontifical Catholic University of Peru, Lima, Peru

S. Mjahed
King Saud University, Riyadh, Kingdom of Saudi Arabia

A. Gupta et al. (eds.), *Sustainability in the Gig Economy*,
https://doi.org/10.1007/978-981-16-8406-7_13

partners[1] because they enable entrepreneurial activity (the gig economy is a solution for many job seekers) (Berger et al., 2019; Burtch et al., 2018), full autonomy over working time and scheduling flexibility (Burtch et al., 2018), and possibilities for earning supplementary income (when the independent contractor keeps working at other jobs or running his/her business) (Berger et al., 2019). Many people prefer using those platforms although they generally provide less stability and financial revenues (Berger et al., 2019). However, a recent and emerging research stream assumes that many factors can contaminate the independent contractors' aspirations and subjective well-being (Henama & Sifolo, 2017).

This work contributes to the literature on the gig economy by unveiling its dark side. More specifically, it focuses on the effects of some of its darker aspects on the independent contractors' job satisfaction and life satisfaction. More specifically, it proposes a comprehensive model that tests the effects of customer aggression, disproportionate customer expectations, and ambiguous customer expectations on emotional exhaustion and, in turn, on job satisfaction and life satisfaction, following Karatepe (2011, 2013) and Dormann and Zapf (2004). Accordingly, this work will provide insightful results that acknowledge different players (e.g. service providers) of the gig economy in regard to potentially detrimental effects of the working conditions of independent contractors or partners in order to, potentially, try to improve those conditions.

2 Hypothesis Development

2.1 Customer Aggression, Disproportionate Customer Expectations, and Ambiguous Customer Expectations and Emotional Exhaustion

"Emotional exhaustion refers to the lack of energy and depletion of emotional resources due to excessive psychological demands" (Karatepe, 2011, p. 282). It forms in stressful work environments, such as where workforce exchanges impose poor working conditions (Belanche et al., 2021). Previous research has reported that customer-related social stressors (customer aggression, disproportionate customer expectations, and ambiguous customer expectations) result in emotional exhaustion (Dormann & Zapf, 2004; Grandey et al., 2004; Karatepe, 2011; Van Dierendonck & Mevissen, 2002). Customer aggression refers to their intentions to inflict harm on workers (Karatepe et al., 2010), while disproportionate customer expectations are "situations in which customers tax or challenge the service that they want to receive from the service provider" (Dormann & Zapf, 2004, p. 75), and "ambiguous customer expectations describe unclear customer expectations" (Dormann & Zapf,

[1] Many of firms in the gig economy work with independent contractors or partners such as Uber drivers.

2004, p. 76). The effects of these factors on emotional exhaustion are explained by the conservation of resources theory (Buchwald & Schwarzer, 2010; Dormann & Zapf, 2004; Karatepe, 2011; Karatepe et al., 2010). This theory highlights the roles of gaining, maintaining, and protecting resources (object, person, condition, and energy) for individuals to engage in appropriate behaviours (Buchwald & Schwarzer, 2010). Several circumstances emerge and demonstrate the theoretical rationale behind people's sensitivity to stressors in the workplace and their incapacity to cope with such stressors that are: (1) the loss of resources, (2) threat of losing those resources, and (3) reaping the expected return on the investment from their scarce resources (Dormann & Zapf, 2004; Hobfoll, 2001; Karatepe, 2011; Karatepe et al., 2010). "Because resources are often hard to obtain and maintain, resource loss according to COR [i.e. conservation of resources] theory is considered to be more salient and of greater impact than resource gain" (Hobfoll, 2001, p. 14,464). As a result, when independent contractors experience customer aggression, disproportionate customer expectations, and ambiguous customer expectations, they lose their scarce resources and tend to experience emotional exhaustion. Accordingly, we propose the following hypotheses:

H1a: Customer aggression has a positive effect on emotional exhaustion.
H1b: Disproportionate customer expectations have a positive effect on emotional exhaustion.
H1c: Ambiguous customer expectations have a positive effect on emotional exhaustion.

2.2 *Emotional Exhaustion, Job Satisfaction, and Life Satisfaction*

Furthermore, conservation of resources theory proposes that once people feel that they have insufficient resources to manage and alleviate their emotional exhaustion, they become less satisfied with their job and life (Karatepe, 2011). Empirical evidence in different settings (e.g. public sector, salesforce, health care, hotel, and banking services) has shown that emotional exhaustion has a negative effect on people's attitudes and behaviours at work. Accordingly, emotional exhaustion for workers in the gig economy has a negative influence on job performance and job satisfaction, since it creates feelings of tiredness and frustration (Gaines & Jermier, 1983). Consistent with the meta-analytic study of Lee and Ashforth (1996) and the results of prior studies (Babakus et al., 2009), emotional exhaustion is reported to negatively affect job satisfaction. In addition, this study also posits that life dissatisfaction is another adverse outcome to emotional exhaustion. Life satisfaction is defined as an emotional state stemming from a person's overall assessment of their life (Karatepe & Baddar, 2006). Once the emotional resources of independent contractors are depleted, they are more likely to report decreased satisfaction with their life. There is evidence showing that

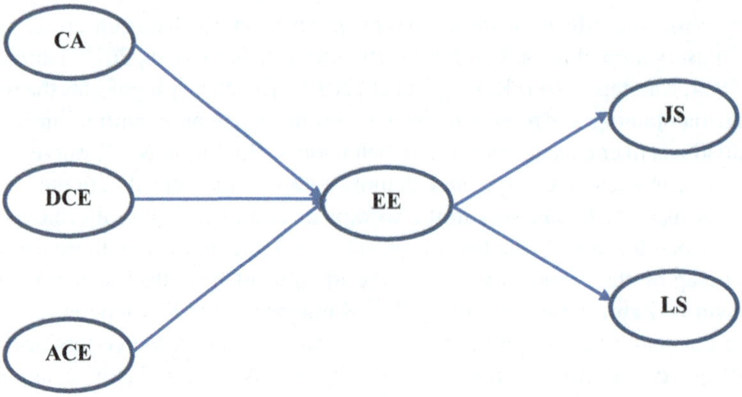

Fig. 1 Research framework. *Notes* CA = Customer aggression; DCE = disproportionate customer expectations; ACE = ambiguous customer expectations; EE = emotional exhaustion; JS = job satisfaction; and LS = life satisfaction

emotional exhaustion leads to decreased life satisfaction. For instance, Demerouti et al. (2000) found negative effects of emotional exhaustion on life satisfaction.

H2: Emotional exhaustion has a negative effect on job satisfaction.
H3: Emotional exhaustion has a negative effect on life satisfaction.

Figure 1 displays the research framework.

3 Method

This work focuses on Uber drivers. Uber is an American technology company and an important player in the gig economy that was founded in 2009 as Ubercab by Garrett Camp, who is a computer programmer (Uber, 2021). Now, its offerings include ride-hailing, package delivery, freight transportation, and food delivery (via Uber Eats) (Uber, 2021). The headquarters are in San Francisco, although Uber is present in more than 71 countries (American continent, Europe, Australia, India, Japan, and a handful of countries in Africa) and more than 890 cities (the USA with 263 cities and Brazil with 131 cities) (Uber Estimator, 2021). Ninety-three million people used Uber monthly, in the fourth quarter of 2020, and five billion rides were delivered in 2020 generating a global net revenue of 11.1 billion US dollars in that year (Statista, 2021).

For this study, the data is collected using a famous online panel company enrolling Uber drivers in France. This technique is well-established in information systems, management, and marketing literature. In addition, it is deemed appropriate because of the lockdown imposed during the COVID-19 pandemic (the time of the study). The final sample is composed of 432 participants.

All concepts are measured using well-established multi-item scales adapted from previous studies (see Table 1). Customer aggression is adapted from Karatepe (2011), disproportionate customer expectations and ambiguous customer expectations from Dormann and Zapf (2004), emotional exhaustion from Karatepe (2013), job satisfaction from Hartline and Ferrell (1996), and life satisfaction from Diener et al. (1985).

4 Results

4.1 Measurement Model

The study uses SmartPLS 3 (Ringle et al., 2015) to test the model. As shown in Table 2, construct reliability and validity is established (loadings, ρA, and AVE values are well above their respective thresholds) in line with Hair et al. (2017). In addition, discriminant validity (Hair et al., 2017) is verified since HTMT values are below 0.9 and are statistically different from 1, as shown in Table 3. Moreover, common method bias is not a critical issue because the first factor accounts for less than 50% of the overall variance (Podsakoff et al., 2003).

4.2 Structural Model

As shown in Table 4, the model explains 69.5% of the variance in emotional exhaustion, 51.1% of the variance in job satisfaction, and 50.7% of the variance in life satisfaction. Customer aggression, disproportionate customer expectations, and ambiguous customer expectations have positive effects on emotional exhaustion ($\beta = 0.173$, CI = [0.098; 0.276]; $\beta = 0.196$, CI = [0.110; 0.290]; $\beta = 0.262$, CI = [0.142; 0.384], respectively). Therefore, H1a–c are supported. In addition, emotional exhaustion has negative effects on job satisfaction and life satisfaction ($\beta = -0.715$, CI = [−0.777; −0.646] and $\beta = -0.712$, CI = [−0.756; −0.643], respectively). Therefore, H2 and H3 are supported. Using the blindfolding procedure, the model has a high predictive power since Q^2 values are well above zero (0.426, 0.344, and 0.380 for emotional exhaustion, job satisfaction, and life satisfaction, respectively).

5 Discussion

The gig economy is radically reshaping the economic landscape by generating new ways of doing business (Burtch et al., 2018; Henama & Sifolo, 2017). These new business models are spreading exponentially and are generating gigantic profits (Cheng &

Table 1 Items

Construct	Items	Source
Customer aggression	"Customers ridicule me" "Customers tell me my thoughts or feelings are stupid" "Customers put me down in front of others" "Customers are rude to me" "Customers tell me I am incompetent"	Karatepe (2011)
Disproportionate customer expectations	"Some customers ask us to do things they could do by themselves" "Customers vent their bad mood out on me" "Customers do not understand that we have to comply with certain rules" "Customers' demands are often exorbitant" "Customers are pressed for time"	Dormann and Zapf (2004)
Ambiguous customer expectations	"Customers' wishes are often contradictory" "It is not clear what customers request from me" "It is difficult to make arrangements with customers" "Customers' instructions can complicate my work"	Dormann and Zapf (2004)
Emotional exhaustion	"I feel used up at the end of the workday" "I feel burned out from my work" "I feel frustrated by my job" "I feel I am working too hard on my job" "I feel like I am at the end of my rope"	Karatepe (2013)
Job satisfaction	"My overall job" "Uber policies" "The support provided by Uber"	Hartline and Ferrell (1996)
Life satisfaction	"In most ways, my life is closer to my ideal" "I am satisfied with my life" "If I could live my life over, I would change almost nothing"	Diener et al. (1985)

Notes CA = Customer aggression; DCE = disproportionate customer expectations; ACE = ambiguous customer expectations; EE = emotional exhaustion; JS = job satisfaction; and LS = life satisfaction

Table 2 Loadings, ρA, and AVE

Items	Loadings	ρA	AVE	Items	Loadings	ρA	AVE
CA		0.798	0.598	EE		0.876	0.657
CA1	0.888*			EE1	0.849*		
CA2	0.900*			EE2	0.845*		
CA3	0.709*			EE3	0.744*		
CA4	0.770*			EE4	0.809*		
CA5	0.753*			EE5	0.801*		
DCE		0.954	0.572	JS		0.809	0.727
DCE1	0.738*			JS1	0.782*		
DCE2	0.769*			JS2	0.892*		
DCE3	0.796*			JS3	0.880*		
DCE4	0.852*			LS		0.873	0.794
DCE5	0.708*			LS1	0.844*		
ACE		0.861	0.696	LS2	0.908*		
ACE1	0.854*			LS3	0.920*		
ACE2	0.809*						
ACE3	0.801*						
ACE4	0.872*						

Notes CA = Customer aggression; DCE = disproportionate customer expectations; ACE = ambiguous customer expectations; EE = emotional exhaustion; JS = job satisfaction; LS = life satisfaction; * = significant ($p < 0.05$), CA = Cronbach' alphas, ρA = rho_A; and AVE = average variance extracted

Table 3 Discriminant validity

	CA	DCE	ACE	EE	JS
DCE	0.772*				
ACE	0.448*	0.641*			
EE	0.594*	0.413*	0.895*		
JS	0.403*	0.648*	0.808*	0.839*	
LS	0.442*	0.622*	0.785*	0.809*	0.862*

Notes CA = Customer aggression; DCE = disproportionate customer expectations; ACE = ambiguous customer expectations; EE = emotional exhaustion; JS = job satisfaction; LS = life satisfaction; and * = statistically different from 1

Jin, 2019). These disruptive technologies and platforms have retained the attention of academia and experts trying to comprehend the factors that encourage its worldwide diffusion (Henama & Sifolo, 2017). In this vein, they enable would-be entrepreneur activities (Berger et al., 2019; Burtch et al., 2018), flexible work hours (Burtch et al., 2018), and additional income (Berger et al., 2019). However, little is known about the dark side of the gig economy (Henama & Sifolo, 2017). In this chapter, we develop

Table 4 Results of the structural model

	β	95% BCa CI
CA → EE	0.173	[0.098; 0.276]
DCE → EE	0.196	[0.110; 0.290]
ACE → EE	0.262	[0.142; 0.384]
EE → JS	−0.715	[−0.777; −0.646]
EE → LS	−0.712	[−0.756; −0.643]
	R^2	Q^2
EE	69.5%	0.426
JS	51.1%	0.344
LS	50.7%	0.380

Notes CA = Customer aggression; DCE = disproportionate customer expectations; ACE = ambiguous customer expectations; EE = emotional exhaustion; JS = job satisfaction; LS = life satisfaction; and BCa CI = bias-corrected and accelerated (BCa) bootstrap confidence interval

a research framework exploring the effects of unfavourable factors (i.e. customer aggression, disproportionate customer expectations, and ambiguous customer expectations) on emotional exhaustion and, in turn, on job satisfaction and life satisfaction on the basis of responses from Uber drivers.

6 Implications

This study shows that customer aggression, disproportionate customer expectations, end ambiguous customer expectations have detrimental effects on Uber driver job satisfaction and life satisfaction. Indeed, these factors increase their levels of emotional exhaustion and, in turn, decrease their job satisfaction and even life satisfaction. These results are in line with other qualitative studies in this field (Berger et al., 2019). This situation is mainly due to the idea of the supremacy of customer sovereignty (Fisk et al., 2010). Indeed, traditional marketing assumptions, such as "the customer is king" and "the customer is always right", can lead Uber drivers to suppress their dissatisfaction and rage and serve customers with a smile even though they do not really want to (Madupalli & Poddar, 2014). Such an approach can be counterproductive in certain conditions because it can generate an unbalanced power relationship between workers and customers, which may make some customers behave improperly (Choi et al., 2014). This work highlights that Uber should be aware that customers are not always right and that in some circumstances they are accountable for causing stress and life dissatisfaction in their drivers (Fisk et al., 2010; Grandey et al., 2004). From a managerial perspective, this work has useful implications for business practices in the gig economy sector.

Uber should invest in improving the skill and ability of its drivers to manage and cope with demanding or aggressive customers. Since the number of drivers is huge, it can record and disseminate internal training videos and case studies (for resolving problems and improving listening skills) on how to efficiently cope with these types of stressful situations. Uber can keep records of customer abuse incidents in order to monitor and understand them and develop successful responses (Karatepe, 2011). The implementation of such training programmes teaches them how to cope with stressful situations (Karatepe et al., 2010).

Uber should also empower their drivers by giving them high levels of the freedom to make decisions (Forrester, 2000). This can be reached by placing dash cams (internal cameras recording the interior of the car that automatically send real-time audio and video to the Uber system). Moreover, Uber can help its drivers file suits against the rudest and the most aggressive customers. It can also reward (tangible and intangible rewards) good performance as recognition of competence and the successful management of customer demands and aggression (Forrester, 2000). Uber should have a more caring and unique relationship with its partners and interact with them more compassionately and consistently to express that it cares for them as it does for its customers. It can communicate supportive messages to its partners (Forrester, 2000). Another solution is to put experienced drivers in touch with younger ones in order to share their experience (failures and successes) regarding customer aggression and discuss the possibility of providing psychological support when needed (via internal chat rooms).

These activities send powerful signals about the presence of an encouraging, sympathetic, and protective environment (Karatepe et al., 2018). Moreover, Uber should obtain periodic feedback from partners to measure their level of emotional exhaustion and identify the factors that have contributed the most to its formation (Karatepe, 2013). In sum and as suggested by Kahn (1990), partners should have protective guarantees to reduce their stress and increase their job and life satisfaction.

References

Babakus, E., Yavas, U., & Ashill, N. J. (2009). The role of customer orientation as a moderator of the job demandburnout-performance relationship: A surface-level trait perspective. *Journal of Retailing, 85*(4), 480–492.

Barile, S., Lusch, R., Reynoso, J., Saviano, M., & Spohrer, J. (2016). Systems, networks, and ecosystems in service research. *Journal of Service Management, 27*(4), 652–674.

Belanche, D., Casaló, L. V., Flavián, C., & Pérez-Rueda, A. (2021). The role of customers in the gig economy: How perceptions of working conditions and service quality influence the use and recommendation of food delivery services. *Service Business*. https://doi.org/10.1007/s11628-020-00432-7

Berger, T., Frey, C. B., Levin, G., & Danda, S. R. (2019). Uber happy? Work and well-being in the 'Gig Economy.' *Economic Policy, 34*(99), 429–477.

Buchwald, P., & Schwarzer, C. (2010). Impact of assessment on students' test anxiety. In P. Peterson, E. Baker & B. McGaw (Eds.), *International Encyclopedia of Education* (3rd ed., pp. 498–505). Elsevier.

Burtch, G., Carnahan, S., & Greenwood, B. N. (2018). Can you gig it? An empirical examination of the gig economy and entrepreneurial activity. *Management Science, 64*(12), 5497–5520.

Cheng, M., & Jin, X. (2019). What do Airbnb users care about? An analysis of online review comments. *International Journal of Hospitality Management, 76*, 58–70.

Choi, C. H., Kim, T. T., Lee, G., & Lee, S. K. (2014). Testing the stressor-strain-outcome model of customer-related social stressors in predicting emotional exhaustion, customer orientation and service recovery performance. *International Journal of Hospitality Management, 36*, 272–285.

Demerouti, E., Bakker, A. B., Nachreiner, F., & Schaufeli, W. B. (2000). A model of burnout and life satisfaction amongst nurses. *Journal of Advanced Nursing, 32*(2), 454–464.

Diener, E., Emmons, R. A., Larsen, R. J., & Griffin, S. (1985). The satisfaction with life scales. *Journal of Personality Assessment, 49*(1), 71–75.

Dormann, C., & Zapf, D. (2004). Customer-related social stressors and burnout. *Journal of Occupational Health Psychology, 9*(1), 61–82.

Duggan, J., Sherman, U., Carbery, R., & McDonnell, A. (2020). Algorithmic management and app-work in the gig economy: A research agenda for employment relations and HRM. *Human Resource Management Journal, 30*(1), 114–132.

Fisk, R., Grove, S., Harris, L. C., Keeffe, D. A., Russell/Bennett, R., Daunt, K. L., Wirtz, J. (2010). Customers behaving badly: A state of the art review, research agenda and implications for practitioners. *Journal of Services Marketing, 24*(6), 417–429.

Forrester, R. (2000). Empowerment: Rejuvenating a potent idea. *Academy of Management Executive, 14*(3), 67–78.

Gaines, J., & Jermier, J. M. (1983). Emotional exhaustion in a high stress organization. *Academy of Management Journal, 26*(4), 567–586.

Grandey, A. A., Dickter, D. N., & Sin, H.-P. (2004). The customer is not always right: Customer aggression and emotion regulation of service employees. *Journal of Organizational Behavior, 25*(3), 397–418.

Hair, J. F., Hult, G. T. M., Ringle, C. M., & Sarstedt, M. (Eds.). (2017). *A Primer on Partial Least Squares Structural Equation Modeling (PLS-SEM)* (2nd ed.). Sage Publications.

Hartline, M. D., & Ferrell, O. C. (1996). The management of customer-contact service employees: An empirical investigation. *Journal of Marketing, 60*, 52–70.

Henama, U. S., & Sifolo, P. P. S. (2017). Uber: The South Africa experience. *African Journal of Hospitality, Tourism and Leisure, 6*(2), 1–10.

Hobfoll, S. E. (2001). Social support and stress. In N. J. Smelser & P. B. Baltes (Eds.), *International Encyclopedia of the Social & Behavioral Sciences* (pp. 14461–14465). Elsevier.

Kahn, W. A. (1990). Psychological conditions of personal engagement and disengagement at work. *Academy of Management Journal, 33*(4), 692–724.

Karatepe, O. M. (2011). Customer aggression, emotional exhaustion, and hotel employee outcomes: A study in the United Arab Emirates. *Journal of Travel and Tourism Marketing, 28*(3), 279–295.

Karatepe, O. M. (2013). High-performance work practices, work social support and their effects on job embeddedness and turnover intentions. *International Journal of Contemporary Hospitality Management, 25*(6), 903–921.

Karatepe, O. M., & Baddar, L. (2006). An empirical study of the selected consequences of frontline employees' work-family conflict and family-work conflict. *Tourism Management, 27*(5), 1017–1028.

Karatepe, O. M., Haktanir, M., & Yorganci, I. (2010). The impacts of core self-evaluations on customer-related social stressors and emotional exhaustion. *Service Industries Journal, 30*(9), 1565–1579.

Karatepe, O. M., Yavas, U., Babakus, E., & Deitz, G. D. (2018). The effects of organizational and personal resources on stress, engagement, and job outcomes. *International Journal of Hospitality Management, 74*, 147–161.

Kost, D., Fieseler, C., & Wong, S. (2020). Boundaryless careers in the gig economy: An oxymoron? *Human Resource Management Journal, 30*(1), 1–12.

Lee, R. T., & Ashforth, B. E. A. (1996). Meta-analytic examination of the correlates of the three dimensions of job burnout. *Journal of Applied Psychology, 81*(2), 123–133.

Lee, K., Hakstian, A.-M., & Williams, J. D. (2021). Creating a world where anyone can belong anywhere: Consumer equality in the sharing economy. *Journal of Business Research, 130*, 221–231.

Madupalli, R., & Poddar, A. (2014). Problematic customers and customer service employee retaliation. *Journal of Services Marketing, 28*(3), 244–255.

Ossig, J., Cramer, S., & Bengler, K. (2021). Concept of an ontology, for automated vehicle behavior in the context of human-centered research on automated driving styles. *Information, 12*, 1–14.

Podsakoff, P. M., MacKenzie, S. B., Lee, J.-Y., & Podsakoff, N. P. (2003). Common method biases in behavioral research: A critical review of the literature and recommended remedies. *Journal of Applied Psychology, 88*(5), 879–903.

Ringle, C. M., Wende, S., & Becker, J.- M. (2015). *SmartPLS 3. Bönningstedt: SmartPLS*. https://www.smartpls.com/

Statista (2021). *Monthly Number of Uber's Active Users Worldwide from 2017 to 2020, by Quarter (in Millions)*. https://www.statista.com/statistics/833743/us-users-ride-sharing-services/

Uber (2021). *Uber's technology offerings*. https://www.uber.com/fr/en/about/uber-offerings/

Uber Estimator (2021). *Uber Cities*. https://uberestimator.com/cities

Van Dierendonck, D., & Mevissen, N. (2002). Aggressive behavior of passengers, conflict management behavior, and burnout among trolley car drivers. *International Journal of Stress Management, 9*(4), 345–355.

Digital Industrial Revolution 4.0 and Sustaining Gig Economy: Challenges and Opportunities Ahead

Om Prakash Gusai, Ankur Rani, and Preeti Yadav

1 Introduction

In today's scenario, gig workers are everywhere. The term gig economy is used in a collective way to elaborate the independent workers or freelancers. In this economy, people work independently, and "the short-term commitment" made by the gig workers, also known as gigs, "is the norm rather than the exception" (Kobie, 2018). A typical classification of employment in the gig economy is based on the interaction of many parties, such as the relationship between a seller and a mediator, as well as the relationship between the seller and the customer (Healy et al., 2017). The seller is generally known as the independent worker who provides the labor and manages the time, but sometimes the seller can be the producer (like in case of a restaurant, the owner is producer as well as seller of the products and services). Essentially, for the purpose of the transaction, arrangements that are focused on a specific objective will be used to achieve a high degree of autonomy or independence (McKinsey Global Institute, 2016). There is a mediator in the middle of the transaction, but who is that mediator? We have to ask ourselves, is not it? The platform firm acts as a go-between when it comes to making arrangements. Connecting customers and vendors requires some degree of participation from the platform company.

O. P. Gusai
Department of Commerce, Motilal Nehru College, University of Delhi, New Delhi 110021, India
e-mail: opgusai@mln.du.ac.in

A. Rani (✉)
Department of Commerce, Baba Mastnath University, Rohtak, Haryana 124021, India

P. Yadav (✉)
Department of Commerce, Kamal Institute of Higher Education and Advance Technology, GGSIPU, New Delhi 110059, India

A. Gupta et al. (eds.), *Sustainability in the Gig Economy*,
https://doi.org/10.1007/978-981-16-8406-7_14

The platform can be tabled in many different ways, and the dependency of platforms is based on the arrangement of jobs among the gig workers. The platforms can be separated in four categories like the transportation platform, platform which is related to crowd work, the different task-oriented platforms, and the digital freelance platforms. There are significant differences among these platforms; for example, crowd work platforms are generally defined by low wages and fewer workers, whereas the transportation and delivery task-oriented platforms focus on higher wages and the digital free land platform deals with higher wages and workers control in a positive spirit (Kalleberg & Dunn, 2016). The correlation exists among the payment and the required skills to carry on the work by gig workers. The gig worker platform companies are often cited as a defining characteristic of the gig economy, but this is not the case according to Kobie (2018) and Hill (2016), who argue that workers with higher skill levels are less reliant on piecework distribution through digitalization than workers with lower skill levels. The economy of the gig worker is not really a new environment, but it is a new designation for the relationship between self-employed people, such as freelancers, independent contractors, and workers who operate on a project-by-job basis.

According to the arguments given by Harris and Krueger (2015), the classification of gig economy is a new pattern of employment in the technologically changing world. It should involve the work for both the digital and non-digital economies. On the basis of above discussion, it is not easy to conclude whether gig economy will expand or stagnate in the future. The gig economy shows the different aspects depending upon the different cultures of the countries. The legal formalities also create the differences in the platforms. The gig work economy is impacted by the culture and traditions of the nation. For example, in Sweden, the nature of jobs done by white-collar workers (those engaged in service industry) is different from that of the jobs done by blue-collar workers (any worker engaged in hard manual labor).

The gig economy has gained a lot of fame and attention from media, and depending upon the widespread popularity of the gig economy, most companies and their stakeholders are looking for efficient and capable gig workers. Whether it is a new concept or old one, the day-by-day expanding gig economy is successful in keeping the trust of stakeholders by serving various cost-effective advantages to the companies.

2 Gig Economy's Timeline

The evolution of gig economy took place during the revolution of industrial sector. Industrial Revolution leads to revolution of mechanization. It was started in the late 1700s. The main characterization of the First Industrial Revolution was defined by the steam engine appearance. During second revolution of industrial sector, electricity took place and it was called as Industry 2.0. In middle of the twentieth century, Industry 3.0 originated in which the information technology collaborated with the production lines. Now, it is the era of Industry 4.0, where the collaboration of digitalization and artificial intelligence is taking place. From past to present day, the gig economy has been an integral part of every Industrial Revolution.

1. **Gig economy's past**: It was necessary to retrospect the Industrial Revolution because, as the evolution arises, the gig economy transforms in a constant way, and now it is present today due to the various developments in the labor market. Labor patterns were changed during Industry 1.0 where productivity gains were accelerated with the technology of steam engine, and massive productivity gains were generated in massive aspects. In today's scenario, the workforce evolves in a dynamic manner because today the demand is for flexible jobs. It is not a new concept that has evolved today; it is acceleration in the transformation from mechanistic field to digital field.
2. **Gig economy's present**: According to the Brookings Institute, the economic area will be grown from 2014 to 2025 with 14 billion dollars and 335 billion dollars, respectively (Yaraghi & Ravi, 2016). It is challenging for the gig economy to the exact statistics related to employment. The estimation done by JP Morgan platform in 2016 was the revenue earned by at least 1% of adults from the digital platform, and it was more than 4% of the workers who worked for 3 years on digital platforms. The traditional workers, which are now been replaced by workers who work on the basis of their time as a guest to the organization, can also use platforms for earning the extra money (Farrell & Greig, 2016).

   There was a survey conducted by McKinsey and Company, for the gig industry workers' motivation. The survey was conducted on the basis of self-employed workers, with the sample size of active population of around 20–30% in the field. The study concluded that from the primary and secondary sources of income, there were many direct participants. Workers in the gig economy were motivated in two ways: by preferred choices and by necessity. By preferred choices, around 49 million free agents were from primary income and 40% casual earners that is 64 million from supplemental income. In the out of necessity category, there were 14% reluctant that is 23 million from primary income and 16% financially strapped that is 26 came from supplemental income (McKinsey Global Institute, 2016, own processing).
3. **Gig economy's future**: The labor market is going to heavily effected from the technological development and use of artificial intelligence. In the coming years, the gig economy will have an impact on the global economy. There are various factors which are possible for the growth of gig services, like the comfort and the flexibility. This flexible work can eliminate the secondary cost of production. The consumer will benefit apart from the price and the choices as compared to the traditional ways of business. In the gig economy, the most powerful aspect is how to balance the cost–benefit together. The flexibility comes in the fundamental trade, which allows the workers to strike for an offset with their work and life together, with the obligations and limitation in the work but from the security aspect, it will not be an easy way of thought. When compared to

more traditional jobs, gig workers may face less protection at their workplaces, which means lower pay and more complicated tax obligations. They may also have difficulty taking advantage of retirement and insurance benefits because they do not have the same level of stability as traditional employees. Studies suggested that various gig activities can impact on the health (Marquié et al., 2014).

The providers and consumers' ability to use technology in an effective manner is the most crucial element of the gig economy. It has to enhance the capital efficiency, but as no gain without pain, it has not come without risk and cost.

3 The Fourth Industrial Revolution

The First Industrial Revolution recognizes the application with steam engine to the production processes with mechanical aspect. The Second Industrial Revolution recognized the standard mechanical production in manufacturing with the use of electricity. The Third Industrial Revolution recognized the application of information technology and electronics together to bring specialization in the manufacturing sector. There was enormous destruction in the production processes and various changes in the cultural and social aspects of the organization. In the development of industries, the Internet is the key innovation for deriving the changes in information management and storing the data. The impact of the Internet and information and communication technology together at a rapid pace is the "Internet of things" era.

The digital connection provides the new possibilities and provides the new possibilities for generating innovations in manufacturing sector that is called 4IR. At the broad level, Industry 4.0 is the integration of various methods of manufacturing or production digitally, that is, the Industrial Internet of Things.

As a result of using robots in the digitalization process, advanced technology like artificial intelligence, big data, cloud computing, and 3D printing is introduced; the workers are expected to work with these technologies. The gig workers are also expected to have skill and knowledge of the machines to handle the assigned task properly. Major disruption happened in manufacturing processes. The innovation in the Industrial 4.0 implicates supply chain, the value chain, the transformation of the manufacturing workers' work from traditional to modern ways of working, and so on. The work in the digital economy is carried out with the use of sensors, robotic conveyor belts, and other such digital technologies that help in tracking the processes of the manufacturing sector and represent the quality control concerns (Federal ministry for economic affairs and Energy 2017; Sniderman et al. 2016). Industry 4.0 has enabled the use of smart work by industries that rely on digital connections with machines, such as outbound logistics and marketing services. It can easily compare with the real-time quality and advantage of the cost factor while comparing with the typical system of production (Kagermann et al. 2013).

Job transformation is tough in Industry 4.0 since machines conduct the work rather than humans, somehow it reaches the gap between the physical and virtual worlds with the new innovation and rated fees of digitalization the production the new business model can also be created for autonomous manufacturing for improving the value chain position (Sniderman et al. 2016).

Hence, the journey of digitalization in the products manufacturing has made many developments and conceptualization in the products recycling (Platform industries 4.0, 2017). It is a seamless collaboration of virtual and physical world that is the row transformation in the gig economy.

4 Reason for Growth of Gig Economy

In today's world, the gig economy is growing at a rapid pace. People prefer freelancing to full-time employment because it allows them more independence and flexibility in their work. Furthermore, gig workers find more work that is adaptable to changing needs. It is growing due to the lifestyle choices that were absent in conventional jobs. Workers can choose the time and location of their work based on their availability to provide services. Companies and organizations are also benefiting from it because less money is spent on the recruitment processes, they do not need to invest in medical coverage, and if the workforce is not suitable, it can easily be replaced. For businesses, there are a wide variety of gig workers who are available to work.

5 Examples of Application of Gig Economy

1. **Lyft**: This app is used for transport purposes and is a bit similar to Uber. The company provides its workers with a connection between drivers and riders and gives them "the prime time pricing" for earning the extra money in peak hours. The claim from the driver side regarding earnings is up to $35 per hour and tries to compete with Uber.
2. **Uber**: Uber is a perfect illustration of how the gig economy is being represented. The app is referred to as the "Uber driver partner's" application. This app allows workers to use the app at their own convenience and on their own time. They may even use their own personal automobiles to access the app.
3. **Amazon Flex**: According to studies, workers who deliver Amazon packages can earn around $20 per hour. This app also provides flexible time and gives the flexibility to make schedules.
4. **Airbnb**: As Uber provides the application for space transport, Airbnb is created for the purpose of housing property. This app allows the owners to post online about the availability of the property for the rental agreement. The referral bonus scheme is also introduced in this app.

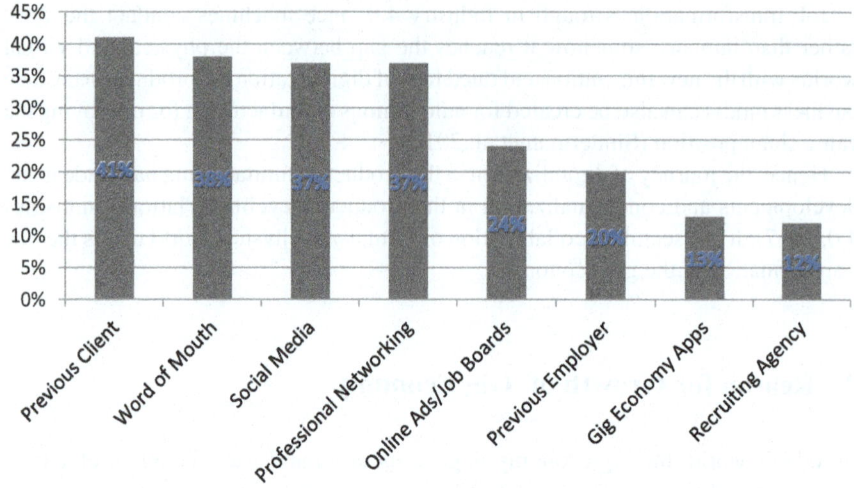

Fig. 1 Sources of gig work. *Source* Author's compilation of various studies

5. **Parking Panda**: In today's time, there is a huge fight for the parking space. Parking Panda app provides an opportunity to the space providers for gaining profits who are providing the perfect space to the customer who requires a space for parking.

6 Sources of Gig Work

It is not easy to get work in a gig economy, and the freelancers are required to build networks, keep themselves updated about the market, and grab the best opportunity available to them. They do not rely on a single source; in fact, there are multiple sources from where these gig workers get jobs which are illustrated in the graph in Fig. 1.

Figure 1 clearly shows that most of the freelancers rely on their networks and previous clients for new work and the rest of them rely upon other sources like recruitment firms, online ads or job boards, and apps for gig work updates.

7 Present Picture of the Gig Economy

The stories of the gig economy might look attractive to people, but in reality, there are risks which one might neglect. Most gig workers do not rely on only gig work for their survival; they maintain some sort of stable work option (primary source) with them. In a certain situation where they do not get work, at least they can have something for their survival in the form of that stable job. The statistics and studies on the gig

Table 1 Use of gig economy platforms by global workers to earn money

Countries	Gig work as primary source of income (%)	Gig work as secondary source of income (%)
USA	4	10
France	3	3
Germany	2	6
Spain	1	6
Sweden	1	3
UK	3	7
Japan	2	5
Brazil	5	13
Indonesia	3	23
India	8	31
China	12	33

Source Author's compilation of various studies

economy highlight the challenges gig workers face while working. Because the work is not stable, gig workers do not get a good monthly income as compared to traditional jobs. With the rapid development in technology, the workers are being replaced by machines, which reduce the existing number of assignments for them. The workers in a gig economy are set up to have a safer primary option, which increases their work burden and stress. The study conducted by various sources shows that in all the emerging global economies, the majority of gig workers consider gig work as their secondary source of income. They cannot totally rely on gig work as their primary source of income. The results of the study shown in Table 1

The study reveals that out of the all players of gig worker economy the majority of workers take gig work as a secondary option specially in the developing nations like India, China, Indonesia, and Brazil; the proportion of gig work dependence is lower as people keep a primary work with them to meet the uncertainties.

Figure 2 clearly shows that the percentage of the people having gig work as secondary source of income is higher than that of primary source. In emerging economies like Brazil, Indonesia, India, and China, the gig work is higher as a secondary source of earning as compared to the developed nations like UK, USA, Japan, and Germany.

8 The Future of Gig Economy in the Era of Digital Revolution 4.0

The Digital Revolution 4.0 is basically concerned with the technological advancements like high-speed Internet, automation and artificial intelligence, big data, and

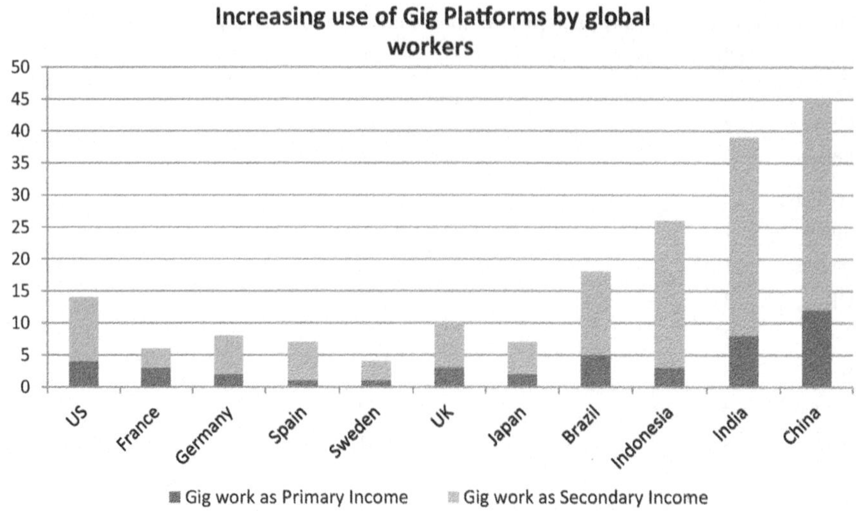

Fig. 2 Use of gig economy platforms by global workers to earn money. *Source* Author's compilation of various studies

cloud technology. These technological developments have significant impact on the employment level. These advancements are important to combat with the rising global competition, but at the same time the technology made by humans for their comfort is replacing human and taking their jobs. Most of the jobs that were earlier done by labors are now done by heavy machines. Global businesses are installing machines in order to reduce the time and cost of production, and this is resulting in a reduction in the demand for a full-time work force in the economy. A study undertaken by McKinsey Global Institute shows that about 20% of the global work force will be affected by the adoption of artificial intelligence and automation, and the most important impact will be on developed countries like UK, Germany, and the USA by 2022. The survey also reveals that by 2022, 50% of companies are going to reduce the number of full-time employees. By 2030, due to advancements in AI and automation, robots will be replacing 800 million workers globally (McKinsey Global Institute, 2016). These figures seem depressing as rising technology is gulping down the existing jobs for humans. These situations can be controlled by better planning and organizing and by grasping knowledge of machine handling. The future is full of opportunities and challenges, but one can combat the same by acquiring more skills and knowledge.

9 Benefits and Threats of the Gig Economy

On the one hand, the gig economy has been rapidly spreading as freelancers get the chance to earn money by performing the tasks on which they have their expertise, and on the other hand, the gig workers do not get regular pay and benefits like retirement, pension, or health insurance plans. Like any work, there are pros and cons to taking an interest in the gig economy.

10 Benefits of Gig Economy

1. **Flexible Approach**: The most attractive and important part of gig work is the flexibility. As a gig worker, the best part is that independent workers can choose the type of work they want to do and the type of people they want to work with. Gig workers can choose to work at the time that suits them best, and they are not forced to work under prescribed conditions nor have to work with people they do not like at all.
2. **Gives a chance to pursue passion**: The gig economy offers work to people based on their skills and talent. Gig workers take on tasks that they feel interested in doing, so they can pursue their passion while making money.
3. **Additional source of income**: Sometimes, gig workers take independent projects to pursue their passion, and it becomes their additional source of earning apart from their permanent job.
4. **Helps businesses in saving time and huge costs**: In a gig economy, organizations may reduce their costs connected to assets like cash and time. Cash is effortlessly saved by recruiting workers for short contracts; the companies do not have to worry about pensions, health insurance, provident funds, etc., for the short-term contractual workers. Moreover, the recruitment and selection process of permanent workers consumes time and cost, and gig workers help companies' save the time and costs involved in these recruitment and selection formalities.
5. **Free from work Politics and discrimination**: The gig economy enables people to work from the comfort of their home, and they do not have to face the discrimination and politics happening in the workplace. People working as gig workers do not have to work in a toxic work environment, and they can focus on their work properly.

11 Threats of Gig Economy

1. **No Benefits like a regular job**: The major problem with gig work is that people who choose to work as gig workers do not have benefits like pensions, provident funds, sick leave, paid leave, etc. They are paid only when they work, and they do not get paid when they do not get the work.
2. **Irregular Income**: In gig economy, payment is made on the basis of completion of a task. The issue arises when the work assigned to gig workers is not

completed on time and can lead to a delay in the payment. Also, when no tasks or assignments are available, these gig workers cannot earn any income.
3. **Overburdening and Stressful**: In order to earn more, gig workers take on multiple tasks at a time. Everyone cannot be good at multitasking, and some people find it difficult to handle multiple tasks at a time, which causes stress and makes the workers overburdened.
4. **Lacks seriousness and discipline**: No doubt, a gig worker feels freedom, but this freedom and independence can make him less serious toward work and, thus, there is a need for self-discipline to maintain the seriousness and focus toward the task assigned to him.
5. **Loneliness and no social interaction**: Most gig workers work from home in social isolation with a risk of not getting work in the future and an unstable income, which can adversely impact their mental health.
6. **Less support from Government**: A big challenge that gig workers might face is that they are not registered in the government's records or the records of regulatory agencies, which makes it difficult to ensure that the help provided by the government reaches them.

12 Conclusion

A sustainable economy is one where people can meet their present needs without harming the needs of the future. But if we look deep into the realities of the gig economy, it does not guarantee a stable income for the people involved in gig work. In a condition of unstable income and uncertainty about work, the gig economy model is not sustainable at all. If the gig workers do not have enough resources to fulfill their present needs, then how are they going to meet their future requirements. Gig workers are dependent on various sources of income and work an average of 40 h per week. One can work upon the following things to grow in a gig work economy:

- Because work methodologies are rapidly changing as a result of technological advancements, continuous learning and knowledge expansion are essential.
- Making good connections with people will help you connect with prospective customers.
- Do not isolate yourself from society because working alone can lead to mental stress and your involvement with society can help you overcome that stress.
- Having expertise in the work assigned.
- Learn the skills required to perform the task efficiently.
- Maintain your self-discipline and take your work seriously.
- Choose the job wisely.

The gig economy is going to be the future of working culture no matter how advanced technology is introduced, because it cannot fully replace the need for human labor. As technological advancements eliminate the need for full-time workers, businesses will rely on gig workers to get their work done at a reasonable cost. This creates scope for the gig worker economy in the future. Companies benefit from the gig worker's lower costs, skilled labor, and efficiency, and their roles cannot be completely eliminated. The integration of innovation and technology is a never-ending aspect, and we can only develop it if proactive strategies are made in advance to meet the demands of a rapidly growing technological world. The government can also play a significant role in monitoring emerging changes and developing policies to protect the interests of gig workers.

References

Farrell, D., & Greig, F. (2016). *Paychecks, paydays, and the online platform economy.*

Federal Ministry for Economic Affairs and Energy. (2017). *Industrie 4.0.* https://www.bmwi.de/Redaktion/EN/Dossier/industrie-40.html

Gleim, M. R., Johnson, C. M., & Lawson, S. J. (2019). *Sharers and sellers: A multi-group examination of gig economy workers' perceptions.*

Harris, S. D., & Krueger, A. B. (2015). *A proposal for modernizing labor laws for twenty-first-century work: The "Independent Worker".* https://books.google.com/books/about/A_Proposal_for_Modernizing_Labor_Laws_html?

Healy, J., Nicholson, D., & Pekarek, A. (2017). Should we take the gig economy seriously? *Labour & Industry: A Journal of the Social and Economic Relations of Work, 27*(3), 232–248.

Hill, A. (2016, October 6). When McKinsey met Uber: The gig economy comes to consulting. *Financial Times.* https://www.ft.com/content/a5419fca-7f24-11e6-bc52-0c7211ef3198

https://hbr.org/2018/03/thriving-in-the-gig-economy

https://medium.com/@maximilian.weiner/the-gig-economy-is-going-to-die-unless-we-make-it-sustainable-60002fa7c6d0

https://www.bcg.com/publications/2019/new-freelancers-tapping-talent-gig-economy

https://www.websiteplanet.com/blog/freelance-stats/

Kagermann, H., Wahlster, W., & Helbig, J. (2013). *Securing the future of German manufacturing industry: Recommendations for implementing the strategic initiatives INDUSTRIE 4.0—Final report of the Industrie 4.0 working group.* Acatech—National Academy of Science and Engineering.

Kalleberg, A. L., & Dunn, M. (2016). Good Jobs, Bad Jobs in the Gig Economy. *Perspectives onWork.*

Kobie, N. (2018, September 14). What is the gig economy and why is it so controversial? Retrieved February 6, 2019, from https://www.wired.co.uk/article/what-is-the-gig-economy-meaningdefinition-why-is-it-called-gig-economy

Kuhn, K. M. (2016) *The rise of the "Gig Economy" and implications for understanding work and workers.*

Marquié, J.-C., Tucker, P., Folkard, S., Gentil, C., & Ansiau, D. (2014) *Chronic effects of shift work on cognition: findings from the VISAT longitudinal study.*

McKinsey Global Institute. (2016). *Independent Work: Choice, Necessity, and the Gig Economy.* McKinsey Global Institute.

Oyer, P. (2020). *The gig economy: Non-traditional employment is a great opportunity for many, but it won't replace traditional employment.*

Platform Industry 4.0 2017. What Is Industry 4.0? http://www.plattformi40.de/I40/Navigation/EN/Industrie40/WhatIsIndustrie40/what-is-industrie40.html

Roy, G., & Shrivastava, A. K. (2020). *Future of Gig Economy: Opportunities and Challenges.*

Schwellnus, C., Geva, A., Pak, M., & Veiel, R. (2019). *Gig economy platforms: boon or bane?*

Sniderman, B., Mahto, M., & Cotteleer, M. J. (2016). *Industry 4.0 and manufacturing ecosystems*. Deloitte.

Sundararajan, A. (2015) *Will the on-demand economy raise global living standards?* World Economic Forum online, September 9, 2015. www.weforum.org/agenda/2015/09/will-the-on-demandeconomy-raise-global-living-standards/.

The five faces of the on demand economy, Intuit, 2016.

The online platform economy in 2018, JPMorgan Chase Institute, 2018.

Ungureanu, A. (2019). *Industry 4.0. The Role of Gig Economy in the Industrial Revolution of the 21st Century*.

Weil, D. (2014) *The fissured workplace: Why work became so bad for so many and what can be done to improve it*. Harvard University Press.

Yaraghi, N., & Ravi, S. (2016). *The current and future state of the sharing economy*.

Operating in Industry 4.0: The Need for Gig-Workers and Systems Approach

Ashutosh Shukla, Ashish Mohan Dubey, and Sunil Kumar Pandey

1 Introduction

Every age is yet another opportunity to revisit our most sustainable values. The values have stood the test of time and are relatively stable for thousands of years. These values have manifested them in different forms of arts, culture, music, architectures, literature and indeed in our scientific progress. One of the values psychology identifies in human beings is that of 'control'. It is our innate desire to control people and things around us; however, we are seldom willing to admit it (Skinner, 1955). All human struggles whether it resulted in creating something valuable for humanity or our most painful lessons of fighting world wars, and it is the intrinsic desire to control which has found its manifestation. The whole equation of life revolves around this intrinsic desire to control. At this stage, it is safe to assume that any act that brings more control in our hands is going to be welcomed by masses. As we move into the newest version of Industrial Revolution, popularly known as Industry 4.0 we have to actively look if it is going to bring more control in human hands or is it going to be perhaps for the first time that we see humans competing with robots or artificial intelligence?

Is Industry 4.0 an obvious extension of Industry 3.0? With computers making a mainstay in almost all the industries and advent of the Internet in connecting the whole world, we could see Industry 3.0 setting the right stage for the next level of revolution. Not only did our phones became smarter but also we witnessed an emergence of a robust and reliable digital platform with incredible capabilities of doing businesses and giving people a powerful alternative to traditional systems of markets, banking and plethora of services from paying bills to health care and

A. Shukla (✉)
School of Management Sciences, Varanasi, India
e-mail: ashutoshshukla@smsvaranasi.com

A. M. Dubey · S. K. Pandey
Birla Institute of Technology Mesra, Patna Campus, Patna, India

A. Gupta et al. (eds.), *Sustainability in the Gig Economy*,
https://doi.org/10.1007/978-981-16-8406-7_15

education. We have to remember that 'smart' in the smartphone is not an adjective, but a comprehensive term of adding plural functions to it. We as a society are trying to achieve even greater capabilities by adding 'smart' to our devices, institutions, governance, production systems and cities. Smart technologies are about bringing integration and interactions into our devices and systems by active use of complex networks and AI.

The ability to network or networking remained as the panacea for small and start-up firms in high-tech industry for abridging physical (geographical) or psychological (knowledge-based) distance to resources, opportunities and capital (Andersson et al., 2013; Brekke, 2015; Coduras et al., 2016). Using text-mining techniques, Jalali et al. (2020) revealed 'networks' among the most relevant ten keywords to describe Industry 4.0. There have been a number of studies supporting the relationship between network and innovations (Partanen et al., 2014); for instance, diverse network relationships have radical internationalization and innovation (Chetty & Stangl, 2010a, 2010b). Network leads to enhancing public sector innovation (Bland et al., 2010). Networks are marked for their contagion characteristics. Be it transmission of an idea or an outbreak of a disease, in a networked world it spreads faster. In a working paper based on an extensive analysis of 1.8 million US patents and their citations in mapping the innovation network and its strength, Acemoglu et al. (2016) found that when there is more past upstream innovation for a particular technology class to build on, then that technology class innovates more. Simply speaking our future is going to be more driven by AI.

2 Evolution of Industry 4.0

A snapshot into the earlier versions of Industry Revolutions:

The great strides in scientific progress made during the past three centuries established science and its varied applications, in the form of reliable technologies to serve mankind in different walks of life. The era of First Industrial evolution came handy with realizing the power of steam and water to power engines that could be used to commute or transport and for doing many things such as production of goods which were earlier being done by humans alone. The Second Industrial Revolution also known as technological revolution featured introduction of assembly lines resulting in mass production and spreading of large rail networks and introduction of telegram. The advent of electricity further resulted in electrification of factories and modernizing production lines. The Third Industrial Revolution dated back to the ending years of the 1960s when first programmable logic control system was built. This revolution is known as the digital revolution. During this time, the role of computers rose to a significant degree in almost every industry and nearly all aspects of society. The biggest game-changer of this era turned out to be Internet which has rightly laid the foundation of the upcoming Industrial Revolution 4.0. At present, we are very much in Industry 4.0, which is in its early stage (Lins and Oliveira, 2020), but the

Table 1 Fourth Industrial Revolution

Industry	Time span	Main thrust
Industry 1.0 Also known as Industrial Revolution	1760–1840	Replacing production by hands to machines mostly powered by steam and water, emergence of factories
Industry 2.0 Also known as technological revolution	1870–1914	Development of assembly lines, construction of large railroad networks, electrification of factories, advent of telegram
Industry 3.0 Also known as digital revolution	Later second half of twentieth century (1969)	Internet, application of electronics and IT to further automate production
Industrial 4.0 Also known as Internet of everything or Industrial Internet	Beginning of the twenty-first century	Smart and autonomous systems backed by big data and machine learning. Rise of smart factories, smart ports, smart cities

institutions and researchers are largely identifying it with creation of smart manufacturing systems built on digital automation and the Internet. Table 1 summarizes the Fourth Industrial Revolution under name of Industrial Revolution, its time span and its main thrust or the changes it introduced in the world.

If we are to evaluate Industrial Revolution 4.0 from its predecessors, we could see that each one resulted in bringing the technology closer to our life. While the earlier versions of revolution were more about 'introductions' such as emergence of factory system, setting up manufacturing facilities, economic systems, factory workers and labour laws, the Industry 4.0 is more about 'integrations', and that makes all difference! It translates to revisiting our views of the world, as a single complex system. It means getting rid of 'silo-based thinking' and learning the art of seeing the whole. It means evolution of virtual platforms making actual changes in our working, spending and overall life styles. The unfolding of Industrial Revolution and its consequences in transforming businesses and social systems are immense but, in this chapter, we shall confine our discussions to three important themes—defining Industrial 4.0, its impact on jobs and, lastly, developing a system approach to operate in Industry 4.0.

3 Defining Industry 4.0

Industry 4.0 is essentially the transformation of manufacturing and production systems by introducing new technologies. The Government of Germany is accredited with using the term Industry 4.0 for the first time, to integrate digital technologies into its national manufacturing strategy. Industry 4.0 is marked by high level of automation, integration of industries (Liu and Xu, 2017) and industrial information integration (Xu, 2020). It is largely based on integration of business and manufacturing processes as well as integration of all actors in the value chain from customers to suppliers (Rojko, 2017).

There has been a number of definitions of Industry 4.0; for instance, Delloite identifies this term with a further developmental stage in the organization and management of entire value chain to its predecessors' versions. It specifically views the Fourth Industrial Revolution on the basis of cyber-physical production systems and merging of real and virtual worlds.

Klaus Schwab (2018) defines it as the fusion of the technologies [AI, big data, IoT, bioinformatics] and their interaction across the physical, digital and biological domains that make the Fourth Industrial Revolution fundamentally different from previous revolutions—diffusing faster and more broadly than any of the previous revolutions. At the heart of Industry 4.0 lies a strong backbone of new and enabling technologies.

Industry 4.0 refers to cyber-physical systems in a connected environment, where physical and software components are deeply intertwined through sensors and actuators connected to a controller. Software controls the physical mechanism with algorithms for decision-making, using data generated from operations. Autonomous vehicles, intelligent process controls, robotics and expert systems are some of the examples of cyber-physical systems. It is clear that Industry 4.0 orchestrates discussing the world as a giant system or a system of systems. One of the defining characteristics of a system is that the whole is greater than the sum of its part. And it requires even more skills to understand the behavioural dynamics of a system. The fact that we shall be moving in a more interconnected world involving complex systems, one of the essential skills would be to start learning more about systems in terms how we work being part of the system and how it responds back.

4 The Technology–Job Relationship in Industry 4.0

Technology has been always seen as a reliable mechanism to automate our systems and processes resulting in greater efficiency and better service capability. At the same point of time, technology is always feared to replace or eliminate jobs in huge numbers. As we move into Industry 4.0, we foresee many of the jobs being eliminated of course, and it would allow for creation of new jobs too, which might have not even existed in any of the previous Industrial Revolutions. But the question remains on the net effect of Industry 4.0 in changing the dynamics of labour market.

In the new order, the jobs requiring unskilled labours will be automated, and therefore, the jobs under unskilled category will be largely replaced (Şener & Elevli, 2017). It is likely to impact countries like India, where some 86% of the workers belong to unskilled or low-skilled job categories as per the unemployment survey of Labour Bureau (2015–2016). Quoting a number of agencies including FIICI, NASCOM (2017) and ILO (2018), Mashelkar (2018) argues that the Industry 4.0

is less likely to affect the informal sector where a significant portion of unskilled workers fall, while the formal or organized sector is more likely to face its larger impact, similar to the experiences of industrial countries. As per the World Bank Report, Industry 4.0 is likely to threaten some sixty-nine per cent of job year on year. Mehta and Awasthi (2019) cautions about the ill-effects of Industry 4.0 in displacing millions of low or unskilled job through automation. World Economic Forum 2017 predicts creation of higher value jobs with altogether different skills and likely job losses in developing and developed countries including India. The picture may appear gloomy at the first go, but one has to assess the question from the perspective of the amount of workforce working in organized sectors, the sectoral break-up of working population and the speed of automation in different industries and sectors in a country. For instance, in India 49% of the workforce is engaged in agriculture which is less likely to be affected by Industry 4.0; in fact, there are studies supporting that the adoption of new technology will also benefit informal sector in the form of higher income and better working conditions (Mehta & Awasthi, 2019).

In a study by the Hays and Oxford Economics, analysing labour trends in 33 countries' report hollowing out of job distribution whereby some middle-skilled jobs will disappear. However, more jobs will be created at both the upper and the lower levels. In line with this, World Economic Forum predicts creation of 133 million new jobs against 75 million jobs lost as a result of Industry 4.0 after a comprehensive study following the roles of 15 million workers in 20 countries. Given that Industry 4.0 shall result in addition of jobs at certain level and deletion of jobs at a different level, it is sometimes referred to create polarization of jobs (Mehta & Awasthi, 2019).

Quantitatively inquiring into the question may result in a net addition or deletions of jobs, but equally important would be to probe into the qualitative changes in the jobs. Gates and Bremicker (2017) highlight a massive transition in employee skills, recruitment and training as a result of Industry 4.0. They reinforce on identifying the new capabilities and skills and identifying the current employees ready to be upskilled, amid the human resources challenges HR leaders likely to confront in the present phase of IR 4.0. As Industry 4.0 foresees creation of more high-end jobs, an open mindset to learn new things and upskilling oneself with changing technology shall become even more crucial. The enabling technologies of Industry 4.0 shall result in creating more virtual workplaces discounting on geographical locations and shall allow to access skilled professionals anywhere from the world. This would trigger a demand for a fluid workforce or gig-workers thriving on the unique and multi-fold opportunities presented by the firms under Industry 4.0.

4.1 Gig-Worker: A Natural Demand for a Networked World

Operating in a world of interacting systems and overlapping domains, Industry 4.0 foresees an increased demand of flexible and autonomous workers. It presents an opportunity to develop a fluid workforce, an access to specialist or super-specialist, and enjoy cost savings and greater productivity. Sundararajan (2016) differentiates two types of work in a gig economy: work on demand, where physical services such as plumbing or child care can be rendered locally by using a simple mechanism of booking or requesting over an app or Internet. Second, 'virtual service' could be performed remotely via Internet such as accounting or translation. It has been estimated that contingent workers will make up nearly half of all US workers in 2020 with 11% working on-demand platform (Huws, 2016). The trend is on rise, with gig economy growing by 26% in 2017 according to Kässi and Lehdonvirta (2018) at Oxford Internet Institute. They further observe India accounting to about a quarter of global gig-workers, Bangladesh at 16%, the USA at 12% and 8% for Pakistan (Fig. 1).

In a networked world, the access to qualified person or teams would be easier for organizations to gain an access to and deliberate jobs. For any given piece of job, there will be a pool of qualified professionals with right blend of experience and expertise. It is not difficult to assume the modalities of their working where the digital platforms shall be connecting the professionals with the companies. In terms of job design, it will be worth assessing the job of a gig-worker using the framework given by J. Richard Hackman and Greg Oldham. It describes any job over five core job dimensions:

Skill variety: It represents the degree to which a job requires a variety of different skills so that the worker can use specialized skills and talents. A gig-worker has specialized skills and talents to offer his services, but he is also going to face an intense competition from professional with same expertise across geographies. He

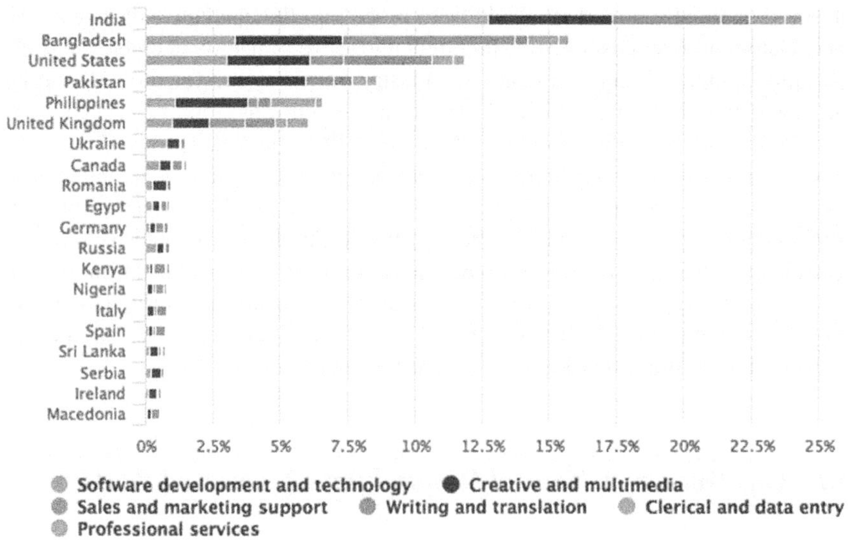

Fig. 1 Opportunities for gig-workers in different countries. *Source* Online Labour Index, *Reprinted with Permission of* Kässi and Lehdonvirta (2018)

has to upgrade himself with a number of professional skills to keep attracting projects and their successful delivery.

Task identity: It refers to the degree to which a job requires completion of whole and identifiable piece of work. Naturally, a gig-worker shall score high on this dimension, given that it would be the same dimension for which the gig-worker is hired.

Task significance: It is the degree to which a job affects the lives or work of others. In a number of projects, a gig-worker would be a part of a virtual team, and therefore, he has to perform his job in a manner that brings collaboration and integration to the flow of work.

Autonomy: One of the key values of freelancers or gig-workers is work autonomy. In other words, a gig-worker experiences a greater autonomy in his work and this allows for crafting jobs with enough discretion power in the hands of one who performs it. However, autonomy is more likely to dilute should a gig-worker becomes part of a working team.

Feedback: Lastly, a feedback about their own performance would allow the gig-workers to make an objective assessment of how well he has performed his job.

In terms of job characteristic model, the job of a gig-worker is a lot more autonomous, high on both task identity and significance, and full of varied skill; however, there are a number of issues which requires an immediate redressal towards making the surrounding conditions conducive for a gig-worker to contribute his services in Industry 4.0.

First, bringing gig-workers under the protection of certain employment laws shall define their working, remuneration, health, safety and welfare concerns. Most of the laws related to factories and labour were introduced during the First and Second Industrial Revolution. We also see a number of amendments in these laws from time to time, with change in nature and demand for the jobs and the workforce. As the Industry 4.0 precipitates newer challenges in human resources, there is a strong need to introduce fresh laws safeguarding the interests of workers and organizations.

Second, as the job becomes more contractual in nature, it would be difficult to assess the ownership of a job. Lack of ownership dilutes the accountability and affects the overall quality of a service; therefore, adding accountability to the work of a gig-worker shall remain an important issue to address while operating in Industry 4.0.

Third, a gig-worker is most likely to be a part of a physical or virtual team that allows for a better coordination and greater interaction. This is likely to make his work less autonomous. And fourth, there is a need for digital leadership to manage gig-workers by giving necessary directions, providing feedback, anticipating and addressing their concerns.

5 Systems Thinking: A Much Needed Framework to Operate in Industry 4.0

Industry 4.0 is rightly positioned to reinforce the work of Peter (1990) about learning organizations. Senge defines learning organization where people continually expand their capacity to create the result, they truly desire, where new and expansive patterns of thinking are nurtured, collective aspiration is set free and people are continually learning how to learn together. Advances in AI and its growing adaptations in different walks of life have definitely made us all to make more informed choices in our life. At the workplace, humans and machines are sharing workspace and more such workplaces will evolve in future. Indeed, it has added to enhance capacity of collectively realizing the desired goals.

Industry 4.0 is more akin to Senge's idea of systems thinking. In a system, it is the interaction among the underlying components that govern the behaviour of the system. The connections and communication become crucial. Here comes the Industry 4.0 where there are components, integrating technologies and complicated networks largely constituting complex systems.

Systems thinking addresses focusing on whole instead of parts. It gives learners an opportunity to seek point of leverage which acts as a key driver in fostering a transformative change. We constantly see evolution of complex systems evolving in today's time. The era of 'specialization' has moved into a space of overlapping domains, relations and interrelations where change in one part of a system has power to evoke different reactions and responses in the different parts of it. An interconnected world operates through network, and it brings forth a seamless capability of fast and wide spread adaptation of newer technologies and tools to make our lives better. The more we become aware of systems under which we operate, the more we become aware of the limitations and pitfalls of running biasness expressed under system archetypes. Our capability may be limited to understand complex systems, but AI could make better assessment in terms of identifying that which nodes of network are relatively more important in impacting the situation at hand and possibly locate a point of leverage which Senge calls the point to act on for bringing systemic and transformative change. For example, AI could possibly predict the outbreak of pandemic well in advance and could warn the whole world before it turns into a crisis.

Systems thinking is about understanding the world in terms of loops where consequence of an action is not just a linear cause and effect relationship, but a series of effects that feeds on through balancing and reinforcing feedback mechanism. Systems approach has its basis in general systems theory which formulates a transdisciplinary science for overcoming the cognitive limitations people have in understanding complex systems and their interconnectedness (Van Assche et al., 2019). This approach discounts on dualism and reductionism to social systems comprehension (Hofkirchner, 2019). In some of the notable classical work, Lawrence and Lorsch (1967) supported the concept of an organization as an open system in interaction with the environment. Systems approach attempts to address the need of science of understanding complex behaviour by providing a strong range of concepts for modelling of complex systems behaviour (Mingers & White, 2010).

As the world moves into Industry 4.0, we have to equip ourselves with right kinds of tools and life. The real challenge is not about learning new things, but about doing away with old patterns of thinking and acting. The methodology of breaking a complex problem into smaller parts might be a success story of yester decades, but it is going to be ineffective and ill-prepared for the future world. Industry 4.0 is unique from its predecessors because AI was not there at all. With Internet of things (IoTs), big data, virtual platforms, cobots and host of devices from mobiles to smart watch, enormous amount of data is being created every day. AI is silently feeding up the vital details in the background right from our health statistics, to our social connections to our interests, buying behaviour, even compulsive or conspiring behaviour that is feared to precipitate a crime. The policing function was largely seen as 'reactive', where it appears only after the crime had taken place, but now it is moving into a 'preventive role', where it could predict the occurrence of crime well in advance and stop it from happening at the first place. For instance, by assessing the word cloud comprising thoughts and likes shared over Twitter and Facebook, suspicious people and activities could be traced. AI has significantly improved the predictive power, and as we march through the Industry 4.0, we could expect a dramatic decrease in breakdowns and accidents in production plants and industry.

Our ability to read systems can be limited by many factors, and Industry 4.0 shall function as a 'system of systems' of multiple domains and fields involving complex networks; however, the power of AI could be harnessed to read these complex systems and identify crucial points or leverages to act upon in a timely manner.

6 Conclusion

Any revolution fundamentally brings forth a number of changes in human systems, and Industry 4.0 is no exception to that. As a matter of fact, it will bring changes marked by both magnitude and variety. With AI taking a forefront, the production and distribution systems will be transformed mandating a fresh review into how jobs are crafted and carried out. The technology–job relationship is most likely to change with increased automation, eliminations of some job levels, newer job designs and demand for gig-workers. It is also likely to precipitate a number of challenges towards sustainability of a system run by gig-workers without having sufficient legislative provisions, concerns about lack of ownership of job and need for digital leadership to provide necessary direction and addressing issues on virtual platforms. As a mechanism to operate in Industry 4.0, systems approach should be developed and practised for a deeper understanding of complex systems leading to improved predictability and better control.

References

Acemoglu, D., Akcigit, U., & Kerr, W. R. (2016). Innovation network. *Proceedings of the National Academy of Sciences,* 113(41), 11483–11488. https://economics.mit.edu/files/13372 accessed January 30, 2021.

Andersson, S., Evers, N., & Griot, C. (2013). Local and international networks in small firm internationalization: Cases from the Rhône-Alpes medical technology regional cluster. *Entrepreneurship & Regional Development, 25*(9–10), 867–888.

Bland, T., Bruk, B., Kim, D., & Lee, K. T. (2010). Enhancing public sector innovation: Examining the network-innovation relationship. *The innovation journal: The public sector innovation journal,* 15(3), 1–17.

Brekke, T. (2015). Entrepreneurship and path dependency in regional development. *Entrepreneurship & Regional Development, 27*(3–4), 202–218.

Bureau, L. (2016). *5th Annual Employment Unemployment Survey 2015–16 conducted by Labour Bureau.* Ministry of Labour and Employment, Government of India.

Chetty, S. K., & Stangl, L. M. (2010a). Internationalization and innovation in a network relationship context. *European Journal of Marketing.*

Chetty, S. K., & Stangl, L. M. (2010b). Internationalization and innovation in a network relationship context. *European Journal of Marketing, 44*(11/12), 1725–1743. https://doi.org/10.1108/03090561011079855

Coduras, A., Saiz-Alvarez, J. M., & Ruiz, J. (2016). Measuring readiness for entrepreneurship: An information tool proposal. *Journal of Innovation & Knowledge, 1*(2), 99–108.

Gates, D., & Bremicker, M. (2017). Beyond thc hype: Separating ambition from reality in i4. 0. *KPMG International.* Retrieved Mayo, 4, 2019.

Hofkirchner, W. (2019). Social relations: Building on Ludwig von Bertalanffy. *Systems Research and Behavioral Science, 36*(3), 263–273.

Huws, U. (2016). New forms of platform employment. *The Digital Economy and the Single Market.*

Industrial Internet Consortium, Industrial Internet Reference Architecture, Version 1.7, 2015.

Industry 4.0: Challenges and solutions for the digital transformation and use of exponential technologies. Retrieved January 21, 2021, from https://www2.deloitte.com/content/dam/Deloitte/ch/Documents/manufacturing/ch-en-manufacturing-industry-4-0-24102014.pdf

Jalali, S. M. J., Park, H. W., Vanani, I. R., & Pho, K. H. (2020). Research trends on big data domain using text mining algorithms. *Digital Scholarship in the Humanities.*

Kässi, O., & Lehdonvirta, V. (2018). Online labour index: Measuring the online gig economy for policy and research. *Technological Forecasting and Social Change, 137*, 241–248.

Lawrence, P. R., & Lorsch, J. W. (1967). Differentiation and integration in complex organizations. *Administrative science quarterly*, pp. 1–47.

Lins, T., & Oliveira, R. A. R. (2020). Cyber-physical production systems retrofitting in context of industry 4.0. *Computers & Industrial Engineering, 139*, 106193.

Liu, Y., & Xu, X. (2017). Industry 4.0 and cloud manufacturing: A comparative analysis. *Journal of Manufacturing Science and Engineering, 139*(3).

Mashelkar, R. A. (2018). Exponential technology, industry 4.0 and future of jobs in India. *Review of Market Integration, 10*(2), 138–157.

Mehta, B. S., & Awasthi, I. C. (2019). Industry 4.0 and future of work in India. *FIIB Business Review, 8*(1), 9–16.

Mingers, J., & White, L. (2010). A review of the recent contribution of systems thinking to operational research and management science. *European Journal of Operational Research, 207*(3), 1147–1161.

Partanen, J., Chetty, S., & Rajala, A. (2014). Innovation types and network relationships. *Entrepreneurship Theory and Practice, 38*, 1027–1055. https://doi.org/10.1111/j.1540-6520.2011.00474.x

Peter, S. (1990). *The fifth discipline. The Art & Practice of Learning Organization.* DoupledayCurrence.

Retrieved January 21, /2021, from https://tulip.co/resources/industry-4-0/
Rojko, A. (2017). Industry 4.0 concept: Background and overview. *International Journal of Interactive Mobile Technologies, 11*(5).
Schwab, K. (2018). The global competitiveness report 2018. In *World Economic Forum* (Vol. 671).
Şener, S., & Elevli, B. (2017). Endüstri 4.0'da Yeni İşKollarıveYüksekÖğrenim. *Engineering Minds Journal*, 25–37.
Skinner, B. F. (1955). Section of psychology: The control of human behavior. *Transactions of the New York Academy of Sciences, 17*(7 Series II), 547–551.
Sundararajan, A. (2016). The sharing economy. The End of Employment and the Rise of. Retrieved February 23, 2021, from https://www.imf.org/external/pubs/ft/fandd/2016/06/pdf/book3.pdf
Van Assche, K., Verschraegen, G., Valentinov, V., & Gruezmacher, M. (2019). The social, the ecological, and the adaptive. Von Bertalanffy's general systems theory and the adaptive governance of social-ecological systems. *Systems Research and Behavioral Science, 36*(3), 308–321.
What does the future of Industry 4.0 mean for your job? Viewpoint—careers advice blog (hays.com) Retrieved February 03, 2021.
Xu, L. D. (2020). The contribution of systems science to Industry 4.0. *Systems Research and Behavioral Science, 37*(4), 618–631.

Ashutosh Shukla is Assistant Professor at School of Management Sciences, Varanasi, India. He holds a Ph.D. in Management from BIT Mesra Ranchi. His research area includes organizational behaviour and human resource management. With more than 12 years into academics, he has published many research papers in international and national journals.

Ashish Mohan Dubey is currently Assistant Professor at Birla Institute of Technology, Mesra, Ranchi (Patna Campus), India. He holds a Ph.D. in Management from the School of Management Studies, Motilal Nehru National Institute of Technology, Prayagraj, India. His research area includes strategic management and strategic human resource management. He has more than 15 years of teaching experience at graduate and postgraduate levels and 7 years of experience in guiding and examining graduate and doctoral thesis in India. Two students have earned their Ph.D. degree under his supervision. His interest lies in strategic management and project management. He serves on the editorial board of various journals. He has published several papers in international and national journals and conference proceedings.

Sunil Kumar Pandey is Assistant Professor at Birla Institute of Technology, Mesra, Ranchi, Allahabad Campus, India. He has more than 20 years of teaching experience in management. His area of interest includes general management, banking and business laws. He has more than 20 years of teaching experience at graduate and postgraduate levels and four years of experience in guiding and examining graduate and doctoral theses in India. He has published several research papers in international and national journals and conference proceedings.

Employer or Owner? The Character of Platform Work

Gábor Mélypataki, Dávid Adrián Máté, Panggih Kusuma Ningrum, and Zsófia Riczu

1 Introduction

The digitalization of labour activities, such as platform work, brings new questions compared to the general labour law phenomena and affects the transformation of the traditional employer–employee hierarchy (Senatori, 2020). In 2020, the worries known on the employees' side had come to the foreground due to the pandemic situation (Acevedo, 2020) has been accelerating this new form of work to gain more popularity.

Therefore, countries worldwide keep exploring platform work regulation. One thing that has been comprehensible about platform workers so far is that they are not the same. Several studies have been conducted which focused on the analysis of Uber and Lyft. However, these app-based ride-sharing services are not very representative in generalizing the platform business practices or the working conditions in the gig economy scope. It is because Uber and Lyft operate in just specific sectors such as transportation-related services. Simultaneously, other gig platform practices are more complex, often covering a wide variety of services that apply to various potential functions across a range of industries and involving many different types of job natures, demographic profiles, and skillsets. Consequently, the gig works may

G. Mélypataki (✉) · D. A. Máté · Z. Riczu
University of Miskolc, Miskolc, Hungary
e-mail: jogmega@uni-miskolc.hu

D. A. Máté
e-mail: jogmate@uni-miskolc.hu

Z. Riczu
e-mail: jogriczu@uni-miskolc.hu

P. K. Ningrum
HeyLaw Indonesia, Kota Tangerang Selatan, Indonesia
e-mail: ningrum@analyticainstitute.com

A. Gupta et al. (eds.), *Sustainability in the Gig Economy*,
https://doi.org/10.1007/978-981-16-8406-7_16

be widely arranged, from ride-hailing drivers, delivery service to freelance computer programmers.

There is no precise definition for the platform work practice (Florisson & Mandl, 2020) and as mentioned earlier that the range of jobs belonging in this work frame cannot be defined clearly (Tóth, 2017). The former studies used several different terms to narrate the platform work practices presented by the flowery euphemisms to sound positive and thrilling (Sundararajan, 2016). Therefore, the terms like "crowdsourcing", "sharing economy", or the "collaborative economy" are usually adopted to describe this phenomenon. More specifically, previous studies revealed that various terms had been used to refer to platform workers, including gig workers Roll (2020a, 2020b), freelancers (Kokkodis & Ipertoris, 2016) (Westregård, 2020), crowdworkers (Deng et al., 2016), driver-partners (Hall & Krueger, 2016), service providers (Allon et al., 2012), or sellers (Moreno & Terwiesch, 2014), depending on context and the authors' academic discipline. For clearer policymaking, the government undoubtedly needs to separate these terminologies for each platform worker segment to formulate appropriate and effective legislation. It is pivotal since recognizing the crucial differentiating factors will give a better understanding of the power relationship between the platform firms and the platform workers, likewise the nature of work in this practice. Thus, each particular characteristic of platform work can be determined because every type of platform work faces different forms of vulnerability.

Responding to this issue, Sergeant highlighted a major characteristic of this platform work that the workers utilize a third party's digital environment (software or hardware) to fulfil their works. It means that the platform firm provides a web-based environment or marketplace where consumers find the sellers from where they want to buy the service (Sargeant, 2017). Conversely, Aloisi described the platform firm as a provider that is offering the "employed" person as a service to the customers or end-users (Aloisi, 2015).

Those arguments depict that this new work frame is formed as a triangular relationship which is somewhat similar to the temporary agency working relation. However, before we can fully address the compatibility of this new work frame to the temporary agency working relation, firstly, we need to answer these tricky questions: What relation`status must be subjected to the platform firm? Is it the platform provider (owner) or the employer? Regardless, it is crucial to have a civil law contract to legally accommodate this new form of relationship so that the involved parties are considered equal and well protected.

Align with Sargeant's opinion, in many platform work practices, the platform firm is an IT company that does not have tools relating to the real services. Uber and Lyft, for instance, do not have cars to provide the taxi service. This underlying reason has led to considering the platform firm as the platform owner because it limitedly provides the marketplace and generally has nothing else to do with the dealing process between the platform worker and the end-user. However, the rating system that the platform firm conducts in order to assess the workers has made the relationship status between the two blurry and questionable. As a result, concerns arise questioning the platform firm's role and how much control it can exert over the platform workers.

Furthermore, the deepness of the practiced commanding, controlling, and monitoring, to some extent, describes the level typical to an employment relationship. The relationship among parties should be qualified to these. The main reason is that the basis in the employment relationship is not the equality between parties alone. It must also encompass the hierarchical relationship to justify the appropriate protection level to safeguard the employees as the more vulnerable party (Rosin, 2020).

Based on the aforementioned points, this current research is grounded in the hypothesis that the platform firms typically define a system of requirements for the workers since they act as the employers per se. To test this hypothesis and achieve the aim of this research, we should primarily observe the platform work practices from the real setting as it is necessary to understand the empirical overview and apprehend the complete picture of this phenomenon. Accordingly, we examined the form of a relationship constructed in this platform work practice both from the legal contractual perspective and the court judgements in various countries.

2 Empirical Overview

2.1 Terms of Service Statement for the Working Relationship

Platform firms illustrate their workers' independence with various depictions. Uber, for instance, depicts its drivers as entrepreneurs "who do not work for Uber", but rather "work with Uber" and retain "complete control over their business". In addition to that, a carpool app-based service provided by Google, Waze, describes their platform as "a platform service that connects drivers and riders who are willing to share a ride" and straightforwardly states in their terms of service that "all carpool arrangements made through Waze carpool are between riders and drivers"; therefore, "Google is not a party to any carpooling agreements". Meanwhile, a competing firm, Handy, states on its website that the platform firm is "not an employer", but acts as "the intermediary which connects independent service professionals with customers" and positions its platform as a "venue for communications". Besides, a crowdsourcing marketplace, MTurk, describes that the workers who perform tasks for requesters in their platform are "working in their personal capacity as an independent contractor and not as an employee". This "independent contractor" status is also found in other labour platforms such as DiDi, Careem, Zimride, Grab, and Gojek, to address their platform workers.

Regardless of the wordings used in describing the business model, it can be seen that there is a similarity in terms of the form of this new working relationship concept. Those statements mentioned earlier always show a triangular relationship between the platform firms as the digital intermediary which facilitates the whole process, the platform worker who performs the service, and the client as the end-user of the services (who may act as an individual consumer or corporation). The work arrangement between the gig worker and the end-user of the services seems ambiguous, which fully depends on the intermediary's business model.

2.2 *The Platform's Degree of Control*

Identifying how the platform firms define their relationship with the workers is not enough to get a clear depiction of this phenomenon. According to Stone (2006), the extent to which an organization or company maintains directive power over the work process is central to legal concepts of work arrangement in developing economies. Hence, determining the platform's degree of control towards the workers is very crucial.

After delving into the labour platforms' business processes, it is found that there are various levels of directive control played by the platform firms towards the workers in running their business. Crowdsourcing platforms like Upwork, Freelancer, and Fiverr serve a marketplace where the workers, who are typically "white-collar" freelancers such as copywriters, graphic designers, and programmers, can showcase their portfolio, services, and rates to attract potential clients. Though constrained by the common laws of supply and demand, workers here have relative control over the jobs or projects they take and over the rates they charge to the clients. In this business model, the platform firm takes a commission but does not directly determine or offer jobs to the workers.

On the other hand, those who perform app-based ride-hailing and delivery services like Uber, Lyft, Careem, DiDi, Grab, and Gojek drivers have a very different relationship with their platform firms. Based on proprietary and in-house algorithms, platform firms offer rides or delivery jobs to workers with several considerations, including the location radius, the time estimation from the driver location to the pickup point, user preferences, driver mode, and other related factors. Besides, the platform firms have an absolute authority to set the prices of each ride or delivery job. Practically, workers are free to accept or reject the jobs offered, but in many platforms, penalty systems are built, which may have adverse effects on the workers with low job acceptance rates.

2.3 *The Independence of Workers*

Regarding the independence of the workers, there are various work designs provided by the platform firms. Generally, workers in labour platforms will actively search among advertised projects with varying scopes and requirements, then choose which to pursue by applying to the project (e.g. Toptal, Lemon.io) or initial bid the proposing projects (e.g. Upwork, WINaTALENT, Freelancer) either with a fixed price for each particular project or an hourly wage.

On other platforms, clients determine price rates, but workers can exercise some choice based on which tasks are more or less appealing to them. MTurk workers, for instance, can search and select among available microtasks advertised at piecework compensation rates set by clients. In comparison, Wonolo workers are sent push notifications of short-term jobs in their areas, complete with the description of the task, location, and skills or equipment required and the pay that the client has set. Furthermore, the workers are free to accept the tasks that they perceive as a good fit.

Compared to the popular supply-driven platforms, only a few platforms can be classified as demand-driven platforms (Ge et al., 2015). Fiverr can be used as the example for this model. Unlike workers on other supply-driven platforms, the Fiverr workers promote and advertise projects or tasks they are willing to perform for a fixed price that they can freely set by themselves. The tasks are ranging from "I will create your logo design for your business or event starting at $95" to "I will create a cartoon voice for your animation project starting at $20." The workers in this kind of platform have substantial autonomy.

However, on many location-based labour platforms, workers are assigned to tasks by the algorithm, and the platform firm also determines the pay rate. This business model can be seen at Uber, Lyft, OLA, Careem, Grab, and Gojek. The firm uses complex algorithms to control the fares charged to passengers and the fees it charges to drivers, which can be possibly changed on short notice. Practically, the driver who receives an alert of a passenger requesting a ride has only a limited time to decide whether to accept it or not.

Meanwhile, errand runner platforms typically offer a standard list of covered services and optional extras at fixed fees set by the firms. For instance, TaskRabbit originally used a bidding model under which a client would post a job description and await bids from contractors or workers, known as Taskers. Furthermore, the system would allow the Taskers to communicate and discuss with potential clients to find out more information about the task to fine-tune their bids. However, it was found that the remunerative work under this auction model was very demanding (Kessler, 2014), and clients used to complain about the time required and how the low-bid Taskers often did not show up to carry out their duties.

2.4 The Job Monitoring, Worker's Performance Evaluation, and Incentives System

Continuous monitoring of worker performance via electronic feedback from customers or end-users is the labour platform's key feature. The reputation feedback on worker incentives primarily depends on how the employee has control over the pay and work process. To some degree, all workers on labour platforms can be seen as having good incentives since they are paid on a piecework basis. For example, the app-based ride-hailing drivers are paid per trip. The platform workers who have limited autonomy and restricted control, such as freelancers, will usually not reap significant benefits associated with superior quality performance or risk-taking, even though they may be disciplined for poor performance as measured by platform algorithms. Particularly if the platform provider wishes that consumers perceive workers as interchangeable so that workers' efforts to create a personal customer base can be actively monitored in the way conventional independent contractors would. Such platform workers can only increase their earnings by working longer hours since they have a certain opportunity to prevent negative consumer feedback, but it is unlikely that outstanding work results can affect dramatically higher incentives.

On the other hand, platform workers with greater autonomy who can make decisions about their compensation and work assignments are likely to benefit materially from their superior skills or performances. These sorts of firm-controlled incentives strategies are framed more positively than the account deactivation strategy, but simultaneously could still be viewed as punishment for failure to obtain high ratings.

Overall, this empirical overview has depicted some characteristics of the platform work practice in real settings. From there, we get the idea and insights that can further be used for the legal analysis.

3 Legal Analysis

3.1 The Analysis of Platform Work from the Contractual Point of View: Platform Work and Temporary Agency Work

The contractual connections between platform workers and platform providers and between the platform provider and customer depend on the country's regulation. The concept of the quality of the relation in this framework depends on regulation and the platform provider's role. Ildikó Rácz argued that platform work bores a strong resemblance to temporary agency work. This argument is based on the fact that the legal relationship of the platform workers can be represented as a three-sided legal relationship (Rácz, 2020).

The framework for the rules on temporary agency work is set out in Directive, 2008/104/EC of the European Parliament and the Council on temporary agency work. According to the directive, 'temporary-work agency' means any natural or legal person who, in compliance with national law, concludes contracts of employment or employment relationships with temporary agency workers to assign them to the user undertakings to work there temporarily, under their supervision and direction. 'Assignment' means the period during which the temporary agency worker is placed at the user undertaking to work temporarily under its supervision and direction (Directive, 2008/104/EC of the European Parliament and of the Council of 19 November 2008 on temporary agency work). It is essential to emphasize a civil legal relationship between the temporary-work agency and the user undertaking, while there is a labour legal relationship between the temporary-work agency and the worker (Takács, 2012). However, in the case of platform workers, neither the traditional employment relationship nor the agency or business relationship framework can fully cover the relationship between the parties. (Rácz, 2020)

We want to point out that the analysis, by definition, covers the comparison of the relevant criteria of the legal relationship and not the compliance with the legal conditions. According to the definition of temporary agency work, it is necessary that the temporary-work agency with the worker enter into the employment relationship. We come across two essential elements in this regard. One of these is the type of the attachment that requires the establishment of an employment relationship.

On the other hand, the purpose of the employment contract must contain the employment contract for temporary agency work purposes. In terms of purpose, the platform work can be considered in some respects as a special temporary agency work relationship. We base this on the fact that the platform operator enters into a contract with the worker then lends it to the service recipient/end-user. However, this is on a fragile footing, as in the case of a traditional taxi company we cannot talk about temporary agency work if it employs workers to provide a passenger transport service to the user in case of a taxi order. In this respect, on the one hand, the aim is lacking the will of the parties to carry out temporary agency work activities. Conversely, the party using the service does not appear as a 'user undertaking' in the legal relationship and does not qualify as an employer. In the case of platform work, the parties' will is therefore not created for temporary agency work, so they are not subject to the type restriction either. As a first step, we start from the presumption that an organization providing a platform that connects labour need takes on the role of temporary agency work (excluding the labour law contract). The directive defines who can be a temporary agent, a natural, or a legal person. This criterion is met by the party providing the platform, so that the basic conditions for being the party of a legal relationship are met.

In the case of the user undertaking, we also start from a similar proposition. The definition in the directive is in some respects equivalent to the party using the service in the context of the work of the platform, as this actor of the legal relationship fills the employment relationship with content. This person is the one who concretizes the work, giving instructions to the worker under whose direction the temporary work is performed. However, it is important to emphasize that there is a significant qualitative difference between the status of the recipient of the service and that of the user undertaking. Namely, the service recipient will be the final consumer and not the person for whose benefit the employee performs the task. Thus, the profit or economic benefit is not realized by the service user, so he cannot be considered a user undertaking. It is also worth emphasizing that if we consider the user of the service as a user undertaking, a different person will take on this role every 10 minutes, challenging to interpret legally.

Furthermore, since the service recipient acts as an individual, it is not easy to bring it under the terminology (Garben, 2017). It is essential, however, that the party using the service only partially has the rights that the user undertaking is entitled to in temporary agency work, so the instruction is also limited to a very narrow circle. Among other things, this is the reason why a party using a service would not, or would only, find it very difficult to interpret it as an employer. It should be emphasized that the service user cannot determine exactly which person will perform the task. This is partly due to the fact that the platform workers decide for themselves when to start when to finish the work, so they have control over their work schedule themselves. The party that provides the platform can orient, for example, by providing higher monetary consideration during specific (peak) periods. This also means the lack of personal character in the legal relationship. The party providing the platform, as an intermediary, only undertakes to assist in connecting the current needs. However, the similarity is further enhanced because the right to terminate the legal relationship belongs to the party providing the platform. However, this is still affected by the assessment of the party using the service.

Moreover, assessing how many "stars" you rate the party performing the activity is based on a somewhat subjective basis. However, it should be noted that even in the case of employment in a traditional employment relationship, the "assessment" of another person who out of the contract may be relevant to the termination of the employment relationship, for an example of consumer complaints against the employee.

The party providing the platform usually considers that it merely provides the platform to the parties and therefore cannot be considered an employer. Based on this, is it worth considering whether we can talk about labour intermediation? In the case of labour intermediation, it is also a tripartite relationship. However, a significant difference can also be observed compared to temporary agency work, as a potential employer instructs an intermediary firm to find suitable labour for it. Following the selection process, the intermediary company connects the client employer and the selected candidate. The legal relationship is established between the latter two, so the employer's rights are not divided between the parties; only the intermediary company takes over selection and recruitment (Kártyás, 2021). A civil law relationship will be established between the intermediary and the principal, and the result of successful intermediation will only be the conclusion of an employment contract between the intermediated employee and the principal employer. In their case, therefore, the legal relationship is established directly, only the intervening of an intermediated person to facilitate the establishment of the employment relationship. The party providing the platform does act as an intermediary but has similar rights as employers, such as the obligation to pay consideration (wages) or the right to terminate the employment relationship. Based on these, we can conclude that we are facing a particular version of intermediation. We need to analyse this specialty in the mirror of the case law as well.

3.2 *The Practice of Platform Work in the Mirror of Case Law*

Many workers see platform work as an innovative form of employment opportunity, although the business model and technology itself are not new. According to Jeremias Prassl, these companies are based on an old business model used to outsource a specific function; therefore, he does not support the separation of the gig economy from the labour market (Prassl, 2018). These companies' concept is practically based on circumventing the traditional employee relationship: promises flexible working hours with free disposal of their own resources; however, it does not guarantee employee rights. In order to examine the qualification of a platform operator as an owner or employer, it is essential to analyse the conditions set by the platform in the light of court decisions.

Regarding the assessment of labour relations in the gig economy context, the most significant is arguably Judgement no 434/15 from the European Court of Justice, concerning Asociación Profesional Elite Taxi v Uber Systems Spain SL. Although it does not specifically address labour law issues, it is relevant to the employment law assessment of this new form of working relations. In 2014, Elite Taxi filed a lawsuit in the Commercial Court of Barcelona. The court found that neither Uber Spain nor the non-professional drivers of the vehicles concerned held the licences and driving licences required by the Barcelona City Taxi Ordinance of 22 July 2004. The case was referred to the European Court of Justice, which ruled based on the information available: Uber's activities constitute a "transport service" within the meaning of Article 2 (2) (d) of Directive 2006/123. Accordingly, Uber's service provides an application through which the service provider communicates with the service user.

Conditions specified by the application operator have been listed as an essential element from the court's point of view, influencing the decision on the merits considering that Uber has a decisive influence on the conditions of service provided by drivers. Among other things, it sets the highest freight rate. The ruling of the European Court of Justice is also significant from a labour law point of view, given that Uber exercises a degree of control over the quality of motor vehicles and their drivers and the conduct of drivers, which may even be interpreted as an employer's right of control (Asociación Profesional Elite Taxi, 2017).

In addition to the growing scope of work, there have also been significant changes on platform workers' part. They are actively fighting to improve their employment conditions, given that their labour problems have recently come to the fore. An article published on the OECD Forum analyses a court ruling in the UK in 2018, drawing attention to the Deliveroo judgement could bring about a significant change in the employment law of those working in the gig economy (Shu, 2018). The judgement examined the Deliveroo application's introduction of a new pricing structure by the operator and the collective action of the suppliers against the measure (Osborne & Butler, 2016). In the Deliveroo dispute, the union behind the workers was a member of the UK's Independent Workers' Union of Great Britain (IWGB), the UK's first union. The Central Arbitration Commission examined the legal status of couriers: although they can be classified as employees in many respects (successful application and test required for the work, as well as a course necessary for the work, wear uniforms, receive training on safe food handling, follow them with the help of the application), Deliveroo allows deliverers to use a substitute. Thus, the lack of a personal obligation to work and the freedom to conduct a business suggests that couriers are indeed self-employed—in the light of this, Deliveroo is present in the legal relationship as an operator and not as an employer (IWGB v Deliveroo—Are

Deliveroo couriers workers and thus entitled to trade union recognition?, 2020). The Supreme Court agreed with the Central Arbitration Committee's (CAC) conclusion that Deliveroo's suppliers could not be classified as employees with the right to bargain collectively. However, it referred to Article 11 of the European Convention on Human Rights. Although the right to bargain collectively for Deliveroo couriers is debatable, the CAC should have considered the right to bargain collectively for couriers and other workers. Subsequently, a law firm called Leigh Day has filed labour court proceedings on behalf of Deliveroo deliverers, demanding better employment conditions, including a minimum wage, sick pay, and access to paid leave (Deliveroo's hiring conditions to face scrutiny by MPs, 2021). In practice, the conflict of interest extended from the issue of employment rights to a human rights issue that brought workers and trade unions closer to victory over companies that build their success on business models of (mostly) platform-based services. This process will pave the way for future gig economy workers.

Regarding the employment rights of those working in the gig economy, another notable case is when the Supreme Court as a worker and not a self-employed person, recognized a heating engineer working for Pimlico Plumbers—thus having more comprehensive employment and social security rights as an employee than full-time employees. Even though the term "applicant" in the agreement refers to the self-employed plumber status, the company (in this case, acting as the defendant) added several clauses in the agreement that made it more relevant to the employer–employee status. Those include the requirement for the workers to wear a uniform decorated with the company's logo, drive a vehicle with a GPS tracker, the obligation to work at least 40 hours a week, be available for on-call work, and report after the work is done. Additionally, the defendant had the authority to terminate the contract following a heart attack by the plaintiff, which is an unlawful reason for the contract termination (dismissal). The defendant also initiated the right to paid leave, sick pay and filed direct disability claims against the defendant. As a result, the court found that the plaintiff was not an employee; however, the Court of Appeal defined the defendant as an employer given its high degree of command, direction, and control. This court decision is significant for future jurisprudence and will set an ample precedent to review similar labour law cases related to employment status in the future (Deliveroo's hiring conditions to face scrutiny by MPs, 2021).

Rebecca Hilsenrath, Director-General of the Committee on Equal Opportunities and Human Rights, said, referring to the above cases: "If you wear the uniform, if you drive the branded vehicle, if you only work for one business, you are employed". Accordingly, workers who meet these criteria are entitled to adequate protection in connection with their work and work safely without endangering their health, meaning thousands of workers can benefit from sick pay and paid leave (Pimlico Plumbers case, 2021).

The aforementioned labour law movements have also encouraged gig economy workers to enforce their labour rights in the other Member States of the European Union. Consequently, The French Court of Cassation finally decided to use the contractual relationship between Uber and the driver providing the service as an employment contract. It recalled that the connection to the digital platform creates a hierarchical relationship between the parties because of the subsuperiority relationship. Thus, Uber is a platform provider and at the same time is also considered as an employer, while the driver performs his work in employee qualification (Cour de cassation - Chambre sociale, 2020). In France, during the FIFA World Cup final, workers from local gig economy workers, Uber Eats, Deliveroo, Foodora, Stuart, and Glovo, organized a protest rally auspices of the Paris Independent Deliverymens' Collective (CLAP In our view, this also sheds light on, that these unions are in a growing force.

In Italy, the Bologna Court ruled that Deliveroo, as an on-demand food delivery platform, discriminated against delivery workers by violating local labour laws (Rider, l'algoritmo discrimina chi si ammala e chi sciopera, 2021). The court ruled by examining the platform's rating system, according to which Deliveroo, as an employer, discriminated against all deliverers who did not undertake delivery, regardless of whether he did not work due to the illness or at his own discretion (Deliveroo Rating Algorithm Was Unfair To Riders, 2020). Beyond the continent, Ethan Sculman, a member of the California Court of Appeals in the USA, ordered the two passenger service providers, Uber and Lyft, to be treated as employees by a court order at the request of the California Attorney General, at the same time guarantee them the rights of workers. The judgement refers to the regulation adopted in 2020 (California Assembly Bill 5 (AB5, 2021)), in which a system of criteria was established to classify workers' status. Under this legislation, a person can only be considered an independent, self-employed person if the employing company does not have the right to instruct and control the activity or if the contractor carries out an activity other than that of the firm. In this case, likewise, the court made its decision based on the conditions of the platform provider and the instructions, command, and control rights of the employer. The verdict could affect the case law of the whole world beyond the borders of the (California Assembly Bill 5 (AB5, 2021))

In the light of the above, we can conclude that the legal status of platform providers and their contractors poses a severe dilemma to legislators and regulators, starting with that this form of work is widespread—they do not guarantee a minimum income or fixed working hours, ignore employee protection and classify workers as subcontractors.

These firms do not fall into the traditional legal categories; they raise several legal issues. It is indisputable that working through the application means or has meant tremendous savings for these companies, as they are exempt from the obligation to pay contributions for the employee. Whether the law can provide forward-looking solutions to further issues raised by companies operating based on an innovative economic model beyond the classical labour law framework and those who work in this sector of the economy, will it help to exploit the potential of the "gig economy" without compromising guarantees of labour and social security conditions? This is significant because EU 2019/1152. Directive on transparent and predictable working conditions aims to protect all EU workers, regardless of their form of employment (Directive (EU) 2019/1152 of the European Parliament and of the Council, 2021). In the light of the above case law, gig economy workers, the so-called grey area actors, are expected to open the door to a broader range of rights to employment and social security, and labour protection. According to statistics from the OECD blog in 2018, court decisions to this effect could affect 4.8 million people in the UK (Department for Business, Energy and Industrial strategy, 2021).

4 Conclusion

Both everyday practice and court judgements show that platform providers generally vindicate such licences for themselves that create a much stronger relationship between the platform firms and the gig workers. The intensity of this relationship is much more critical than in a business or a self-employing relationship. We cannot talk about equality between the parties since the gig workers depend on the platform owner's business design. So, the platform owner exercises property rights and the employer's rights as well. Answers found by both theory and practice show that the platform firm is more than just an owner or marketplace provider. It widely exercises the triplet of the right to command, control, and monitor. The exercise of these rights may also extend to the performance of the concrete task or another circumstance. Nevertheless, exercising the right supposes the labour law relationship. As it has been found in the cases of Uber and Deliveroo more times, the rights of the service provider create inequalities. Inequality originates from that the employer exercises its rights, but it does not fulfil its obligations, saying it is not an employer. After reviewing the agreement, the form of working relationship, the theory and case law, we realized a contradiction in the industrial practice regarding this issue as the companies tended to escape from the employment-relating obligations, which consequently caused a vulnerable situation for the workers. This phenomenon perfectly captures a vital difference between the employer and platform owner status. It relies on the level of the rights and authority owned by platform firms and workers, even though the border is fragile, and platform firms do not consider it. Especially when the platform firms come up with the demand of classic exercise of rights, they tend to hide and utilize this maximally, which leads to such an unfair practice that labour law regulations should solve.

References

Acevedo, D. D. (2020). *The rise and scope of gig work regulation.* Cambridge University Press.

Act AB5. (2021). *California assembly bill 5 (AB5), superior court of the State of California: No.CGC-20–5884402.* Forrás. https://www.scribd.com/document/472020392/Order-on-People-s-Motion-for-Preliminary-Injunction-and-Related-Motions.

Allon, G., Bassamboo, A., & Cil, E. B. (2012). Large-scale service marketplaces: The role of the moderating firm. *Management Science, 58*(10), 1854–1872.

Aloisi, A. (2015). Commoditized workers. Case study research on labour law issues arising from a set of "on-demand/gig economy" platforms. *Comparative Labor Law & Policy Journal, 37(3),* 653–690.

Asociación Profesional Elite Taxi. (2017). *Judgment C 434/15 (Court of justice of the European Union 2017)*. Forrás. http://curia.europa.eu/juris/document/document.jsf;jsessionid=5F9C6CF583160ED278E2BF0796859B65?text=&docid=198047&pageIndex=0&doclang=hu&mode=lst&dir=&occ=first&part=1&cid=21938981.

California Assembly Bill 5 (AB5). (dátum nélk.).

Cour de cassation - Chambre sociale. (2020). Forrás. https://www.courdecassation.fr/jurisprudence_2/chambre_sociale_576/374_4_44522.html.

Deliveroo Rating Algorithm Was Unfair To Riders. (2020). Forrás: Italian Court Rules. https://www.forbes.com/sites/jonathankeane/2021/01/05/italian-court-finds-deliveroo-rating-algorithm-was-unfair-to-riders/?sh=57c094c922a1.

Deliveroo's hiring conditions to face scrutiny by MPs. (2021). Forrás. https://www.theguardian.com/business/2018/jun/18/deliveroos-hiring-conditions-to-face-scrutiny-by-mps.

Deng, X., Joshi, K., & Galliers, R. (2016). The duality of empowerment and marginalization in microtask crowdsourcing: Giving voice to the less powerful through value sensitive design. *MIS Quarterly, 40*(2), 279–302.

Department for Business, Energy and Industrial Strategy. (2021). Forrás: The Characteristics of those in the gig economy. https://assets.publishing.service.gov.uk/government/uploads/system/uploads/attachment_data/file/687553/The_characteristics_of_those_in_the_gig_economy.pdf.

Directive (EU) 2019/1152 of the European Parliament and of the Council. (2021). Forrás. https://eur-lex.europa.eu/legal-content/HU/TXT/PDF/?uri=CELEX:32019L1152&from=HU.

Directive 2008/104/EC of the Eurpoean Parliament and of the Council of 19 November 2008 on temporary agency work. (2008). (dátum nélk.). Article 3.

Florisson, R., & Mandl, I. (2020. 12 15). *Platform work: types and implications for work and employment*. Eurofound Working Papers.

Garben, S. (2017). Protecting workers in the online platform economy: An overview of regulatory and policy developments in the EU. *European Risk Observatory Discussion Paper*, 16.

Ge, H., Caverlee, J., & Lee, K. (2015). Crowds, gigs, and super sellers: A measurement study of a supply-driven crowdsourcing marketplace. In *Ninth international AAAI conference on web and social media.*

Hall, J. V., & Krueger, A. B. (2016). An analysis of the labor market for Uber's driver-partners in the United States. In *NBER WORKING PAPER SERIES Working Paper 22843*. NATIONAL BUREAU OF ECONOMIC RESEARCH. https://doi.org/10.3386/w22843.

IWGB v Deliveroo – Are Deliveroo couriers workers and thus entitled to trade union recognition? (2020). Forrás: Are Deliveroo couriers workers and thus entitled to trade union recognition? https://pjhlaw.co.uk/2017/11/24/iwgb-v-deliveroo-deliveroo-couriers-workers-thus-entitled-trade-union-recognition/.

Kártyás, G. (2021). *Kölcsönzés vagy közvetítés?* Letöltés dátuma: 2021. 03 31, Forrás: https://ado.hu/munkaugyek/kolcsonzes-vagy-kozvetites/.

Kessler, S. (2014). Pixel and dimed: On (not) getting by in the gig economy. *Fast Company*. Letöltés dátuma: 2021. 04 27, Forrás: https://www.fastcompany.com/3027355/pixel-and-dimed-on-not-getting-by-in-the-gig-economy.

Kokkodis, M., & Ipertoris, P. G. (2016). Reputation transferability in online labor markets. *Management Science, 62*(6), 1687–1706.

Moreno, A., & Terwiesch, C. (2014). Doing business with strangers: Reputation in online service marketplaces. *Information Systems Research, 25*(4), 865–886.

Osborne, H., & Butler, S. (2016). Collective action via social media brings hope to gig economy workers. *The Guardian*. Letöltés dátuma: 2021. 01 17, Forrás: https://www.theguardian.com/money/2016/aug/19/collective-action-via-social-media-brings-hope-to-gig-economy-workers.

Pimlico Plumbers case (Supreme Court 2021). (2021). Forrás: https://www.hrdept.co.uk/birmingham-central-south/blog/supreme-court-rules-favour-workers-rights-pimlico-plumbers-case.

Prassl, J. (2018). *Human as service*. Oxford University Press.

Rácz, I. (2020). *A digitalizáció hatása a munkajog egyes alapintézményeire*. Ph.D. Thesis, 66. Budapest.

Rider, l'algoritmo discrimina chi si ammala e chi sciopera. (2021). Forrás: https://www.ilfattoquotidiano.it/in-edicola/articoli/2021/01/02/rider-lalgoritmo-discrimina-chi-si-ammala-e-chi-sciopera/6053273/.

Roll, K. (2020a). *Gig work at the base of the pyramid: considering*. UCL Institute for Innovation and Public Purpose, Working Paper Series (IIPP WP 2020–05).

Roll, K. (2020b). *Gig work at the base of the pyramid: considering dependence and control*. UCL Institute for Innovation and Public Purpose.

Rosin, A. (2020). Platform work and fixed-term employment regulation. *European Labour Law Journal*. https://doi.org/10.1177/2031952520959335

Sargeant, M. (2017). The gig economy and the future of work. *E-Journal of International and Comparative Labour Studies, 2017/6. 4*, 1–12.

Senatori, I. (2020). The European framework agreement on digitalisation: A whiter shade of pale? *Italian Labour Law Journal, 13*(2), 159–175. https://doi.org/10.6092/issn.1561-8048/12045

Shu, L. (2018). *European war on labour rights*. Forrás. https://www.oecd-forum.org/posts/37023-european-war-on-labour-rights?channel_id=722-digitalisation.

Stone, K. V. (2006). Legal protections for atypical employees: Employment law for workers without workplaces and employees without employers. *Berkeley Journal of Employment and Labor Law*, 251–286.

Sundararajan, A. (2016). *The sharing economy: The end of employment and the rise of crowdbased capitalism*. MIT Press.

Takács, G. R. G. (2012). A munkaerő-kölcsönzés és az iskolaszövetkezeti munka szerepe a fiatalok foglalkoztatásában. *Budapest*, 44.

Tóth, H. (2017). A munkajog új kihívásai: a "gig" gazdaság munkavállalói csoportjai. In V. Szimora, & É. Török (szerk.), *Ünnepi tanulmányok Csécsy György 65. születésnapja tiszteletére I.-II. kötet* (Ünnepi tanulmányok Csécsy György 65. születésnapja tiszteletére I.-II. kötet. kötet, old.: 393-400). Debrecen: Debreceni Egyetem Állam- és Jogtudományi Kar.

Westregård, A. (2020). Digital collaborative platforms: A challenge for both the legislator and the social partners in the Nordic model. *European Labour Law Journal, 11*(2), 142–153. https://doi.org/10.1177/2031952520905154

Gábor Mélypataki Ph.D., assistant professor. University of Miskolc, Faculty of Law, Department of Agriculture and Labour Law

Dávid Adrián Máté 2nd year Ph.D. student, Deák Ferenc Doctoral School in Law and Political Science, University of Miskolc, supervisor: Gábor Mélypataki Ph.D. assistant professor, associate professor, University of Miskolc, Faculty of Law, Department of Agricultural and Labour Law

Panggih Kusuma Ningrum Researcher. HeyLaw Indonesia (HeyLaw id), PT. Prawira Bahagia Selalu and Co-Founder Analytica id

Zsófia Riczu 1st year Ph.D. student, Deák Ferenc Doctoral School in Law and Political Science, University of Miskolc, supervisor: Gábor Mélypataki Ph.D. assistant professor, University of Miskolc, Faculty of Law, Department of Agricultural and Labour Law

Industry 4.0: A Paradigm Shift in Technological Approach for Business Organization and Society

Reetika Sehgal, Anukaran Khanna, Ashish Mohan Dubey, and Prateek Khanna

1 Introduction

In last few decades, our daily lives have been influenced by a variety of technological advancements. The most common examples are using Internet and mobile phones made it possible for people to be connected everywhere. Technologies have transformed the traditional economy in an innovative economy characterized by the prompt sharing of knowledge, speedy information on products, price, sale, feedback of consumers, tracking information, etc. The economy has turned to be fast-growing economy where consumers are aware about market and demand fast delivery of quality products. To cater the emerging and dynamic demand of consumers and market, the business entities are started to restructure the mode of business, models of manufacturing and deliverance of goods.

Gradual changes in technology and the changes in lifestyle of people resulted in industrial revolution (Brettel et al., 2014). The invention of steam engines and powered machines was triggered during the First Industrial Revolution which increases the rate of production. After the First Industrial Revolution, the second

R. Sehgal (✉)
Department of Management, United College of Engineering ,and Management D-II, UPSIDC Industrial Area, Prayagraj, Uttar Pradesh, India
e-mail: reetikasehgal@united.edu.in

A. Khanna
Department of Electrical and Electronics Engineering, Birla Institute of Technology and Science, Pilani, India

A. M. Dubey
Department of Management, Birla Institute of Technology, Mesra, Ranchi (Patna Campus), Patna, Bihar, India

P. Khanna
Department of Business Administration, Shambhunath Institute of Engineering and Technology, Prayagraj, Uttar Pradesh, India

A. Gupta et al. (eds.), *Sustainability in the Gig Economy*,
https://doi.org/10.1007/978-981-16-8406-7_17

revolution was related to mass production of goods and electricity. Third revolution was related to the use of electronics in manufacturing which again increased the production activities and reduced the need of the labor. The three revolutions were given a name of "revolution" as they brought a significant transformation in the working of industries resulting in its welfare and growth.

Industry 4.0 is regarding the revolution characterized by giving services and manufacturing through innovation. The prime purpose of Industry 4.0 is to develop "smart factories" and "cyber-physical systems" (CSP). By smart-driven factories, we mean the factories having autonomous advanced machines which can serve routine works as well as exceptional jobs or situations whenever required. They can intimate the time for replenishment of inventory and maintain minimum inventory level to switch and manage different tasks at a time. According to Kagermann et al. (2013), the new industrial revolution is driven by nine technologies. These are industrial Internet of Things (IoT), big data and analytics, cybersecurity, autonomous robots, cloud, simulation, horizontal and vertical integration, additive manufacturing, augmented reality (AR) and virtual reality (VR). These technologies are already working but still required more advancement to achieve the objectives of Industry 4.0. (Li et al., 2019). For instance, intelligent robots are common in today's world, but there would be more development in the technology when these robots do not need human involvement in the process of decision making. The role of sensor-based technology and artificial intelligence (AI) has the ability to make things easy for human being in real life. Technology has brought a tremendous change in our lifestyle. The way of thinking has changed with respect to manufacturing. The new concept of predictive maintenance will be followed instead of preventive maintenance. By "preventive maintenance," we mean predicting the time when machines will be required and maintenance to be scheduled rather than preferring periodic maintenance.

Industry 4.0 is different from other revolution in many ways as compared to the past three industrial revolutions. There many reasons for it. First, it has an explicit start date as it was announced in 2011. The name was given in Germany; it is adopted by many other countries later on (Mosconi, 2015). Second, it is an industrial revolution which worked over the Internet. Third, it is an industrial revolution which is associated with various independent and autonomous machines. While machines were controlled by humans in earlier industrial revolutions, in the Fourth Industrial Revolution it was not the case; we can say, here, human were controlled by autonomous and intelligent machines for manufacturing. Thus, the control is more over the machines in the process of manufacturing.

The effect of Industry 4.0 is transforming the countries in terms of their manufacturing, providing services and the way of doing work. In 2016, a study conducted by Price Waterhouse Cooper (2016) on more than 2000 participants in 26 different countries reveals that companies are likely to invest $907 billion per year on advanced digital technologies like connectivity devices, sensors, intelligent robot and software for manufacturing process. Moreover, expect $421 billion reduction in cost and $493 billion increment in terms of annual revenues. The study conducted by Boston Consultancy Group (BCG, 2015) assumed that the new industrial revolution will create a production system which will be 30% faster and 25% more efficient in output. Further, it will also create more than 390,000 new jobs and investment of 250 billion Euro specific to manufacturing sector (Bhalla & Kohli, 2016).

The role of technology push inventions and innovations has increased with the role of Industry 4.0. Technological penetrate has accelerated the productivity through the value chain, demand for new products and services and investments in new capacities (Bai & Thuemmler, 2017). There are positive trends from the demand aspects also because in case of global networks communication, and the logistics and transportation costs (Barreto et al., 2017) have declined significantly which will facilitate the development of new markets and boost investment and overall growth.

2 Background of Industrial Revolutions

In an industrial perspective, a revolution can be defined as a remarkable growth and transformation in technology. It is basically associated with the scientific growth in perspective of different theories and its application. The First Industrial Revolution (1750–1870) resulted in enhancing the application of science in industry (PWC, 2016). There was a change in production pattern which majorly transformed from agrarian-based production to handicraft production with the aid of machineries. With the different sources of energy, the man-powered tasks were replaced by machines, for example, production of steam by burning coal.

The First Industrial Revolution, in addition with the change in science and technology, also brought a remarkable change in the economy, culture, social life and politics. A new customer base was created with a large-scale production where products were produced at lower prices. There was a change in standard of living as people followed urbanization.

There are different views regarding the dates of industrial revolution. It is difficult to ascertain the exact dates of beginning and end of the industrial revolution. Figure 1 represents a timeline with the most agreed dates. For instance, the date of beginning in the textile industry was developed in Britain. The invention of electricity and process of steelmaking was witnessed in the end of the nineteenth century. The Second Industrial Revolution was facilitated by these inventions which in turn enabled the mass production and eased the manufacturing process. It can be assumed that the second revolution lasts until the beginning of World War I (WWI) in 1914 although its effects can be observed in the initial years of the Third Industrial Revolution.

The technology continued to expand in the whole world even during the period of two World Wars and the Cold War. Digital computers and the Internet are the two important inventions for the world witnessed at that time. By the 1950s, the use of digital computers became prominent in many sectors especially in manufacturing sector. Conversely, the starting of the Third Industrial Revolution is credited to the discovery of programmable logic controller (PLC) in the year 1970. PLC had a huge impact on mechanization and automation in the manufacturing sector worldwide.

In the late 1980, the influence of computers for business purpose was observed which even resulted in the use of programmable logic controller in manufacturing.

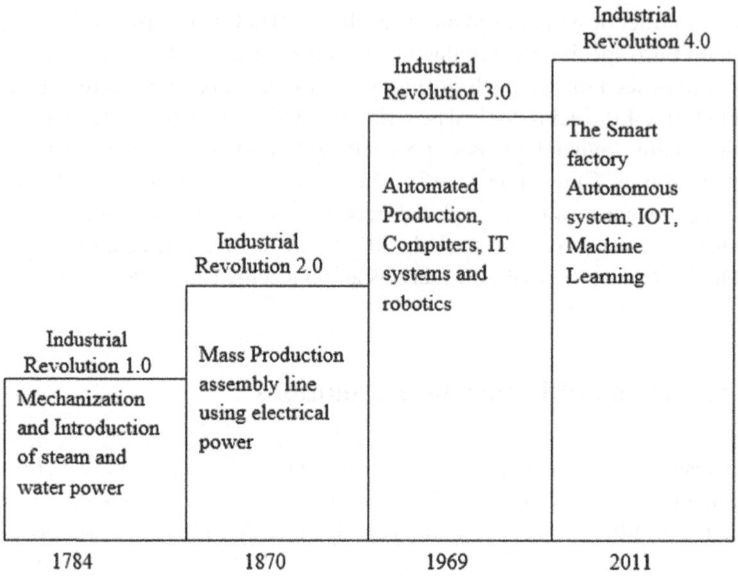

Fig. 1 Industrial revolution timeline. *Source* Authors'

In 1960s, swiftness was observed in computer networking that permitted computers to communicate. In 1980s only, the circulation of this technology and its commercialization was noticed. But later in this era, there was an evolvement of Internet which became the well-known medium of communication and megastore of information. The huge transformation in the economy was witnessed with the invention of personal mobile phones and later on the smartphones. Finally, the era ended and the name given to this era is Information and Communication Technologies (ICT).

The benefit of this era was that systems of manufacturing improved significantly with the help of ICT. The automated machines eliminated the wastage of time (Ghemawat, 2017). Just the pressing of buttons facilitated the production process in minutes. Today, the manufacturing process happens in such a manner with adequate controlling (Roblek et al., 2016). The main idea in the fourth revolution is to control the manufacturing process with the aid of smart machines. Industry 4.0 technologies aim to achieve the objective of "smart factories" whose prerequisites are awareness and rational decision making.

Further, there is a debatable question that whether Industry 4.0 is an industrial revolution? Some experts say "yes" to this question. Many nations have adopted this philosophy to reshape and structure their manufacturing process. It will be accurate to mention that with the current existence of advanced technology, we are in the age where the products are demanded differently as compared to the previous age. The products are manufactured according to the customer's specification in terms of quality, color, taste, shape, configuration, etc. Industry 4.0 can be regarded as

Table 1 Cause and impact of industrial revolution

Revolution	Causes	Impact
First revolution 1750–mid-1800	Steam engine came into existence	Mechanized production
Second revolution 1870–1914 (Start WWI)	Electricals energy-driven motor	Mass production, large-scale manufacturing
Third revolution (1970–2011)	Electronics circuits, digital logic, PLC and IT	Automated production with human intervention
Fourth revolution (2011–Present Time)	CPS, automation and intelligent robots, AI, IOT	Smart and advanced manufacturing connected with various businesses

Source Authors'

a revolution in the industry. It is phenomenon which manages the end demand of consumers by managing, producing and transporting final products.

At present, we are in the age of Retail 4.0 (Gla & Lukert, 2018), Telecommunication 4.0 (Mosconi, 2015) and Health 4.0 (Stentoft et al., 2020). The emergence of these ideas is based on Industry 4.0. Japanese government introduced with the new idea which is reshaping and redesigning the society, named Society 5.0. The idea behind Society 5.0 basically to develop a new form of societies. Causes and impact of the Fourth Industrial Revolution are summarized in Table 1. After third revolution, we have seen the new form of industry which is very different compared to the past. "Smart digital signals" are available which can decide what to do next, and machines are there for conversion.

There is a process of transformation of manufacturing; technological advancement allows us to convert a result in an effective and efficient ways.

3 Backbone of Industry 4.0

Industry 4.0 is the digitization of production or manufacturing-based industries with the integration of cyber-physical system into manufacturing technologies. Industry 4.0 transforms and creates the whole manufacturing process as the smart factory that are not only interconnected (BCG, 2015) but communicate, analyze and use information to drive productivity, improve efficiency and eliminate human errors (Li, 2018). There are nine fundamentals of Industry 4.0 as shown in Fig. 2.

3.1 Cyber-Physical Systems (CPS)

One of the most important fundamentals of Industry 4.0 is cyber-physical system. A CPS is a mechanism controlled and monitored by computer-based algorithm. CPS or

Fundamentals of Industry 4.0	Cyber Physical System
	Vertical and Horizontal systems Integration
	Immersive Technology
	Cloud Computing
	Internet of Things
	Additive Manufacturing
	Big Data Analytics
	Artificial Intelligence
	Cyber Security

Fig. 2 Pillars of Industry 4.0. *Source* Authors'

smart system is a close association between cybernetics, mechatronics, design and process science, or in other words it can be defined as an integration of physical and cyber components, hence known as cyber-physical system (Jarrahi et al., 2017).

All the cyber-physical system is working on information processing and advanced computing system which is embedded into a different product like airplane, smart grid, biomedical, car and other smart devices. These advanced computer systems are useful in handling specific task in a more efficient way as compared to human controls. So for instance, embedded system in a car would be the anti-lock braking system, to control the brake of the car first. Question comes! How it works? These advanced computer systems work together with physical environment through sensor-based technology and actuators which together called embedded system. In CPS, embedded systems share the data through communication network like Internet with cloud computing, and in this manner, data from any embedded system can be gathered and analyzed. We can create system of systems. Connected embedded system can be controlled and decentralized via one computational unit; here data can be analyzed automatically or by human–computer interface (HCI). In Fig. 3, complete architecture of CPS is shown.

3.2 *Vertical and Horizontal Systems Integration*

In relation to business growth strategies, horizontal integration means mixing two companies at the same level of the value chain, whereas vertical integration is the opposite of horizontal integration, and in this, two companies in two different stages of the value chain are getting together. However, in terms of Industry 4.0 horizontal and vertical integration have different meaning altogether as depicted in the Fig. 4.

To attain a seamless and agile plant to enterprise connectivity, businesses need to establish a real-time collaborative work environment enabled by convergence across various areas linking shop floor structure with industry and execution system aids in achieving vertical integration. The bottom line here is to make all data available to the decision makers in real time for effective enterprise resource planning and transformation. Horizontal integration for value chain is related to connecting manufacturing factory with bigger ecosystem and flawless communication among all the entities. It

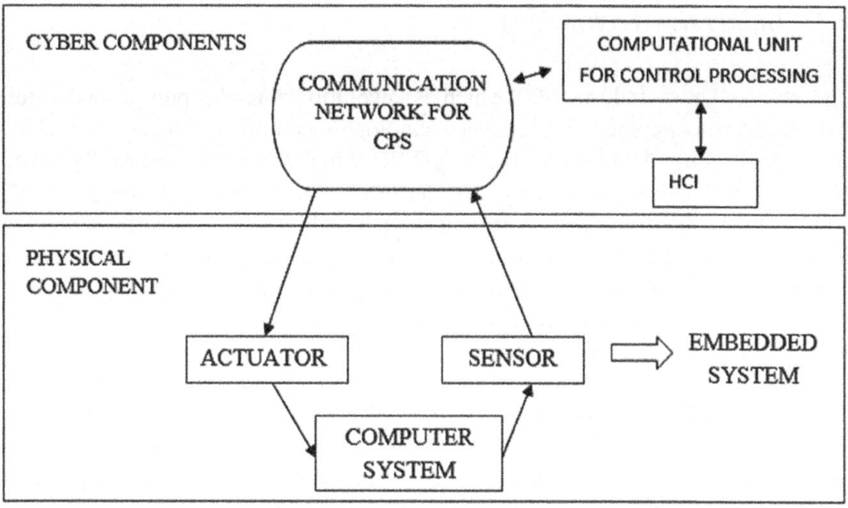

Fig. 3 Architecture of cyber-physical system. *Source* Authors'

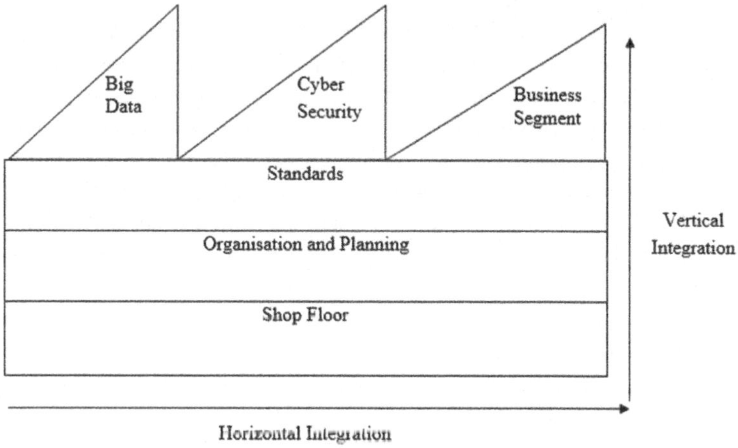

Fig. 4 Horizontal and vertical integration with respect to Industry 4.0. *Source* Authors'

will facilitate clear and holistic outlook of product planning and development all the way up to plant operations and logistics.

3.3 Immersive Technology

The next pillar of Industry 4.0 which is revolutionizing the present and future is immersive technology. Immersive technologies comprise virtual reality (VR), augmented reality (AR) and mixed reality (MR), which are among the fastest growing and emerging technologies today. So, question comes: What is immersive technology? Immersive technology creates or extends reality, which is done by immersing the user in a digital environment, and it has application in different areas such as health care, transportation, construction, education, gaming, etc. Now this advanced technology is gaining quick pace with the passage of time and transforming us to reimagining the future possibilities.

Virtual reality (VR) uses special type of headsets to create a simulator environment and helps an individual to immerse into it to experience an entirely different reality. A lot of companies like Amazon, Apple, Google, Sony, Samsung, Intel and others are investing billion dollars in VR sector. Some of the VR products are Sony play station, Lenovo mirage, Oculus Go and many more. These gadgets enable an individual to immerse in a digital environment to experience a world which is different from reality.

Next is augmented reality (AR); Azuma (1997) states that it is a technology that projects computer generated augmentation on top of reality helping us to perform task better and in efficient way. AR which comes in between reality and virtual reality is a procedure utilized to render real-world data and presented consciously, so that virtual elements bear a resemblance to the present reality to an extent. AR is giving brands the power to provide their customer with unique experiences that can prove to be difference between purchase and dropouts. From Pokemon Go to training future surgeons, AR is starting to infiltrate many industries and even the society today. But what exactly AR is? Looking into the most popular application of AR is location-based AR maps like Google maps. Google maps which place digital direction on top of real world show where to go. We also have Google lens, it is another application that enhances the user search experience, and with Google lens we need not type anything, just open the lens and aim at what you want to learn about. It will identify the object and give us all the essential information and detail about it. Facebook has planned to build AR glasses to create 3D maps of the world.

Next in the line of immersive technology is mixed reality. MR is blending the real world with VR. Unlike AR, user can interact with virtual objects in MR, which was nearly impossible a few years ago and was limited to our imagination like interacting with our favorite superhero is now possible because of MR technology. MR can be called as AR 2.0. MR is still in its early stage and will take a while to reach consumers. MR has vast uses in the field of health care, education, constructions and even on space missions. Though many cases are in testing phase, this idea is not far-fetched by any means.

So immersive technologies are quickly becoming a part of our daily life, and they are here to stay. They are not only enhancing human experience but helping brands market their products effectively and successfully to attract their target customer.

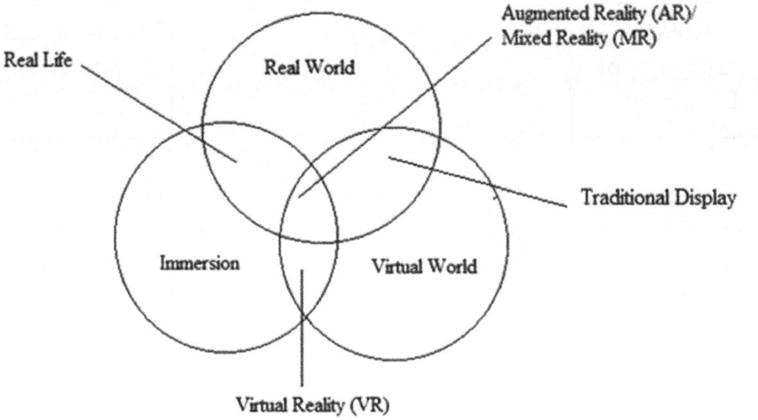

Fig. 5 Immersive technology. *Source* Authors'

From gaming to buying furniture, immersive technologies are taking the world by storm.

Figure 5 represents the relation among different immersive technologies where VR, AR and MR are connected with real and virtual world.

3.4 *Cloud Computing*

Cloud computing can be explained as the utilization of a network of remote servers organized on the Internet to handle, store and process data as compared to a local server. In other words, it can be said as computing services like software, networking, servers and databases are delivered over the Internet. The data is stored and accessed with the aid of Internet. The companies which offer such service are called cloud providers. These companies such as Amazon Web Service and Microsoft Azure provide the capability to control services and applications with the aid of a global network.

There are multiple benefits of cloud computing such as:

(a) Speed: Enormous amount of computing resources can be accessed instantaneously.
(b) Cost reduction: It reduces the expenditure of purchasing computer software and hardware.
(c) Scalability: It is easy to either scale up or scale down the cloud capacity as and when required.
(d) Accessibility: With cloud computing, it is easy to access data from anywhere across the globe as long as we are connected to Internet.
(e) Security: The data remains secured as it is stored in a centralized location with cloud.

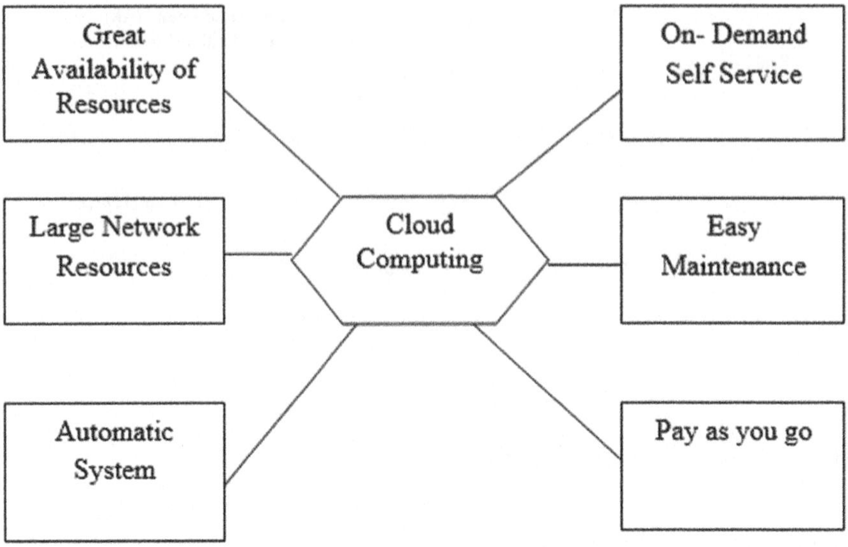

Fig. 6 Advantages of cloud computing. *Source* Authors'

The benefits or advantages of cloud computing can be explained explicitly with the help of a figure. Figure 6 represents the advantages of cloud computing.

Almost every kind of organization today is using cloud computing service. For example, healthcare companies are utilizing the cloud service for better and personalized treatment of individual patients. Financial service provider is using the cloud for real-time fraud detection and prevention. Video game makers are using the cloud to deliver online games to millions of players around the world.

3.5 Internet of Things (IoT)

Internet has the capability to connect all around through various means like laptop, phone, TV, refrigerator or even electricity bulbs too. Internet of Things (IoT) means the collection of devices that have the capability to connect to the Internet and share data (Gilchrist, 2016). Hence, it is named as Internet of Things. We can also say that with the help of sensors and actuators, data is collected from our surroundings through this device and send it to Internet for its processing. An example can be washing machines, watches, laptops, cars, watches, cars or even the entire home can be a part of IoT too. The architecture of IoT is shown in Fig. 7.

IoT works in four different layers. The first layer is sensing device. It is regarded as the "thing" portion of IoT (Sommer, 2015). It is primarily the embedded device that has sensors and actuators which is helpful in collecting the data from surroundings relying on definite function such as light temperature, humidity and pressure. After

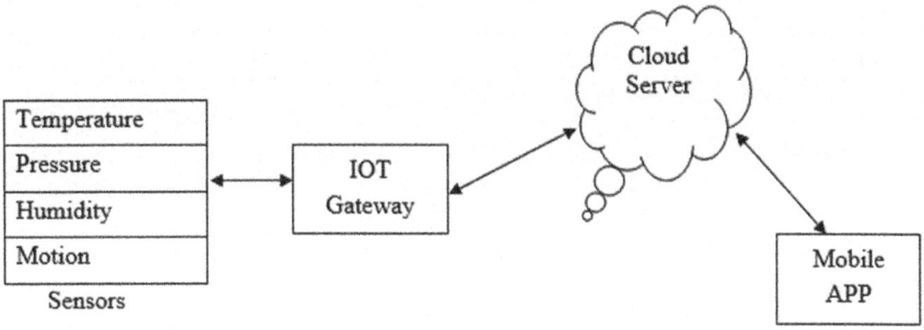

Fig. 7 Architecture of IoT. *Source* Authors'

the collection of data through sensing device layer, it is sent to the embedded device which is further sent to connectivity layer. This connection is usually made through the techniques like RFID, Bluetooth, Wi-Fi, etc., with the aid of Internet. After this, the data is transferred to processing layer. After the data is reached to cloud, it undergoes the very important process, that is, its analysis part to reach to the significant insight so that an adequate decision may be taken. When this process is completed, the outcome of the conclusion is communicated to the IoT device. The last layer is user interface and application. This is the layer which is more visible to us. This layer deals with IoT device through buttons or touch screen on device.

So, question comes why do we need IoT? In short, it can be said that it makes our lives comfortable and easy. Let us take an example of smart house. There will be many features of smart house. Automatic lighting system may be its one of the examples. It detects the presence of anyone in the room, and the light gets switched on automatically. We can conclude that it makes our lives lavish and comfortable.

On a broader basis, it is also beneficial for industries and society on a large scale. One of the examples may be healthcare sector where it facilitates the remote interface between patient and doctor. It is also beneficial for farming industry as it is helpful in escalating productivity with the innovative techniques like smart tractors or analysis devices. It can help us to get a better data. The analysis of soil can be conducted in a better way which can further be helpful in suggesting the farmer about the best crop to be grown in the preferred land. Then, there are manufacturing industries which are also opened to IoT following replacement of many unskilled jobs with high automation. With the aid of IoT, the overall efficiency and productivity are increased for manufacturing industries. The education sector is also benefitted by IoT. One of the examples is augmented reality which makes a significant difference in the class by exposing the students to the practical world by providing the real experience. It can be concluded that IoT will remain significant to individual, industry and society as a whole.

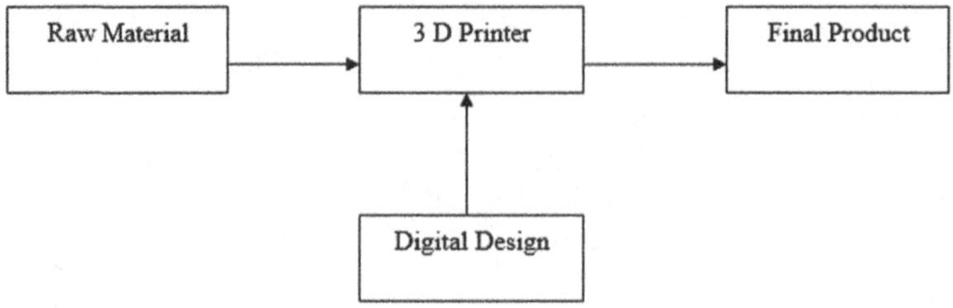

Fig. 8 Flow diagram of additive manufacturing. *Source* Authors'

3.6 Additive Manufacturing

Additive manufacturing is also acknowledged as 3D printing. It is a procedure through which a digital design is created with a physical object. The object to be made is first designed using aided design or CAD software. After the 3D design file is separated into thin layers, it is uploaded to an addictive manufacturing technique. When the slim layer of metal powder is swept throughout the platform in the beginning of manufacturing procedure, a heat source like electron beam or laser dissolves the primary layer of the 3D design. The flow diagram of addictive manufacturing is shown in Fig. 8.

Additive manufacturing allows us to produce parts that are lighter, stronger and more durable than conventionally made parts. Build times are faster, and precise features and complex geometries can be easily added without any extra cost. This type of manufacturing reduces material waste by 95% and reduces the production time as well. Additive manufacturing is changing the whole horizon of manufacturing process; it is redefining the manufacturing in areas like aerospace, medical, transportation, energy and consumer products.

3.7 Big Data Analytics

The world is becoming increasingly digital space today, and we manage, share and store our lives online. Data is gathered from our devices like computers, smartphones, GPS devices and sensors installed all over, and 2.5trillion bytes of data or information are generated everyday through our surrounding devices. An obvious question which revolves around our mind is what can be done with his huge data. To get answer of this, big data analytics comes into picture. It is an analysis of enormous quantity of data with the purpose of extracting meaningful information and behavior pattern to facilitate industries and government.

There are four varieties of big data analytics, namely the descriptive, the diagnostic, the predictive and the prescriptive. The descriptive analytics explains what took place in the past but not what will happen in future. The diagnostic analytics attempts to analyze the reason of any event that took place in the past. The predictive analytics is helpful for companies as it analyzes the data in order to forecast the future that could take place in future. Last but not least, the prescriptive analytics is the development of the previous approach aiming on automation and providing recommendations on how to proceed further with the system.

One real-life example is big data. Netflix gathers customer behavior data from over 100 million of its subscribers. This data facilitates Netflix in exploring the needs of individual subscriber. On the basis of this analysis, it suggests TV shows, web series and movies which are preferred by the subscribers to watch. As a result, the consumer is contented and delighted because he is able to watch things of his interest without even looking for it. On the other hand, Netflix is happy because it has made its customer satisfied which will result in higher consumer retention. Big data analysis is considered to establish explicit business value, as its analysis and processing will assist an organizational growth by reducing cost.

3.8 Artificial Intelligence

Artificial intelligence is a combination of two words: artificial meaning anything that is made by human that are not natural and intelligence is the capacity to comprehend, think and understand. Artificial intelligence is a wide area of computer engineering; it is the study of how to make computers do the things which at present human can do better. The primary aim is to build a machine which thinks like human and can independently take decision as well. Lot of research is still going on in this field, but it is also true that in recent past, various machines and robots are made, and they are used in various sectors ranging from health care, robotics, marketing, business analytics and many more.

3.9 Cybersecurity

The onset of digitalization era has opened up lot of opportunities for everyone especially business and enterprises from mobile banking to online shopping. The safety and security of confidential data are as risk with the higher dependence on digital assistance. There is a big challenge for companies to secure their confidential data. For this purpose, the companies rely on cybersecurity.

Cybersecurity is an integration of methods and procedures process and practices intended to safeguard networks, data, computer programs and or mishandling of authorized asset. The objective of cybersecurity is to decrease the risk of digital and virtual insecurity and defend the individuals and companies from any sort of exploitation of technology.

As discussed above, Industry 4.0 is backed by innovative technologies. These technologies are used in constructive manner, and then it will be a boon for business organizations and society as well. However, as every coin has two sides, in the next section we will discuss the potential threat which may arise from implementing Industry 4.0 in future.

4 New Social Normalities in Industry 4.0

As already discussed, technology and social context are two such entities that interact with each other at any phase of growth of the humankind. In actuality, in comparison with the technological change, the consequence of social aspect on economic growth and development is more diversified. The social normalities, in reference to the partially modified source (Wiesner et al., 2018), can be expected to be affected by six global trends until 2050. The trends are as follows:

1. Demographical change
2. Movement of masses to urban areas
3. Growth of middle class
4. Struggle for limited natural resources
5. Growth of secondary and fall of primary economies
6. Advent of extremism

1. ***Demographical change***. As expected, the world population would be approx. 9.7 billion by 2050, as compared to what it was about 7.3 billion back in 2015. Africa would be the most affected, having almost 54% of net increase. Except Africa and Middle-East, all the other geographies will suffer workforce shrinkage and aging population. The major challenge in front of less developed parts of the economy would be the difference in demographic trends along with less ability for job creation.

   The disruption of the labor market because of the competence of innovative technologies, like industrial robots, would make the previous problems worse only. With the increasing substitution of automation for labor, the bridge between return to capital and labor income might be exacerbated with the replacement of human resource by industrial robots. This creates segregation of the labor markets into low-skill low-pay and high-skill high-pay segments, which ultimately breaks the social harmony. Larger beneficiaries of these technological breakthroughs are the investors, innovators and shareholders, who are the providers of intellectual and financial capital. While the less educated workers possessing lower competence are the bigger losers in terms of income.
2. ***Movement of masses to urban areas***. With reference to the allocation of population between urban and rural areas, we have reached the break-even point in 2006 in terms of world population. More than 50% of the population of the world resided in cities. The urban areas of North America, South America and Europe are populated by almost two-thirds of population these days. In Asia and Africa, in particular, it is expected that the speed of urbanization will pick up the pace between now and 2050. More than 80% of world population could be projected to be living in 600 megacities in the next 25–30 years from now.

For the increase of output, productivity and standard of living, urbanization is a real powerful force. But to bring this structural change, sectors like transportation, urban planning, waste management and renewable energy sources need huge investments based on the philosophy of circular economy.

3. ***Middle-class expansion***. In this era of emerging economies, if there is any outcome of sustainable and comprehensive economic growth, it is the expansion of the middle class. It is projected that by 2050, a big chunk of the population of world, say about 41% of people in number, might fit in to middle or upper class. The economic history tells that the social and economic growth and development have been empowered by the appearance of large middle class. A strong middle class, anywhere, ensures adding up of pressure on the politicians to be accountable and to maintain their promise and results in tangible outcomes.
4. ***Competition for limited natural resources***. The relationship of growth with the growing consumption of natural resources is resulting in the depletion of their reserves (Ray et al., 2017). In this scenario, it is really challenging for the world to maintain the demands of the ensuing new middle and upper and middle while choosing the current lifestyle of western consumers. So the question arises: Would the people throughout the world choose it, or by choosing newer technologies like "green energy", "circular economy," etc., they would agree to acquire different lifestyles that would be less demanding to the earth?
5. ***Rise of secondary and fall of primary economies***. Currently, the economic power is undergoing major changes across the economy. It is projected that by 2050, Asia alone will generate over about half of the global GDP, about three-fourths of worldwide productivity will be in the rising economies. Because of this, worldwide domination, particularly multinational financial organizations, requires transformation according to the current needs and practicality of global economy.
6. ***Advent of extremism***. In this information era, the social media platforms are used by more than 30% of the global population to share, connect and learn information. Often there are a few extremists, who take the advantage of slow development of economy resulting in conflicts and tensions, supporting impractical expectations.

The geopolitical landscape has now come up with new phenomenon of violent non-state actors, which are a severe danger for the security of the global because the procedure of economic growth and development may get interrupted by them. Requirement of actions to constraint the effect of geopolitics on nation becomes very important to combat this serious threat, so that inclusive growth models can be promoted more to lift up peoples' expectations in relation to the rule of law, economic integration and non-violent resolution of deep rooted differences. The latest industrialization based on highly developed manufacturing has impacted strongly and positively. But if new normalities are not considered and managed well, they could result in the negative situation in case of "poor policy regime."

5 Conclusion

Although, in the short run, technological changes can be tremendously disrupting, and this disruption can continue in the long run also if it becomes difficult for the companies and economies to adapt with the changes. But ultimately, in the long run, the technological advancement is a good phenomenon for one and all. Every industrial revolution brings enormous opportunities with it along with some challenges. The industrial revolution, i.e., Industry 4.0 extremely influenced us and the way we are working including our lifestyle, consumption pattern, privacy and safety, balance between work and spare time, etc. The list is never ending as its determinants are human thoughts and imagination. Emerging technology, no doubts, has changed our way of behaving and approach toward demand, industries and overall market. Our choices are mostly influenced by technological aspects and managed capitalism which is different from heterodox way of industries.

References

Azuma, R. T. (1997). A survey of augmented reality. *Presence: Teleoperators and virtual environments, 6*(4), 355–385.

Bai, C., & Thuemmler, C. (2017). *Health 4.0: How virtualization and big data are revolutionizing healthcare*. Springer. https://doi.org/10.1007/978-3-319-47617-9.

Barreto, L., Amaral, A., & Pereira, T. (2017). Industry 4.0 implications in logistics: An overview. *Procedia Manufacturing, 13*, 1245–1252.

BCG. (2015). Industry 4.0: The future of productivity and growth in manufacturing industries. https://imagesrc.bcg.com/Images/Industry_40_Future_of_Productivity_April_2015_tcm9-61694.pdf

Bhalla, M., & Kohli, H. S. (2016). The world In 2050: Striving for a more just, prosperous, and harmonious global community. *India Quarterly, 72*(4), 425–428.

Brettel, M., Friederichsen, N., Keller, M., & Rosenberg, M. (2014). How virtualization, decentralization and network building change the manufacturing landscape: An Industry 4.0 perspective. *World Academy of Science, Engineering and Technology, International Journal of Information and Communication Engineering, 8*(1), 37–44.

Ghemawat, P. (2017). Globalization in the age of Trump. *Harvard Business Review, 95*(4), 112–123.

Gilchrist, A. (2016). *Industry 4.0: The industrial internet of things*. Apress.

Gla, B. R., & Leukert, B. (2018). *Retail 4.0: The digitization of retail-strategies, technologies, transformation (1st ed.)*. Springer International Publishing AG.

Jarrahi, F., Pezzotta, G., Cimini, C., & Gaiardelli, P. (2017). Smart service strategies in Industry 4.0: a proposal of a readiness assessment methodology. In S. West, Gebauer, H., & Baines, T., (eds.) *Proceedings of the spring servitization conference 2017 "Internationalisation through Servitization"* (pp. 232–240). Lucerne University of Applied Sciences and Arts, May 15–17, ISBN 978-1-85449-418-4.

Kagermann, H., Wahlster, W., & Helbig, J. (2013). Recommendations for implementing the strategic initiative Industrie 4.0: Final report of the Industrie 4.0 Working Group. *Communication Promoters Group of the Industry-Science Research.*

Li, D., Fasth, Fast-Berglund, Å, Paulin, D. (2019). Current and future Industry 4.0 capabilities for information and knowledge sharing: Case of two Swedish SMEs. *The International Journal of Advanced Manufacturing Technology,* 105:3951–3963.

Li, Z. (2018). *Telecommunication 4.0: Reinvention of the communication network.* Springer.

Mosconi, F. (2015). *The new European industrial policy: Global competitiveness and the manufacturing renaissance.* Routledge.

Pwc (2016). Industry 4.0: Building the digital enterprise. https://www.pwc.com/gx/en/industries-4.0-building-your-digital enterprise-april-2016.pdf

Roblek, V., Meško, M., & Krapež, A. (2016). A complex view of Industry 4.0. *SAGE Open.* https://doi.org/10.1177/2158244016653987.

Sommer, L. (2015). Industrial revolution—Industry 4.0: Are German manufacturing SMEs the first victims of this revolution? *Journal of Industrial Engineering and Management, 8,* 1512–1532.

Stentoft, J., Wickstrøm Jensen, K., Philipsen, K., Haug, A. (2020). Drivers and barriers for Industry 4.0 readiness and practice: empirical evidence from small and medium-sized manufacturers. In *Proceedings of the 52nd Hawaii international conference on system sciences, production planning & control* (pp. 5155–5164).

Wiesner, S., Gaiardelli, P., Gritti, N., Oberti, G. (2018). Maturity models for digitalization in manufacturing—Applicability for SMEs. In: *IFIP international conference on advances in production management systems (APMS)* (pp. 81–88), Aug 2018.

Zhong, R. Y., Xu, X., Klotz, E., Newman, S. T. (2017). Intelligent manufacturing in the context of Industry 4.0: *A Review [J].Engineering, 3*(5):616–630.

Reetika Sehgal is working as Assistant Professor in Department of Management at United College of Engineering and Management, Prayagraj. She holds Ph.D. in Management from Birla Institute of Technology, Mesra, Ranchi (Allahabad Campus). Her research area includes public policy, public administration, strategic management and human resource management. She has more than 9 years of teaching experience at graduate and postgraduate levels. She has published more than seven research papers in national and international journals in the area of public policy and public administration.

Anukaran Khanna is currently pursuing Ph.D. from Birla Institute of Technology and Science, Pilani, India. He has more than 5 years of teaching experience in engineering education. He contributed various articles and published research paper in national and international journals. He has presented various research papers in the national and international conferences. His area of interest lies in aerospace and control engineering.

Ashish Mohan Dubey is currently Assistant Professor at Birla Institute of Technology, Mesra, Ranchi (Patna Campus). He holds a Ph.D. in Management from the School of Management Studies, Motilal Nehru National Institute of Technology, Prayagraj, India. His research area includes strategic management and strategic human resource management. He has more than 15 years of teaching experience at graduate and postgraduate levels and 7 years of experience in guiding and examining graduate and doctoral thesis in India. Two students have earned their Ph.D. degree under his supervision. His interest lies in strategic management and project management. He serves on the editorial board of various journals. He has published several papers in international and national journals and conference proceedings.

Prateek Khanna is currently working as Associate Professor in the Department of Business Administration, at Shambhunath Institute of Engineering and Technology, Prayagraj, Uttar Pradesh. He has more than 10 years of teaching experience in management education. He contributed various articles and published research papers in national and international journals. He has presented various research papers in the national and international conference. His area of interest is consumer behavior, sensory branding and digital marketing.

Gig Economy Gets Technology Tick: Stories from India

Ritika Gugnani

1 Introduction

'Gig' is a word coined initially by Jazz musicians. It is a short word used for 'engagement'. 'Gig' is a word coined for each piece of paid task or work which involves an individual. 'Gig economy' that has gained popularity based on this present context involves freelance work or temporary contractual job which might be only on project to project basis. So gig economy encompasses those independent contractors, consultants, content creators, social media marketers, food and beverages experts, movie producers, art and design professionals, etc. It involves temporary or part-time work force instead of permanent workforce. Typically gig workers involve millennials, experienced professionals, skilled craftsman, artisans and multitaskers. The overall importance of non-standard forms of employment (hereinafter 'non-standard employment', or 'NSE') as referred by the International Labour Organization (ILO) has increased in labour market of both advanced and emerging economies. As per a report of International Labour Organization (2016), NSE can be of four different types (Rodda & Lubman, 2014). The first one is temporary employment which involves fixed-term contracts, including project- or task-based contracts; seasonal work; casual work, including daily work. This type of employment is not open ended. Second type is part-time and on-call work, including zero-hours contracts which normally involves fewer than full-time workers; on-call work. Third type is 'multi-party employment' relationship like also known as 'dispatch', 'brokerage' and 'labour hire', temporary agency work; subcontracted labour. The last and fourth type is disguised employment/dependent self-employment, sham or misclassified self-employment (International Labour Organisation, 2016). The term 'non-standard employment' repeatedly combines the concepts of labour market of 'precarious work' and 'gig work' (Labour Market Information Council, 2020). These three

R. Gugnani (✉)
Department of Economics, Jaipuria Institute of Management, Noida, Uttar Pradesh, India
e-mail: ritika.gugnani@jaipuria.ac.in

A. Gupta et al. (eds.), *Sustainability in the Gig Economy*,
https://doi.org/10.1007/978-981-16-8406-7_18

concepts are frequently used interchangeably in various literature available, but they are distinct. The ILO defines precariousness as 'risky' job that includes low pay (i.e., earning at or less than poverty line), uncertainty in job continuation and few or no job protections guaranteed under law or collective agreements. Because there is no universally agreed upon definition of gig work, the relationship between non-standard employment and gig work (and between precocity and gig work) is more complex and beyond scope of this work.

The gig economy typically includes two types of work, firstly 'crowd work' and secondly 'work on-demand via apps' (Cardon & Casilli, 2015; International Labour Organisation, 2016; Kessler, 2015; Said, 2015; Smith & Leberstein, 2015). The term 'crowd work' is usually referred to activities that indicate completing a sequence of tasks through online platforms (Bergvall-Kåreborn & Howcroft, 2014; De Stefano, 2015; Felstiner, 2011; Howe, 2006). Usually, technology platforms try to on board a large number of organizations or clients and workers through the Internet hence increasing the reach. 'Work on-demand via apps' helps in executing daily routine activities such as cleaning, delivering; some forms of clerical jobs are also channelized through apps which tries to set some minimum norms and standards for quality of workforce and services provided by them (Aloisi, 2015; Dagnino, 2015; Rogers, 2015).

In India, gig economy encompasses of two broad classifications. One is physical gig economy which includes low to semi-skilled workers who normally offer their services through 'work on-demand' platforms like UrbanClap, Ola, Uber, etc. (Pant & Krishna, 2021). On the other hand, the digital gig economy includes semi- to high-skilled workers like freelancers, consultants and other knowledge workers who work directly for companies through technology platforms (Kuppili, 2020). ASSOCHAM (2020), predicted the size of India's gig economy at compound annual growth rate (CAGR) of 17 percent to $455 billion by 2023. However, it is also a fact that though gig economy is growing fast, but is at an early stage in India. There are two plausible impacts of pandemic COVID-19 that firstly demand for gig work will decrease during the crisis and secondly companies in order to consolidate on their cost later will shift to gig workers in comparison to hiring conventional workforce.

2 Changing Landscape of Gig Economy in India

The upsurge of gig economy in India owes to technological and demographic shifts which are evolving interaction among companies and job aspirants. Increased digitalization has facilitated remote working options. Use of technology means that many who otherwise would have worked previously in unorganized sectors can now reach better employment opportunities in organized sectors in India, though for short term only. The workforce is becoming more diverse in constitution because millennials and generation Z are joining labour markets. Co-working spaces and co-living are emerging in cities like Bangalore, Delhi, etc. which facilitate individual connect and better utilization of human talent. Increased digitization has increased acceptability of remote working options amongst HR (Human Resources) professionals in India (Lund et al., 2020). However, this might get unfolded in future only that how wages will evolve according to free market principles. India is now at fifth position globally after USA, China, Brazil and Japan regrading flexible staffing. As per a survey report by Noble House (2019), at least 53% of employers surveyed have absorbed 5 to 20% of gig workers in their organization in last two years indicating increasing fondness for gig workers.

3 Technology Platforms Bridging the Gap

The idea of work from home or employing someone who is remotely situated remained foreign to most of the companies in India. Nevertheless, technological improvements in internet and wireless communication technologies (ICTs) have changed the landscape. But as the time has gone by, data infrastructure was put in place improving connectivity globally. High-speed Internet computers, sophisticated collaborative tools, and above all smartphones proved to be game changer and increased possibility of remote collaboration. ICT and smartphones have tried to fill the void left by loss of in person and face to face meetings due to the Covid-19 pandemic undoubtedly impacting on-demand workers. The platforms like Freelancer, Truelancer, Fiverr, Upwork, Workex have created a platform where skilled professionals (or white collar workers) can be hired for specific projects for graphic design, web design, coding, writing and many more specialist jobs for short-term projects. The unique thing about these platforms is that they bridge the gap between demand and supply of short-term contractual jobs by connecting gig workers and even managing their payments. Platforms like Uber, Airbnb, Upwork, Swiggy, Fiverr, People per hour are helping in creating a novel business model where unskilled workforce (or blue collar workforce) were hired through apps and online market place based on client or customer ratings. Interestingly, the pandemic posed an interesting trend where giggers (someone who works in the gig economy) crowded the customer service segment. The inclusion of giggers eventually has pushed corporates to be more agile. These technology platforms with the help of artificial intelligence and big data algorithms have been responsible for matching recruiters' requirement with the suitable employee skill set enabling employers to hire the correct skill set and talent in a timely and cost-efficient manner. Of course, this has enabled the rise of freelancing companies opening opportunities for gig workers. In a study by McKinsey authored by Manyika et al. (2016), it is estimated that 20–30% of the workforce in developed countries is already self-employed or employed as independent worker. As per a report by ICRIER authored by Kathuria et al. (2017), India is home to the second largest market of freelance professionals (about 15 million), in comparison to the USA (nearly 53 million) which contributes about 40% of total freelance jobs available globally. The technology platforms are helping India in solving four major concerns like job search, skilling underemployed, increasing women participation in workforce and migration and loss of jobs due to pandemic. As per survey from a human resource firm TeamLease Service as quoted by Salman and Bansal (2019) in an Indian Newspaper Mint, Delhi (the Capital of India) added 560,660 people to its gig economy by March, 2020 showing almost 88% jump from 298,000 people.

3.1 Wishup: The Virtual Employee Company

Wishup, started in July 2015 by Neelesh Rangwani and Vivek Gupta, is a chat-based concierge, trying to solve a unique problem of joining businesses with experienced professionals who are interested in working remotely. Wishup uses different selection procedures, interviews to collate talent pool and matches it with demand of their clients. Wishup changed its model from chat based to virtual assistant service in 2017 (Debolina, 2018). It reformed further to become Virtual Employee (VE) company. According to founders, it started with identifying 50 to 70 online tasks which a Virtual Employee can perform. There are two sides, i.e., client side and a VE side. Clients of Wishup raise various demands and requirements (Debolina, 2019). They explain the kind of tasks and requirement of skill sets. On Virtual Employee side, they receive applications from professionals, 90% of them are married women with children, from Tier-I and Tier-II cities having age between late 20s and late 40s. Their resume highlights the skill sets that these applicants possess. Applicants have to undergo rigorous selection process, testing and evaluating them on at least 30 parameters focusing on communication skills, internet skills and problem solving skills. Normally, only out of 500 applications 2–4% are shortlisted. After selection, all the applicants need to undergo 4 weeks rigorous training for upgradation of their skill set by mangers at Wishup. Now VE with maximum matching skill sets is introduced to the clients, who then choose and pay. The platform also tracks the performance and time taken by each VE to complete a task on a daily and monthly basis. In coming time, Wishup wanted to do away with extensive recruitment process and reduce its hiring costs. It wants its clients to able to just log in and choose a set of VE and hire immediately. This technology platform has accomplished wide range of tasks which can be completed by virtual employees in client management, sales, recruitment support and e-mail marketing, CRM tools, invoice creation, follow-ups arranging services and secondary research. So the organizations which wants to grow among the pandemic hiring a good and strong team can easily complete their tasks through these virtual companies as they offer virtual assistants which can manage routine and technical matters at a very low cost. Wishup has recognized easy availability of various types of professional appropriate for various computer-based tasks. These professionals for various reasons cannot take a regular office-based jobs and hence prefer to work remotely.

3.2 *Flexiple: The Freelancing Game Changer*

Flexiple started in 2016, is a Bengaluru-based start-up who wants to change the freelancing game in India. Flexiple started by Karthik, Hrishikesh and Suvansh has received support from Centre for Innovation Incubation and Entrepreneurship (CIIE) of IIM-Ahmedabad.

Good-quality technology talent consisting of developers and designers is very tough to find in an unorganized market of freelancers. Hence, finding good talent with right skills and right attitude is what Flexiple tries to provide to its clients. When a company wants to hire a freelancer (software developer or designer), the problem that they face is to dig very deep to find right kind of talent. They select freelancers based on reviews or rating which might not be the best way of selecting the talent. Flexiple developed a unique internal screening process which resulted in increased competition when on boarding of any freelancer starts at Flexiple. Furthermore, their transparent pricing solves the other problem of organizations which wanted to hire developers and designers on project basis only to reduce the cost. So right pricing, increasing number of applicants and a strong internal screening process help Flexiple in attaining client satisfaction.

The freelancers of Flexiple consist of seasoned and proficient software professionals across seven countries who have earlier worked with top companies like Amazon, Adobe, Microsoft, Ola, Goldman Sachs, etc. They are now self-employed and independent freelancers. The clients are those enterprises who are looking for software developers, UX experts, illustrators and designers with diverse skill sets. Clients interested in hiring freelancers have to fill a form available on Flexiple website. After this, team from this start-up gets in touch to verify and understand the requirements of the client. The clients are then offered three recommendations for their requirements. After this step, client is normally given a week to try and check freelancer's job fit . Once the trial period is over, the Flexiple works around payments and other contractual formalities. Flexiple team tries to maintain high level of transparency with quickest turnaround time which significantly lowers the cost for the clients. They also assign a 'customer happiness manager' for each project to avoid any potential problem between client and the freelancer. Flexiple is now planning to expand abroad with more foreign clients.

3.3 *Refrens: Managing and Tracking Payments*

Burgeoning freelancers force in India face challenging issues such as managing and tracking payments and planning their finances. There are a lot of technology solutions which are coming through Fintech, B2B software and SaaS. Refrens founded by Naman Sarawagi and Mohit Jain offers an online platform for free invoicing software and payment collection for freelancers and helps them to collect payments from their clients. The tool is free for those looking for work. Both the founders came up with this idea in June 2019 only when they themselves were working as freelance consultants for multiple start-ups on Internet products. Many freelancers still manage their payment details in excel sheets and convert them into invoices and sometimes this become a tedious task for them. Refrens which is a free web-based SaaS solution tries to solve this very problem of freelancers (Sindhu, 2019). The platform works with freelancers and small agencies working as B2B service providers in the fields of software development, design, public relations (PR), sales and marketing, co-working spaces, housekeeping agencies, etc.

Refrens optimizes on multiple opportunities in workflow software, financial services by bringing innovative ways of collecting payments through reputation management. Once a member avails free service for generating an invoice on platform three to four times, they are able to see the network available on the platform. Each member can offer a referral commission which other members can see. Since its launch, this start-up is able to on board 500 clients who use the platform at 1–2 times a week. They are able to generate a small revenue through online payments done on the platform. Usually, a fee of 0.1 percent is collected on online payments. Many freelancers are using Refrens for dollar invoicing. Refrens can be used for 37 currencies for generating invoices across 100 countries.

3.4 Lemonop: Skilling India's Youth

Lemonop, Bengaluru-based start-up by Swaroop Chand, Ramkiran Bhat and Sateesh Havannavar, was created to provide multiple opportunities. The projects are exclusive for Students and fresher. The platform which is also available in the form of mobile application is created through multiple technologies (Shubham, 2019). Short-term work or gigs can solve economy's biggest problem of skilling youth. The platform offers short-term work or gigs ranging from few hours to maximum of 90 days. As claimed by the platform, more than 185 reputed companies have given them assignments and more than 17,000 users have done more than 300 short-term jobs through the platform. The platform is completely free for giggers but charges companies through pay per post or subscription model. Interestingly, the gigs available on platform are not only related to designing, software development, administrative routine jobs but also food photography, coding, travel blogging, music bands, event management and stand-up comedy also. Earlier gig was applicable to entry-level low order skill sets. Now platforms like Lemonop are trying to change the game. Students and freshers will now get a chance to upskill themselves and expose to network of companies which are on this technology platform (Deepthi, 2019).

3.5 *Opportunities and Future Drivers of Gig Economy*

The gig economy is relatively in its early stage in India, but like the other global trends its growth is also fueled by many factors like a shortage of talented and skilled workforce, preference of workers toward more work/life balance and requirement of on-demand workforce (Franklin, 2020). The information and communication technologies have fueled the presence of gig economy. All the above-said platforms are short stories of changing landscape of gig economy in India. The shift from on-demand apps (taking care of cabs, drivers, cooks and other low end jobs) to technology platform (hiring developers, marketers, administrators and other complex tasks) is very clear. These technological platforms have given immediate ready access to talent marketplaces and will fuel hiring of gig knowledge workers (Agile-One, 2018). The platforms like Lemonop is helping young India to bridge its learning gaps with more industry interface and upskill their current game in job market. Online platforms with their technology have started bending and challenging norms of traditional workplaces. They are moving the labour market from low flexibility with high security toward high flexibility with low security (Cieslak, 2020).

Interestingly in a green paper published by Cottam (2020) has coined a term 'Nanobusiness' which employs less than one full-time worker and includes businesses that sells products, creative solutions, services, influence, labour or commercial sharing of assets owned by any business or its owner. The gig economy is considered part of 'Nanobusiness' (Cottam, 2020). The presence of Nanobusiness is fueled by ICT companies only. The ICT is helping delivery of labour and services irrespective of location and is pushing new forms of flexibility at work places and is opening newer opportunities for workers who earlier found it hard to work in a more formal 9–5 job scenarios or traditional work places (Aditya, 2021). This is giving newer opportunities to students (work while studying), parents (balancing child care with jobs) especially women and older work force wanting to work beyond their retirement age. The platform like Refrens is telling a hidden trend which is catching the world silently that is selling services to Nanobusiness, a part of which are gig workers. These gig workers are also consumers of many products and services. These gig workers rely on their mobile phones to sell their labour, services and creativity. Hence are becoming an upcoming market segment for ICT companies as they are creating B2B on-demand economy and need to communicate, collaborate and consume various cloud-based solutions. As these gig workers' number increases in any economy, they will also demand services like tax solutions, legal and contractual services, cloud-based solutions, working spaces and many more (Arruda, 2020). The companies using technology platforms like Wishup and Flexiple would require a thorough assessment of their internal processes and a step-by-step approach in order to blend gig workers with their existing work force. They need to adopt steps that institutionalize enabling factors in their current ecosystem like giving short-term trainings on firm-specific standards, developing strict non-disclosure and secrecy agreements and adopting facilitating technology. Though this has also become clear after the second wave of pandemic that job matching platforms for gigs need to give time to companies to sail through the current slowdown. This time should be utilized by gig providers to explore and learn newer possibilities (Hundekari et al., 2020).

4 Ensuring Social Sustainability to India's Portable Workforce

However, all is not well with the gig economy and gig workers in India. It is not a utopian state that we are living with unemployment levels being down, recorded by Centre for Monitoring Indian economy (CMIE) in December 2020 at 9.1%, but inequality and 'dystopia of sham self-employment' (Wright, 2018).

The pandemic COVID-19 has increased already existing income inequalities present in Indian society. The pandemic has forced lot informal sector workers out of job. The viewpoint that the rising gig economy is full of entrepreneurs who love their casual work in the pleasant surroundings of their homes with flexible schedules has its another side. The fact that these are risky workers showcased to the world as gig workers shifting all responsibility away from the companies is an element that should not be overlooked. In the absence of regular pay outs, sick leaves, health insurances and other social security benefits, the financial risks are very high. During lockdown, the income of gig workers falls sharply. Post COVID-19 also, how gig workers will be affected remains a burning topic for future researches. However, this is very clear that in the absence of special legislations gig workforce remain out of reach of benefits like minimum wages, shift timing, overtime payment, sick leave, etc. and even access to financial services available to most forms of standard employment. However, technology platforms through their digital infrastructure can help in tracking payments on weekly, monthly or after completion of projects. It is important for governments to track the exact size of gig economy to infuse 'formality' into this informal sector. Smahi Foundation has recommended creation of a National Registry of Platform-based workers. With increased digital infrastructure (based on Aadhaar or creation of unique social security number), the target benefits provided by states and central governments can easily be reached with minimum governance and efforts. This could help in achieving seamless on boarding process of gig workers also. However, still this remains disputed that whether government through revised labour reforms should increase monitoring of the technology platforms as this will lead to increased cost for budding companies or start-ups. Experts in labour reforms have recommended a social security fund for gig workers. The recommendation is to deduct some amount from their payouts and should be contributed to a fund which will be portable in nature. These funds can be managed like provident funds where payout can be granted after attaining a certain age. So recently, Government of India (GOI) presented Social Security Code 2020 (also known as SS Code) in front of Parliament and received presidential acceptance. The SS Code recognizing gig workers has proposed a social security scheme and electronic registration for them. The proposed fund will be run by contributions of government, technology platforms and corporate social responsibility funds.

The draft proposes that unorganized workers, platform workers and gig workers are supposed to be registered with Aadhaar on a self-declaration basis. The technology platforms will link their databases with the Aadhaar number. The Indian Federation of App-Based Transport Workers (IFAT) is a worker union representing app-based transport workers feels that SS code can ensure eligibility for various benefits but cannot force companies due to lot of open lacunas in the code (Indian Federation of App-based Transport workers (IFAT) and International Transport Workers' Federation (ITF, 2020). If Sustainable Development Goal 8 aims at 'promoting sustained, inclusive and sustainable economic growth, full and productive employment and decent work for all', then collecting more data related to non-standard form of employment and their working conditions from gig platforms and bringing relevant regulatory changes can make gig economy more sustainable. It can contribute significantly to providing productive employment opportunities and decent work for all. It can be mandated that these on-demand app and technology platforms need to share information with government. These data points can help the government to bring significant changes in regulatory framework to include more gig workers (working in low-skilled jobs).

5 Future Implications

The COVID-19 pandemic has pushed many Indian companies to accept the feasibility of the idea of having casual and temporary staff in their current workforce. This will give rise to acceptance of non-standard forms of employment in India. This condition will push acceptance of gig workers along with traditional workforce. Surely future technological developments will influence the way the humans work and labour force will be organized. Technological platforms dealing with online outsourcing will be playing a bigger role in terms of fulfilling on-demand talent (providing a specific skill set not required on permanent basis). However, the impact of pandemic is not similar across industries and professions indicating the diversity of Indian economy. The difficulties faced by gig workers during the pandemic due to future employment and job loss have pushed them to unionized. Indian Federation of App-based Transport workers (IFAT) and International Transport Workers' Federation (ITF, 2020) believes that COVID-19 has forced everyone to think that even independent contractors or free agents are required to be brought under social security schemes. Regulators in India and globally are now thinking of inclusion of gig workers for different financial assistance programs and social security schemes. The companies and organizations using extensively independent workforce or free agents need to incorporate these social security schemes in their current business model.

As the gig economy will mature in India, there are certain trends which can be easily observed like adoption of more technology and automation-oriented solution will be the need of the hour. The choices regarding automation and technology adoption made by different companies will decide their survival and resilience during and after the pandemic. Work from home (WFH) has proved that some complex and high end roles will also become part of gig economy. Technology platforms like Wishup, Flexiple, Virtual Employee, Acelerar Technologies, Webcenture and many more are going to reduce many biases and stigmas attached to gig workers. This will increase their acceptability and size in Indian economy. As the gig workers will rise in the economy regulations will be redrafted to take care of this part of the economy.

6 Conclusion

It is for sure that in future, gig workers will be hired for complex tasks across industries. This disruption has created opportunities as well as challenges in front of India. The technology platforms will play a strong role in providing opportunities to young generations and bringing the gap in female participation in work force. It will long time and perseverance on part of both job providers and job seekers before gig economy reaches next stage of development. The gig economy has broken a long established belief that informal work will be all 'unskilled'. There is definitely shift in demand toward more 'high-end skilled jobs' in marketing, human resource, finance domain, etc. which has changed the tenor and texture of gig economy. Indian labour reforms need to address diverse spectrum presented by gig economy. Failing to address this could prove counterproductive and hence ruin the advantage of India's demographic profile. Only time will tell whether the new labour model provided by gig economy with more flexibility and low on security will lift millions out poverty or not? But the ownership is on societies to rethink and redefine the social contracts defining responsibilities of organizations and individuals working with them.

References

Aditya, G. (2021). *Gig economy & the future of work*. Available Via, Productivity Hub, Accessed on February 1, 2021. https://productivityhub.org/2019/07/02/gig-economy-the-future-of-work.

Agile-One. (2018). *The new gig economy, what's at stake?* (White Paper), AGILEONE-WP-GIGECON-V2, Retrieved via www.agile-one.com. Retrieved on April 21st, 2021. https://agile-one.com/media/1590/2018-agileone-whitepaper-new-gig-economy-us-final.pdf.

Aloisi, A. (2015). Commoditized workers: Case study research on labor law issues arising from a set of on-demand/gig economy platforms. *Comparative Labor Law and Policy Journal, 37*, 653.

Arruda, W. (2020). *6 trends that will shape the gig economy in the 2020s, Forbes*, Accessed on April 23, 2021. https://www.forbes.com/sites/williamarruda/2020/07/12/6-trends-that-will-shape-the-gig-economy-in-the-2020s/?sh=2117289c1565.

ASSOCHAM. (2020). *National conference, gig economy aligning consumer preferences: The way forward, January 24, 2020*. Background Note, Associated Chambers of Commerce and Industry of India. Accessed on February 5, 2021. https://books.google.co.in/books?id=YxerzQEACAAJ.

Bergvall-Kåreborn, B., & Howcroft, D. (2014). Amazon Mechanical Turk and the commodification of labour. *New Technology, Work and Employment, 29*(3), 213–223.

Cardon, D., & Casilli, A. (2015). *Qu'est-ce que le digital labor?* Ina.

Cieslak, N. (2020). *Future of work report, appjobs Institute.* Available Via www.institute.appjobs.com. Accessed on April 25th, 2021. https://irp-cdn.multiscreensite.com/ec5bfac6/files/uploaded/AppJobs%20Institute%20Future%20of%20Work%20Report%202020.pdf.

Cottam, T. (2020). *Nanobusinesses—A new business category* (Green Paper). Available Via www.Omnisperience.com. Retrieved on 1 Feb 2021.

Dagnino, A. (2015). *Transcultural writers and novels in the age of global mobility.* Purdue University Press.

De Stefano, V. (2015). *The rise of the just-in-time workforce: On-demand work, crowd work, and labor protection in the gig-economy.* Conditions of Work and Employment Series No. 71.

Debolina, B. (2018). Wishup connects businesses with virtual employees who can take care of their every task. Available Via *Yourstory.* Accessed on February 7, 2021. https://yourstory.com/2018/11/wishup-aims-help-mums-balance-careers-family-work-home-options.

Debolina, B. (2019). *Bengaluru-based start-up Flexiple is changing the freelancing game, one gig at a time.* Available Via *Yourstory.* Accessed on February 7, 2021. https://yourstory.com/2019/07/startup-iim-alumni-bengaluru-flexiple-freelancing-gig-economy.

Deepthi, S. (2019). *Short-term jobs could be the next big thing among students.* Available Via *Times of India,* Accessed on February 10th, 2021. http://timesofindia.indiatimes.com/articleshow/68868850.cms?utm_source=contentofinterest&utm_medium=text&utm_campaign=cppst.

Felstiner, A. (2011). Working the crowd: Employment and labor law in the crowdsourcing industry. *Berkeley Journal of Employment and Labor Law, 32,* 143.

Franklin N (2020) Organisations still adjusting to reality of gig economy, insight magazine. Accessed on April 22, 2021. https://workplaceinsight.net/organisations-still-adjusting-to-reality-of-gig-economy/.

Howe, J., (2006). The rise of crowdsourcing. *Wired Magazine, 14*(6), 1–4.

Hundekari, N., Tuli, R., & Sinha A. (2020) Corporate gigs a 'new normal' post-covid, Mint. Accessed on April 23 2021. https://www.livemint.com/opinion/online-views/corporate-gigs-a-new-normal-post-covid-11589537795340.html.

Indian Federation of App-based Transport workers (IFAT) and International Transport Workers' Federation (ITF) (2020) *Locking down the impact of COVID-19: Appraising state and private measures for app-based transport and delivery workers.* Accessed on February 21, 2021. https://cis-india.org/raw/files/ifat-itf-locking-down-the-impact-of-covid-19-report.

International Labour Organization. (2016). Non-standard employment around the world: Understanding challenges, shaping prospects.

Kathuria, R., Kedia, M., Varma, G., Bagchi, K., & Khullar, S. (2017). *Future of work in a digital era: the potential and challenges for online freelancing and microwork in India.* Indian Council for Research on International Economic Relations. http://hdl.handle.net/11540/11066.

Kessler, S. (2015). The gig economy won't last because it's being sued to death. *Fast Company, 17,* 2015.

Kuppili, S. P. (2020). *The rise of gig economy in India, Start-up stories.* Available Via Start-up Stories, Retrieved on February 7, 2021. https://www.startupstories.in/stories/inspirational-stories/articles/the-rise-of-gig-economy-in-india.

Labour Market Information Council0 (2020). *Non-standard Employment, WorksWords.* Retrieved on February 10th 2020. https://lmic-cimt.ca/projects/work-words/non-standard-employment

Lund, S., Madgavkar, A., Manyika, J., & Smit, S. (2020). What's next for remote work: An analysis of 2000 tasks, 800 jobs, and nine countries.

Manyika, J., Lund, S., Bughin, J., Robinson, K., Mischke, J., & Mahajan, D. (2016). Independent work: Choice, necessity, and the gig economy. *McKinsey Global Institute, 2016,* 1–16.

Noble House. (2019). *The gig readiness survey of corporate India.* Excitement, Doubts, mark Corporate Readiness (White Paper), Retrieved Via www.thinknoblehouse.com

Pant, B., & Krishna, G. D. (2021). *COVID-19 and gig workers: Need to democratize the gig economy in India.* Available Via ETGovernment.Com. Retrieved on January 31,

2021. https://government.economictimes.indiatimes.com/news/economy/covid-19-and-gig-workers-need-to-democratize-the-gig-economy-in-india/78567292.

Rodda, S., & Lubman, D. I. (2014). Characteristics of gamblers using a national online counselling service for problem gambling. *Journal of Gambling Studies, 30*(2), 277–289.

Rogers, B., (2015). The social costs of Uber. *U. Chi. L. Rev. Dialogue*, *82*, 85.

Said, C. (2015). Growing voices say gig workers need protections, benefits. *SFGate*. http://www.sfgate.com/business/article/Growing-voices-say-gig-workers-needprotections-6079992.php.

Salman, S. H., & Bansal, V. (2019). Delhi, and not Bengaluru, is the place to be for gig economy workers. *Mint*, April 11, 2019. Retrieved on February 10th 2021. https://www.livemint.com/companies/start-ups/delhi-and-not-bengaluru-is-the-place-to-be-for-gig-economy-workers-1555013405684.html.

Shubham S. (2019). *Lemonop, app that helps students find paid part-time gigs (Web Log Post).* Retrieved on February 9th, 2021. https://www.newsbytesapp.com/news/business/how-lemonop-is-kick-starting-student-fresher-careers/story.

Sindhu, K. (2019). *This start up by former free charge exec is providing a faster payment gateway for B2B service providers*. Yourstory. Retrieved on February 8th, 2021. https://yourstory.com/2019/09/startup-payment-gateway-refrens-b2b-freecharge.

Smith, R., & Leberstein, S. (2015). *Rights on demand. Ensuring workplace standards and worker security in the on-demand economy.* National Employment Law Project, Washington DC.

Wright, M. (2018). Gig economy: Construction vs Reality. *Critical Reflections: A Student Journal on Contemporary Sociological Issues*, (6), Leeds Becket University.

Future Challenges of Sustaining a Gig Economy

Potential Impact of 3D Printing on Gig Economy

L. C. Raghavan, Sumathi Chakravarthy, Sindhu Bharathi Mandharachalam, and Badri Narayanan Gopalakrishnan

1 Introduction

The application of 3D printing or additive manufacturing is expanding as a means of producing products that have greater customization while lowering costs. 3D printers have also become more accessible to a wider range of potential users through the production of smaller printers for use by hobbyists and designers. At a time when major organizations and the labor force are preparing to gain the most out of the emerging "gig" economies, disruptive technologies like 3D printing are anticipated to bring about a disruption in the incumbent labor market.

The study aims to capture the overall impact on employment when 3D printing and other Industry 4.0 technologies are rolled out rapidly. Initially, a detailed empirical study is carried to identify and capture the cost benefits, productivity enhancements, and other savings that industries can gain by deploying 3D printing and other additive manufacturing techniques. The analysis reveals that the deployment of 3D printing technology in the aerospace industry would save 50% cost apart from reduction in time for casting and machining processes. While such processes typically consume more than three months, using 3D printers would reduce the time to 35 h. Apart from casting and machining, aerospace companies can acquire benefits from using the technology to produce tooling equipment like jigs and fixtures and it has been proven that such printers can reduce the lead time by 95% and overall costs by 40%.

The analysis revealed that employing 3D printers in prototyping to produce light fixtures in automotive industries would reduce the lead time significantly and that a 3D-printed part proved to cost 50% less than a conventional counterpart. A study of the benefits and savings that result from the deployment of 3D printing in the production of industrial goods revealed the fact that industrial OEMs are shifting their operations to deploy 3D printing to amplify the agility of the process as well

L. C. Raghavan · S. Chakravarthy · S. B. Mandharachalam · B. N. Gopalakrishnan (✉)
Infinite-Sum Modeling Inc., Washington, USA
e-mail: badri@infisum.com

A. Gupta et al. (eds.), *Sustainability in the Gig Economy*,
https://doi.org/10.1007/978-981-16-8406-7_19

as to reduce the costs. A leading bearing manufacturing company in the UK transformed the production process by using 3D printers, and that such bearings had a 7% increased load-bearing capacity and an increased working life up to 500%.

Following the empirical analysis, the paper employs a Computable General Equilibrium model to analyze the benefits of disruptive technologies on the macro-economic indicators including GDP, employment, output, trade, and so on. The Global Trade Analysis Project (GTAP) database is used for analysis, and the results of the empirical analysis are fed as shocks.

The results reveal that an increase in the adoption of 3D printing technologies, additive manufacturing techniques, and other disruptive technologies for various industrial applications in India would result in a GDP increase of 1.26%. A sector-wise analysis of the output reveals that there will be an increase in the output of manufacturing industries, metal product manufacturing, automotive industries, the aerospace sector, and construction, apart from a 2.36% increase in the total output of the country. The model also predicts that the employment opportunities would increase by 2.38% due to an increase in automation in the afore-described sectors.

2 3D Printing and Its Applications

This technology is based on an additive manufacturing process and builds the product in layers with the help of cross-sectional slices. It uses powder instead of ink and forms an image on the layers. It helps in producing small quantities of customized products at a low cost. It is one of the most disruptive technologies and can transform the landscape of manufacturing (Kunovjanek & Reiner, 2020). It helps the companies to operate with little or no unsold inventory of finished products (Rajan et al., 2016).

There may be a negative effect of this technology as it will reduce the importance of the factory workers. It may also give rise to free moving parts products that do not have the need to be assembled. 3D printing can be used for "office or consumer versions of rapid prototyping machines that are relatively low-cost and easy to use" (Casey, 2009).

There are various varieties of 3D printing technologies which have been developed for different functions. 3D printing technologies can be divided into seven groups including binding jetting, material jetting, directed energy deposition, material extrusion, powder bed fusion, sheet lamination, and VAT photopolymerization; this categorization is according to the ASTM standards (ASTM, 2012). The application of 3D printing has been no longer limited to prototyping usage; it has been also used for making a variety of products.

The first technology uses a jet chemical binder for layer formation (Low et al., 2017). It can be used for producing casting patterns and can print a variety of materials like sands, metals, and ceramics. It is simple and fast and can produce large products, and the powder is glued together. The second technology droplets of photosensitive material are dispensed under ultraviolet light which solidifies layer by layer (Yap et al., 2017). The third technology is a complex printing process. It has a high degree of control of the grain structure. It is used either to repair or to add extra material to the existing components (Tofail et al., 2018). The quality of the object is maintained. The fourth technology can be used to print multi-color plastics, food, or living cell (Kunovjanek & Reiner, 2020). It can help in producing low-cost fully functional parts of the products or the complete product (Tofail et al., 2018). The fifth technology includes "electron beam melting, selective laser sintering, selective heat sintering" techniques of printing. It can be used on a wide range of materials like ceramics, metals, polymers, etc. The sixth technology has sheets of materials bonded together to produce a product (Yap et al., 2017). It can print colorful items and is simple, cheap; recycling is possible. The last technology uses laser or ultra violet light (Low et al., 2017). Time of exposure, wavelength, and amount of power supply play a very crucial role in this technology. It is used to make high-quality detailed products.

3D printing has been used in the aerospace industry as it provides unlimited design in components and products. It helps in producing light weighted components, spare parts, engines, and improved geometries. It can help in reducing the energy and fuel requirements and resources (Maghnani, 2015). In the automobile sector, it can help in producing fast, lighter, and complex structures. One example is OLLI which is "the driverless electric recyclable and extremely smart 3D-printed bus". It has been frequently used by car manufacturers like Ford, AUDI, and BMW and has reduced the cost and time of these brands (Maghnani, 2015). It has also helped the ceramic industry as it is very suitable for future construction and buildings (Baldassarre & Ricciardi, 2017). It can produce and process the desired shape of food materials (Brunner et al., 2018). It can produce healthy food as it allows the customers to adjust the ingredients without reducing taste or nutritional levels (Caulier et al., 2020; Brunner et al., 2018). It can print shoes, jewelry (Yap & Yeong, 2014) consumer goods, and clothing (Chittaro & Corvaglia, 2003). It has led to short processing time, reduced costs related to inventory and packaging (Tu, 2011).

3 Modeling Framework

The paper uses a Computable General Equilibrium model to estimate the cost and benefits of 3D printing on the Indian economy. The impact of disruptive technologies at the country level is predicted through a standard GTAP model. GTAP is a publicly funded project based at the Center for Global Trade Analysis, Purdue University, USA. This multi-region, multi-sector CGE model (Hertel, 1997) is widely used for the global-scale assessment of economic policies. It combines economic theory and empirical data and accounts for all trade flow interactions among industries, consumers, and countries globally while simultaneously ensuring theoretical and accounting consistency. It assumes perfect competition, constant returns to scale and profit, and utility-maximizing behavior in both firms and households.

The data used in this study is from version 10 of the GTAP database [the most recent version available, documented in Aguiar et al., (2016) and Aguiar et al., (2019)]. The reference year for this database is 2014.

Based on version 10 of the standard GTAP model which is a multi-regional, CGE model of world trade and investment, markets are perfectly competitive, industry technologies are linearly homogeneous, and traded goods are imperfectly substitutable. This captures the interaction of interdependent components: industries, households, investors, governments, importers, and exporters, and the flow-on effects and interactions of each country and/or region with detailed inter-industry links.

The GTAP database is exhaustive, covering 141 countries and 65 sectors. The 141 countries in the database are aggregated into 2 regions—India and the rest of the world—as the focus of the study is on analyzing the impact of 3D printing technology and additive manufacturing on the macro-economic factors.

The model is shocked by the findings from the empirical analysis that revealed productivity enhancements and cost savings in applications in aerospace industries, the automotive sector, and manufacturing industries. The anticipated cost savings—40% cost reduction in the aerospace industries and the 50% cost reduction in the automotive sector curated at the end of the empirical analysis—were fed to the model attributes.

The cost benefit estimated in the previous section for the aerospace and defense sector, industrial goods, and the automotive sector is fed as a shock to the model, and the change in macro-economic indicators including GDP, output, trade, and employment is observed. The analysis is performed considering an increase in the adoption of such technologies by 10%.

4 Results and Analysis

The model is shocked with a 40% cost reduction in the aerospace industries and 50% cost reduction in the automotive sector, and the results are analyzed for a 10% increase in the adoption of 3D printing technologies and additive manufacturing techniques. As it can be inferred from Table 1, the model estimates that the overall GDP would increase by 1.26%, apart from a 2.36% increase in the overall output of the country. This could be attributed to the increase in manufacturing output that results from reduced industrial lead times, cost-saving benefits, productivity, and

Table 1 Percentage change in macro-economic indicators

Indicators	% Change
GDP	1.26
Output	2.36
Exports	4.71
Imports	7.57
Employment	2.38
Investment	3.43

Source Authors' estimations from GTAP model simulations

efficiency enhancements that result from the deployment of such technologies. There might be a 2.38% increase in employment as automation would enable efficient, productive utilization of the labor force that is otherwise been to carry out mundane tasks. Upskilling of unskilled labor and reskilling of skilled labor might enable and equip them to be engaged more productively resulting in an increase of employment opportunities across the country. This could gain significance in a gig economy where organizations are strategizing ways to engage the labor force productively, given the rapid pace of digitalization and the emergence of futuristic technologies ensuing the Fourth Industrial Revolution. The emergence of new technologies like 3D printing would lead to the introduction and institution of new job roles, as such technological operations would demand altogether different skills and competencies.

Because executing complex tasks by harnessing these disruptive technologies reduces the time frame of critical, complex operations, the employee shall take up other contract works, and the employer might also hire full-time employees to whom he has to shell out fixed salaries every month. It would be a mutual win for the employer and the employee.

Deployment of new techniques and disruptive technologies would attract investments, and the model predicts that there will be 3.43% increase in investments. It also predicts that there might be an increase in exports and imports by 4.71% and 7.57%, respectively. The export of industrial goods and the manufacturing sector would endure an increase while there would also be an increase in import of raw materials, technological attributes, machinery, and other resources that may be required for the successful deployment of disruptive technologies (Table 2).

An analysis of the output by sector reveals that automotive industries, aerospace applications, manufacturing sectors, metal products manufacturing, public administration, and defense, construction, education, training, transportation sector, would experience an increase while agricultural and food processing sectors would endure a decline. The former could be attributed to the increase in benefits, productivity, and efficiency apart from a decline in manufacturing cost, while the latter could be due to the migration of endowment commodities like labor from agricultural sectors to the manufacturing industries.

5 Conclusion and Future Implications

3D technology helps in producing three-dimensional objects. In the beginning, it focused on prototyping, but with the enhanced capabilities, the problems of cost, accuracy, and strength have been overcome to a great extent. It provides a large variety of multi colored products with varying designs and material choices. As 3D printing helps in reducing timeframe, there will be additional opportunities for the employees as the process will become more simple and more automated. It may give rise to more contract workers offering their services to multiple organizations. It would be a mutual win for the employer and the employee. Deployment of this new technology would attract investments, and the model estimates that there might be an

Table 2 Change in output sector-wise

Sector	% Change	Base value (in millions USD)	Change values (in millions USD)	Final value (in millions USD)
Paddy	−0.57	44,637	−253,447	−208,810
Wheat	−1.14	18,847	−214,491	−195,645
Cereal	−0.96	4911	−47,046	−42,135
Vegetables	−0.95	46,185	−438,096	−391,910
Oil	−3.98	8170	−325,037	−316,866
Sugar	−1.08	13,938	−150,437	−136,500
Plant-based	−4.95	9544	−472,131	−462,588
Crops	−0.98	49,058	−480,218	−431,160
Bovine	−1.91	9830	−187,833	−178,003
Animal	−0.28	9677	−27,005	−17,327
Raw	0.95	63,491	603,994	667,486
Wool	−4.05	5859	−237,077	−231,218
Forestry	−0.61	39,519	−239,368	−199,850
Fishing	0.17	19,976	33,367	53,343
Coal	−2.59	35,593	−921,418	−885,825
Oil	−5.22	21,728	−1,134,259	−1,112,531
Gas	−8.94	4265	−381,238	−376,973
Minerals	2.04	11,768	−239,833	−228,065
Bovine	−5.56	8503	−472,648	−464,145
Meat	−0.08	1688	−1267	421
Vegetable	−4.90	35,745	−1,752,406	−1,716,661
Dairy	0.73	32,843	239,741	272,584
Processed	−0.74	58,588	−435,352	−376,764
Sugar	−1.36	18,892	−257,803	−238,912
Food	−0.67	69,560	−467,268	−397,708
Beverages	0.37	25,374	94,260	119,635
Textiles	−3.26	109,386	−3,565,560	−3,456,174
Wearing	−4.94	38,734	−1,912,164	−1,873,430
Leather	−6.11	19,185	−1,171,500	−1,152,315
Wood	−1.03	12,278	−126,999	−114,721
Paper	−3.93	25,013	−983,339	−958,326
Petroleum	−0.57	245,485	−1,404,395	−1,158,910
Chemical	−4.77	101,030	−4,816,905	−4,715,874
Basic	−5.54	28,622	−1,584,669	−1,556,047
Rubber	−1.74	50,527	−879,086	−828,559

(continued)

Table 2 (continued)

Sector	% Change	Base value (in millions USD)	Change values (in millions USD)	Final value (in millions USD)
Mineral	1.32	55,560	735,024	790,584
Ferrous	0.08	101,618	85,511	187,129
Metals	−7.27	32,354	−2,351,685	−2,319,331
Metal	1.19	86,020	1,020,804	1,106,824
Computer	−5.53	47,082	−2,601,971	−2,554,888
Electrical	−3.08	47,136	−1,452,368	−1,405,232
Machinery	−2.84	92,771	−2,633,387	−2,540,616
Motor	25.85	73,310	18,950,471	19,023,781
Transport	246.00	41,703	102,587,855	102,629,558
Manufactures	−3.98	92,003	−3,661,282	−3,569,279
Electricity	−0.14	217,340	−308,992	−91,652
Gas	−0.69	8112	−55,868	−47,756
Water	0.64	34,466	221,437	255,903
Construction	3.02	457,200	13,787,321	14,244,521
Trade	1.06	362,475	3,829,622	4,192,097
Accommodation	1.21	93,607	1,128,480	1,222,087
Transport	0.68	231,192	1,569,425	1,800,618
Water	−3.67	17,641	−647,639	−629,997
Air	−3.43	6694	−229,441	−222,746
Warehousing	0.01	56,086	6882	62,967
Communication	−2.76	65,295	−1,802,847	−1,737,553
Financial	0.98	108,503	1,062,014	1,170,517
Insurance	−0.84	27,369	−230,142	−202,773
Real	−0.27	38,422	−103,454	−65,033
Business	−6.15	122,647	−7,543,850	−7,421,203
Recreational	−1.66	10,107	−167,766	−157,659
Public	0.26	75,875	200,606	276,480
Education	0.28	63,567	176,157	239,724
Human	0.58	108,913	635,757	744,670
Dwellings	1.29	110,064	1,417,971	1,528,034

Source Authors' estimations from GTAP model simulations

increase in investments in years to come. The study also estimates that there might be an increase in exports and imports of nations. The export of industrial goods and the manufacturing sector would endure an increase while there will be an increase in import of raw materials, technological attributes, machinery, and other resources that may be required for the successful deployment of disruptive technologies.

The results of the study indicate that scholars and policymakers should continuously monitor and forecast the 3D manufacturing domain. It is a new technology, and thus, there is a need for experimental learning for the managers adopting the technology. They should cautiously invest in these technologies after validation. Scholars can further use our results for the future study of 3D printing and the emerging macro-economic relationships including employment and growth. While there is a continuous improvement in technology, 3D printing is in its infancy. There is a need for a regulatory framework to lay down the conditions of using this disruptive technology for the betterment of society (Pirjan & Petrosanu, 2013) and the environment (Piccioni et al., 2021).

The scenarios of the study are grounded on quantitative data which can be further supported by qualitative data. There can be studies to differentiate the various types of 3D technologies and their impact on the labor force. The GTAP framework can be combined with the econometric analysis of the usage of the technology across industries.

References

Aguiar, A., Chepeliev, M., Corong, E., McDougall, R., & van der Mensbrugghe, D. (2019). The GTAP data base: version 10. *Journal of Global Economic Analysis, 4*(1), 1–27.

Aguiar, A., Narayanan, B., & McDougall, R. (2016). An overview of the GTAP 9 data base. *Journal of Global Economic Analysis, 1*(1), 181–208.

Baldassarre, F., & Ricciardi, F. (2017). The additive manufacturing in the Industry 4.0 Era: the case of an Italian FabLab. *Journal of Emerging Trends in Marketing and Management, 1*(1), 105–115.

Brunner, T. A., Delley, M., & Denkel, C. (2018). Consumers' attitudes and change of attitude toward 3D-printed food. *Food Quality and Preference, 68*, 389–396.

Casey, L. (2009). Prototypes pronto. *Packaging Digest, 46*(8), 54–56.

Caulier, S., Doets, E., & Noort, M. (2020). An exploratory consumer study of 3D printed food perception in a real-life military setting. *Food Quality and Preference*, 104001.

Chittaro, L., & Corvaglia, D. (2003, March). 3d virtual clothing: from garment design to web3d visualization and simulation. In *Proceedings of the eighth international conference on 3D web technology* (pp. 73–ff).

Hertel, T. W. (1997). Global trade analysis: Modeling and applications. Cambridge University Press, Cambridge, United Kingdom.

Kunovjanek, M., & Reiner, G. (2020). How will the diffusion of additive manufacturing impact the raw material supply chain process? *International Journal of Production Research, 58*(5), 1540–1554.

Low, Z. X., Chua, Y. T., Ray, B. M., Mattia, D., Metcalfe, I. S., & Patterson, D. A. (2017). Perspective on 3D printing of separation membranes and comparison to related unconventional fabrication techniques. *Journal of Membrane Science, 523*, 596–613.

Maghnani, R. (2015). An exploratory study: The impact of additive manufacturing on the automobile industry. *International Journal of Current Engineering and Technology, 5*(5), 1–4.

Piccioni, F., Casenave, C., Lemaire, B. J., Le Moigne, P., Dubois, P., & Vinçon-Leite, B. (2021). The thermal response of small and shallow lakes to climate change: New insights from 3D hindcast modelling. *Earth System Dynamics, 12*(2), 439–456.

Pirjan, A., & Petrosanu, D. M. (2013). The impact of 3D printing technology on the society and economy. *Journal of Information Systems and Operations Management, 7*(2), 360–370.

Rajan, V., Sniderman, B., & Baum, P. (2016). 3D opportunity for life: Additive manufacturing takes humanitarian action. *Delight Insight, 1*(19), 1–8.

Standard, A. S. T. M. (2012). Standard terminology for additive manufacturing technologies. *ASTM International F2792-12a.*

Tofail, S. A., Koumoulos, E. P., Bandyopadhyay, A., Bose, S., O'Donoghue, L., & Charitidis, C. (2018). Additive manufacturing: Scientific and technological challenges, market uptake and opportunities. *Materials Today, 21*(1), 22–37.

Tu, K. N. (2011). Reliability challenges in 3D IC packaging technology. *Microelectronics Reliability, 51*(3), 517–523.

Yap, Y. L., Wang, C., Sing, S. L., Dikshit, V., Yeong, W. Y., & Wei, J. (2017). Material jetting additive manufacturing: An experimental study using designed metrological benchmarks. *Precision Engineering, 50*, 275–285.

Yap, Y. L., & Yeong, W. Y. (2014). Additive manufacture of fashion and jewellery products: A mini review: This paper provides an insight into the future of 3D printing industries for fashion and jewellery products. *Virtual and Physical Prototyping, 9*(3), 195–201.

Integrating Blockchain Technology to Populate Gig Workers into Human Capital Management of Indian Organizations

R. Kiruba Nagini, R. Venkatesakumar, and S. Riasudeen

1 Introduction

Blockchain of Industrial Revolution 4.0, is an emerging technology which is widely used in the banking and financial sector currently. But researches hold that the technology is fine enough to be implemented in most of the sectors in the near future, in places wherever security is a major concern. Gig economy is one another trends in India in the recent past, with its second rank globally, standing next only to the USA. The growing stress in all sectors of employment and the prevailing unemployment problem has pushed the blue-collar job workers to take up gig works, which is now seemingly the surprising trend with the professionals too. With the outset of an online platform where every specific group of professionals get an opportunity to pitch in, the trend of being a temporary worker is becoming the new permanent choice of work. Organizations need to maintain a skills inventory of such gig workers for such talent sourcing. This research article suggests a conceptual model to build a technological framework to populate gig workers into the human capital of organizations using blockchain technology.

1.1 Gig Economy

Gig economy, which was once considered only for blue collar jobs, has made a paradigm shift toward the white collar jobs. Stringent work environment, legal bindings, workhours, targets in jobs, insecurity in jobs in spite of high performance, and similar negative impacts have converted the idea of being temporary as the new permanence. The term "freelancer" has stuck to many fields of work, not only from

R. K. Nagini · R. Venkatesakumar · S. Riasudeen (✉)
Department of Management Studies, Pondicherry University, Pondicherry, India

A. Gupta et al. (eds.), *Sustainability in the Gig Economy*,
https://doi.org/10.1007/978-981-16-8406-7_20

craftsmen, but also to consultants. People who want to be their own bosses choose to be giggers.

1.2 Blockchain Technology

Popularly called the FinTech, blockchain is one of the finest implementations of the distributed database management systems, empowered with hi-end hashed data structures, which ensure data security and seamless access to data by the users. Applications pertaining to banks and other financial transactions were built, combining the other technologies like cloud computing, pervasive computing, and the secure network tokens. Block is the new name given for records, and the name blockchain is justified since the records are created as interrelated chunks, connected by tokens for verification which happens at different storage points, at different intervals. Since the data is verified at a different point, any discrepancy in the data being transferred throws error. The digital signatures attached to the input data and the sender's name alone are passed through the network, which are finally checked and validated. Upon validation, the required core transaction happens.

1.3 Human Capital Management

Human capital management views human resources as assets on whom investments must be made to reap benefits in terms of productivity, revenue, market share, and market value. The term was coined by Schultz (1961) who built the concept in 1981 as follows: "Consider all human abilities to be either innate or acquired. Attributes… which are valuable and can be augmented by appropriate investment will be human capital." Also, Davenport (1999) comments that: "People possess innate abilities, behaviours and personal energy and these elements make up the human capital they bring to their work. And it is they, not their employers, who own this capital and decide when, how and where they will contribute it. In other words, they can make choices. Work is a two-way exchange of value, not a one-way exploitation of an asset by its owner." Human capital contributes to their owner's capital to build shareholder value. It provides guidance to devise HR strategies and design practices to enhance the effectiveness of the human resources involved.

1.4 Objective of the Study

- To develop a technological framework for the sustenance of gig workers in India,
- To design and implement the same using blockchain technology.

2 Review of Literature

With these objectives set to study for the research, the previous works on all the three dimensions were explored. There are studies on the use of the technologies bundled under Industrial Revolution 4.0, such as AI in HR practices, and chatbots, with the robotic automation technologies, automated HR general practices, AI enabled HRIS, and the like. Blockchain technology is primarily recommended for the recruiting practices, (Michailidis, 2018). With growing loss of employment, due to automation, digitalization, and other technical debuts on HR practices, a good number of skilled employees are turning out to be gig workers. The emerging phenomenon of gig economy is found to be a challenging one, with no definite structure for implementation and maintenance (Fleming, 2017; Kässi & Lehdonvirta, 2018; Moisander et al., 2018). It is thought about the gig workers as the self-employed, rather than employees of any organizations, albeit they are hired by organizations for technical and skill related works (De Stefano, 2015; Tassinari & Maccarrone, 2017; Woodcock, 2016). There are digital platforms available globally, which intermediate the gig workers and earn a profit as commission from each of the beneficiary (Paolacci et al., 2010; Silberman, 2015; Silberman & Irani, 2016).

Labor power may be treated as a commodity in the online platforms, which mediate the demand and supply of the gig workers (Gandini, 2019). Such labor which is used for creative works has to be upheld with career sustainability (Alacovska, 2018). By 2017, there was 1.1 million gig workers at Britain (Balaram et al., 2017), which has increased by 4 times, to 4.7 million workers, as the study by The Guardian Times stated on June, 27, 2019. Individuals treat themselves as individual mini-enterprises (Gandini, 2019). The essentiality of organizing the gig workers through online platforms, with proper strategies, is the need of the hour (Graham et al., 2017). There are problems like rejection of works done by gig workers (Silberman & Irani, 2016). To solve such issues, a properly updated platform (Milland, 2017). Sarina and Riley (2018) suggest that a cooperative formed for the gig workers can save their interests. Day by day, the classification in the gig workers is moving from skilled workers to intelligence workers, with many professionals flocking into such online platforms (Lobel, 2017). There are legal issues that make the gig economy troublesome to get into practice at organizations (Aloisi, 2015; Sanders & Pattison, 2016). Studies on classification of gig workers find it difficult to effect or enforce the legislations regarding the rights and privileges of gig workers (Dubal, 2017). Such systems that try to regularize the gig economy must be rule-based, rather than the trending models of business (Cherry & Aloisi, 2016; Lowe, 2017; Sen & Saxena, 2019; Stewart & Stanford, 2017).

Most of the Uber drivers are the examples of gig economy in India, who offer the "demographic dividend" of gig economy in India (Prabhat et al., 2019). Various methods of characterizing the gig workers on the Uber platform are a novel step in maintaining the gig workers who use the platform (Rosenblat & Stark, 2016; Sanders & Pattison, 2016). The legal aspects of the gig workers that make them stand outside the boundary of an employee are rendering them helpless in issues rising due to payments and contracts (Page-Harris, 2018; Oranburg, 2018; Tickell & Ritchie, 2020). Ways to handle the decline of wages and welfare issues are common in volatile workplaces (Berg, 2015; Nica, 2018). The loss of benefits as a corporate employee in comparison with the independent contractor is viewed as a negative aspect of the gig economy (Khan, 2020). The surge in the number of gig workers and their contribution to the organizations has risen the interests of the governmental bodies that have stepped in to categorize and regularize the gig workforce (Donovan et al., 2016; Johnston & Land-Kazlauskas, 2018). The role of online platforms and the migration decisions of workers on the performance of the gig workers reveals whether the job has to be handled by a gig worker or not (Dunn, 2018).

Blockchain technology can be adapted for implementing a platform for job seekers, where they can share their CVs in a secured manner (Salah et al., 2020). Blockchain technology will help create a non-biased, secure, efficient, and transparent environment through its distributed ledgers and can create a new milestone in the recruitment processes (Morkunas et al., 2019; Onik et al., 2018; Sharmila et al., 2019). Blockchain can be seen as a boon to develop and redefine the basic and extended activities of any organization, in a highly secure way, eliminating costs, and avoiding indulgence of outside resources as internal sources (Tapscott & Tapscott, 2017). Blockchain technology can rule out many legal issues rising in the recruitment, compensation, and genuine selection processes, and with digitalization in place at many countries across continents, it is easy to implement the system using blockchains (Koncheva et al., 2019). Empirical studies prove how technology and knowledge-based HRM practices can impact the intellectual capital of an organization leading to higher levels of innovation and performance (Kianto et al., 2017; Nieves & Quintana, 2018; Novikov et al., 2019). The classification of gig workers is categorized into people depending on freelancing jobs for primary income, and supplemental income and their characters are studied (Manyika et al., 2016). Intellectual capital, in which human capital is one of the components, can be measured to find how performance of an organization is enhanced through tapping out the best solutions from the available human talents (Palacios-Marqués & Garrigós-Simón, 2003). Conceptual frameworks are being developed for measuring the increased employee engagement and organizational performance, due to human capital management practices (Patil & Swapna, 2017; Zeb et al., 2018, 7). Humans as a service is considered as the future of work in the online platforms that increase competitiveness and efficiency in workers (Prassl, 2018), with special mention to the platforms like Uber, TaskRabbit, and so on (Prassl & Risak, 2015).

Blockchain technology is the one that handles the "blocks" or the public ledgers that carry information of the customers, with an approved consensus mechanism to access the information, thereby providing an incontrovertible record (Puthal, et al., 2018).

Automation and digitization is the primary step to implement blockchain (Hegadekatti, 2016). Blockchain technology can take up different disguises to be implemented at both public and private sectors (Hegadekatti, 2016, 2017). Also, the problems in creating a cryptocurrency for the organizations for HR practices are viewed (Hegadekatti, 2016; Hegadekatti & SG, 2016). Blockchain technology is viewed as one technology that can kill the traditional form of organizations by its strong and secure transaction power (Coita et al., 2019).

The strategic human resources management practice including the sustainability of the organization centered by the human capital to achieve competitive edge over other organizations is highly a possible practice (Hamadamin & Atan, 2019; Hayton, 2003). Human capital is viewed as the collective capability of an organization in extracting the best out of the knowledge of its individuals (Bontis, 1998). The method to assess knowledge as an asset for the human capital was discussed (Bontis, 2001a), and the mode of managing it as the organization knowledge is also found (Bontis, 2001b). The measuring and maintaining of human capital by calculating its ROI was also found to be better way to improve the intellectual capital (Bontis & Fitz-enz, 2002; Baron & Armstrong, 2007). The typology to review different category of work arrangements and the mode of capturing them in the existing data setup was formed (Abraham et al., 2017; Hamzah et al., 2017). Aremu (2020) studies on how human capital practices could improve job performance of employees. The human capital management is a reciprocal relationship where the performance is brought out by the employees and the organization has to recognize it through benefits to employees (Boroujerdi et al., 2014; Chatzkel, 2004; Thomas, 2002). Probing into the human capital is one best way to realize the company's true value (Edvinsson, & Malone, 2007). Also, including the gig workers will bring out challenges in existing social policies (Friedman, 2014). Gibbins (2018) explores how the gig workers could be protected by extending the protection policies available for the regular employees.

Since the paper tries to study the gig economy in India, the following section deals with the current scenario of the same.

3 Gig Economy in India: A Snapshot

India stands second in the population of gig workers, with an amazing number of 15 million, compared to its predecessor USA, where the gig population is around 53 million. The population of gig workers is increasing at a rate of 17% globally, with an expected number of around $455 million in the year 2023. The Government of California and of the European Parliament have also passed bills favoring the law setting minimum rights and transparency to the gig workers. In India, the Code on Social Security Bill 2020, passed by the Ministry of Labor and Employment, recognized the gig workers and their genuine contribution, thereby providing legislator protection to their services. Puri (2017) has explored the rise of gig economy in India in the sectors like IT, transportation services like Ola and Uber, data scientists, digital marketers, and social media enthusiasts. The report says that there has been a steady decrease in the number of freelance workers. The challenges pointed out were job insecurity, fulfillment of financial requirements, family circumstances, structural barriers, structured gap, and gender preferences. A detailed study on the Uber cult in the society has been made and the study reveals the challenges lying ahead to regularize, legalize, and provide support to the gig workers (Prabhat et al., 2019).

Though the gigworking platforms are open to all, the Female Labor Force Participation (FLFP) has not increased in India. The international platforms like UpWork are finding an upsurge from Indian freelancers, from which they gain employment opportunities, income, upskilling, international exposure, and career progression (D'Cruz & Noronha, 2016).

The recent Social Security Code 2020 extends the benefits any organizational employee would receive in case of life and disability cover, accident insurance, health and maternity benefits, crèche, and old age protection. But at the dark side gives a shocking revelation that the costs of these benefits would be a part of the pie that the freelancers earn by gig works. With TDS already parting away a 10% of earnings, this would add to the reduction of the take-home of the freelancers. The issues regarding the availability, time of work, quality of service, and so on must be considered before this Social Security Code 2020 can take off. To counter these challenges, this paper proposes a model by which the government can launch a site, where the gig workers can register themselves, and a unique id can be provided to them, which they can use to register for any job at any gig work portal. The aggregators may lose their role as an aggregator, and have to remodel their roles, if such a governmental platform is designed and implemented. As another option, the sites of the aggregators may be recognized by the government and then their links could be included in the website. This will ensure the presence of both the aggregator, gig worker, and the organization that sought gig workers as well.

With a population of around 1332 millions, the work group age falling between 16 and 65 years is around 890 millions, which forms around 51.8% of the total population. The gross value of the market for gig workers is estimated to be $34 billion (approx.). The article by The Economic Times (Jan 6, 2020) explores the population of around 3 million registered gig workers in India. In terms of Economics, the low price of the gig economy has created a consumer surplus, with a multiplier effect on income and employment generation. Using ICT, the online platforms where the gig workers register form the base of data on the gig workers. But this data lacks stability, since gig workers may abruptly move out of the gig workers' population.

3.1 Need for the Study

After analyzing the research works on gig economy, HCM, and blockchain technology, the following research questions were identified, which necessitated the modeling of this concept:

1. Can gig economy be a valid option to fit into the human capital management practices?
2. Apart from artificial intelligence implementations, could blockchain technology be a viable option to be integrated into HR practices?

3. Is the technological strength of Indian infrastructure strong enough to host a model which integrates blockchain technology with gig economy and human capital management?

To analyze these questions, the following model was created, which is named gig society, incorporating the features of blockchain into human capital management reinforced by gig economy.

4 The Conceptual Model

With that portrayal of the Indian scenario of the gig workers, this section discusses how the blockchain technology can be adopted to populate gig workers into the human capital management systems of organizations. The conceptual model is called the gig society, which is explained in the following paragraphs.

4.1 Building the "Blocks"

The primary dimension to be considered in a gig economy is their skillset or area of expertise. All the other essential information of the giggers are to be designed and maintained as a database, stored on a distributed database or a cloud.

4.2 Building the Platform of Gig Society

Now, let us see how a gig worker be populated into the human capital of the organization. Using a common platform, the gig workers should be given a unique identification number, which they can use across any headhunting platforms, which seek freelancers. The common platform shall be named the gig society, an online community, where all gig workers and professionals can register themselves, giving their basic details and professional details. A dashboard can be allotted to each of them, where they can update their current status of availability for being hired. This status will help the HR people to choose from the best possible talents available. The gig workers can upload proof of their work on their dashboard, which will help the HRs to decide on whether to select the gig worker or not. The gig worker can update their pricing also for their works, which will also help the HRs to decide on the cost occurred for the job/project/task, whatever the case may be. The background checks for the certifications done by the gig workers are to be approved by the concerned organizations, which will help the HRs to decide on the quality of the professional qualification received by the gig worker.

The aggregators or the online platforms that provide the freelance opportunities to the gig workers can be included into the network, who can work closely with the certifying authorities for the updates or upgrades in the certification processes. In this way, the organizations can keep track of the gig workers in their loop. Also, the security issues that the Social Security Code 2020 encounters can be solved, by this integration of entities involved in the gig economy. The article published on the Social Security Code 2020 by the Bloomberg Quint, on October 6, 2020, described the major concerns of including the gig workers into the mainstream workers. But the authenticity is questionable, since there may emerge a few solutions to solve the ideology issues of gig economy.

Coming to the security issues of the documents uploaded by the gig workers, the security component of the blockchain technology comes into play. The hash identifiers of the encoded block and the previous block together are taken into consideration for generating the block codes. Similarly, the blocks of the gig workers can be secured through the secure cryptography followed in blockchain for the hashed blocks. Until the input into the blocks remain same, the output hashed block remains the same. In case any data is changed in the middle of the chain, the output hashed block will change. This will reveal any purposeful or malicious hampering done to the data in the block. Therefore, the further processing of the block can be stopped and the hampered location can be backtracked, canceling the current transaction and requesting for acknowledgment from the first location where the transaction originated. If the hashed block is received at the destination with the timestamps of all the respective nodes for authentication, then the actual transaction can be initiated. In this case of the blocks of the gig workers, the educational certifications may be valid only for a finite time, beyond which they require renewal of the same. In such cases, the source and destinations fixation can happen from the user dashboard, to the concerned qualifying authorities to whom they can apply and get their renewal process done online, with a new renewal number or a new certificate, which will be available on the public domain. In such cases, the hashed blocks created will have a different/new information encrypted. Using this facility, the HRs can ensure that the gig workers are providing updated information about them.

Let us now associate the gig society with the available online platforms for sourcing talents like Naukri, Shine, where the eligible candidates register themselves and apply for jobs. Gig society can include the members of the other job seeking sites, based on the keywords they provide to describe their skillsets and qualification. Such association will broaden the boundary of the gig workers and increase their visibility.

So, when all these are set, the HRs can create a ranking or reviewing technique to choose the gig worker for them. Though the reviews given by the other people, ranking provided by the earlier hirers, may be present for the gig workers, the HRs should identify specific measures to evaluate the gig workers and hire them for their projects on a priority basis. Such a priority should be set by the gig workers in their dashboard, for the types of freelancing jobs they would like to take up. HRs can match their priorities with that of the gig workers and choose to hire them. Similar to succession planning, a strategy can be devised to populate the contactable gig workers

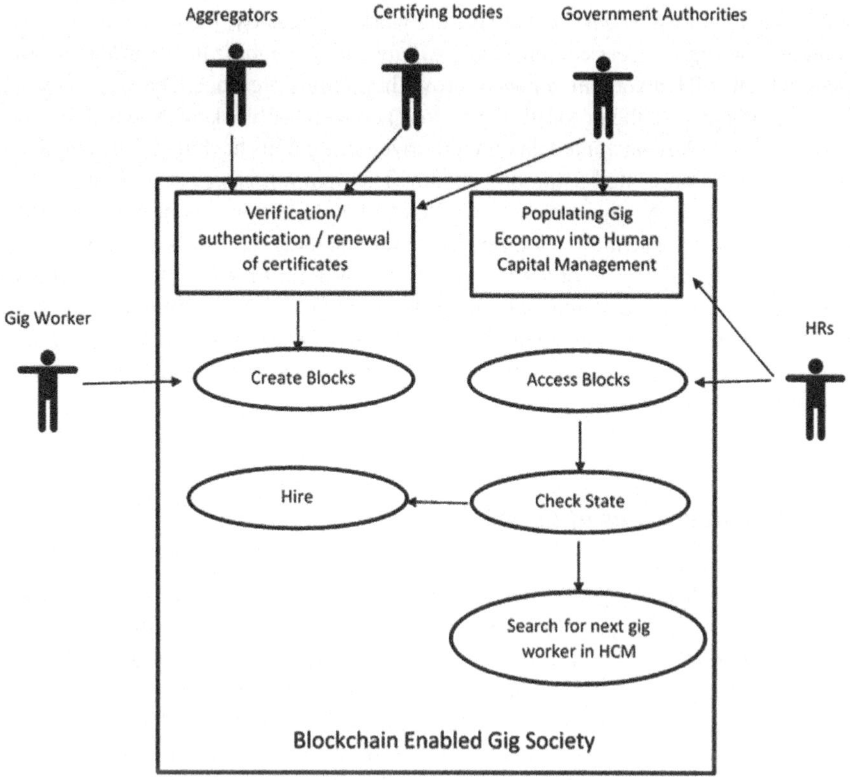

Fig. 1 Use case diagram of the gig society. *Source* Author

by the organizations. The common platform gig society can be relied upon to choose the reliable talents for their projects. With that focus on the interconnection among the three dimensions of study, let us take a look at the advantages of this system (Fig. 1).

4.3 Advantages in Using Blockchain Technology in the Model

The previous section described the proposed system in detail. The main advantage lies in *secure document update and safe display of blocks.* An automated renewal check of the certifications, the availability of workers, their prices, agreement terms and engagements, opening and closing of contracts, earnings from each project, the tax liability, and other legal provisions if any could be added as features to these blocks. The HRs could provide *star ratings* for the gig workers, which would improve the quality of job or service rendered by them. Such authentic referencing will open up more avenues and help the gig workers to choose the best that suits their routine. The gig workers can provide *feedback on the organizations* and their practices, which will help organizations improve their online presence. These services can be found equated to the proof of work (PoW) concept of blockchain, which enables the consensus. Any unwanted and unauthorized, malicious hacking of the employee records can be prevented using blockchain. The *taxation issues* at both the ends—the company and the gig worker as well—can be made transparent with respect to the income tax department. In case any reimbursements are to be authorized, the validity verification could be done through this system. Fraud prevention, cybersecurity, cross-border payments, and mobility could be ensured by implementing the blockchain technology. The contracts made by the gig workers and the organization are no more a secret. Since all transactions gain transparency, the auditing and legal compliance is not an issue any more.

4.4 Disadvantages of the Model

The foremost disadvantage is the unavailability of data regarding the gig workers in India, which demands visibility of their availability. Registration in this platform may be reflected in all connected websites of the aggregators, leading to multiple entries. Due to network failure, the blockchains may be lost in the network, with the blocks simply wandering in the network. Since they contain confidential data, they are prone to insecure access. Legal restrictions may prove fruitful in the initial stages, but in spite of all these regulations, there may be non-compliance, insecurity of jobs, and similar issues. There may be an identity crisis occurring due to the multiple talents and skillsets that the gig workers develop in course of time. The certifying authorities may fall prey to illegal certifications and approvals.

5 Managerial Implications

The blockchain enabled human capital system, gig society can become a revenue generating model for the government. The users could be charged a nominal subscription to avail the services mentioned in the system. Similarly, the aggregating bodies, the authenticating authorities, the certifying bodies, all could be made to become a registered users for a nominal amount as a subscription. The subscription should be a renewable one, which ensures the continual inflow of revenue. The infrastructure cost could be broken even in a short span of time, given the large number of organizations, the aggregators, and the certifying bodies.

Apart from a revenue generating model, this system can provide authenticated information about the giggers, and all the stakeholders operating around them. Such foolproof system can bring in job opportunities to giggers from international market, which will again rise their status. Since India has such a large expertise, the GDP can see a marginal increase if not a substantial one. The diversion of the wasted human power in any country could be streamlined into a positive revenue generating possibility, thereby increasing the personal disposable income and the GDP as well.

From the viewpoint of the corporates who look for authenticated sources, this system would be a centralized, yet distributed database of the available workforce in any stream. From this database, the organizations could source competitive workforce, at a reasonable cost. Though it is seen as cost cutting measure, the legal security provided through the country's laws will ensure a secure work environment for the giggers.

6 Future Scope of the Work

Since blockchain technology is included in this system, this could be extended to any level of network. The scope of extension includes the stored volume of records of each registered user, the services of each stakeholder (apart from the gigger) would provide to the gigger, the volume of transactions that would be carried out at any single point of time, at various locations. A probable analytical module included may be provide insight into the optimal usage of the platform, and other data on how efficient the system is in weeding out the unemployment problem of the country. With the inclusion of cloud storage, the cost of investment for the model could also reduce. Dividing the modules and implementing them at different locations as a measure of increasing the time and cost efficiency of the system would provide a better means to limited access to the giggers, but the database may be available at the background, which increases only the storage base, and the transactions. This reduction in the number of transactions would increase the speed in which the system would work. The updates on the database and the other services could be included from time to time, making the system highly competitive.

7 Conclusion

The research has modeled an implementable platform for the gig workers and organizations, using blockchain technology. The governmental implications on this model could be sorted out before implementation. The model will help government to plan for skill development programs; the HRs of organizations in talent sourcing; and the authorized entities to ensure authenticity of certification. This system will enhance the social infrastructure development in any country. The unutilized manpower could be finding a proper channelized utilization, resulting in revenue generation through different registrations and subscriptions. This will eventually result in increase of GDP, personal disposable income, and the market would boom. The various economic factors like purchasing power of the people will increase, thereby decreasing the purchasing power parity. The foreign currency exchange would gain momentum. The standard of living would increase, resulting in better life style, better infrastructure, better economic status, and the like.

With the extremely poor economic situations prevailing in the country, the dormant and unutilized manpower should be put to use in a proper channel, that it supports the upliftment of the society. This system would help in upskilling the prospective workforce, given that it is in place with the interests of the nation to increase its economic indices, by identifying the required skillsets of the industry, framing policies to include the youth into the social infrastructure development. The women workforce could also safely find lots of opportunities to increase their family income, thereby capable of increasing their economic independency. The rippling effect of this economic independency could be found in leading a higher standard of living. Ultimately, every nation tries to increase the standard of living of the people, giving them a prosperous life, excellent education.

References

Abraham, K., Haltiwanger, J., Sandusky, K., & Spletzer, J. (2017). Measuring the gig economy: Current knowledge and open issues. *Measuring and Accounting for Innovation in the 21st Century*.

Alacovska, A. (2018). Informal creative labour practices: A relational work perspective. *Human Relations, 71*(12), 1563–1589.

Aloisi, A. (2015). Commoditized workers: Case study research on labor law issues arising from a set of on-demand/gig economy platforms. *Comparative Labor Law and Policy Journal, 37*, 653.

Aremu, M. O. (2020) Human capital management practices and employees' job performance in Oyo State, Nigeria. *Editorial board*, 337.

Balaram, B., Warden, J., & Wallace-Stephens, F. (2017). *Good gigs: A fairer future for the UK's gig economy*. RSA.

Baron, A., & Armstrong, M. (2007). *Human capital management: achieving added value through people*. Kogan Page Publishers.

Berg, J. (2015). Income security in the on-demand economy: Findings and policy lessons from a survey of crowdworkers. *Comparative Labor Law and Policy Journal, 37*, 543.

Bontis, N. (1998). Intellectual capital: an exploratory study that develops measures and models. *Management Decision*.

Bontis, N. (2001). Assessing knowledge assets: A review of the models used to measure intellectual capital. *International Journal of Management Reviews, 3*(1), 41–60.

Bontis, N. (2001b). Managing organizational knowledge by diagnosing intellectual capital: Framing and advancing the state of the field. In *Knowledge management and business model innovation* (pp. 267–297). IGI Global.

Bontis, N., & Fitz-enz, J. (2002). Intellectual capital ROI: A causal map of human capital antecedents and consequents. *Journal of Intellectual capital*.

Boroujerdi, R. Y., Siadat, S. A., Hoveida, R., & Khani, S. (2014). The study of the nature of human capital management and its strategic role in achieving competitive advantage for the organization. *International Journal of Scientific and Research Publications, 4*, 1–4.

Chatzkel, J. (2004). Human capital: the rules of engagement are changing. *Lifelong learning in Europe*, 138–145.

Cherry, M. A., & Aloisi, A. (2016). Dependent contractors in the gig economy: A comparative approach. *Am. UL Rev., 66*, 635.

Coita, D. C., Abrudan, M. M., & Matei, M. C. (2019). Effects of the blockchain technology on human resources and marketing: an exploratory study. In *Strategic Innovative Marketing and Tourism* (pp. 683–691). Springer, Cham.

Davenport, T. O. (1999). Human capital. *Management Review, 88*(11), 37.

D'Cruz, P., & Noronha, E. (2016). Positives outweighing negatives: The experiences of Indian crowdsourced workers. *Work Organisation, Labour and Globalisation, 10*(1), 44–63.

De Stefano, V. (2015). The rise of the just-in-time workforce: On-demand work, crowdwork, and labor protection in the gig-economy. *Comparative Labor Law and Policy Journal, 37*, 471.

Donovan, S. A., Bradley, D. H., & Shimabukuru, J. O. (2016). *What does the gig economy mean for workers?*

Dubal, V. B. (2017). Winning the battle, losing the war: Assessing the impact of misclassification litigation on workers in the gig economy. *Wis. L. REv.*, 739.

Dunn, M. (2018). *Making gigs work: career strategies, job quality and migration in the gig economy.*

Edvinsson, L., & Malone, M. S. (2007). *Intellectual capital.* Harper Business.

Fleming, P. (2017). The human capital hoax: Work, debt and insecurity in the era of Uberization. *Organization Studies, 38*(5), 691–709.

Friedman, G. (2014). Workers without employers: Shadow corporations and the rise of the gig economy. *Review of Keynesian Economics, 2*(2), 171–188.

Gandini, A. (2019). Labour process theory and the gig economy. *Human Relations, 72*(6), 1039–1056.

Gibbins, P. (2018). Extending employee protections to gig-economy workers through the entrepreneurial opportunity test of FedEx home delivery. *Wash. UJL & Pol'y, 57*, 183.

Graham, M., Hjorth, I., & Lehdonvirta, V. (2017). Digital labour and development: impacts of global digital labour platforms and the gig economy on worker livelihoods. *Transfer: European Review of Labour and Research, 23*(2), 135–162.

Hamadamin, H. H., & Atan, T. (2019). The impact of strategic human resource management practices on competitive advantage sustainability: The mediation of human capital development and employee commitment. *Sustainability, 11*(20), 5782.

Hamzah, N., Hassan, H., Saleh, N. M., & Kamarudin, A. (2017). Intellectual capital management practices: The case of Malaysian private hospitals. In *18th European Conference on Knowledge Management (ECKM 2017).* Academic Conferences and publishing limited.

Harris, S. D. (2018). Workers, protections, and benefits in the US gig economy. *Global Law Review (Sept. 2018, Forthcoming).*

Hayton, J. C. (2003). Strategic human capital management in SMEs: An empirical study of entrepreneurial performance. *Human Resource Management: Published in Cooperation with the School of Business Administration, the University of Michigan and in Alliance with the Society of Human Resources Management, 42*(4), 375–391.

Hegadekatti, K. (2016). *Automation Processes and Blockchain Systems.* Available at SSRN 2890435.

Hegadekatti, K. (2017). *The KY Paradox: Problems in Creating a Centralised Sovereign Backed Cryptocurrency on a Decentralised Platform.* Available at SSRN 2942914.

Hegadekatti, K., & SG, Y. (2016). *The KY Protocol: The First Protocol for the Regulation of Crypto Currencies (Eg-Bitcoin).* Available at SSRN 2735267.

Johnston, H., & Land-Kazlauskas, C. (2018). Organizing on-demand: Representation, voice, and collective bargaining in the gig economy. *Conditions of work and employment series, 94.*

Kässi, O., & Lehdonvirta, V. (2018). Online labour index: Measuring the online gig economy for policy and research. *Technological Forecasting and Social Change, 137*, 241–248.

Khan, M. A. A. (2020). Gig economy: Value comparison against noncontingent income and corporate employment benefits. *Global Journal of Management and Business Research.*

Kianto, A., Sáenz, J., & Aramburu, N. (2017). Knowledge-based human resource management practices, intellectual capital and innovation. *Journal of Business Research, 81*, 11–20.

Koncheva, V. A., Odintsov, S. V., & Khmelnitski, L. (2019, December). Blockchain in HR. In *International Scientific and Practical Conference on Digital Economy (ISCDE 2019)*. Atlantis Press.

Lobel, O. (2017). The gig economy & the future of employment and labor law. *USFL Rev., 51*, 51.

Lowe, M. (2017). *Uber's Gambit: Reassessing the Regulatory Realities of the 'Gig Economy'*.

Manyika, J., Lund, S., Bughin, J., Robinson, K., Mischke, J., & Mahajan, D. (2016). *Independent-work-choice-necessity-and-the-gig-economy*. McKinsey Global Institute.

Michailidis, M. P. (2018). Hie challenges of AI and BLOCKCHAIN on HR recruiting practices. *Cyprus Review, 30*(2).

Milland, K. (2017). *Slave to the keyboard: the broken promises of the gig economy.*

Moisander, J., Groß, C., & Eräranta, K. (2018). Mechanisms of biopower and neoliberal governmentality in precarious work: Mobilizing the dependent self-employed as independent business owners. *Human Relations, 71*(3), 375–398.

Morkunas, V. J., Paschen, J., & Boon, E. (2019). How blockchain technologies impact your business model. *Business Horizons, 62*(3), 295–306.

Nica, E. (2018). Gig-based working arrangements: Business patterns, labor-management practices, and regulations. *Economics, Management, and Financial Markets, 13*(1), 100–105.

Nieves, J., & Quintana, A. (2018). Human resource practices and innovation in the hotel industry: The mediating role of human capital. *Tourism and Hospitality Research, 18*(1), 72–83.

Novikov, S., Kazakov, O., Kulagina, N., & Ivanov, M. (2019, March). Organization of data gathering and preparing on the basis of blockchain for the supporting system of making decisions in the sphere of developing human capital of region. In *IOP Conference Series: Materials Science and Engineering* (Vol. 497, No. 1, p. 012046). IOP Publishing.

Onik, M. H., Miraz, M. H., & Kim, C. S. (2018). *A recruitment and human resource management technique using blockchain technology for industry 4.0.*

Oranburg, S. C. (2018). Unbundling employment: Flexible benefits for the gig economy. *Drexel L. Rev., 11*, 1.

Page-Tickell, R., & Ritchie, J. (2020). Presence and pretence: Trade unions and the gig economy. In *Conflict and Shifting Boundaries in the Gig Economy: An Interdisciplinary Analysis*. Emerald Publishing Limited.

Palacios-Marqués, D., & Garrigós-Simón, F. J. (2003). Validating and measuring IC in the biotechnology and telecommunication industries. *Journal of Intellectual Capital.*

Paolacci, G., Chandler, J., & Ipeirotis, P. G. (2010). Running experiments on amazon mechanical turk. *Judgment and Decision making, 5*(5), 411–419.

Patil, B. S., & Swapna, H. R. (2017). Human capital management practices and employee productivity: A conceptual framework with new dimensions. *International Journal of Engineering and Management Research (IJEMR), 7*(3), 140–145.

Prabhat, S., Nanavati, S., & Rangaswamy, N. (2019, January). India's "Uberwallah" profiling Uber drivers in the gig economy. In *Proceedings of the Tenth International Conference on Information and Communication Technologies and Development* (pp. 1–5).

Prassl, J. (2018). *Humans as a service: The promise and perils of work in the gig economy*. Oxford University Press.

Prassl, J., & Risak, M. (2015). Uber, taskrabbit, and co.: Platforms as employers-rethinking the legal analysis of crowdwork. *Comparative Labor Law and Policy Journal, 37*, 619.

Puri, R. (2017). Gig economy: The road ahead. *IMI KonnectVolume, 6*(5).

Puthal, D., Malik, N., Mohanty, S. P., Kougianos, E., & Das, G. (2018). Everything you wanted to know about the blockchain: Its promise, components, processes, and problems. *IEEE Consumer Electronics Magazine, 7*(4), 6–14.

Rosenblat, A., & Stark, L. (2016). Algorithmic labor and information asymmetries: A case study of Uber's drivers. *International Journal of Communication, 10*, 27.

Salah, D., Ahmed, M. H., & ElDahshan, K. (2020). Blockchain applications in human resources management: Opportunities and challenges. In *Proceedings of the Evaluation and Assessment in Software Engineering* (pp. 383–389).

Sanders, D. E., & Pattison, P. (2016). Worker characterization in a gig economy viewed through an Uber centric lens. *Southern Law Journal, 26*(2), 297.
Sarina, T., & Riley, J. (2018). Re-crafting the enterprise for the gig-economy. *New Zealand Journal of Employment Relations, 43*(2).
Schultz, T. W. (1961). Investment in human capital. *The American economic review, 51*(1), 1–17.
Sen, S., & Saxena, M. J. (2019). Temporariness the new permanency: Evaluating the pros and cons of gig workforce. *JSSGIW Journal of Management.*
Sharmila, K., Kamalakkannan, S., Devi, M. R., & Shanthi, M. C. (2019). *A comprehensive study on blockchain with its components, taxonomy and consensus.*
Silberman, M. (2015). Operating an employer reputation system: Lessons from Turkopticon, 2008–2015. *Comparative Labor Law & Policy Journal, 37*, 505.
Silberman, M., & Irani, L. (2016). Operating an employer reputation system: lessons from Turkopticon, 2008–2015. *Comparative Labor Law & Policy Journal, Forthcoming*.gan
Stewart, A., & Stanford, J. (2017). Regulating work in the gig economy: What are the options? *The Economic and Labour Relations Review, 28*(3), 420–437.
Tapscott, D., & Tapscott, A. (2017). How blockchain will change organizations. *MIT Sloan Management Review, 58*(2), 10.
Tassinari, A., & Maccarrone, V. (2017). *The mobilisation of gig economy couriers in Italy: some lessons for the trade union movement.*
Thomas, R. (2002). *U.S. Patent Application No. 09/877,474.*
Woodcock, J. (2016). Deliveroo and UberEATS: organising in the gig economy in the UK. *Connessioni precarie.*
Zeb, A., Hazana Abdullah, N., & Javaid, M. (2018). Impact of human capital management practices on employees' job performance. *JPhCS, 1049*(1), 012020.

R. Kiruba Nagini is a Research Scholar of Department of Management Studies in Pondicherry University. She has a work experience of more than nine years in teaching Computer Science and Management at B-Schools. Her areas of expertise include Human Capital Analytics and technology-oriented implementations in Ports.

Dr. R. Venkatesakumar is Research Guide and Professor of Department of Management Studies in Pondicherry University. He is a Renowned Technical Trainer in Data analytics and other computing platforms using SPSS, R Programming, SmartPLS, AMOS, Tableau, etc. His areas of interests include marketing analytics, optimization techniques, and technology-oriented operations research Marketing Analytics, Optimization Techniques and Technology-Oriented Operations Research.

Dr. S. Riasudeen is Associate Professor of Department of Management Studies in Pondicherry University. He retired as Airforce Personnel; his faculty includes Soft Skills Training, Placement Training, and Personality Development Trainings for the government officials. As Associate Professor, he focusses on Transformative Pedagogy, stimulating higher order of thinking among learners.

The Future of GIG Workforce

Istadeva Mishra and Anhsu Yadav

1 Introduction

Technology has been driving change for ages. It can be undoubtedly argued that technology has gifted humanity with comfort and happiness. People have adopted technology to make their lives easier. In this process of making harmony with technology, we have aligned our way of thinking and working with technology (Allamnakhrah, 2013). Every such effort of making harmony with technology has changed us slowly and steadily. Technology has been changing our traditional way of working. The gig economy has been made possible using technology in the workplace. The face of the workplace has been changing, and it needs academic understanding and analysis to make the best out of the new face of the workforce (Healy et al., 2017). With the advent of the Internet, the face of the industry has changed drastically. It has made collaborations easier over the Internet with less time and effort. The power of aggregators is quite evident for everyone to see. The immense potential that the aggregators offer in every industry be it be hospitality, education, retail, healthcare, and whatnot. The unique role the platforms play today is that of permissive potentate that delegates responsibility and control over economic transactions but still commands it end to end. It is this capability of the platform that calls for the alignment of the regulatory framework for the betterment of workers and other competitors operating in the traditional economy (Vallas & Schor, 2020). Companies are willing to hire a crowd of mini entrepreneurs instead of permanent workers because of the incentive this culture offers not only in the form of tax-related gains but also ease of compliance. The gig workers are classified under five broad categories. The first category includes professional that is essentially driven by the intention to become one's own boss. They make up around one-third of the total gig worker. The second category

I. Mishra (✉) · A. Yadav
Amity Business School, Noida, Uttar Pradesh, India

A. Yadav
e-mail: ayadav2@amity.edu

A. Gupta et al. (eds.), *Sustainability in the Gig Economy*,
https://doi.org/10.1007/978-981-16-8406-7_21

of workers includes the ones who are following their passion. The third category are of the people who have been using gig to learn more and add to their careers. The fourth category is made up of the individuals who choose gig to earn extra as a side income, whereas the individuals in the fifth category use gig till the time they land a traditional job (Bose, 2017).

2 The Realignment

The future of gig economy lies in its ability to keep pace with the demand of time. An adjustment is needed to support the ecosystem. A failure to align the interest of stakeholders toward mutual success has been creating unrest in the system. As per the annual report of ETUI (Simon et al., 2020), more than 325 protests have been reported across the world between 2015 and 2019 against online platforms. India is no exception; the year 2020 has witnessed many protests against platform operators Zomato, Ola, Swiggy, Flipkart, and Amazon (Rakheja, 2020). It is crucial for the success of the gig economy that the concerns raised by various stakeholders are addressed in the nascent phase of the gig economy. This realignment is required among the goals of all the stakeholders.

2.1 Organizational Calibration

To reap the benefits of the gig economy and to avoid unnecessary friction among the stakeholders, the goals of an organization and the gig worker must be aligned. Technology has been enabling collaboration, but organizations need to harness this gift of technology. Organizational culture has been playing a vital role in keeping employees' effort toward the shared goal. The study by Nikpour (2017) reaffirms the claim that organizational culture has a direct impact on organizational productivity. In many cases of gig workers, the contract is of short duration; hence, acculturation of an employee is difficult in short duration. Most of the time the advantages offered by the gig also bring with it the challenge for the Human Resource Team. A new-age platform-based company is in an advantageous position here. It is always relatively easy to build an organization afresh based on the realities of today's market. But it is relatively painful to transform an organization that has been able to thrive and endure the test time. Affirmative action is required for the traditional organizations to be able to acquire, retain, and grow in the gig economy. The calibration is required, specifically in the following domain.

2.1.1 Task Restructuring

If you look at platform economies, the key to success lies in dividing a task into a group of microtasks and being able to assign these microtasks to different gig workers as opposed to the traditional organization where the task is assigned to a team in its entirety (Ginès i Fabrellas, 2019). The challenge lies in dividing such microtasks in a manner that these microtasks are profitable to support the livelihood of gig workers.

2.1.2 Ensuring Fair Pay

Competition is forcing organizations to reduce the cost. It has implications on the employees involved in gig work. Organizations are forcing the employees to reduce the compensation. However, gig work does not guarantee regular employment. It is reported by Apouey et al. (2020) that gig workers' income saw the sharpest decline in France during the lockdown even if they were working during the lockdown. Gig economy is bringing new opportunity for every section of society, and it is also bringing new challenges. Some of the unfair practices existing in the traditional workforce have precipitated into the gig workforce also. It has been revealed in the study by Renan Barzilay and Ben-David (2018) that women working in the gig economy are getting paid lesser compared to the male counterparts, whereas they spend more hours at work. It requires a more innovative and robust response for the person with a disability (Harpur & Blanck, 2020). Hence, ensuring fair and equitable pay to all is a challenge that is extremely important to achieve long-term sustainability. These studies also argue that the gig work profiles are marked by less pay and insecurity. The insecurity of job profile and less pay cannot be overlooked because the gig economy offers disruptive innovation and micro-entrepreneurship (Prassl, 2018).

2.1.3 Keeping the Partners Healthy and Motivated

The study by Jabagi et al. (2019) presents how an employer can innovatively motivate their employees in a virtual platform-based job environment. The study by Burbano (2019) explains that employees can be motivated to put in extra efforts and spend more time by communicating charity works the gig employer is doing. Several studies have been done to understand the implication of platform economy over the health of gig workers. Various frameworks have been provided to uncover and resolve the sleep difficulties of people working in the platform economy (Crain et al., 2020). It has been highlighted in the study over time that the gig economy raises concerns over employee rights in the gig economy. It has been found that the drivers working in the platform economy face a severe risk of collision and damage (Christie & Ward, 2019). To sustain gig for a longer duration, these challenges should be handled strategically toward the long-term success of an organization.

2.1.4 Ensuring Compliance

To avoid labor regulations, the study by Kelly (2020) reveals that employers are misclassifying their workforce as contract employment. In absence of a well-defined classification, employers are taking undue advantage due to which such employees are also claiming unemployment compensation from the governments. Over the years, various organizations have been fighting legal battles to protect workers from bogus self-employment. One such case is of Independent Workers of Great Britain (IWGB) which has been fighting such bogus self-employment claims for Foster Care workers (Kirk, 2020). It is important to have clear classification and regulation for online platforms and gig workers. It is also important to clarify as to what is paid work or unpaid work and how should the earning from gig work and sharing assets be treated (Koutsimpogiorgos et al., 2020).

2.2 *Community*

The online resources not only enabling the gig economy but also ensuring that the worker can support each other through online workers' communities. However, these communities are distinct for distinct location and work profile, etc. (Wood et al., 2018). The absence of power to negotiate a better working condition and other benefits makes workers' life tough; however to ensure collective bargaining power, studies have shown various strategies that gig workers are using. One of them is through using platforms and communities to unionize. These platforms can be worker centers, cooperatives, and online forums (Johnston & Land-Kazlauskas, 2018). The nature of the gig economy offers lesser trust as opposed to the conventional workforce but studies have found that the work is completed well in time because such gig workers are also embedded in the interpersonal network of trust (Wood et al., 2019b). It has also enabled the companies to get various incentive offered by the government policies.

2.3 *Government*

The gig economy rescues organizations from overhead costs on the workforce. One of the severe adverse impacts of the gig economy comes in the form of transfer of responsibility of social security and training expenses back on employees. The study by Adams et al. (2018) calls for changing the law to bring such a workforce under some regulation. This calls for increasing the role of the government in ensuring that the workforce is brought under the social security net (Ministry of Law & Justice India, 2020). Social Security Code 2020 is one of the important steps toward the same. The public interests are at stake by the advent of platform economy; there is a need to develop a general framework for the local, state, and national governments to guide their actions to deal with the challenges that arise due to the new development. It calls for looking into the concerns of labor protection, tax compliance, privacy protection, and consumer protection (Frenken et al., 2020).

3 The Way Forward

The expansion of the gig economy is enabling the integration of innovation and creativity in the job market that helps organizations enter into innovative product categories and new markets. (UNGUREANU, 2019). Several studies have highlighted that the incumbent entering the industry may bring innovative business models; the most common of them are sharing business models which can make retention and diffusion of entire business model in the economy (Ciulli & Kolk, 2019).

It has been found in the research on piece-rate workers in the USA that the piece-rate work hurts the most vulnerable class of workers such as women, minority, and low-income group workers (Davis & Hoyt, 2020).

There is a strong buzz on gig economy; its short-term and long-term effects must be studied in a holistic manner taking care of all aspects relating to society. Several studies have been done to understand the implication of platform economy on the health of gig workers. On the other hand, several studies have discussed how technology is helping health promotion by the innovative use of online application platforms in promoting the health of the subject (Morales et al., 2019). It has been found that the consumers are willing to pay extra to ensure that the workers working in the gig economy can earn equivalent to their counterparts in the traditional economy, but the consumers have very little awareness of the working condition of worker in the gig economic model (Smith et al., 2021). The need for fair working conditions in platform-based companies has been highlighted by the fair work foundation which has engaged with app-based companies in India and South Africa to encourage a fair working state for the workers in these industries. The study also proposes to begin a yearly ranking of the gig concept-based worker's conditions in these companies (Graham et al., 2020). In the case of bikers on the contrary, the stress level was recorded to be lower than the other samples.

It may however be concluded that the job satisfaction of gig workers relies on the quality of platform they have opted for the work. The better the quality of the platform, the more autonomy and job satisfaction (Kim et al., 2018).

On the other hand, one section of thought leaders believes that the gig economy is not considered in a silo, but the tasks in gig work format should be matched to the similar tasks in the traditional workforce. By clubbing such activity will ensure that the workers in both the format are treated equally (De Stefano, 2016).

Platform-based algorithm control moderates the job in remote gig works, whereas it offers a variety of advantages such as flexibility, complexity, task variety, and autonomy; it also brings with it various challenges such as sleep deprivation, over time, unhealthy and unsocial working hours and less pay, etc. (Wood et al., 2019a).

Another incentive that the gig economy offers is the freedom from office politics and micromanaging boss (Bughin et al., 2016).

The study by Gleim et al. (2019) classifies gig workers into two classes, i.e., sharers and sellers, and concludes that sellers have a higher level of self-congruity and lover level of commerciality leading to organizational trust and job satisfaction, but sharers feel exactly the opposite. It is the need of the hour that the new motivation techniques should be opted to ensure that the employee remains motivated during the platform-based work where it is very little, or no interaction is possible with the employer. Studies have highlighted that the study on organizational attraction, job satisfaction, and attrition is not incompatible with the gig economy rather it requires a deeper understanding of such aspects in the gig economy (Kuhn, 2016).

The celebratory mood toward the gig economy is prevailing in the industry; today some studies (Davis & Hoyt, 2020) believe that is just de-standardized form of traditional work and the companies offering gig are a new form of insecure enterprises.

Some scholars believe that the gig economy has only changed the way we transact in an economy. Work is to be done the old way. It is only that millions of smartphones, some virtual interaction platforms, and a data center have been added to it, and hence, it should be only an enabler and should be regulated the same way (Graham & Shaw, 2017).

4 Dealing with Concerns

The concerns that gig workers face can be summed up in four distinct categories—collective bargaining, economic inclusion, intermediate value chain, and upgrading (Graham et al., 2017).

For the gig economy to succeed, new social security policies must be implemented. The need for new policies arises because the gig economy shifts many of employers' responsibility toward workers back to the workers themselves. Hence, the social security policies must be tweaked to meet the emerging demand of the workforce (Friedman, 2014).

Workers are vulnerable to various health issues in the globalized platform economy. Bajwa et al. (2018) classified such vulnerability of gig workers in three distinct classes, i.e., platform vulnerability, occupational vulnerability, and precarity. To deal with such uncertainty and to provide policy response to the above-mentioned vulnerability, it is required that the definition of employer, employee, and work be broadened to include gig workers. Policies and regulations concerning the relationship between employer and employee are amended to include a new work format that emerged in the form of the gig economy (Stewart & Stanford, 2017). To prepare a suitable regulatory response, the statistics concerning the labor market must be available for the policymaker to refer to. The available labor statistics do not represent online gig worker; hence, Kässi and Lehdonvirta (2018) developed an online labor index which provides a near-real-time index on online labor market situation.

The study by Burtch et al. (2018) finds one of the latent contributions of the gig platforms that it is reducing unviable startups by offering an alternate platform to the unemployed and underemployed workforce. However, it also contributes to the entrepreneurial activity by offering flexibility for people with entrepreneurial mindsets to support the entrepreneurial venture in the nascent phase.

The HRM practices should be implemented upon gig workers also; Meijerink and Keegan (2019) explain that the three actors involved in the gig economy, i.e., gig workers, intermediate technology, and the requesters, are not only the recipient of such policies but also involved in implementing them.

5 Growth Prospects

As per ASSOCHAM (India, 2020), the gig economy is expected to grow 17% CAGR by the year 2023. The five companies with maximum market capitalization Apple, Microsoft, Alfabet, Amazon, and Alibaba are all platform businesses with a total market capitalization of about $6.3 trillion in 2020.

Various studies have shown that gig economy is only going to grow to occupy more share of the total workforce. Study by Upwork (Ozimek, 2019) shows that gig workforce is gaining ground; it has grown around 35% of adult in the USA reported having involved in some of the other forms of gig work. It has also been explained in the same study that the number of workers taking gig as full-time employment is only increasing, but the ones taking is part-time is shrinking each year.

References

Adams, A., Freedman, J., & Prassl, J. (2018). Rethinking legal taxonomies for the gig economy. *Oxford Review of Economic Policy, 34*(3), 475–494. https://doi.org/10.1093/oxrep/gry006

Allamnakhrah, A. (2013). Learning critical thinking in Saudi Arabia: Student perceptions of secondary pre-service teacher education programs. *Journal of Education and Learning, 2*(1). https://doi.org/10.5539/jel.v2n1p197

Apouey, B., Roulet, A., & Solal, I. (2020). Gig Workers during the COVID-19 Crisis in France: Financial precarity and mental well-being. *Journal of Urban Health, 97*(4), 776–795.

Bajwa, U., Gastaldo, D., Di Ruggiero, E., & Knorr, L. (2018). The health of workers in the global gig economy. *Globalization and Health, 14*(1), 124. https://doi.org/10.1186/s12992-018-0444-8

Bose, S. (2017, May 30). *5 Faces of the Gig Economy: New Study Reveals All (Infographic)—Small Business Trends*. Retrieved April 25, 2021, from Small Business Trends website: https://smallbiztrends.com/2017/05/types-of-freelancers.html

Bughin, J., Manyika, J., Lund, S., Robinson, K., Mischke, J., & Mahajan, D. (2016). Independent Work: Choice, necessity, and the gig economy. *McKinsey Global Institute*, (October), 1–119. Retrieved from https://www.mckinsey.com/~/media/McKinsey/FeaturedInsights/EmploymentandGrowth/IndependentworkChoicenecessityandthegigeconomy/Independent-Work-Choice-necessity-and-the-gig-economy-Full-report.ashx

Burbano, V. C. (2019). Getting gig workers to do more by doing good: Field experimental evidence from online platform labor marketplaces. *Organization & Environment*, 108602661984645. https://doi.org/10.1177/1086026619846455

Burtch, G., Carnahan, S., & Greenwood, B. N. (2018). Can you gig it? An empirical examination of the gig economy and entrepreneurial activity. *Management Science, 64*(12), 5497–5520. https://doi.org/10.1287/mnsc.2017.2916

Christie, N., & Ward, H. (2019). The health and safety risks for people who drive for work in the gig economy. *Journal of Transport and Health, 13*, 115–127. https://doi.org/10.1016/j.jth.2019.02.007

Ciulli, F., & Kolk, A. (2019). Incumbents and business model innovation for the sharing economy: Implications for sustainability. *Journal of Cleaner Production, 214*, 995–1010. https://doi.org/10.1016/j.jclepro.2018.12.295

Crain, T. L., Brossoit, R. M., Robles-Saenz, F., & Tran, M. (2020). Fighting fatigue: A conceptual model of driver sleep in the gig economy. *Sleep Health, 6*(3), 358–365. https://doi.org/10.1016/j.sleh.2020.02.004

Davis, M. E., & Hoyt, E. (2020). A longitudinal study of piece rate and health: Evidence and implications for workers in the US gig economy. *Public Health, 180*, 1–9. https://doi.org/10.1016/j.puhe.2019.10.021

De Stefano, V. (2016). The rise of the «just-in-time workforce»: On-demand work, crowdwork and labour protection in the «gig-economy». *Conditions of Work and Employment Series,* (71), 43. Retrieved from https://www.ilo.org/publns%0A, http://www.ilo.org/wcmsp5/groups/public/-ed_protect/-protrav/-travail/documents/publication/wcms_443267.pdf

Frenken, K., van Waes, A., Pelzer, P., Smink, M., & van Est, R. (2020). Safeguarding public interests in the platform economy. *Policy and Internet, 12*(3), 400–425. https://doi.org/10.1002/poi3.217

Friedman, G. (2014). Workers without employers: Shadow corporations and the rise of the gig economy. *Review of Keynesian Economics, 2*(2), 171–188. https://doi.org/10.4337/roke.2014.02.03

Ginès i Fabrellas, A. (2019). The zero-hour contract in platform work. Should we ban it or embrace it? *IDP Revista de Internet Derecho y Política,* (28), 29–43. https://doi.org/10.7238/idp.v0i28.3176

Gleim, M. R., Johnson, C. M., & Lawson, S. J. (2019). Sharers and sellers: A multi-group examination of gig economy workers' perceptions. *Journal of Business Research, 98*, 142–152. https://doi.org/10.1016/j.jbusres.2019.01.041

Graham, M., & Shaw, J. (2017). Towards a fairer gig-economy. *Meatspace Press* (pp. 13–14). Retrieved from https://issuu.com/meatspacepress/docs/towards_a_fairer_gig_economy

Graham, M., Woodcock, J., Heeks, R., Mungai, P., Van Belle, J.P., du Toit, D., Fredman, S., Osiki, A., van der Spuy, A. and Silberman, S.M. (2020). The fairwork foundation: strategies for improving platform work in a global context. *Geoforum, 112*(May 2019), 100–103. https://doi.org/10.1016/j.geoforum.2020.01.023

Graham, M., Hjorth, I., & Lehdonvirta, V. (2017). Digital labour and development: Impacts of global digital labour platforms and the gig economy on worker livelihoods. *Transfer, 23*(2), 135–162. https://doi.org/10.1177/1024258916687250

Harpur, P., & Blanck, P. (2020). Gig workers with disabilities: Opportunities, challenges, and regulatory response. *Journal of Occupational Rehabilitation, 30*(4), 511–520. https://doi.org/10.1007/s10926-020-09937-4

Healy, J., Nicholson, D., & Pekarek, A. (2017). Should we take the gig economy seriously? *Labour & Industry: A Journal of the Social and Economic Relations of Work, 27*(3), 232–248. https://doi.org/10.1080/10301763.2017.1377048

India, T. A. C. of C. and I. of. (2020). *GIG ECONOMY Aligning Consumer Preferences: The Way Forward*. Retrieved from https://www.assocham.org/userfiles/GIGREPORT_2020.pdf

Jabagi, N., Croteau, A. M., Audebrand, L. K., & Marsan, J. (2019). Gig-workers' motivation: Thinking beyond carrots and sticks. *Journal of Managerial Psychology, 34*(4), 192–213. https://doi.org/10.1108/JMP-06-2018-0255

Johnston, H., & Land-Kazlauskas, C. (2018). Organizing on-demand: Representation, voice, and collective bargaining in the gig economy. *International Labour Office*, (94), 54. Retrieved from https://www.ilo.org/wcmsp5/groups/public/-ed_protect/-protrav/-travail/documents/publication/wcms_624286.pdf

Kässi, O., & Lehdonvirta, V. (2018). Online labour index: Measuring the online gig economy for policy and research. *Technological Forecasting and Social Change, 137*, 241–248. https://doi.org/10.1016/j.techfore.2018.07.056

Kelly, J. M. (2020). The low end of the gig economy. *Journal of Rural Studies, 75*(February 2019), 229–236. https://doi.org/10.1016/j.jrurstud.2020.02.004

Kim, S., Marquis, E., Alahmad, R., Pierce, C. S., & Robert, L. P. (2018). The impacts of platform quality on gig workers' autonomy and job satisfaction. In *Proceedings of the ACM Conference on Computer Supported Cooperative Work, CSCW* (pp. 181–184). https://doi.org/10.1145/3272973.3274050

Kirk, E. (2020). Contesting 'bogus self-employment' via legal mobilisation: The case of foster care workers. *Capital and Class, 44*(4), 531–539. https://doi.org/10.1177/0309816820906355

Koutsimpogiorgos, N., Slageren, J., Herrmann, A. M., & Frenken, K. (2020). Conceptualizing the gig economy and its regulatory problems. *Policy & Internet, 12*(4), 525–545. https://doi.org/10.1002/poi3.237

Kuhn, K. M. (2016). The RISE of the "Gig Economy" and implications for understanding work and workers. *Industrial and Organizational Psychology, 9*(1), 157–162. https://doi.org/10.1017/iop.2015.129

Meijerink, J., & Keegan, A. (2019). Conceptualizing human resource management in the gig economy. *Journal of Managerial Psychology, 34*(4), 214–232. https://doi.org/10.1108/JMP-07-2018-0277

Ministry of Law and Justice India. (2020). *The Code on Social Security, 2020*. (DI), 116.

Morales, J., Inupakutika, D., Kaghyan, S., Akopian, D., Yin, Z., Evans, M., & Parra-Medina, D. (2019). Technology-based health promotion: Current state and perspectives in emerging gig economy. *Biocybernetics and Biomedical Engineering, 39*(3), 825–842. https://doi.org/10.1016/j.bbe.2019.07.006

Nikpour, A. (2017). The impact of organizational culture on organizational performance: The mediating role of employee's organizational commitment. *International Journal of Organizational Leadership, 6*(1), 65–72. https://doi.org/10.33844/ijol.2017.60432

Ozimek, A. (2019). *Report: Freelancing and the economy in 2019*. Retrieved January 26, 2021, from Upwork website: https://www.upwork.com/press/releases/freelancing-and-the-economy-in-2019

Prassl, J. (2018). Humans as a service: The promise and perils of work in the gig economy. In *Humans as a service: The promise and perils of work in the gig economy*. https://doi.org/10.1093/oso/9780198797012.001.0001

Rakheja, H. (2020, December 29). *2020 In Review: From Zomato And Swiggy To Ola And Uber – A Year Of Protests By India's Gig Workers*. Retrieved April 25, 2021, from https://inc42.com/infocus/year-end-review-2020/from-swiggy-to-ola-a-year-of-protests-by-indias-gig-workers/

Renan Barzilay, A., & Ben-David, A. (2018). Platform inequality: Gender in the gig-economy. *SSRN Electronic Journal*. https://doi.org/10.2139/ssrn.2995906

Simon, J., Neumann, D., Trappmann, V., & Umney, C. (2020). *A global struggle: Worker protest in the platform economy*. Retrieved from https://www.etui.org/publications/policy-briefs/european-economic-employment-and-social-policy/a-global-struggle-worker-protest-in-the-platform-economy

Smith, B., Goods, C., Barratt, T., & Veen, A. (2021). Consumer 'app-etite' for workers' rights in the Australian 'gig' economy. *Journal of Choice Modelling, 38*, 100254. https://doi.org/10.1016/j.jocm.2020.100254

Stewart, A., & Stanford, J. (2017). Regulating work in the gig economy: What are the options? *The Economic and Labour Relations Review, 28*(3), 420–437. https://doi.org/10.1177/1035304617722461

UNGUREANU, A. (2019). Industry 4.0. The role of gig economy in the industrial revolution of the 21st century. *USV Annals of Economics & Public Administration, 19*(2), 77–84. Retrieved from https://search.ebscohost.com/login.aspx?direct=true&db=buh&AN=142506516&site=ehost-live

Vallas, S., & Schor, J. B. (2020). What do platforms do? Understanding the gig economy. *Annual Review of Sociology, 46*(1), 273–294. https://doi.org/10.1146/annurev-soc-121919-054857

Wood, A. J., Graham, M., Lehdonvirta, V., & Hjorth, I. (2019). Good gig, bad gig: Autonomy and algorithmic control in the global gig economy. *Work, Employment and Society, 33*(1), 56–75. https://doi.org/10.1177/0950017018785616

Wood, A. J., Graham, M., Lehdonvirta, V., & Hjorth, I. (2019). Networked but Commodified: The (Dis)Embeddedness of digital labour in the gig economy. *Sociology, 53*(5), 931–950. https://doi.org/10.1177/0038038519828906

Wood, A. J., Lehdonvirta, V., & Graham, M. (2018). Workers of the Internet unite? Online freelancer organisation among remote gig economy workers in six Asian and African countries. *New Technology, Work and Employment, 33*(2), 95–112. https://doi.org/10.1111/ntwe.12112

Managing Generation Z in Gig Economy: Towards an Integrative Framework of Talent Management

Mohammad Faraz Naim

1 Introduction

The digital disruption leading to non-conventional ways of working is termed as a 'Gig' economy (Manyika et al., 2016). It supports the concept of free-market, offering temporary jobs and short term assignments to the workers. This digitally assisted economy has challenged the status quo of organisations by demanding the complete transformation of existing human resource practices meant for full-time workers. The forthcoming gig workers with superior control over their work and life will challenge the conventional ways of leveraging talent. It will change the way organisational resources are leveraged to satisfy varying needs of a diverse workforce. It has transformed existing business models and market operations in an unprecedented manner (Manyika et al., 2016). Additionally, the progression of Millennial employees to the senior management roles and the emergence of Generation Z (born between 1995 and 2002) have added a new dimension to the contemporary workplaces (Naim, 2021). Most organisations are realising that their conventional practices of talent management will no longer serve the demands of younger workforce segments, particularly, of Generation Z (hereafter will be referred as Gen Z) workforce.

Nonetheless, several studies have demonstrated the Gen Z display distinct characteristics, needs, preferences, expectations relative to their senior counterparts at workplace (Chillakuri & Mahanandia, 2018) Grow & Yang, 2018; Turner, 2015). This workforce segment with high aspirations and self-belief has altogether different expectations from their employers. The inconsistencies between the aspirations of Gen Z, and the opportunities offered by the organisations in the gig economy, pose serious challenges for organisations. It often leads to employees feeling less engaged with work and inclined to leave jobs frequently. Therefore, it is a business imperative

M. F. Naim (✉)
Department of Management, Birla Institute of Technology & Science Pilani, Pilani, India

A. Gupta et al. (eds.), *Sustainability in the Gig Economy*,
https://doi.org/10.1007/978-981-16-8406-7_22

for organisations to embrace innovative HR practices, particularly talent management strategies, commensurate to the idiosyncratic needs and preferences of Gen Z employees.

Importantly, the extant literature on Gen Z is limited, and at the nascent stage, a few studies focus on personality traits and workplace attitudes of Gen Z; however, a sustainable talent management strategy is largely unexplored yet. To bridge this gap, the current study embarks upon developing a conceptual framework of talent management of Gen Z. This conceptual study is an attempt to explore distinct characteristics of Gen Z and help the organisations to attract, engage and retain the best of talent in the gig economy context. The proposed framework makes several theoretical contributions to academia and helps HR practitioners to transform their talent management practices for the upcoming workforce.

2 Gen Z Characteristics

The term 'generation' is defined as a group which shares significant events in the same year of birth and other critical development within those events (Kupperschmidt, 2000). The environment and surrounding values affect the individual basic social values and consuming habits of each generation (Seckin, 2000). Gen Z, born after 1995 (Chillakuri & Mahanandia, 2018; Lanier, 2017) with a high exposure to the digital platforms, also known as Net generation and I generation (Seemiller & Grace, 2017). They grew up with technology along with the World Wide Web, YouTube, cell phones, and, iPods (Kapil & Roy, 2014).

An early exposure to an uncertain and complex environment made an impact on their work attitudes and behaviours (Bursch & Kelly, 2014). Gen Z tends to have more realistic expectations and like to make informed decisions while sharing their ideas and opinions (Schawbel, 2014). They prefer ethical organisations that work on the principle of justice and equity (Seemiller & Grace, 2017) with a proclivity towards a diverse work culture (Ozkan & Solmaz, 2015). Additionally, they give more importance to financial security and peaceful life (Seemiller & Grace, 2017; Turner, 2015). Moreover, their entrepreneurial drive makes them seek freelancing, which gives them autonomy and less degree of supervision from the direct managers (Grow & Yang, 2018).

This generation is not inclined towards a full-time commitment and hence does not intend to work for an organisation for a long period. A normal routine job seems dull and monotonous to them, compelling them to look for a challenge and creativity in work. They believe in gathering experience of multiple organisations, besides learning diverse skills (O'Malley, 2006). Gen Z members display a strong preference for autonomy, flexible workings hours, upward mobility, trust, supportive work environment and financial stability (Grow & Yang, 2018). They demonstrate respect for authority and organisations' protocols but liked to be involved in the organisations' important decisions (Seemiller & Grace, 2017). They also believe in knowledge sharing, getting access to instant information and are comfortable with virtual meetings and teamwork (Turner, 2015). Though technology is their identity, they somehow lack problem-solving skills with weak analytical power for taking a decision (Goh & Lee, 2018). With an entirely different perspective of their ideal job; they desire mentoring, and learning and development opportunities (Bridges, 2015; Turner, 2015).

Gen Z is an outgoing generation with an inclination towards social media, used for sharing and gathering information while connecting with friends simultaneously (Turner, 2015). With a dependence on technology, they believe to find an answer on the internet and prefer to solve their problems independently without asking for anyone's advice (Goh & Lee, 2018). Though this generation has a short attention span, they can create innovative tools and applications faster than their previous generations (Mueller & Lovell, 2015). Gen Z exhibits proficiency in multitasking but their short attention span creates a problem for processing complex information (McCrindle, 2006). This generation has a proclivity towards social causes too and they like to be actively involved in initiatives, for instance, working for the rights of the LGBT community and a concern towards climate change (Levine & Dean, 2012).

3 Talent Management in Gig Economy

Despite the slow pace of gig economies in the world, it is expected to be strengthened in future. It is estimated that 80% of the workforce will be comprised of gig workers by 2030 (Forbes, 2019). Even in Asia, the gig economy is accelerating at a higher speed, with countries like China and India which are going to have a huge proportion of contingent workers shortly.

Gig economy involves an increasing number of contingent workforce that work on projects temporarily to meet specific deadlines. To retain the agility of organisations, employers are required to participate in gig economy while embracing its workforces without losing the expertise and competencies of Gen Z, the upcoming workforce. Here comes the role of talent management practices of an organisation which involves the deliberate efforts of HR to attract, develop, engage and retain employees to meet present and future needs (Goh & Okumus, 2020). Though attracting and retaining talent has always been the priority of organisations, it would be challenging to manage Gen Z in new work dimensions. Since the gig economy functions altogether differently so organisations must prepare themselves to fulfil the aspirations and expectations of its workforce with their less level of commitment and engagement. It will require updating outdated job profiles and recruitment practices to accommodate the working patterns and preferences of Gen Z as they are future of the workforce and possess a unique psychological profile.

Various multinational companies are already working in the direction of attracting and effectively engaging their gig workers. For example, Ernst and Young have created an online platform named as 'GigNow' solely involved in recruiting contingent workers for their assignments. Based on the report of McKinsey, such platforms have the potential of reducing the recruitment cost by 7%, besides they can effectively manage other talent management functions for Gen Z. An effective employer branding with unique employer propositions aligned with changing gig economy trends would be effective. Use of online portals with machine assisted algorithms can help in bringing the recruiters and gig workers together. An effective engagement and commitment of remotely located workers demand constant support from their leaders and employers too. A work environment with open channels of communication, mutual respect and trust would be a crucial factor for bringing geographically dispersed teams together. Building an online culture with the help of virtual tools for exchanging views and opinions with online meeting platforms gives them a sense of belongingness (Vaujany et al., 2020). Their collaboration with reciprocation for fellow team members will challenge the old hierarchical organisational structures; hence, a system of clear reporting and accountability should be established. Since these workers are paid on task completion, an equitable and performance-driven reward system with additional benefits can engage its contingent workforce. A system for providing regular feedback and keeping the gig workers informed about their progress ensures that they are equally significant and visible like their full-time workers (Sharma, 2019).

If an organisation expects its upcoming workforce to be engaged, then embracing them as full-time workers is essential. As organisations accept that this new generation of the contingent workforce will take over the jobs of full-time workers, a significant transformation of the current talent management practices is inevitable. Additionally, the upcoming Gen Z with its proclivity towards freelancing, collaboration, integrity, flexible working hours, autonomy, task variety, high dependency on technology and innovation (Tapscott, 2009), suits so well in this temporary digitally-driven gig culture (Manyika et al., 2016). Therefore, organisations need to prepare themselves considering, the unique profile of Generation Z with their distinct impact on the work environment from previous generations.

4 Conceptual Framework

Each generation has its personality traits shaped by different social, cultural and historical events with other personal experiences of life (Strauss & Howe, 1991). Based on the generation cohort theory, the cohort's shared values, beliefs and experiences have a deep influence on his/her personality. This generational cohort perspective is the most widely used in the generational scholarship for understanding the generation's traits and their impacts on their career choices, aspirations, expectations, work motivations and rewards preferences (eg. Gabrielova & Buchko, 2021, in press; Nichols & Wright, 2018; Padayachee, 2017). It also influences our understanding of different talent management practices of organisations for accommodating Gen Z in the gig economy context. Organisations are experimenting with different talent management models, incorporating multiple work formats and robust career path for their workers. They are supposed to shape their workforce strategically by customising plans for Gen Z employees, different from Millennials. Based on the extant literature and understanding of Gen Z perspectives and expectations, organisations should consider the following mentioned strategies for their sustainable talent management. The author classifies the whole talent management process into three broader categories: talent attraction, talent development and talent engagement and retention. All suggested strategies given under these dimensions will take into consideration the commonalities between Gen Z and gig culture.

Gen Z with heavy dependence on social media, frequently access online platforms to gather information about different organisations, work culture and potential job vacancies. They seek emotional and psychological connection with their work and employer; they prefer to work for a place only if their values and aspirations are aligned with it. Consequently, it is important to enhance the employee value proposition (EVP) for attracting and engaging the workers (KPMG, 2018; Naim & Lenka, 2018). This generation believes in the idea of justice and equity; hence, a diverse and inclusive work environment will fascinate and engage them for a long time. They prefer to work for an open culture which facilitates autonomy and nurture their entrepreneurial drive. Organisations can target this generation, immediately after graduation as they wish to gather work experience than pursue higher education. Moreover, organisations can sponsor their international and professional courses while providing security for the job. Gen Z's desire to get an experience of multiple jobs makes them suitable for rotational programs within the organisation. HR professionals must provide a strong learning and development environment to this generation for their effective engagement and retention. A well-crafted approach should be adopted for addressing the requirements of geographically dispersed employees. Organisations can collaborate with international learning organisations for up skilling and reskilling these Gen Z workers. Since they have a short attention span, self-paced learning programs should be provided with inner mentoring opportunities from their previous generation. Jobs should be enriched with motivational factors with scope for better exposure and work–life balance. Organisations must try to give them opportunities for open communication with their team members and to develop congenial work relations (Elmore, 2014). Since this generation seeks financial security, offering lucrative remuneration packages with extra benefits will give them a reason to stay and contribute more. HR professionals must try to create provisions for innovative rewards and welfare services for their retaining them. A culture of fairness with instant feedback, recognition for the achievements, opportunities for mentoring and for career advancement also lead to engagement and retention of Gen Z workers (Fig. 1).

Gig economy				
		Talent Management		
Gen Z characteristics		**Attraction**	**Development**	**Engagement and retention**
Entrepreneurial Drive Tech-savy Sense of immediacy Sense for Social Justice and Equity Need Autonomy Quest for Learning and Development Short Attention Span Sense of Purpose	⇨	Use of Social Media Diverse and Inclusive workplace Alignment of Personal Goals with Organisational Vision	Knowledge sharing Self Paced Learning Nurture Competency and Experience mapping	Rotational Jobs Competitive Salary Innovative Rewards Work-Life Balance Mentoring and Coaching Instant Feedback for Performance Opportunities for advancement

Fig. 1 Conceptual framework of talent management strategies for Gen Z

5 Discussion and Implications

The gig economy has already altered a significant portion of work, making it inevitable for the organisations to actively engage in revamping their conventional talent management practices. Meanwhile, the emergence of a workforce segment with a distinct psychological profile, and emphasis on technology use, workplace flexibility, sense of immediacy, autonomy, and multitasking, make engagement and retention of this generation more challenging (Naim & Lenka, 2017). This generation seeks new job experiences to become engaged and committed. Therefore, organisations should consider these generational differences while framing their strategies, as one single approach which will fit all has lost its relevance. Therefore, generation-specific talent management practices are needed more than ever (Festing & Schäfer, 2014).

In this line of thought, the proposed conceptual framework illustrates talent management strategies in the light of Gen Z's peculiar traits and gig culture. Gen Z has a high reliance on technology and believes in accessing information and sharing ideas online to gain knowledge and a sense of affiliation (Seemiller & Grace, 2017). Hence, utilising social media platforms for the employer branding would help attract this workforce. Additionally, it is essential to make them aware of organisations' values and goals at the time of hiring, so that they can align their purpose with that of the organisation, with a clear understanding of organisations vision and strategic goals (Chillihari and Mahanandia, 2018). Besides, Gen Z with a proclivity towards ethical practices selects an organisation based on its values and culture rather than innovative products (Moore & Frazier, 2017). Therefore, HR professionals must highlight organisations' social initiatives (e.g. CSR activities) and values, in their talent attraction practices.

Gen Z prefers continuous learning and development and wants to upgrade their knowledge base for improving their worth in the market (Naim & Lenka, 2015). Additionally, they expect their managers to give them opportunities for collaborative learning where they can from peers and superiors (Schroth, 2019). Workplace collaboration also includes the sharing of knowledge and expertise leading to a conducive learning environment for Gen Z. It is also crucial for their career advancement and influence their engagement and retention (Kirchmayer & Fratricova, 2020). The technological dependence of Gen Z allows them to get first-hand experience and make them dynamic learners. Due to their short attention span, they crave self-paced learning and online courses. Organisations must try to create an environment with autonomy, flexibility, transparency and honesty as it facilitates their entrepreneurial drive. It satisfies their social, psychological, and cognitive needs. They should also be provided with mentoring as its help them to develop their personal, professional and other social skills. Moreover, a complete mapping of their competencies should be done before assigning them any task. Since they are more comfortable with their virtual teamwork over the offline meetings; hence, organisations should try to give more importance to virtual interactions. Gen Z prefers to derive meaning from their work; hence tedious and mundane jobs do not excite their spirit and decrease their engagement at the workplace. They need a sense of purpose that makes them connected to the mission of the organisation (Chillakuri & Mahanandia, 2018). Their preference for the job and financial security demands competitive salary and innovative rewards on part their employers (Lanier, 2017). This generation seeks instant and real-time feedback for their performance so that they can take corrective measures for improving it, instead of waiting for the yearly review (Chillakuri, 2020a, 2020b). Though this workforce prefers attractive salary and extra benefits, work–life balance is equally significant for them. Organisations must ensure suitable arrangements for flexible work settings helping them to maintain better work–life balance, which, in turn, leads to their retention (Chillakuri & Mahanandia, 2018).

This study offers implications for both academia and practitioners. Since the extant literature lacks a comprehensive framework for addressing all the dimensions of Gen z's talent management in the gig context. Thus, this study extends the understanding of distinct talent management dimensions for these cohorts. While going through the literature, it has been found that there is a dearth of academic studies in the context of talent management practices for Gen Z. Majority of the literature revolves around Gen Z traits and their respective workplace attitude. To the best of the knowledge of the author, no academic work presents a comprehensive talent management framework taking into consideration the psychological profile of Gen Z in the context of the gig economy. Therefore, this chapter expand the literature on Gen Z, gig economy, and talent management. Moreover, this study also provides an integrated picture of Gen Z characteristics, imperative for designing an appropriate holistic talent management strategy. Additionally, it also contributes to the literature of HRM in progressing the understanding of Gen Z, to revamp existing talent management models for the attraction, development, engagement, and retention of this young workforce segment.

This study also has managerial implications as it provides a holistic picture of attraction, development, engagement, and retention of Gen Z talent. Though the conceptual framework warrants empirical validation, it provides limited practical applications. However, understanding the psychological profile of Gen Z members in the context of the gig economy equip organisations to effectively manage this upcoming talent. Besides, it gives an insight to HR professionals about the expectations and aspirations of Gen Z employees, which make them distinct from their preceding generations. They can use these expectations for formulating innovative HR practices like figuring out suitable career paths, designing an employee job and organisation fit, and fulfilling the learning needs of this workforce. This understanding has further implications on the culture of an organisation as it will surely affect the interpersonal relations between Gen Z and employees of other cohorts (Dwivedula et al., 2019). Though, the emergence of this generation may create serious threats for HR professionals; but there effective development and engagement can lead to successful outcomes. Organisations need to construct and adopt robust career paths for this workforce and should provide them with collaborative learning and development opportunities. An innovative performance management system, competency mapping for creating strong employee value propositions, mentoring with effective leadership development can equip an organisation to face the future workplace challenges posed by Gen Z in the gig economy.

6 Limitations and Future Scope of Research

This chapter provides a conceptual understanding of the domain; however, it lacks empirical validation. Though the study has tried to provide an integrative framework for Gen Z characteristics and strategies for talent management, it cannot be generalised to other generational cohorts including Gen X, Gen Y, and so on. Additionally, strategies such as rotational jobs, opportunities for learning and development may vary across cultural settings. Moreover, the perceptions of individuals may vary towards different HR practices like as job rotation, learning and development, autonomy and work–life balance. In addition to it, the influence of previous generations on the perception of Gen Z about their organisations seems an interesting area to be explored. Furthermore, the role of leaders' effectiveness in managing multigenerational workforce can be examined. Since this generation has a unique psychological profile, examining any variations within the Gen Z cohort is a valuable stream for future researches. Moreover, the role of organisational culture in attracting, engaging, and retaining the Gen Z is another one potential area to be studied.

7 Conclusion

Organisations have realised that Gen Z has already entered the workforce and is ready to take over its previous generation. Their talent management is becoming quite challenging in the context of gig economy. This new generation with a unique set of preferences and aspirations seek distinct ways of finding their purpose in life. This workforce demands personalisation in terms of their talent management, leading to a complete overhaul of existing models. Their characteristics and work preferences should get consideration while framing HR policies for their better engagement and retention. It will be beneficial if organisations endeavour to recognise the priorities and expectations of Gen Z employees. Moreover, building a culture with a clear role and responsibilities with measurable performance is crucial. HR professionals should try to create a fair, flexible, transparent, and inclusive work culture. Though money is a significant motivator for Gen Z, their entrepreneurial drive, freedom, and a quest for learning and development hold equal importance. Giving due recognition to their contribution, mutual respect, and keeping them informed about the development of their work engage them more effectively. Consequently, organisations embrace this new generation, i.e. Gen Z with a digitally driven gig culture, by transforming their conventional talent management strategies for an effective attraction, development, engagement, and retention. It is giving an opportunity to our organisational leaders to leverage the changes bought by this generation and making most out of it.

References

Bridge, T. (2015). 5 ways the workplace needs to change to get the most out of generation Z. Retrieved from http://www.fastcoexist.com/3049848/5-ways-theworkplace-needs-to-change-to-get-the-most-out-of-generation-z

Bursch, D., & Kelly, K. (2014). Managing the multigenerational workplace. UNC executive development. Retrieved from http://www.kenan-flager.unc.edu/~/media/Files/documents/executive-development/managingthe-multigenerational-workplace-white-paper.pd

Chillakuri, B. (2020a). Fueling performance of millennials and generation Z. *Strategic HR Review, 19*(1), 41–43.

Chillakuri, B. (2020b). Understanding Generation Z expectations for effective onboarding. *Journal of Organizational Change Management, 33*(7), 1277–1296.

Chillakuri, B., & Mahanandia, R. (2018). Generation Z entering the workforce: The need for sustainable strategies in maximizing their talent. *Human Resource Management International Digest, 26*(4), 34–38.

De Vaujany, F. X., Leclercq-Vandelannoitte, A., & Holt, R. (2020). Communities versus platforms: The paradox in the body of the collaborative economy. *Journal of Management Inquiry, 29*(4), 450–467.

Dwivedula, R., Singh, P., & Azaran, M. (2019). Gen Z: Where are we now, and future pathways. *Journal of Human Resource Management, 22*(2), 28–40.

Elmore, T. (2014). How generation Z differs from generation Y. Retrieved July 01, 2020, from http://growingleaders.com/blog/generation-z-differs-generation-y/

Festing, M., & Schäfer, L. (2014). Generational challenges to talent management: A framework for talent retention based on the psychological-contract perspective. *Journal of World Business, 49*(2), 262–271.

Forbes. (2019). Hiring top talent from generation Z: 14 essential recruitment tips. Retrieved February 15, 2021, from https://www.forbes.com/sites/forbeshumanresourcescouncil/2019/08/05/hiring-top-talent-from-generation-z-14-essential-recruitment-tips/?sh=2adce083421e

Gabrielova, K., & Buchko, A. A. (2021, in press). Here comes generation Z: millennials as managers. *Business Horizons*, (n/a, n/a).

Goh, E., & Lee, C. (2018). A workforce to be reckoned with: The emerging pivotal generation Z hospitality workforce. *International Journal of Hospitality Management, 73*, 20–28.
Goh, E., & Okumus, F. (2020). Avoiding the hospitality workforce bubble: Strategies to attract and retain generation Z talent in the hospitality workforce. *Tourism Management Perspectives, 33*, 100603.
Grow, J. M., & Yang, S. (2018). Generation-Z enters the advertising workplace: Expectations through a gendered lens. *Journal of Advertising Education, 22*(1), 7–22.
Kapil, Y., & Roy, A. (2014). Critical evaluation of generation Z at workplaces. *International Journal of Social Relevance and Concern, 2*(1), 10–11, 10–14.
Kirchmayer, Z., & Fratričová, J. (2020). What motivates generation Z at work? Insights into motivation drivers of business students in Slovakia. *Proceedings of the Innovation management and education excellence through vision* (pp. 6019–6030).
KPMG. (2018). Generation Z talent how the new generation of workers will reshape talent management. https://advisory.kpmg.us/content/dam/advisory/en/pdfs/generation-z-talent.pd
Kupperschmidt, B. R. (2000). Multigenerational employees: Strategies for effective management. *The Health Care Manager, 19*(1), 65–76.
Lanier, K. (2017). 5 things HR professionals need to know about generation Z. *Strategic HR Review, 16*(6), 288–290.
Levine, A., & Dean, D. R. (2012). *Generation on tightrope: A portrait of today's college student*. Wiley.
Manyika, J., Lund, S., Bughin, J., Robinson, K., Mischke, J., & Mahajan, D. (2016). Independent work: Choice, necessity, and the gig economy. *McKinsey Global Institute, 2016*, 1–16.
McCrindle, M. (2006). New generations at work: Attracting, recruiting, training and retaining.
Moore, K., & Frazier, R. S. (2017). Engineering education for generation Z. *American Journal of Engineering Education (AJEE), 8*(2), 111–126.
Mueller, M. B., & Lovell, G. P. (2015). Theoretical constituents of relatedness need satisfaction in senior executives. *Human Resource Development Quarterly, 26*(2), 209–229.
Naim, M. F. (2021). *Exploring learning preferences of Gen Z employees: A conceptual analysis*. In Applications of work integrated learning among Gen Z and Y student (pp. 1–14), IGI, USA.
Naim, M. F., & Lenka, U. (2018). Development and retention of generation Y employees: A conceptual framework. *Employee Relations, 40*(2), 433–455.
Naim, M. F., & Lenka, U. (2017). Linking knowledge sharing, competency development, and affective commitment: Evidence from Indian Gen Y employees. *Journal of Knowledge Management, 21*(4), 885–906.
Naim, M. F., & Lenka, U. (2015). Mentoring as an HR intervention to engage Gen Y employees. *Global Research & Development Services, 2*(1), 1697–1715.
Nichols, T., & Wright, M. (2018). Generational differences: Understanding and exploring generation Z. *Officers President President-Elect*, 177.
Ozkan, M., & Solmaz, B. (2015). The changing face of employees-generation Z and their perceptions of work (A study applied to university students). *Procedia Economics and Finance, 26*, 476–483.
O'Malley, S. (2006). Attracting and retaining generation Y employees. *Insurance Advocate, 117*(24), 27–30.
Padayachee, K. (2017). The myths and realities of generational cohort theory on ICT integration in education: A South African perspective. *The African Journal of Information Systems, 10*(1), 4.
Sharma, A. (2019). What Gen Z expects from the workplace. Retrieved January 10, 2021 from https://www.peoplematters.in/article/life-at-work/what-gen-z-expects-from-the-workplace-23751
Schawbel, D. (2014). Gen Z employees: The 5 attributes you need to know. Retrieved from www.entrepreneur.con/article/236560
Schroth, H. (2019). Are you ready for gen Z in the workplace? *California Management Review, 61*(3), 5–18.
Seckin, S. F. (2000). Turkiye'nin Kusak Profili. *Capital Journal, 12*, 100–106.

Seemiller, C., & Grace, M. (2017). Generation Z: Educating and engaging the next generation of students. *About Campus, 22*(3), 21–26.

Strauss, W., & Howe, N. (1991). *Generations: The history of America's future, 1584 to 2069.* Learner orientations among baby boomers. William Morrow and Company.

Tapscott, D. (2009). *Growing up digital: How the net generation is changing your world*. McGraw-Hill.

Turner, A. (2015). Generation Z: Technology and social interest. *The Journal of Individual Psychology, 71*(2), 103–113.

The Future of the Gig Professionals: A Study Considering Gen Y, Gen C, and Gen Alpha

M. Anand Shankar Raja, A. V. Akshay Kumar, Neha Makkar, Senthil Kumar, and S. Bhargav Varma

1 Study Setup

This study intends to explore the various reviews on the gig economy and trace the factors leading to the gig economy's success. There is a massive shift in the economy due to the enormous influence of gig jobs. Top organizations worldwide have started to look forward to extending gig job opportunities to makeover the cost. The situation has been more flexible for the Millennials to be a gig worker. In general, Millennial's personality, behavior, and attitude have been a base factor contributing to the gig economy's growth. For this purpose, we have depended on various white and gray secondary sources of data. The study concluded that Millennials are very proactive and agile to new changes and have the mentality and physical ability to explore new opportunities. Information technology has been a source of motivation for the gig millennials to learn, explore, and benefit from the given available resources compared to Gen X.

M. A. S. Raja (✉)
Department of Commerce, CHRIST (Deemed To Be University), Bangalore, India
e-mail: anand.shankar@christuniversity.in

A. V. A. Kumar
Department of Commerce, Jain College, Vasavi Campus, Bengaluru, India
e-mail: akshay.av@res.christuniversity.in

N. Makkar
Institute of Innovation in Technology and Management, Janakpuri, Delhi, India

S. Kumar
Professor of Research & Business Analytics, School of Management, Presidency University, Bangalore, India
e-mail: drsenthilkumar@presidencyuniversity.in

S. B. Varma
Department of Economics, Meghanad Desai Academy of Economics, Mumbai, India

Ottoman's Turkish Restaurant, Chennai, India

A. Gupta et al. (eds.), *Sustainability in the Gig Economy*,
https://doi.org/10.1007/978-981-16-8406-7_23

On the other hand, Gen Z (Born after 1996) is just entering the corporate world and is more influenced by information technology. However, Gen Z, Gen C, and Generation Alpha will dominate the gig economy in the future. The present gig economy is built with Millennials' efforts and slowly creates a new revolution in the global job market. Automation and new digital technologies have accelerated the growth of the gig economy, creating vast opportunities. Talent-related technology platforms are for individual workers; however, the organization also prefers the traditional full-time workers. Thus, standalone gig workers depend on technology and are tech-pro (*mc1.pdf*, n.d.). Usage of technology for survival has become a mega demographic trend associated with gig workers (Lai, 2019). Independent work (gig work) is facilitated through the digital platform. The gigs are paid based on the task, assignment, project, sales, etc. It is more choice-based flexibility rather than a necessity says (Bughin et al., 2016). The majority of these gig jobholders are Gen Z and Gen C, but Gen Alpha will soon be taken over. This research will also be an opportunity to understand Gen Alpha and draw a road map to visualize them as gig workers.

2 The Mystery Behind the Growth of Gig

Though there are many factors behind the growth of gig, there are two major economic factors responsible for the development of the gig economy in the past decade. Though there are many secondary factors, being the reasons for the growth of gig, the primary reason is the great economic recession. Moreover, the present global health crisis "COVID-19" is also a reason for the forced gig effect. The majority of the gigs occupying a significant chunk are Gen Y, X, and C. Millennials and baby boomers dominate the gig work market, comprising 37% and 35% because they are tech-savvy (Mitic, 2020). The Gen Alpha, due to various reasons, will dominate the future. In this research, we will discuss the characteristics of each generation and their contributions to the gig economy.

3 The Great Economic Recession

In 2008, major countries did not bring in new economic reforms behind the great economic crisis, especially regarding the job market. This imagery and reality of life experienced and realized by many stimulated them to quit their permanent job and chose to freelance. This crisis was also a major shift, making the firms rethink and realign their payment strategies because of the fund shortage. The unemployment dynamics during this recession can be one of the major forces to drive gig economic success (Choudhry, 2010). Moreover, the unemployment in OECD countries reached peak position (Islam & Verick, 2010), which may be one of the major causes of fear in the minds of several millennials. (Borbely, 2009); in his article, many job leavers quit their job and started to look for something better during the great economic crisis of 2008. (Legge & Legge, 2018), Also, workers forced to leave and voluntary termination due to less salary and wages received due to the crisis in 2008. Post-crisis, in 2010, there was major growth in gig jobs in the USA. (Iacurci, 2020). The Ministry of Manpower Singapore also says that people started to depend on gig jobs between the years 2010 to 2016, though gig jobs took shape after 2017 (Matters, 2020). Little research work also proposes the same logic that the great recession is one of the primary forces to drive the growth of gig or the on-demand task (Kacher & Weiler, 2017).

4 Covid-19 the Global Pandemic

The global pandemic COVID-19 has taken back the job opportunities due to the fewer funds and inability of the management to pay wages and salary. The governments of various countries have made efforts to support those who have lost their jobs. However, this cannot continue for months (Jain, 2020), (Express, 2020). India has income disparity because of a massive gap in skill possessed by various employees (un-skilled, semi-skilled, and highly skilled). Highly skilled will manage the pandemic, and the post-pandemic will not be miserable for them as they have the exposure to "work from home". However, the work-from-home population may just a tiny portion among the other working class; they are tech-savvy and can manage their daily bread. In the COVID-19 pandemic, the Millennials, who are the parents of Gen Alpha, find it very difficult to manage them as they are at home and need mobile and laptops with Internet connection for games. The pandemic has put the millennials in the worst crisis as they earn for themselves and their children.

Moreover, not all the millennials are highly qualified and are tech-savvy, many do not have the basic education, and they are the ones majorly affected due to the lockdown. Millennial parents are actively into parenting blogs, which means they have exposure to the Internet, and few studies even state that they encourage their children to be on social media. They are multi-taskers, busiest people, active in social media, and digital natives (Sweeney, 2006). The millennials dominate the world at present when compared with Gen X and baby boomers (Fig. 1).

5 Gig Economy an Overview

Social security, job security, insurance, and other benefits, which are less than expected, motivate the young generation to be freelancers considering this opportunity to earn better. Earning better here has to be understood in two views, i.e., to spend better and to save better for the future (first perspective) and to earn in a comfort zone (second perspective). Moreover, the deskwork stuck with loads of commitments demotivates an individual to spend time for personal life. It brings

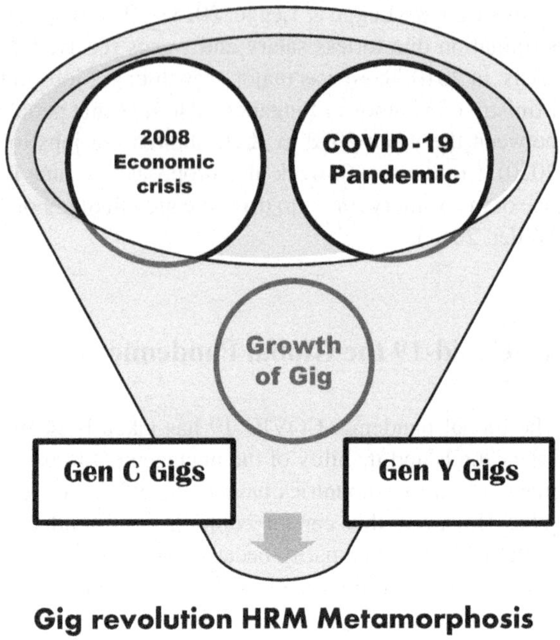

Fig. 1 Gig revolution "HRM metamorphosis". *Source* Author's

in many health issues and family issues due to work–life balance (WLB). Considering the national unemployment rate in 2017–2018 as 3.4% of the citizens find a decent job with a fair wage and salary has become a significant challenge. This could have been one reason people search for a job for day-to-day living, and there is an increase in the gig workers category. After digitalization and technological advancement, India has opened up new opportunities for women who need freelancing and part-time work. Online platforms such as Ghar Se Nakuri "JobsForHer" have created a positive remark announcing job vacancy for women who return to the job market after 1–3 years of break. Gig workers are the male community who get the exposure to connect with new clients and firms and even the women empowered to search, execute and achieve the desired outcome from the gig work. India leads the gig economy with 24% in the online labor market. Other job opportunities are seen for software builders, market researchers, and creative marketing professionals.

The author says that gig work is for those who look for a freelancing job. This profession is bound with positive factors such as flexibility, good pay, and new career opportunity. The gig economy has risen because of the negativities seen in the white-collar profession, which functions on a full-time basis. Moreover, a country like India, which has grown in leaps and bounds in digital upgradation gig jobs, is numerous. According to this article, it is said that gig work has increased in India because of the crisis and its impact on the professional arena providing job opportunities.

Moreover, the article clearly states that 9–5 jobs are not preferred, and hence, the youth are now preparing themselves for gig work. Automation, digital technology, artificial intelligence, machine learning, etc., have affected traditional jobs. Those who know how to use technology like to be flexible earn a fair income and live a decent life without overburden. Those who make use of IT for survival are good gigs, and the others who struggle are the bad gigs (Manyika & Taylor, 2017). There are many job opportunities for gig workers in India, such as Swiggy delivery boys, Big Basket delivery workers, OLA and Uber taxi drivers, Domino's pizza delivery, etc. Now, the world is moving toward two concepts, i.e., minor entrepreneurs and part-time workers. Having a flexible job contract with two or more firms has become the modern trend. It is pretty shocking to know that Deloitte's survey says that 81% of Gen Z will be joining the gig market. Earning more money and work–life balance are the two significant factors. In India, a highly connected mobile workforce drives the trend as people have started to consider gig jobs. In the initial days, the freelancing job was associated more with creativity and design, but now it is due to the stress and depression in the full-time employment. Freelancers or independent contractors have found a new way to save money for retired life, such as being a gig worker. According to this article, the gig economy is creating negative and positive effects on the American economy.

Here are the best example quotes: the Uber drivers, Airbnb, and Door Dash, which employs workers as freelancers. All these individuals' income falls under self-employed and has many tax benefits. Mental well-being and stability is the essential factor for any professional in any given job. Traditional paid work has many restrictions, and gig job has no such norms, which increases self-confidence. Gig jobs allow getting specialized in various skills and meeting new people, and new offers accepted as a challenge makes a person strong and confident. Gig economy goes to the highly positive side, leaving a good impact on the economy and may include confessions of part-time prostitutes that may also consider gig workers have a negative effect. Overall, gig jobs are filled with flexibility, have many new opportunities, and will be helpful to earn additional income. All these factors (flexibility, opportunity, and extra income) are pretty impossible in full-time employment. Hence, the three driving forces behind the success of the gig economy to grow in large heights have been presented below (Fig. 2).

Fig. 2 Three core variables behind the gig growth. *Source* Author's

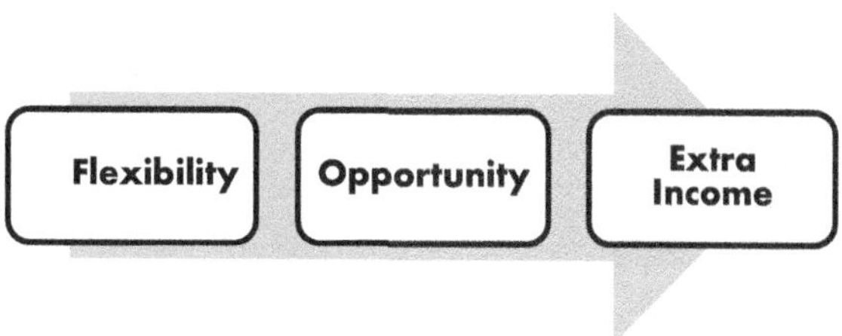

Understanding (Gig economy)

Author/year	An overview on gig economy
Economy (2019)	Considering the highest demographic dividend in India, the authors say that income disposal has increased in recent times. Organizations have made their functions very simple by replacing men with machinery and computerized tools. Gen Y has become the popular gigsters in India. They have concluded that India needs strong laws to protect the freelancer's job
Accenture digital economy I.T.'S TIME TO REIMAGINE, (n.d.)	The usage of information technologies likes artificial intelligence, robotics is replacing humans, and the nature of skills expected in the industrial world is unimaginable. Corporate firms are keen on using the employees' selected skills when there is a need/want. Digital technology-based applications and websites connect the freelancers and the firms that need gig work. Thus, IT has been one of the primary reasons for the growth of the gig economy
Gross & Musgrave, (n.d.)	A flexible employment pattern has been one of the reasons for the growth of gig jobs. The authors further say that gig's development is to be appreciated. However, this will affect the well-being and mental health of the employees in the future
Talent & Economy, (n.d.)	Gig jobs and their fast growth are considered a threat to the traditional full-time jobs because of their preexisting issues such as workplace gender discrimination, unfair payment of wage/salary, improper work culture, rigid work policy, etc. Instead of using the low-skilled workers and struggling to get the work done, which involves a massive cost, corporates think it wise to consider gigsters whenever needed. Thus, forced job shrinking and job enlargements for gigs are a new trend
2020 Global Marketing Trends, (2020)	The USA has predicted that by the year 2020, it will witness 42 million gig workers actively seen across various sectors. Reward strategies play a significant role and act as a source of motivation for all categories of employees. Few who are full-time employees prefer being a gig; a person can also earn extra income and hence gig and take up freelancing jobs where opportunities are

(continued)

(continued)

Author/year	An overview on gig economy
Is the gig Contents, (n.d.)	Cross-industrial talent acquisition has become a significant need in the competitive world for which the firms use the gigsters. This theme is called industrial fusion or fusion of skills needed to enhance the work for the success of an organization
Gen Z and the Gig Economy It's time to gig in or get out. IS GIG ALWAYS GREENER ? Gen Zers have split down the middle on whether (2019)	A research report states that 54% of Gen Z will prefer full-time jobs because of certain factors such as stability in job, regular payment, committee members, etc., and only 46% of the employees will prefer to be gigs. Gen Z prefers certain benefits from employment such as public holidays, regular pay, cash rewards, bonus, public recognition, etc. We understand that Gen Z's children will be opposite to them, preferring to be a gig

6 Das Kapital's M-C-M and the Gig Economy (Theoretical Underpinning)

Theoretical underpinnings are essential in research work to introspect various underlying themes which can be understood, connected, analyzed, appreciated, criticized, and also modified as per the present trend. The most famous theory proposed by Karl Marx, known as Das Kapital, has been considered. The modern economic understanding of the economy and world considering the gig workers is a new dimension in this research. We all know that capital is a very important factor, which contributes to economic growth. First, we have to understand the meaning of capital. Capital is the source of wealth or money to buy something, in simple terms, to strike a transaction.

Moreover, capital is not just a current wealth; it is a value created throughout many years. To earn this capital or to accumulate the capital, the role of laborers plays a major role. The rate of profits depends on the commodities and raw materials used in producing a final product and the influence of labor to convert the raw materials into a finished product. The economy has grown in leaps and bounds only with the help of human assets. To understand capital maximization, there is a need to understand the factors associated with it. Karl Marx "Das Kapital" stated M-C-M (money-commodity-money), which means we buy to sell. Here, money is the capital. There are two phases, which are involved in M-C-M. The first phase is when money transfer into a commodity, and the second phase is the transfer of a commodity into money. There is money for money in the M-C-M theory, and the capital investment is being drawn back, which is called money "reflux". This is because the cycle of buying and selling is endless. In the process of M-C-M, the money becomes the starting point again but has reflux at the time of selling, which makes "M = M + excess." This excess of money is called the surplus value. Now, keeping the surplus value will understand the multiplier effect and its role in the M-C-M model. The multiplier effect provides the numerical estimate of the reflux; the multiplier effect can be calculated (change in income/change in money). A change in income is the reflux of money, and a shift in spending is the capital amount spent by the buyer. In the M-C-M model, the multiplier effect plays a key role by calculating the buyer's money and the profit he gained during selling. This makes the possessor a capitalist. The basic idea of the M-C-M model is to invest and gain profit out of the investment without loss. The process of money-commodity-money may differ based on where it is used. However, the nature of the model remains the same.

Men (labor) play a significant role in the multiplier effect. If labor cost is cut, then the results may be negative. The majority of the organizations are doing that in the name of gig jobs. Thus, making the ultimate product of M-C-M is money. William R. Tracey defines human resources as "The people that staff and operate an organization, as contrast with the financial and material resources of an organization". When an HR is recruiting an employee, specific policies are put forth, which areas of guidelines, protocol, and the employee's working hours—and later exploited by assigning target projects per day and not being paid for the overtime done by the employee. There is no compromise in gig economy boosting the economy, but if we consider gig workers and the rigid HR policies by the gig employer, which is based on exploitation and circumvention. We have to maintain the advantages the model offers but at the same time improve more bargaining power and regulate the bad aspects. The gig economy is a category of work that is still largely undefined and unrecognized by many governments, from the local to federal level.

Nevertheless, the gig economy is growing, influencing how humans view work, which poses several challenges for countries. The old theories say that the more time laborers spend time in production will be paid more. However, in modern days, the fewer work hours are preferred by firms considering cost-saving mechanisms. This is the concrete reality applicable for the gig workers. Money from the HR department on employees (gig workers) is well used in the right way, right time without wastages. Labor value is defined in terms of smart work, quick work, and good work.

7 Shifting Mindset of Work

The gig economy's growth represents a shift in the way employees view work, instead of a more traditional system where a worker works full-time for only one employer. Some workers choose to enter the gig economy for the spirit of more flexibility, freedom, and personal fulfillment. In addition to this, freelancing may offer people an increased chance to select companies and projects that attract them. Findings from the Global Gig Economic by Staffing Industry Analyst include marker estimates for the 18 countries representing approximately 90% of global temporary agency work spend and per type of contingent worker. Total global gig economy spending hit an estimated $4.5 trillion in 2018. Employers are increasingly using gig workers to lower costs and meet project need for the companies. Gig worker is often viewed as "economy" to hire. The desire to cut down overheads will not likely disappear in the next few years. Besides, with the rise of technology for communication and remote collaboration, it may no longer even make intelligence is required to do the work. Poor HR policies could lead to an increase in employee turnover. Many organizations do not follow a process of exit interviews. An exit interview is where the HR talks to the employee who voluntarily leaves an organization. Usually, exit interviews are conducted to know why a worker leaves the organization to build upon the gaps, which that employee states. However, many organizations do not follow exit interviews and, in turn, sometimes will have yearly based contracts where the free will of the employee is restricted.

8 Absence of Employee Protection

Some organizations do not give life insurance pays if an event such as death occurs in the works. This leads to insurance gaps and fear of fewer pension funds and results to ensure tech companies, which may play a significant role in nudging people. Concluding the economic perspective of gig economic, we would have to stretch on few points on the benefits of the employee and define as to where there is more psychological peace and ample amount of time for the employee to learn a new skill set and spend sufficient time with his/her family. They can also work on free will, and there is the workplace safety act, which also protects the employee. However, the lack of life insurance and the gap in the pension and funds seem to be an ear of only corn. Taking the basic idea of the Das Kapital M-C-M model, there is a money multiplier effect, which increases credit growth. Nevertheless, the employer does not spend the excess money on the insurance of the workers. Instead, it uses the money on R&D projects, which would create more job opportunities for the GIG economy workers.

9 Review of Literature (Tracing the Various Perspectives on Gig Work/economy)

Inc, FieldEngineer, (2018) says that the gig economy has another name called the on-demand work. The highlight of being a gig worker is to get involved in short-term work for a short duration. The gig economy has grown due to the growth in technology, networking using smartphones and mobile applications, artificial intelligence, and big data. Moreover, the development of gig economy is due to a digital and technological revolution. (KPMG report (White paper), 2018), The report clearly states that the changes in the labor market have given rise to self-employment and freelancing task. Seeking alternative career paths and flexible work management has motivated individuals to get into the gig revolution. The report says that a few factors have to be introspected to avoid this disruption. They are: Evaluate the HR policy, bringing in the concept of gig in regular employment, redefining employee's value proportion, etc. Seeking more flexibility. (The Prudential Insurance Company of America, Newark, NJ., 2017), the report mentions in detail the pros and cons of gig employment. As there is a resource, flexibility, the employer can save many costs, which positively impacts. Simultaneously, gig work is an unpredictable work stream where the employees may not be available throughout the period, and the workforce is not constant; it keeps changing. (Phair, December 2016) says that gig work is a short-term work opportunity to earn money (financial incentives), primarily independent or contingent. The report also mentions an important term, "contingent work," which means employment with less employee protection. In simple, we have to understand that there is no job security. (lives, Jobs transforms, 2016), In this white paper, the authors have mentioned that the gig revolution has changed the recruitment landscape. Work flexibility is the most advantageous factor for a gig employee, but at the same time, an insecure way of working is a significant disadvantage. The gig economy is a platform where individuals can experiment before choosing their careers. In simple, location of skill and comfort zone is possible. (Roma Puri, 2017) says that gig work occurs in specific domains such as restaurants, production units, and educational institutions. Millennials are more attracted to gig because of work flexibility, aspiration to money, and more work–life balance. Creating a team for gigsters and getting the work done is a great challenge in today's gig revolution. Quoting the examples of Uber and its competitors in the market, the author says that the rise of gig economy is in leaps and bounds. Career is vanishing where every worker becomes a freelancer where labor transaction is a one-night stand. Fluctuations in demand led to shift in work and improper work schedules, which is an essential factor, creating gig employment. (Abdhuliahi Muhammed, October 2018) wrote commenting on the problems in the gig economy, stating that identity is a fixed job and specialization for any individual. In gig economy individuals, finding a sense of identity will be pretty tricky. Moreover, the employment legislation is very murky, and no many policies, rules, and regulations have been framed and implemented to control the gig economy. (Nidheesh M. K., 2019 February) says when there is a lot of opposition to get into permanent jobs, the availability of short-term contracts is called a gig job. Because people are desperate to take up a job to make the daily bread, they search for a short-term job. Moreover, the success of gig jobs is seen only in specific industries and sectors, and it is not successful in other domains. Says that an expanding portion of all the employed persons is also a big success. Creating own hours to work gives a sense of comfort, which is the main success of the gig economy/revolution. Saving for own retirement, paying on own for health insurance, and not being dependent on the employer are a basic understanding of a gig job. Based on the literature reviews, a model is built titled "The Four Dimensions of Gig Jobs."

10 Generation Y (Millennials as Gig)

William Strauss, who authored a book titled "The History of America's Future, 1584 to 2069," coined Millennials' term (Home & Strauss, 2018). They were born and raised when there was a rapid change in the economy, which witnessed liberalization, privatization, and globalization. Indeed, they had the opportunity to be agile to the new technological advancements. Though Gen X had seen these recent changes, they are not agile to the changes. Thus, Millennials are considered tech-savvy and tech-pro. However, this technological impact will have a negative effect on the Millennials. The Internet has caused a massive change in the behavior of Millennials negatively and positively depending upon various factors. Research by (Myers, 2016) explored the impact of the Internet on millennials and concluded that Millennials had been tuned to use the Internet several times a day. Several routine activities like meal consumption, during the time of interaction with family members, etc. In a way, these millennials are addicted to using the Internet as a practice.

Moreover, they are educated and stay connected using technologies (Zachos, 2015). Internet and digital tools have allowed the Millennials to be smart, knowing the industrial trends and expectations. Millennials are more technology agile and embrace digital life when compared with the other Generations of X and Z (Vogels, 2019). Millennials do not adapt to technology; instead, they deal and interact with technology, which has caused a social change among this generation. There are several advantages, which they enjoy, like knowledge updating, interaction, global networking, opportunity-seeking, etc. However, information technology (IT) is a hindrance to productivity (Au-Yong-Oliveira, 2018). They are also considered lazy because of the technological attraction and addiction and not much concentration for career development and life progression (Joyner, 2016). Millennials are looking forward to a relaxed life compared with Gen X. Over the competition, fewer full-time opportunities have also pushed the millennials to be active gig workers. Most of the gig work has become highly flexible and is preferred by the millennials. Many studies conclude that gig work has more flexibility and is highly welcomed in the era of forced work–life balance. An article by (Monahan et al., 2020) mentions few advantages enjoyed by the millennials of being a gig worker as follows,

- An opportunity for the women millennials to be a freelancer and to earn an extra income.
- The Millennials find it easy to grab gig jobs as per their expectations.
- Gig jobs have emotional agility and have allowed being free from a heavy workload.

In addition to this, (Leeds University, 2017) studied the gig economy and its impact on the millennial generation. The study clearly understood a particular factor such as skill development, opportunity to do several new projects, and work–life balance attracting the millennials. From the study, it was also concluded that many people had a favorable opinion about the gig economy and the gig jobs. In contrast, only a very

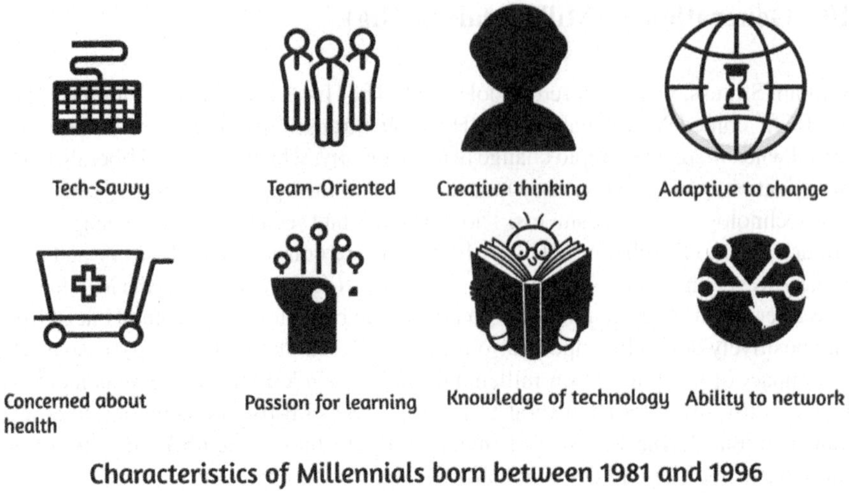

Fig. 3 Forces behind millennial gig's

few people had a negative preference toward gig. However, there is a need for a well-framed structure to regulate the gig economy. People prefer gig jobs because they do not have to work on a routine schedule from morning nine to evening five; instead, they can work as a freelancer depending on the opportunities they get (Hazarika & Joshi, n.d.). The Millennials are highly time-bound and do not like to spend overtime working in the office premises. To be more precise, Millennials prefer relaxation and do not like to be overburdened with too much workload. Adding to this, a write-up by (Palaniappan, 2019) on "Are millennials lazy and afraid of hard work?" is thought-provoking to understand the characteristics, behavior, and personality of the Millennial group before exploring their like toward the gig jobs. (Gilchrist, 2019) says Millennials prefer a fundamental change in the job setting, such as the need for flexibility, opportunity to reshape knowledge, emphasis on self-development, etc. The future economy will be driven toward growth majorly depending on the Millennials contribution of being a gig because millennials are the most significant representation of the workforce (Pofeldt, 2018) (Fig. 3).

11 Gen C (Technology Connected People as Gigs')

Not all Millennials are tech-savvy; few have not preferred to use technology until and unless there is a need for it. However, many people are over associated with technology. They can also be called "technology-driven people" called Generation C (Sims, 2017). It is to be noticed that Gen C is automatically attracted to technology and has its footprints in social media, and I look forward to exploring something new.

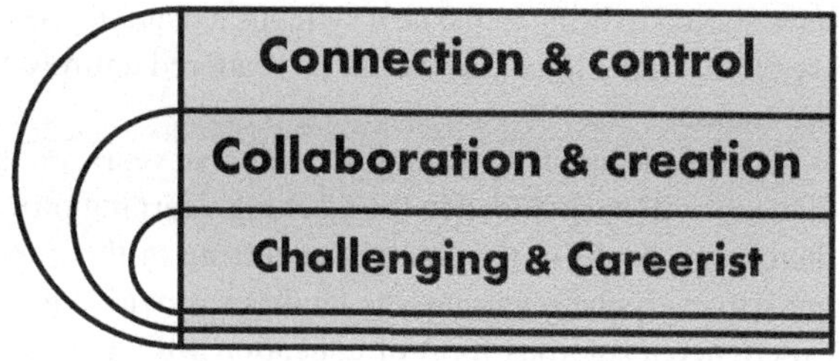

Fig. 4 Six features of generation C. *Source* Author's

They have a lot of enthusiasm for technology, digital tools, and applications, electronic gadgets, etc. The digital revolution has been made the best use not by everyone but rightly by Gen C (Preisler, 2015). Gen C is hyperactively connected and is good at networking, and is preferred by the HR managers. An article by (Zarom, 2015) states that there has been a technological shift in the workplace as Gen C has started to use technology and digital tools to make the task simple and more effective. Thus, the HR managers are now responsible for accelerating more technological adoption in the organizations. We understand that the contemporary work culture is fused with technology even for internal communication within the organizations. People are no more interested in holding a face-to-face meeting or conversation but prefer digital communication. The six important variables (connection, control, collaboration, and creation) are already introduced in the past challenging and careerist has been introduced in this research. It is to note that more than age, the mindset to adapt to technology is considered to define Gen C. Gen C has become hyper-agile and intelligent, and they make use of technical skills and digital skills to progress in their career. Since they know how to deal with IT, they challenge the hurdles and take the risk to explore new areas. Hence, challenging and careerist has been added to the existing Cs. Keeping oneself updated and networking is very important for a person to be successful. A report by (Google, 2013) mentions that 88% of Gen C have social media profiles, and 65% are hyperactive and keep updating their profiles. Social media these days are a platform to grab job opportunities as we see many advertisements frequently, and a majority of the jobs are freelancing jobs (Google, 2013) (Walters Whitepaper, n.d.) (Fig. 4).

12 Gen Alpha the Future Gig's

Technology and technical skills are one of the prime factors to be a successful gig worker. Even during the COVID-19 crisis, tech-pro managed those who did their job through the online platforms operating meetings in the clouds and tried to do some online-based jobs for survival. The others who did not have the essential technical skills faced many challenges, as they had to nurture themselves from the scratches to be exposed to fundamental technologies. In that way, education, exposure, skills, practicality play a significant role in shaping a child. The educational institutions have started to bring in the new syllabus to cater to the needs of the smart generation. By 2030, Gen Alpha kids would be scattered entirely from nursery to graduation in the country.

On the one hand, the youngest being five years, on the other hand the eldest being 20 years will be included in the teaching–learning process as per the new policy, and there is no doubt in the changes occurring in this process. Yet, it is a big question mark to everyone regarding the facilities provided in education to Gen Alpha. They experience a rigorous form of education with a constant change in the educational technology used in the institutions in the teaching–learning process. But the major factor causing an issue is, providing a skilled and efficient workforce to train Gen Alpha. As this generation is very close to technology from their childhood, they are very intimate. They have a greater experience in handling technology when they are adolescents and grown-ups, which will create an imbalance in the education sector. Most of the faculties with partial information and expertise in technology would face an immense problem in handling Gen Alpha and create a gap in their teaching–learning relation. The fact to be discussed is that the faculties who train Gen Alpha in higher education are technically from the previous generations. At times, they fail to understand the new concepts or learning models that Alpha kids are used to from their initial stage of the educational process. Definitely, at this point, it is crucial to focus on Gen Alpha, who is still at the primary level of education, study their learning behaviors through education technology, and try to initiate the changes required as per the study. Millennials (Gen Y) and Centennials (Gen Z) should focus on Gen Alpha's educational process apart from their common behaviors at home. This would help in understanding their requirements and further enable the same information for developing better software, tools, and technology to cater best services to the Gen Alpha. By the time Generation Alpha reached their higher education, they would have experienced drastic exposure to technologies available. There is no doubt that most of the Gen Alpha will be freelancers and pursue their higher education as they would like to explore numerous skills. In the same vein, they will dominate the gig economy in the future with their expertized skills and Pro approach in technology.

However, there is a doubt about multi-tasking in the workplace. Gen Alpha will be a relaxed population with more technological dependency. For example, the game-changer policy introduced by the government of India in the educational sector is going to change the phase of education in the country and help aspiring youngsters to excel in their field of study. And it is achieved by providing a multidisciplinary education system that gives importance to the student's technical development through the new curriculum structured in the further education policy 2020. The government of India has decided to provide a technology-driven education (based on artificial intelligence, cloud computing, and data coding) to all parts of the country, including disadvantaged groups starting from the primary education of an individual to their post-graduation. The Union Cabinet chaired by Prime Minister Shri Narendra Modi approved the National Education Policy 2020 (July 29, 2020) as an adjoining stride toward education for the twenty-first-century kids in the country. Thus, in all means, the Gen Alpha has an opportunity to be associated with technology in a very advanced way (Fig. 5).

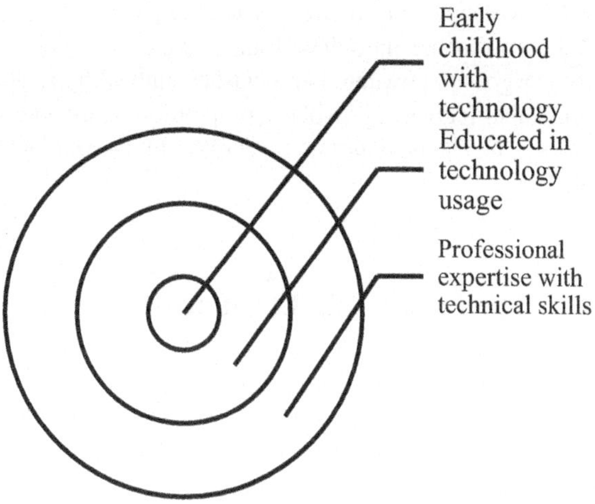

Fig. 5 Tree major elements of Alpha generation. *Source* Author's

13 Discussion

It is well understood from the analyzed results that the gig workers do not enjoy certain benefits, which the full-time employees enjoy. To highlight a few, they do not want the art of learning people's psychology in the organizational setup. Moreover, they do not enjoy other benefits such as compensation schemes given by the top management as a token of appreciation. In some emergencies, the full-time employees depend on the top management to get help, whereas the gig workers do not enjoy these facilities. They instead rely on and seek help from society, and hence, the term social balloons have been rightly framed by Etzioni. As researchers have understood from this article through the data collection and vast interactions with many gig workers spread across many industries, when a person is not considered an employee itself, it is very depressing. The question of why gig workers are not considered employees has no solution (Parent, August 2019). All these negative feelings are piled up and lead to a lot of emotional disorders. Sometimes due to the market demand, the gig workers enjoy continuous assignments, and sometimes, there are no assignments available which provoke anxiety. During an interaction, a gig worker said, "In case if I do not get employment for a couple of months, I would have to put myself in a shameful situation to borrow money from my friends and relatives to take off a lot of expenses." Anxiety may look like a very simple standard variable but holds many sentiments and hidden emotions (Puranik, November 2017), (Ruth Hoffman Cooper, July 2016). Eventually, these employees sometimes go blank without even knowing what to do next for the daily bread and searching for a psychologist. Moreover, it is not all freelancers get a job!

Only a very few. This has been captured from a conversation with a gig worker working as a website designer. He says, "Branding oneself once to clear an interview and to sit in a full employment is easy: but not to brand oneself every day to fetch a freelancing task." This is a compelling statement, and if introspected deeply, it carries a deep emotion. True! Not all gig workers are bestowed with a good job, but a few are fortunate enough with skills and talents (Gallier, May 2017). Workplaces can trigger gossip, unwanted ego clashes, unhealthy relationship, and work climate but remember it always provokes competition. Until a person gets to work as a full-time worker, he/she does not come across "Intensive Competition to Grow and Sustain" ICGS.

14 The Future Gig Economy

There is evidence showing that the future job market will have many gig employees working as freelancers. Loss of work due to unexpected crises like the economic recession or the COVID-19 might be reasonably possible in the post-2021, and the world economy will be a massive hit. However, the business units will have to function to ensure fund flow in the industry and within the economy. HR managers will find it challenging to pay a fancy salary/wages, force themselves to reduce the job vacancies, and cut down unwanted job posts. In few important place's freelancers, part-time workers will be employees, and the concept of full-time employees will minimize. Firms will stop long-term investments in Human Assets soon. Because uncertainty is significant fear and the upcoming generation may not stay with one firm for a longer time. Thus, investing in human assets and providing them training and development programs to equip them is a waste of time, money, and energy. The smart strategy is to give importance to gig jobs whenever there is a need.

Moreover, the younger generation (Gen Alpha) will not prefer to be full-time employees, and this is purely because of their unstable nature and behavior. Henceforth, gig economy will boom in post-2021. The present Millennials are full-time workers as well as gigsters. Word economies have to think and bring in new legislative policies to regulate the gig market. Few highlights of future gig:

- The present gigsters (millennials) and the future Alpha Generation who are born and brought up with technology will dominate the future gig economy.
- The gig economy is now redefining the job profile and related aspects such as job description, job specification, job security, etc.
- The economy may face health disasters and other unexpected crises soon and will not be in a position to hold full-time employees. Thus for a cost control, gig will be preferred.
- The attitude of the present Millennials has changed to prefer gig jobs, and this may be due to several reasons.
- Future gig employees will have an opportunity to learn from the new jobs but will not enjoy the chance to a part of a workstation family and organizational culture.
- The gig economy in the future, if regulated by a new legislative BILL, then the gigsters will benefit from few policies, regulations, and schemes for gig workers.

15 Scope for Future Study

Future researchers can explore the relationship between the present unorganized job market and its impact on full-time worker's decision to be gigs. For a country like India, China, Vietnam the job, market needs major reform; if not, people may lose interest in their respective careers. The applicability of human resources management in these developing countries needs to be relooked to comfort the employees in organized and unorganized sectors. Hence, future researchers can explore the present job market and predict the future trend. In this regard, the growth of the gigs is one of the trends. Thus, there is scope for research from the industrial development and labor reforms point of view. The organizations are now hyper-agile and are ready to adapt to any changes due to internal or external forces. The organization's keen budgeting decisions have led to a drastic cut in the full-time job because of the spill-over experiences. Smart organizations are promoting gig jobs, and hence, there is a need to study the expectations of organizations from the gig workers. There are many themes in HRM, like job analysis, job evaluation, performance appraisal, etc., that can be explored exclusively from the gig employee's point of view. The fundamental and universal laws proposed by great business scientists who have introduced models like POSDCORB may not be applicable in general because managing the dual workforce needs more managerial skills and new managerial functions. Hence, leadership styles and organizational skills to deal with the gig economy can be a new study. The other few areas to be explored by future researchers are:

- Employer branding for gig workers,
- Economic reforms and labor reforms to accommodate gig workers,
- Technological impact on gig growth,
- Bright future of freelancers and the work–life balance and quality of life satisfaction of being a gig.

16 Conclusion

The gig jobs will drive the future job markets and lead to economic progression, especially by the Gen Alpha. There is no doubt that business organizations have to bring in new agile and well-structured reforms to face uncertainty. The gigs have been used to the comfort which they get being a part-time or a freelancer. They are not answerable to the heavy workloads and are entirely free from a rigid organizational climate. Though many new changes are happening in HRM, like green HRM, virtual training and development, work-from-home flexibility, no one likes to be dominated or will not want to have an imbalance between work and family. Though the gigs know that there is no proper governing body or a legislative rule to monitor and govern the gig employee's benefit, they still prefer it because of the comfort and flexibility.

Moreover, it does not mean that only those who are tech-savvy will be successful gigs; but those who are tech-savvy may grab the opportunities more smartly. At present, Gen C is dominating the gig market, especially in specific industries like information technology, etc. In the future, Generation Alpha will naturally dominate the gig economy. The concept of "job for life" is slowly vanishing, and the idea of "work with comfort" is accepted and appreciated. Gigs look for new opportunities, refresh their skills and talents, revive their thirst for knowledge, and at the same time, try to strike a perfect balance between work and family. Maslow's need theory is not being reversed because people these days like to live with minimalistic needs and enjoy joy and happiness. The is always a big market for unskilled workers as they dominate the majority of the unorganized sectors. Hence, though the gig economy has few advantages, it is not the future but a part of the future.

References

Au-Yong-Oliveira, M. (2018). The social impact of technology on millennials and consequences for higher education and leadership. *Telematics and Informatics, 35*(04), 954–963. Retrieved from https://www.sciencedirect.com/science/article/abs/pii/S0736585317303465

Borbely, J. M. (2009). U.S. labor market in 2008: Economy in recession. *Monthly Labor Review, 132*(3), 3–19.

Bughin, J., Manyika, J., Lund, S., Robinson, K., Mischke, J., & Mahajan, D. (2016). Independent work: Choice, necessity, and the gig economy. McKinsey Global Institute, (October). Retrieved from https://www.mckinsey.com/~/media/McKinsey/Featured Insights/Employment and Growth/Independent work Choice necessity and the gig economy/Independent-Work-Choice-necessity-and-the-gig-economy-Full-report.ashx

Choudhry, M. T. (2010). Financial crises and labour market performance. International Atlantic ..., (March), 1–24. Retrieved from http://www.researchgate.net/publication/228337563_Financial_Crises_and_Labour_Market_Performance/file/9fcfd50b71c9b6bbc4.pdf

Economy, G. (2019). *Gig Economy and Its Impact on India, 8*(9565275702), 3177–3188.

Express, T. I. (2020). 122 million Indians lost jobs due to pandemic, these skills can help them be employed again. Retrieved from https://indianexpress.com/article/jobs/122-million-indians-lost-jobs-due-to-pandemic-these-skills-can-help-them-be-employed-again-6510032/

Gen, Z. (2019). The Gig Economy It's time to gig in or get out IS GIG ALWAYS GREENER ? Gen Zers are split down the middle on whether, (pp. 1–11).

Gilchrist, K. (2019). How millennials and Gen Z are reshaping the future of the workforce. Retrieved from CNBC.COM website: https://www.cnbc.com/2019/03/05/how-millennials-and-gen-z-are-reshaping-the-future-of-the-workforce.html

2020 Global Marketing Trends. (2020). Accenture digital economy I.T.'S TIME TO REIMAGINE. (n.d.).

Google. (2013). Introducing Gen C—The YouTube Generation.

Gross, S., & Musgrave, G. (n.d.). Wellbeing and mental health in Policy Perspectives on Precarity.

Hazarika, S., & Joshi, M. (n.d.). Major Research Project Report on Gig Economy: How it has revolutionized the meaning of work.

Home, N., & Strauss, W. (2018). Millenials rising : the next generation. *Small Business and the City*. https://doi.org/10.3138/9781442696501-014

Iacurci, G. (2020). The gig economy has ballooned by 6 million people since 2010. Financial worries may follow. CNBC.COM. Retrieved from https://www.cnbc.com/2020/02/04/gig-economy-grows-15percent-over-past-decade-adp-report.html

Islam, I., & Verick, S. (2010). The great recession of 2008–09: Causes, consequences and policy responses. *From the Great Recession to Labour Market Recovery: Issues, Evidence and Policy Options, 4934*, 19–52. https://doi.org/10.1057/9780230295186

Jain, K. (2020). COVID-19 pandemic impact: 50 lakh salaried jobs lost in July, 1.8 crore since April, says CMIE. DNA Web Team. Retrieved from https://www.dnaindia.com/business/report-covid-19-pandemic-impact-50-lakh-salaried-jobs-lost-in-july-18-crore-since-april-says-cmie-2838404

Joyner, J. (2016). Millennials: The Lazy generation. Mirlinechronicle.Com. Retrieved from http://marlinchronicle.vwu.edu/?p=7212

Kacher, N., & Weiler, S. (2017). Inside the Rise of the Gig Economy. (April).

Lai, R. (2019). How e-commerce and the gig economy is transforming Southeast Asia. (December).

Leeds University. (2017). The gig-economy and the impact on the millennial generation. Dissertation Leeds University.

Legge, J. M., & Legge, J. M. (2018). The great recession and the Eurozone crisis. *Economics Versus Reality*, 121–140. https://doi.org/10.4324/9781351295680-7

Manyika, J., & Taylor, M. (2017). Rethinking the workplace: Flexibility, fairness, and enlightened automation. *McKinsey Quarterly, 2017*(4), 44–53.

Matters, P. (2020). The rise of gig economy. Retrieved from https://www.magzter.com/article/Business/People-Matters/THE-RISE-OF-THE-GIG-ECONOMY

Mitic. (2020). Gig economy statistics 2020: The new normal in the workplace. Fortunly.Com. Retrieved from https://fortunly.com/statistics/gig-economy-statistics/#gref

Monahan, K., Schwartz, J., & Schleeter, T., (2020). Decoding millennials in the gig economy. Retrieved from Deloitte website: https://www2.deloitte.com/us/en/insights/focus/technology-and-the-future-of-work/millennials-in-the-gig-economy.html

Myers, K. (2016). Generation and its impact on family interaction.

Palaniappan, S. (2019). Are millennials lazy and afraid of hard work? Retrieved from Peoplematters.in website: https://www.peoplematters.in/article/talent-acquisition/organizing-gig-workers-the-crowdsourcing-way-23980

Pofeldt, E. (2018). Millennial employees want flexibility & benefits. can they have it all? Retrieved from Workest website: https://www.zenefits.com/workest/millennial-employees-want-flexible-schedules/

Preisler, A. (2015). Learn how to engage gen C (It's not just millennials). Retrieved from Content Marketing Institute website: https://contentmarketinginstitute.com/2015/11/engage-gen-c-millennials/

S, K. L. L. P. U. (n.d.). Plugging into the gig economy.

Scott Sims. (2017). 5 Things you need to know about gen C. Retrieved from https://www.socialmediatoday.com/news/5-things-you-need-to-know-about-gen-c-2/513102/

Sweeney, R. (2006). Millennial behaviors and demographics. Newark: New Jersey Institute of Technology. Accessed On.

Talent, T., & Economy, G. (n.d.). The New Freelancers.

Vogels, E. A. (2019). Millennials stand out for their technology use, but older generations also embrace digital life. Retrieved from Pewresearch.org website: https://www.pewresearch.org/fact-tank/2019/09/09/us-generations-technology-use/

Walters Whitepaper, R. (n.d.). Using social media in the recruitment process introduction.

Zachos, E. (2015). Technology is changing the millennial brain. Retrieved from Publicsource.org website: https://www.publicsource.org/technology-is-changing-the-millennial-brain/

Zarom, R. (2015). Creating a 'Generation Connected' workplace. Workforce.Com. Retrieved from https://www.workforce.com/news/creating-a-generation-connected-workplace

M Anand Shankar Raja works with the Department of Commerce, Christ University, Bangalore, India. He holds a Ph.D. in Commerce from SRM University (SRM Institute of Science and Technology) Chennai, Tamil Nadu. His area of focus is on mystery shopping and mystery shoppers' profession. His doctoral dissertation was on enhancing job satisfaction through motivation and emotional intelligence, a study concerning mystery shoppers. His other research focus is on work–life balance, gig economy, consumer purchase behavior, etc. He has presented his research article at AMA American Marketing Association Conference as an extended feather to his cap.

AV Akshay Kumar works with the Department of Commerce, JAIN COLLEGE, VASAVI CAMPUS, BCU, Bangalore, India. He has completed Master of Commerce in Christ (Deemed to be University), Bangalore, Karnataka. Has participated in various national and international conferences and has been awarded "Best Paper" "—" Role of quality teaching and a new start-up in Entrepreneurship," in a One Day National Symposium, "New India- Emerging Challenges and Evolving Strategies". Added to this, he is an aspiring candidate to publish research work in A Grade or reputed journals and excel in the field of research. At present, the area of research is Generations and, in specific, Generation Alpha.

Neha Makkar works as Assistant Professor with the Department of Management, IITM, Guru Gobind Singh Indraprastha University, Delhi. She has three years of academic experience and is an active researcher with several articles to her credit. She is a master in Commerce and a bachelor in Commerce from the University of Delhi. Her areas of interest are interdisciplinary, including human resources, entrepreneurship development, corporate social responsibility. Her current research focus is on succession in family business, choice of a successor—internal versus external.

Senthil Kumar is working as Professor of Research and Data Science at the School of Management Presidency University, Bangalore. He has 21.5 yrs of teaching experience, 1 yr of industry experience, and 5 + yrs of research experience. In total, he has 27.5 yrs of work experience. He has presented and published papers at the national and international conferences. He has published more than forty papers in the national and international journals. He has been a resource person and delivered a lecture in different colleges in the area of research methods.

S. Bhargav Varma is a graduate of Commerce from SRM University, Chennai. Being an enthusiastic learner, he has enabled him to develop a strong understanding of various subjects. His undergraduate degree aided him in building a strong and funnel approach to problem-solving and developing a critical outlook on social and economic issues. Bhargav has presented three papers at international conferences on business, economics, and knowledge Management. He is the co-founder of Ottoman's Royally Served, a Turkish restaurant in Chennai. His interests in astronomy, psychology, technology, and science have helped him immensely in understanding the future evolution of economics. At present, he works as Developer in Infosys Bangalore.

Revisiting the Gig Economy: Emergence, Challenges and COVID-19 Implications

Mark Ratilla, Sandeep Kumar Dey, and Miloslava Chovancova

1 Introduction

The gig economy depicts a system that brings together the demanders (hirers) and suppliers (independent workers) of human resources and/or personal services through information technology. It occupies a prominent position in the overarching economic phenomenon known as the sharing economy. It is exemplified by companies like Uber, Airbnb and TaskRabbit which are adopting technology-based business models to link freelancers, contractual or part-time workers to the consumers. There are three parties involved in a basic gig work arrangement, namely: the customer, online platform provider and service provider. The service provider engages in the online platform and prescribes the capacity and intent to provide services to clients. Meanwhile, the customer (user) specifies a service request and selects a "best fit" provider for actual service delivery. The online platforms mainly serve as intermediary facilitating the transaction between the supplier and demander of services. Online platform providers (*also called on-demand companies*) solely rely on jobs listed on their platform and, thus, generate income through commissions from customers and providers using the platform (Donovan et al., 2016). In return, service providers are offered with greater possibilities to secure jobs and work flexibility. It is noted that gig work is a deviation from traditional employment as organizations have less control over the workers and employment relationships are nonexistent (Duggan et al., 2020). This work arrangement utilizes a technology-based platform that acts as an intermediary for independent contractors to provide personal services to customers (Koutsimpogiorgos et al., 2020).

M. Ratilla (✉) · S. K. Dey · M. Chovancova
Faculty of Management and Economics, Tomas Bata University in Zlin, Zlin 76001, Czech Republic
e-mail: ratilla@utb.cz

A. Gupta et al. (eds.), *Sustainability in the Gig Economy*,
https://doi.org/10.1007/978-981-16-8406-7_24

Participation in the gig economy is rapidly increasing in both advanced and developing economies. Indeed, it has laid more possibilities for income generation. Nevertheless, its recognition and legitimacy are still being deliberated. As gig workers are considered "contractual workers," existing employment protection laws and regulations may not be fully enforceable resulting to an increase in workers' vulnerability. Chen et al. (2020) specify that more implications are expected in the times of crisis as gig workers' eligibility for employment assistance from the state remains blur. For instance, the COVID-19 health crisis has severely hurt the gig economy. However, the utility of on-demand delivery services has become apparent as pandemic-related restrictions are enforced. Recent evidence suggests that new gig jobs are opening alongside with the incidence of the health crisis, thus inciting the need for support from policy makers in the post-crisis (Umar et al., 2020).

In view of the ongoing discourse of the gig economy, this chapter reviews the concepts' emergence, platform control strategies and the critical issues needed of resolution especially in the post-pandemic recovery period.

2 Emergence and Relevance

The emergence of gig economy is believed to be a response to reduce the adverse effects of the economic crisis in 2008 (Kuhn & Galloway, 2019). Following the recession, people lost their jobs and incomes which concurrently increase their awareness to global issues on population growth and resource scarcity (Agarwal, 2019). People engaged in multiple part-time jobs to augment income and sought for possibilities to utilize tangible and intangible resources more efficiently and generate income out of it. These have spawned the so-called gig economy which captures freelancing jobs and self-employment offered through IT-based platforms (KPMG, 2018). Meanwhile, the growing attitude toward greater freedom and work flexibility among existing and forthcoming workers is espousing the relevance of the gig economy as an option for employment. Oyer (2020) indicates that more people in the USA are deliberately liking the work independence in the gig economy. Individuals who prefer to work on short period of time or to work with great independence would suit gig work arrangements. With the adoption of technology among gig companies, people now have the freedom to choose how, where and for whom they are willing to work (Dunning, 2017). Individuals can take into account one's own passion or simultaneously try different jobs for career exploration (Torpey & Hogan, 2016). It promotes what is known as "*commoditized matching*," wherein technology allows the effective matching of customers' needs and service offerings (Oyer, 2020). However, though working in the gig economy presents several advantages, it cannot be ignored that this work arrangement entails income inconsistency and lost benefits that can be usually derived in traditional employment routes.

A growing number of start-ups and even large companies are integrating flexible staffing to address business needs. Tapping the gig economy is considered to be advantageous as it is easier to craft labor contracts for short-term workers, support cost reduction initiatives and acquire the best talents who prefer to work in contractual basis (Oyer, 2020; Vitaud, 2015). Meanwhile, it can considerably support start-ups by means of expanding labor choices, hastening onboarding processes and developing flexibility in case of downsizing. Growth forecast reveals that the gig economy will expand over the succeeding years. Its inherent advantages over traditional employment are encouraging more people to pursue gig work. Findings from LinkedIn (2007) Survey reveal that on-demand platforms offer possibilities for workers to supplement their traditional jobs. Most of them are satisfied in performing gig jobs as it supplements their traditional income sources, support work-life balance, encourage work independence and scheduling. Lepanjuuri et al. (2018) reported that among European countries, the UK has the most people engaging in gig work. They indicated that in 2017, about 2.8 million people are working in the gig economy and are expected to increase to over 5 million people by 2022. Nevertheless, researchers note that the values only make up 0.5 percent of total employment on these countries and will not displace traditional employment (Duggan et al., 2020; Eurofound, 2017; Katz & Krueger, 2016). Meanwhile, PwC projections on its revenue show that it will reach 63 billion USD globally in 2020 (Green, n.d.). Top thriving occupations propelling its growth are associated with art and design, computer and information technology, construction and extraction, media communications and transport and delivery (Torpey & Hogan, 2016).

Moreover, the integration of technology-born demographic cohorts (i.e., millennials, generation Z, generation alpha) into the workforce is expected to increase its growth in the coming years. These generations highly value work flexibility and freedom in innovation and manifest strong entrepreneurial spirit (KPMG, 2018). All these behavioral patterns match to what gig economy can offer to its workers. Accordingly, the gig economy will in some way be relevant to organizations seeking for short-term labor and/or having difficulty in filling out available jobs (Grensing-Pophal, 2019).

3 Challenges Ahead and Implications to Organizations

Despite the freedom and flexibility that the gig economy is proposing to its service providers, it is also besieged with a number of issues which restrain people in this type of work arrangement. One major concern is the absence of benefits and protection that organizations usually provide to workers via traditional employment. Full-time gig workers also suffer from greater income variability due to the uncertainty and continuity of gigs (Oyer, 2020). They are not entitled to minimum wage rates, overtime pay, unemployment compensation including family and medical leave benefits (Donovan et al., 2016). This only means that working in the gig economy may not be suitable for everybody. To relinquish what traditional employment can provide may considerably impede people to solely rely on contractual jobs.

Flexible staffing is gradually becoming relevant to large organizations especially for project-oriented tasks (Oyer, 2020). Apart from possible low labor cost, it eases the process of accessing limited and high-end talent across the globe (Dunning, 2017). Furthermore, it raises issues in the organization's employee retention policies as gig workers just come and go. Likewise, it challenges human resource management practices pertaining to direct supervision and monitoring which are commonly implemented within the confines of the organization (Graham et al., 2017). Gig workers are considered as independent contractors by gig companies. Together, they form work relationships by specifying the terms and agreements in the contract in the provision of services to the hirers. Nevertheless, gig workers' work quality remains critical. Problems arise when contracted jobs are poorly accomplished or when communications are cut off with the client. Moreover, failing to complete the task within the time frame assignment may warrant further extension; however, the service provider may have already secured other commitments.

Also, concerns regarding confidentiality, security, legal liability and management should be taken into account as organizations decide to outsource talents from online marketplaces (Vitaud, 2015). Grensing-Pophal (2019) stresses that the gig economy will not entirely replace traditional employment. Instead, organizations should be able to achieve balance in sourcing workers from traditional and non-traditional channels. Incorporating both traditional and gig workforce should be exploited as competitive differentiator (KPMG, 2018). Likewise, in response to the changing workforce attitude toward work independence and flexibility, organizations can instead infuse "gig culture" on its working environment. This could be done by redesigning employee value proposition in a way that it enforces entrepreneurial spirit on organizational roles, allow virtual flexibility and design roles that manifest autonomy, require analytical thinking and problem solving skills (KPMG, 2018). In cases when required talents can only be sourced from the gig economy, companies need to re-evaluate human resource policies and modify compensation and benefit packages to attract and retain them. Phillips (2019), however, specifies that providing incentive to gig workers to fully employ them in the organization may be unreasonable. Instead, it is suggested that firms create a positive working environment to gig workers so as to establish loyalty in the company and encourage their respective networks to do the same. Meanwhile, Vitaud (2015) mentions that talented individuals recognize their capabilities; thus, they have full control to choose which projects to work on. The author further indicate that they seek employers with appealing organizational culture, wherein the elements of problem solving, accountability, trust and work independence are highly emphasized.

Meijerink and Keegan (2019) mentioned that there exists a degree of "interdependence and multilaterality" in the value creation process among gig economy actors (p. 220). Reaping the benefits brought about by the positive synergy among players can be realized if they work complimentarily. A player's failure can cause adverse impacts to other players in the gig ecosystem. This happens when service providers leave the gig platform and significantly reduce the supply of on-demand services made available to clients. As a result, some clients leave or seek for alternative platforms where they can obtain the needed services. Thus, they emphasize that it is important to exercise control and coordinate efforts in the entire gig ecosystem.

4 Keeping in Control: The Role of Platform Provider

A well-functioning gig ecosystem requires platform providers to demonstrate some degree of control on the engagement between users and service providers. In situations when the demand for services is higher than the supply, clients will likely experience delay in accessing the requested services. Consequently, this will affect their usage of the platform. In this regard, platform providers carry out strategies to entice and onboard more service suppliers. Airbnb and Uber demonstrate strong traction in the industry which discern that more service providers are needed to satisfy the demand requirements. Intensive marketing campaigns highlighting the advantages that can be derived from participating in the gig economy is needed to support this purpose. Mandloi (2020) stipulates that independent contractors are seeking to find meaning on what they are working and it should be reflected on company's vision and mission. Therefore, aside from highlighting the economic incentives, it is also important to emphasize work flexibility, autonomy and work ownership advantages. In addition, the promotion of economic benefits can go along with granting rewards to well-performing service providers. This is owing to the findings from extant studies acknowledging the significance of economic incentive as a driver to participate in the sharing economy in general (Valente et al., 2019; Wilhelms et al., 2017). However, reward programs in popular gig platforms such as Uber and Airbnb are not yet pronounced clearly. Airbnb's Superhost program is most likely the most evident at present. Service providers having satisfactory performance are granted with badges (Jabagi et al., 2019). This offers greater possibilities for hosts to earn more by means of attracting more guests. Criteria for top performance include the following: (1) 4.8+ average rating from past year, (2) completed 10+ stays in the past year, (3) with less than 1% cancelation rate and (4) 90% response rate within 24 h. As for the case of Uber, drivers can take advantage of surge pricing when the demand increases. Algorithms automate price increases based on demand information and notify other drivers (*even those dispersed in other locations*) to render services. Similarly, it is necessary to maintain regular communication (even in virtual means) and feedback mechanisms to contractual employees to account their needs and concerns (Mandloi, 2020).

Another advantage to the prospective service providers is the capability and flexibility to set the price of service offerings. For instance, taskers in TaskRabbit are the ones setting hourly rates. Then, the gig platform sets a 15% service fee from the total price of the service. In setting the hourly rates, taskers determine how much is it worth to perform the task based on requesters' bids or rely on the gig platform's own estimates. To secure jobs easily, it would be better to set rates equivalent or closer to the bids for the tasks. Too expensive rates might dissuade requestors; meanwhile, cheap rates may signify low-quality services. Meanwhile, Airbnb follows the same case. Pricing solely depends on the service providers; however, the company sets up a smart-pricing tool to assist them in setting prices. Airbnb will only get hold of 3–5% commission fee for the platform services to customers and hosts. Hosts also offer other services to earn money like laundry, cleaning, tour, equipment rental, etc. Conversely, most ride-hailing platforms compensate their drivers distinctively. Aside from the standard base fare + per minute/per-mile rates, they are also offered possibilities to earn more in locations where demand is high. Price surges are generated allowing drivers to earn more by taking additional passenger pickups.

Most importantly, the quality of services needs to be maintained despite the delicate control of platform providers over gig workers and their performance. Quality assurance processes should be in place even upon registration of service providers in the online platform. Information provided during registration should be verified prior to onboarding. Uber already took this initiative as it implements a screening before drivers are deployed on the road. It involves thorough background checks to determine any records of driving violations, driving impairment or violence or crimes committed by prospective drivers. Annual rescreening procedures are also implemented, and customer reviews are accounted for to ensure safety and smooth delivery of quality services. Meanwhile, some gig platforms also assign jobs solely to qualified service providers. As some jobs require special skills or language, only those with appropriate qualifications can be hired. Existing and prospective service providers take their own initiatives to advance qualifications and skillset. Ever since, platform providers neglected the initiative to offer career advancing opportunities to gig workers as they merely consider them as independent contractors. Hence, gig companies may pursue a more proactive approach on improving the totality of service quality by focusing more attention to service providers.

Platform providers supersede traditional businesses through the adoption of a real-time performance monitoring technology. For example, ride-hailing platforms such as Uber and Grab use telematics to remotely monitor real-time driving patterns among drivers. Embedded in the mobile app, it captures information about driver's location, driving speed, braking performance, idling time, fuel consumption and other driving habits and information (Carino, 2018). These are utilized to assure high driving safety performance among drivers. For poor performing drivers, the company gave advices to achieve 5-star ratings. In extreme cases, when poor ratings are not reverted, drivers accounts may be subjected for deactivation. They will no longer be able to use the platform and render services. Drivers who continuously decline requests are penalized by imposing temporary account deactivation (e.g., 10-min deactivation period). Meanwhile, gig platforms allow users to evaluate the quality of services delivered by providers (gig workers). These are outrightly captured and stored in the platform ecosystem. Prospective users, therefore, are able to distinguish independent contractors who are delivering quality services to customers. High ratings and positive client reviews are associated with service providers' reliability, trustfulness and accountability.

5 The Institutional Role: The Need to Protect Gig Workers

The gig economy prospects are promising given the dynamic nature of the key industries that rely on gig manpower. These primarily include public, domestic, social and auxiliary services apart from the conventional sectors like events and catering (Statista, 2018). Studies in the past have focused on the relationship between employer of gig services and gig workers, which in emerging economies remain a gray area (Stewart & Stanford, 2017).

The gig worker community comprise a range of generational cohorts and skill sets which are often highly sought after by different sectors of the economy. For example, during the harvest season, young persons are commissioned by farm owners to conduct various agricultural activities. Likewise, during large-scale events, managers look for casual staff to man critical aspects of the event. Extant literature indicates that short-term employer–employee interactions are not necessarily a contractual nature, thus making the gig worker vulnerable to exploitation and barring access to statutes on labor welfare (Todolí-Signes, 2017).

Due to the largely de-centralized nature of the sharing economy and the associated peer-to-peer autonomy that comes with it, the status quo of public institutions in regulating manpower supply has been a challenge (Frenken et al., 2020). While this situation has reduced red tape and diversifies labor supply, it poses question on the locus of workers under such arrangements. The institutional theory recognizes the central role played by state regulatory agencies in streamlining and leading social processes through isomorphism (rationalized myths about the idea of an ideal organization), decoupling (adaptations to the rationalized myths) and coercion (organizational change by force) (Marquis & Tilcsik, 2016).

The discourse is expanded by commentaries and observations from studies like Graham et al. (2017) who have contested the position of regulatory authorities in the access economy context. There exist two paradigms pertinent to the debate—one advocates the interference of public bodies to shield manpower from predatory practices and the second who view institutions as barrier to labor mobility (Minter, 2017). It will be up to future scholarships in the domain to provide for working solutions in order to balance welfare mechanisms and labor market forces in the gig economy.

6 What's Next After COVID-19?

The incidence of COVID-19 has prompted dramatic shifts in different facets of human activity. As the pandemic-related measures are enforced, people have no other choice but to cope up with the "new normal" modalities of work and other aspects of day-to-day living. Work from home and self-isolation became the norms owing to the fear of exposure to the virus. Peoples' engagement toward the gig economy has also not been spared. A survey from AppJobs Institute reported that the overall number of available jobs in the gig economy has substantially declined (Prevallet-Kinstle, 2021). However, an evident increase in demand is noticed on delivery and free-lancing services. Similarly, Polkowska (2020) observed this development in Poland as food delivery services became relevant as an alternative source of income for people who lost their jobs during the crisis. Lee (2020) also noted that gig-economy style of work is gaining favor in South Korea, especially for those workers severely hit by the pandemic. Economic pressures pushed full-time workers to assume additional jobs to augment incomes. Despite the initiative to stay afloat in the face of the pandemic, issues and concerns commonly ascribed in gig work arrangements become more apparent. Katta et al. (2020) emphasized that hazards and risks associated with gig jobs particularly on mobility services are always present. However, these are magnified as workers continue to deliver services to customers and increasing their chances of viral contagion during the pandemic. The observations of Apouey et al. (2020) indicate that gig workers' physical health outcomes deteriorated along with the decline in income during the COVID-19 crisis. Even more, protection, benefits and assistance commonly derived from traditional employment are nonexistent as platform providers claim gig workers as independent contractors. AppJobs Institute Survey indicates that gig workers have expected furtherance from gig companies and governments during the crisis (Prevallet-Kinstle, 2021). However, it may seem that little attention is given due to employment classification. This has placed gig companies to the spotlight and set-off inquiries that threatens their business model's viability and legitimacy. Gig companies embrace pressure on providing workers' protection irrespective of employment classification at present. Henderson (2020) recounted that the state of California took the first initiative to craft policies pushing gig companies to extend assistance through healthcare contribution and setting minimum wage requirement for its gig workers. Spurk and Straub (2020) stipulated that it is critical for gig companies to pay attention to its gig workers through enhancing working conditions, job security, workforce quality and work performance to stay in business in the long run. The gig economy is expected to thrive as the pandemic ends (De et al., 2020). Its significant role and concomitant concerns have been well recognized in turbulent times. Therefore, it is imperative and timely for gig companies and policy makers to concentrate on the revolving issues and accordingly design strategies that offer the greatest benefits for the society in diverse circumstances.

7 Conclusion

With the rapid technological advances and the concurrent social change, the "gig economy" emerges as an economic phenomenon that encapsulates the commodification of human resources. It reflects a kind of arrangement that enfolds the exchange of human resource-related services between the service provider and customers via online platforms. Its disposition toward work freedom, autonomy, flexibility and the pursuit for a sense of work ownership is espousing its relevance as an alternative employment option. However, the setup refutes the standard employment relationship, thus presenting distinct employment-related issues. Greater vulnerabilities are induced to gig workers as employment benefits and protection in the traditional employment are nonexistent in gig work arrangements. As a result, stakeholders persistently deliberate the subsisting issues and raising questions on the existence and legitimacy of gig companies. Meanwhile, infusing a gig culture in organizations may not be steadily seamless as matters on work quality, work continuity, worker's reliability and accountability arise. Organizations should also account for issues concerning confidentiality, security, legal liability and management when integrating gig workers to its workforce.

Against the backdrop of issues and concerns emanating in the gig economy, it appears that it is still gaining favor among people. Extant studies reveal that workers are largely enticed to participate in the gig economy because of economic incentives. However, it is crucial to maintain a right balance of demand and supply of human resource services to stabilize functions in the gig economy. This shoves gig companies (platform providers) to assume the role that ensures coordination, cooperation and control of efforts in different activities in the gig ecosystem. As the demand for gig services is increasing, gig companies entice and onboard more service suppliers to maintain bearable supply–demand conditions. This could be done by carrying out intensive marketing campaigns and highlighting all the possible economic and social incentives to entice more service suppliers. More importantly, service quality needs to be ensured. Service quality surveillance and monitoring embedded in gig platforms (i.e., ratings, reviews, real-time performance monitoring) must be continuously improved. Simultaneously, more attention is needed in developing gig workers' knowledge, skillset and overall competency to raise the bar of service quality offered to clients.

The COVID-19 pandemic has caused extreme distress in several industries across the globe. Its economic and employment implications are even more agonizing. A significant reduction in the available gig jobs is observed; however, jobs in the delivery services and freelancing became more relevant. The pandemic has even more exposed the vulnerabilities of gig workers, thereby revitalizing the concerns in relation to employment protection and accountability of gig companies. Both policy makers and gig companies need to reflect on these matters and accordingly design and execute interventions that pose the greatest benefits to the society.

Acknowledgements The authors are thankful to the Internal Grant Agency of FaME TBU in Zlín No. IGA/FaME/2020/002 (The impact of digital transformation on customer behavior and firm's sustainable performance) and IGA/FaME/2021/003 (Consumer behaviour and performance management of firms in a competitive digital world) for financial support to carry out this research.

References

Agarwal, P. (2019). *The gig economy*. https://www.intelligenteconomist.com/gig-economy/

Apouey, B., Roulet, A., Solal, I., & Stabile, M. (2020). Gig workers during the COVID-19 crisis in France: Financial precarity and mental well-being. *Journal of Urban Health, 97*(6), 776–795. https://doi.org/10.1007/s11524-020-00480-4

Carino, J. (2018, January 15). *Uber driver tracking and telematics*. Geotab web site. https://www.geotab.com/blog/uber-driver-tracking/

Chen, G., Cheng, M., Edwards, D., & Xu, L. (2020). COVID-19 pandemic exposes the vulnerability of the sharing economy: A novel accounting framework. *Journal of Sustainable Tourism, 0*(0), 1–18. https://doi.org/10.1080/09669582.2020.1868484

De, R., Pandey, N., & Pal, A. (2020). Impact of digital surge during covid-19 pandemic: A viewpoint on research and practice. *International Journal of Information Management*. https://doi.org/10.1016/j.ijinfomgt.2020.102171

Donovan, S., Bradley, D., & Shimaukuro, J. (2016). *What does the gig economy mean for workers?* Congressional research service. https://fas.org/sgp/crs/misc/R44365.pdf

Duggan, J., Sherman, U., Carbery, R., & McDonnell, A. (2020). Algorithmic management and app-work in the gig economy: A research agenda for employment relations and HRM. *Human Resource Management Journal, 30*(1), 114–132. https://doi.org/10.1111/1748-8583.12258

Dunning, J. (2017). *Gig economy: What exactly is it?* HRZone web site. https://www.hrzone.com/lead/future/gig-economy-what-exactly-is-it

Eurofound. (2017). *Automation, digitisation and platforms: Implications for work and employment*. Publication office of the European Union. https://www.eurofound.europa.eu/sites/default/files/ef_publication/field_ef_document/ef18002en.pdf

Frenken, K., Vaskelainen, T., Fünfschilling, L., & Piscicelli, L. (2020). *An institutional logics perspective on the gig economy* (pp. 83–105). Emerald Publishing Limited. https://doi.org/10.1108/s0733-558x20200000066005

Graham, M., Hjorth, I., & Lehdonvirta, V. (2017). Digital labour and development: Impacts of global digital labour platforms and the gig economy on worker livelihoods. *Transfer, 23*(2), 135–162. https://doi.org/10.1177/1024258916687250

Green, A. (n.d.). *How is the gig economy affecting HR?* [NEHRA Northesast HR Association]. Retrieved April 23, 2020, from https://www.nehra.com/page/GigEconomy/How-is-the-Gig-Economy-Affecting-HR.htm

Grensing-Pophal, L. (2019, July 18). *Know the perils of the gig economy*. Society for Human Resource Management Web Site. https://www.shrm.org/resourcesandtools/hr-topics/talent-acquisition/pages/know-the-perils-of-the-gig-economy.aspx

Henderson, R. (2020). How COVID-19 has transformed the gig economy. In *Forbes*. https://www.forbes.com/sites/rebeccahenderson/2020/12/10/how-covid-19-has-transformed-the-gig-economy/?sh=421f0cfa6c99

Jabagi, N., Croteau, A.-M., Audebrand, L. K., & Marsan, J. (2019). Gig-workers' motivation: Thinking beyond carrots and sticks. *Journal of Managerial Psychology, 34*(4), 192–213. https://doi.org/10.1108/JMP-06-2018-0255

Katta, S., Badger, A., Graham, M., Howson, K., Ustek-Spilda, F., & Bertolini, A. (2020). (Dis)embeddedness and (de)commodification: COVID-19, Uber, and the unravelling logics of the gig economy. *Dialogues in Human Geography, 10*(2), 203–207. https://doi.org/10.1177/2043820620934942

Katz, L., & Krueger, A. (2016). *The rise and nature of alternative work arrangements in the United States, 1995–2015*. National bureau of economic research. https://www.nber.org/papers/w22667.pdf

Koutsimpogiorgos, N., Slageren, J., Herrmann, A. M., & Frenken, K. (2020). Conceptualizing the gig economy and its regulatory problems. *Policy & Internet, 12*(4), 525–545. https://doi.org/10.1002/poi3.237

KPMG. (2018). *Plugging into the gig economy: The truth about the gig economy and how it is influencing the future of talent management*. KPGM LLP. https://advisory.kpmg.us/content/dam/advisory/en/pdfs/gig-economy-future-of-work.pdf

Kuhn, K. M., & Galloway, T. L. (2019). Expanding perspectives on gig work and gig workers. *Journal of Managerial Psychology, 34*(4), 186–191. https://doi.org/10.1108/JMP-05-2019-507

Lee, Y. (2020). Pandemic woes bring U.S.-style gig economy to South Korea. In *Bloomberg*. https://www.bloomberg.com/news/articles/2020-12-13/pandemic-woes-bring-u-s-style-gig-economy-to-south-korea

Lepanjuuri, K., Wishart, R., & Cornick, P. (2018). *The characteristics of those in the gig economy*. Department for Business, Energy and Industrial Strategy. https://assets.publishing.service.gov.uk/government/uploads/system/uploads/attachment_data/file/687553/The_characteristics_of_those_in_the_gig_economy.pdf

Linkedin. (2017, February 21). *How the freelance generation is redefining professional norms*. https://www.linkedin.com/profinder/blog/freelance-generation-redefines-modern-workplace.

Mandloi, R. (2020, January 13). *Making the most of talent in the gig economy*. Harvard Business School Publishing. https://www.harvardbusiness.org/making-the-most-of-talent-in-the-gig-economy/

Marquis, C., & Tilcsik, A. (2016). Institutional equivalence: How industry and community peers influence corporate philanthropy. *Organization Science, 27*(5), 1325–1341. https://doi.org/10.1287/orsc.2016.1083

Meijerink, J., & Keegan, A. (2019). Conceptualizing human resource management in the gig economy: Toward a platform ecosystem perspective. *Journal of Managerial Psychology, 34*(4), 214–232. https://doi.org/10.1108/JMP-07-2018-0277

Minter, K. (2017). Negotiating labour standards in the gig economy: Airtasker and Unions New South Wales. *Economic and Labour Relations Review, 28*(3), 438–454. https://doi.org/10.1177/1035304617724305

Oyer, P. (2020). *The gig economy: Non-traditional employment is a great opportunity for many, but it won't replace traditional employment*. IZA World of Labor. https://wol.iza.org/uploads/articles/523/pdfs/the-gig-economy.pdf

Phillips, P. (2019, October 16). *The evolving role of HR in a gig economy*. Forbes. https://www.forbes.com/sites/forbeshumanresourcescouncil/2019/10/16/the-evolving-role-of-hr-in-a-gig-economy/#1fc1b18c61a3

Polkowska, D. (2020). Platform work during the COVID-19 pandemic: A case study of Glovo couriers in Poland. *European Societies*. https://doi.org/10.1080/14616696.2020.1826554

Prevallet-Kinstle, A. (2021). Coronavirus vs. gig economy—many left jobless. In *AppJobs Institute*. https://www.appjobs.com/blog/coronavirus-effect-on-gig-economy

Spurk, D., & Straub, C. (2020). Flexible employment relationships and careers in times of the COVID-19 pandemic. *Journal of Vocational Behavior, January*. https://doi.org/10.1016/j.jvb.2020.103435

Statista. (2018). *Gig economy: Industries where gig economy workers are currently employed*. https://www.statista.com/statistics/915951/gig-economy-industries-where-gig-economy-workers-currently-employed/

Stewart, A., & Stanford, J. (2017). Regulating work in the gig economy: What are the options? *The Economic and Labour Relations Review, 28*(3), 420–437. https://doi.org/10.1177/1035304617722461

Todolí-Signes, A. (2017). The end of the subordinate worker? The on-demand economy, the gig economy, and the need for protection for crowdworkers. *International Journal of Comparative Labour Law and Industrial Relations, 33*(2).

Torpey, E., & Hogan, A. (2016). *Working in a gig economy: Career outlook*. U.S. Bureau of Labor Statistics. https://www.bls.gov/careeroutlook/2016/article/pdf/what-is-the-gig-economy.pdf

Umar, M., Xu, Y., & Mirza, S. S. (2020). The impact of covid-19 on gig economy. *Economic Research-Ekonomska Istrazivanja, 0*(0), 1–13. https://doi.org/10.1080/1331677X.2020.1862688

Valente, E., Patrus, R., & Córdova Guimarães, R. (2019). Sharing economy: Becoming an Uber driver in a developing country. *Revista De Gestão, 26*(2), 143–160. https://doi.org/10.1108/REGE-08-2018-0088

Vitaud, L. (2015). *HR Professionals: What does the rise of the gig economy mean for you?* Medium. https://medium.com/switch-collective/hr-professionals-what-does-the-rise-of-the-gig-economy-mean-for-you-60a5b2a6e158

Wilhelms, M.-P., Henkel, S., & Merfeld, K. (2017). You are what you share: Understanding participation motives in peer-to-peer carsharing. In G. Meyer, & S. Shaheen (Eds.), *Disrupting mobility* (pp. 105–119). Springer International Publishing. https://doi.org/10.1007/978-3-319-51602-8_7

Ing. Mark Ratilla is a Ph.D. candidate in the Department of Management and Marketing at the Tomas Bata University in Zlin, Czech Republic. His research interest spans on sharing economy participation, e-commerce and cross-cultural consumer behavior. He is also co-investigating university-funded research projects, namely: (1) the use of behavioral nudging strategies towards healthier food choices in the Czech Republic and (2) the analysis of consumer behavior in the age of digital transformation

Sandeep Kumar Dey is a Ph.D. candidate in the Department of Business Administration at the Tomas Bata University in Zlin, Czech Republic. His research interest centers around sustainable consumption in the tourism and hospitality industry.

Doc. Ing. Miloslava Chovancová CSc., is Associate Professor in the Department of Marketing, Tomas Bata University in Zlin, Czech Republic. She also chairs the academic senate of the Faculty of Economics and Administration in the same university. Her research focus covers the fields of cross-cultural consumer behavior, brand management and entrepreneurship. She has an excellent track record in publishing several research outputs in reputable journals.

The manufacturer's authorised representative in the EU is Springer Nature Customer Service Centre GmbH, Europaplatz 3, 69115 Heidelberg, Germany. If you have any concerns regarding our products, please contact ProductSafety@springernature.com

Printed and bound by CPI Group (UK) Ltd, Croydon, CR0 4YY
30/09/2026
02225329-0014